EL PASO

Juan de Oñate taking possession of the Kingdom of New Mexico, 1598.
(José Cisneros)

EL PASO

A Borderlands History
by W.H. TIMMONS

Foreword by David J. Weber

Illustrations by José Cisneros

The University of Texas
at El Paso

FIRST EDITION
  Second Printing
Library of Congress Catalog Card No. 88-050545
ISBN 0-87404-207-0 (cloth)
ISBN 0-87404-213-5 (paper)

 The paper used in this publication meets the minimum
requirements of American National Standard for
Information Sciences.
Permanence of Paper for Printed Library Materials,
ANSI Z39.48-1984

Cover art: "El Paso before it was",
by José Cisneros, 1989

Design by Vicki Trego Hill

For Laura

Contents

Foreword

E L Paso's story is, in microcosm, the story of the United States-Mexican border region, and no one has told it better than W. H. Timmons. The written record began in the 1500s, when Spaniards following the Rio Grande inevitably traveled through the *paso del norte* where the Great River slices through two mountain ranges. In the 1600s, the fertile El Paso valley became the site of missions, a town, and a fortification, as well as a stopping place along the trail that connected Santa Fe and Chihuahua. El Paso's strategic setting on that north-south trail, together with its central location, between the Pacific and the Gulf of Mexico, made it pivotal to events on the northern fringes of Spain's New World empire and subsequently, from 1821-1848, on the northern extremities of independent Mexico. After the United States acquired the region at mid-century, a new El Paso developed on the American side of the Rio Grande. For a variety of reasons, so well explained in this book, El Paso grew to become the most sizeable border community on the United States-Mexican boundary and, with its Mexican counterpart, Ciudad Juárez, part of the largest of the twin-city complexes on the border.

As El Paso-Ciudad Juárez grew, historians were there to tell the story. Indeed, local events figured into the first published history of the region, the *Historia de la Nuevo México* by Gaspar Pérez de Villagrá, printed in Spain in 1610. Since Villagrá, historians have continued to chronicle and interpret El Paso's ongoing story. They have written primarily, however, about *aspects* of the city's development. Only on rare occasions has a historian been bold enough to try to put the *whole* story together, as did the distinguished historian C. L. Sonnichsen, in his *Pass of the North: Four Centuries on the Rio Grande.* Published in 1968 by Texas Western Press, it carried the narrative to 1917, and a second volume, published in 1980, summarized the recent years.

Now W. H. Timmons has produced a fresh overview in his *El Paso: A Borderlands History.* Since Sonnichsen's first volume was published, a revolution in historical sensibility and an explosion of historical scholarship have occurred, and Professor Timmons has taken advantage of both. He has, for example, sketched out the stories of blacks, Jews, Chinese, Syrians, and *mexicanos* – ethnic groups whose existence was not of special interest to most historians a generation ago. To accomplish that task, he has consulted the latest scholarship, some of it published in El Paso itself (most notably in the El Paso Historical Society's journal *Password*, and in Texas Western Press's Southwestern Studies Series), and some of it published outside the region (such as Mario T. García's *Desert Immigrants: The Mexicans of El Paso, 1880-1920*, published by Yale University Press). In addition, Professor Timmons has examined a staggering number of unpublished sources, including doctoral dissertations, master's theses, private and public correspondence, census reports, and taped interviews, as well as seldom-consulted imprints ranging from old newspapers to the United States census.

Out of this welter of materials, Timmons has woven a fresh and well-balanced work, as up-to-date in coverage as it is in interpretation. A master craftsman, Timmons has skillfully threaded El Paso's story into the larger fabric of American and Mexican history, deftly outlining the national events in both countries that made developments along the border more comprehensible. In El Paso itself, it is the patterns that stand out vividly, for Timmons has avoided the common pitfall of regional historians who often spin tales of purely local interest in excruciating detail. No reader will put this book down without a clear sense of the dominant themes in El Paso, such as its quest for water and federal dollars, the linkage of its economy and culture to that of Ciudad Juárez, and the bicultural nature of a city where *mexicanos* have formed the majority of the population for the last half century.

Familiar characters and episodes are all here, from Cabeza de Vaca to the Chamizal controversy, from the Chihuahua Trail to the Chicano Movement, but even those *paseños* who know their history well will find much that is new. Professor Timmons has a fine eye for quotations and anecdotes. Rather than editorialize, he often allows people to speak for themselves in ways that are revealing. He notes, for example, that the election of Raymond Telles in 1957 as the city's first Mexican-American mayor, prompted an El Paso businessman to lament, "How can we hold our heads up in the State of Texas when we have a Mexican mayor?"

This fine study of El Paso's life and times, then, is worthy of the city's long and fascinating history. Anyone interested in El Paso or in the larger border region that it dominates, whether resident or outsider, scholar or general reader, will find that W. H. Timmons' *El Paso* is the first book they will want to consult.

The merits of this urban biography will be readily apparent to readers. Less obvious are the merits of the author, who has helped remake the history of El Paso even as he has recorded and interpreted it. Wilbert H. Timmons is professor emeritus at The University of Texas at El Paso, where he taught for nearly thirty years, from 1949 when he received his Ph.D. in history from The University of Texas at Austin, until his retirement in 1978. Trained in the history of Latin America, he is well known among Mexican specialists for books such as *Morelos of Mexico: Priest, Soldier, Statesman* (1963), *Tadeo Ortiz: Mexican Colonizer and Reformer* (1974), and *J. F. Finerty Reports Porfirian Mexico* (1974), as well as for his scholarly articles and for his supervision of ambitious microfilming projects in Chihuahua and Durango.

Since his retirement from teaching a decade ago, Bill, as he is known to his friends, has become increasingly identified with the history of El Paso. He has published several articles on the city, a *History of the University Presbyterian Church* (1983) and, most intriguingly, served as El Paso's "Mr. History." In the late 1970s, Bill Timmons conceived of and promoted the idea that El Paso should celebrate it quatrocentenary in 1981, commemorating the four hundred years since the first European set foot in the El Paso Valley. With a grant from the Texas Committee for the Humanities, he became "Mr. History" in 1981. In that capacity he talked to numerous public and private schools and civic groups, gave public lectures, made TV appearances, arranged for the placement of historic markers, wrote articles for the *El Paso Times*, and edited a textbook: *Four Centuries at the Pass*. In some of his public appearances,

"Mr. History" cut a remarkably striking figure in a turn-of-the-century costume that included a top hat, frock-tail coat, green vest, and gold chain, designed for him by his wife and collaborator, Laura. As Bill once explained, he sometimes wore that costume "to dramatize 'Mr. History' and give him identity." An accomplished jazz pianist since his days as a naval officer during World War II, Bill would conclude a presentation with a rendition of "Happy Birthday, El Paso," if a piano happened to be nearby.

In his lectures as in this book, Bill Timmons does not simply celebrate his adopted city. He points to its impoverished barrios and its comfortable suburbs, its brothels and its country clubs, its crooked politicians and its political visionaries, its prejudice and its biculturalism, as well as its ambivalent relationships with the federal government, the state of Texas, and with Mexico. Above all, he has helped to foster a sense of perspective, place, and identity in a city whose rapid population growth had threatened to thrust it into the future with a case of historical amnesia. In this sense, Professor Timmons has made history as well as recording it. Few historians have served their community with such energy, dedication, and imagination. El Paso is fortunate to have not only this book by Bill Timmons, but "Mr. History" himself!

David J. Weber
Dedman Professor of History
Southern Methodist University

Introduction

THE term Borderlands, which historian Herbert Eugene Bolton introduced in 1921 in his seminal volume, *The Spanish Borderlands*, has never been clearly defined and thus has remained largely a subject for interpretation. In Bolton's view the term included all the territories within the limits of the United States which Spain had held, from Florida to California. Others have used the term in a more restricted sense to include only the Spanish provinces from Texas to California, or the Spanish Southwest, pointing out that Louisiana and Florida historically are more closely related to the Caribbean than to northern Mexico. A third concept of the Borderlands, one which has gained wide acceptance within recent years, encompasses the north Mexican provinces, most of which Spain itself included in its reorganization of the frontier as the Provincias Internas late in the eighteenth century.[1]

This study accepts this larger concept of Borderlands, as defined in a recent publication—"an areal domain consisting of a parallel tier of political-legal administrative units (U.S. and Mexican states) lying in juxtaposition along a previously determined arbitrary binational boundary that extends from the Gulf of Mexico to the Pacific Ocean." In simpler terms, the Borderlands is an area that lies astride the United States-Mexican boundary, comprising the six northern Mexican states— Tamaulipas, Nuevo León, Coahuila, Chihuahua, Sonora, and Baja California Norte—and the four states that make up the American Southwest—Texas, New Mexico, Arizona, and California.[2]

According to Borderlands scholars, these ten states are the fastest-growing regions within their respective countries, with the result that this area has come to be regarded as one of the most important in the world. If it were politically independent, says one specialist, it would be the world's ninth largest nation in size and the thirteenth in population. Despite the area's importance and natural affinity, little planning has taken place either between border states on each side of the border or across the border.[3]

Although an international boundary of some two thousand miles in length divides the Borderlands politically, scholars have come to view the area as a cultural unit, the Western Hemisphere's major zone of Anglo-Hispanic convergence. "While the Mexican-United States boundary is an official dividing line," writes Stanley Ross,

> there is no insurmountable barrier. Rather there are important frontiers, including a cultural one. In this sense the border separates two different cultural worlds—not only between Mexico and the United States, but also between Latin America and Anglo America. Despite the natural tendency to emphasize what is different, there is a unique mixture of Mexican and American heritages and cultures along the border[4]

Sharing this common border are the United States, a rich and powerful industrial nation, and Mexico, a member of the Third World. Nowhere, it has been noted, does a political barrier separate two nations with a greater economic disparity. Even though some border sections in the United States are the poorest in the country, and some border sections in Mexico are relatively well off compared to the rest of the republic, the imbalance of the economies which meet at the border is enormous. As one specialist has noted, "neither the per capita gross national product nor the per capita income of any country in the world even comes near the *amount of difference* in per capita income between the United States and Mexico."[5]

Although the Borderlands at one time was largely the province of historians, the area recently has drawn the attention of physical scientists, social scientists, engineers, and specialists in mental and physical well-being. Thus, the Borderlands has become a veritable research laboratory for specialists in a wide range of disciplines whose expertise will be in increasing demand in the future search for solutions to border problems. Hopefully, both nations will recognize that the problems of the border region are national in scope and deserving of national and international attention.[6]

Located approximately in the geographic center of the Borderlands is the international metropolitan complex of El Paso, Texas, and Ciudad Juárez, Chihuahua. With a combined population of one and a half million, it is the largest concentration of people on the United States-Mexico border, and by the year 2000 may well have close to two million. Like the Borderlands generally, the El Paso-Ciudad Juárez complex is the product of the interaction of two cultural traditions—those of the Spanish-Mexican North and the Anglo-American Southwest, and the resulting convergence of the two during the Mexican period, 1821-1848.

El Paso's four hundred years of history begins with the arrival of the first Spanish expedition from the south in 1581. As they approached the Rio Grande, the Spanish saw two mountain ranges rising out of the desert with a deep chasm between. This site they named El Paso del Norte (the Pass of the North), the future location of two border cities—Ciudad Juárez on the south bank, and El Paso, Texas, on the opposite side of the river. In 1598 in a ceremony at a site near present-day San Elizario the colonizing expedition of Juan de Oñate took formal possession of the territory drained by the Rio Grande. Thus was laid the foundation of more than two centuries of Spanish rule over the Borderlands area.

The traditional date for the founding of the mission of Nuestra Señora de Guadalupe, still standing in downtown Ciudad Juárez as the area's oldest historic landmark, is 1659. Near this mission in the early 1680s Spanish and Tigua refugees from the Pueblo Revolt in New Mexico established El Paso del Norte (the future Ciudad Juárez), San Lorenzo, Senecú, Ysleta, and Socorro in a chain along the south bank of the river. By the end of the eighteenth century more than five thousand people lived in the area, the largest concentration of population on the Spanish northern frontier. The area was a trade center on the historic Camino Real, or Royal Highway, and agriculture flourished, particularly the vineyards, producing wine and brandy said to rank in quality with the best in the realm. For the protection of the settlers against the raiding Apaches, the presidio of San Elizario was established in 1789.

With the winning of Mexican independence from Spain in 1821, the El Paso area and what is now the American Southwest became

a part of the Mexican nation. It was the principal target of the
United States' growing interest in territorial expansion during the
1840s. This became known as Manifest Destiny, a providential dic-
tate that justified the extension of American institutions and control
to the Pacific. The resulting clash of cultures between the Anglo
and the Mexican came in May 1846 with the outbreak of hostilities
between the United States and Mexico. In December Col. Alexander Doniphan and his Missouri volunteers defeated the Mexicans
at the Battle of Brazito, entered El Paso del Norte, then defeated the
Mexicans again at the Battle of Sacramento. They took the city of
Chihuahua in February 1847. Following the entry of Gen. Winfield
Scott's army into Mexico City in September 1847, the two nations
signed a peace treaty.

In accordance with the Treaty of Guadalupe Hidalgo of 2
February 1848, the boundary between the two nations was fixed at
the Rio Grande, the Gila, and the Colorado, westward to the
Pacific. All territory north of that line, known as the Mexican
Cession and comprising half of Mexico's national domain, became a
part of the United States, which paid Mexico the sum of $15
million. Within a year, aided by the gold rush to California, Anglo-
Americans founded five settlements along the left bank of the river.
Joining these were the three Mexican towns of Ysleta, Socorro, and
San Elizario, placed on the American side as a result of the shifting
of the river south of the old channel. Ysleta, founded in 1682, thus
claims to be the oldest town in Texas.

Momentous changes had taken place in the El Paso area as the
Mexican period came to a close, reaching a climax in the year 1848.
Before that date there were six Mexican settlements in a chain
along the right bank of the Rio Grande. But in 1848 the river
became an international boundary and El Paso del Norte, the future
Ciudad Juárez, became a border town. The five settlements founded
by Anglo-Americans along the left bank, together with the three
Mexican settlements placed on the Texas side by the shifting river,
clearly established the bicultural, bilingual foundations of the future
El Paso, Texas. An east-west traffic axis soon supplanted in large
measure the older north-south axis – the historic Camino Real.
Tantamount to a political, commercial, and cultural revolution,
therefore, were the changes that occurred on the Rio Grande at the
Pass of the North in the 1848-1849 period.

The arrival of the railroads in 1881 transformed the little adobe village of El Paso (formerly Franklin) into a flourishing frontier community. Its geographic location as a gateway to Mexico, its proximity to the mining areas of northern Mexico, New Mexico, and Arizona, its mild climate, its ample natural resources, and an abundance of cheap labor assured its future as an important mining and transportation center. The construction of Fort Bliss in its present location in 1893 enhanced El Paso's reputation as a military town. Plans announced in 1906 for the building of Elephant Butte Dam, with its promise to make El Paso's valleys green, convinced investors that the city had a future. This provided the economic base for developing an impressive downtown and attractive residential areas, with many buildings designed by the talented architect, Henry C. Trost.

A major characteristic of El Paso, the border town, is its special relationship with Mexico in general and Ciudad Juárez in particular. Historic developments such as the Taft-Díaz meeting of 1909; the taking of Ciudad-Juárez by the revolutionary forces of Francisco Madero in 1911; the exploits of Francisco "Pancho" Villa; the smuggling and bootlegging activities during Prohibition; the Chamizal dispute and its settlement; the growing interdependence of the cities; and the shaping of a distinctive border culture – all attest to the unique relationship between the two cities.

The post-World War II years marked an era of spectacular growth in the city of El Paso, as its population increased from 130,000 in 1950 to a half million in 1987. Sharing this growth was its twin sister across the river, its population figure by 1960 matching that of El Paso for the first time. By 1985 Ciudad Juárez's population was 800,000, and by the year 2000, as has been noted, this international metropolitan area will have a population close to two million. Thus, as this area approaches the twenty-first century, the challenges will be great, but so will the potential of what promises to be one of the world's most dynamic regions.

El Paso's rich and colorful past has fascinated historians and writers for more than half a century. In 1923 Owen P. White blazed the trail with his delightful *Out of the Desert*. Others have made significant contributions to the telling of the El Paso story, particularly C. L. Sonnichsen, whose *Pass of the North*, written in a popular style, has become a classic. Of the considerable number of monographs published in recent years, most are confined to topics

dealing with the nineteenth and early twentieth centuries and emphasize El Paso solely as a product of the Anglo-American Southwest.
With a few exceptions, such as Rex Strickland's *The Turner Thesis
and the Dry World*, they are short on analysis and interpretation.

On the other hand, the Spanish and Mexican periods have
largely been ignored, with the exception of Anne E. Hughes' scholarly *The Beginnings of Spanish Settlement in the El Paso District*, a doctoral dissertation written under the direction of Herbert E. Bolton.
Cleofas Calleros wrote pamphlets and articles in the 1950s on El
Paso's missions, but the full-length monograph he envisioned failed
to appear, leaving half of the El Paso story untold. This study,
therefore, attempts to present a comprehensive view of both of El
Paso's cultural traditions culminating in the blend of the two in recent years. Finally, an examination of the bibliography at the close
of the narrative should convince readers that there is no dearth of
material for telling the El Paso story.

To the many people who have shared their expertise, performed
the numerous tasks in preparing a manuscript for publication, and
offered advice, support, and encouragement, I am deeply indebted
and extremely grateful. My special thanks to two distinguished
Borderlanders—David J. Weber for his gracious remarks in the
Foreword, and José Cisneros, without whose superb pen and ink
sketches no Borderlands study would be complete.

I extend my sincere thanks to Dale Walker, director of Texas
Western Press, a craftsman in the Hertzog tradition; to G. L. Seligmann, who read the entire manuscript and made countless suggestions for its improvement; to Nancy Hamilton for her painstaking
editorial skills and knowledge of local history; to Mary Sarber, Main
Branch librarian of the El Paso Public Library and dean of its
fabulous Southwest Collection; and Lucy Fischer West, perfectionist
editor-typist.

Thanks also go to the readers of chapters for their numerous
helpful suggestions—Conrey Bryson, John A. Ferguson, Frank
Mangan, and Emily Whitaker; to UTEP librarians and archivists
César Caballero, Rebecca Craver, Hatsuyo Hawkins, and Bud New-
man; to Sue Cook, the best of everything the title "Administrative
Secretary" implies; and to the staffs of the Texas State Library,
Barker Texas History Center, New Mexico State Records Center

and Archives, and the Coronado Room of the Zimmerman Library of the University of New Mexico.

Finally, this book is dedicated to my wife Laura for ten years of note taking, translations, proofreading, and support and encouragement, especially when it was needed. To all of the above I extend my heartfelt gratitude and appreciation.

W. H. Timmons
Professor Emeritus of History
The University of Texas at El Paso

I. The Legacy of the
Spanish-Mexican North

Founding of Guadalupe Mission, 1659.
(José Cisneros, 1980)

CHAPTER ONE

The Pass of the North:
First Settlements

THE El Paso-Ciudad Juárez area lies at the northern end of the Mexican Central Plateau within a desert zone which includes western Texas, southern New Mexico, southern Arizona, northern Sonora, and northern Chihuahua. Ranging from 2,500 to 5,000 feet in elevation, this high altitude desert zone features a wide, shallow basin, or bolson, which is walled in by parallel ranges of steep, rugged, bare mountains. As a result, drainage basins are formed containing lakes, or *lagunas*, in which seasonal waters collect and then evaporate, leaving a salt crust which hinders the growth of plant life. Thus the desert environment in which the El Paso-Ciudad Juárez area is located presents a number of natural obstacles to extensive human occupation. Among them are barren mountains, inadequate rainfall, temperature extremes, relentless winds, sand and dust storms, and limited vegetation. Given these conditions, it is difficult to conceive of a region that has less to recommend it for human occupation.[1]

Historically, some measure of compensation for the rough and raw elements of this desert environment has been offered by the Rio Grande. One of the great rivers of the world — a river which El Paso writers have on occasion compared to the ancient Nile — it has been a fundamental factor in the history of the El Paso-Ciudad Juárez area. Rising in the mountains of southern Colorado and fed by tributaries along its 1,250-mile route, the Rio Grande flows southward through New Mexico to the El Paso region where it slices between the Franklin Mountains and the Sierra de Juárez. Sixteenth- and seventeenth-century explorers named the site El Paso del Norte (the Pass of the North). It was the future location of Ciudad Juárez on the south or right bank of the Rio Grande, and El Paso, Texas, on the opposite side of the river.[2]

Geologist Earl Lovejoy has described the characteristics of this river in graphic terms:

> During most of the year the river was a gentle source of life and sustenance, its placid waters unique in this harsh Chihuahua desert, its flat flood plain a fertile valley in which generous vineyards flourished and cattle grazed on rich stands of lush grass. But during the spring, the river's normal trickle swelled to a torrent which raged for weeks, spreading rampaging flood waters far north into what is now...downtown El Paso, separating the settlements on each side of the river by a wide stretch of impassable flood, destroying man's works, carrying huge volumes of silt and unused water to the sea, and changing its course from one part of the valley to another.[3]

In spite of periodic flooding and droughts, however, this river has been the life blood that created an oasis in the El Paso area and made it possible for human occupation to survive. The three peoples who have lived on its banks — Indian, Spanish-Mexican, and Anglo-American — occupied this oasis and utilized the river's resources for over ten thousand years.[4]

Moreover, as Lovejoy hastens to point out, the Rio Grande has not always flowed to the sea. Rather, millions of years ago it ended in the El Paso region and formed a lake, which the geologists, in a gesture to please the historians, named for the first European in the area, Cabeza de Vaca. For millions of years, writes Lovejoy, the ancestral Rio Grande poured flood waters and river alluvium into this region, thus forming a broad, shallow sheet of water. In dry seasons it would completely evaporate, but during rainy times the lake would spread and deepen. Although the lake is gone, its sediments had filled the basins at great depths and underlie Fort Bliss, International Airport, and the Hueco bolson east of the Franklins, as well as the area west of the Upper Valley. Deposits of river sands almost 1,500 feet thick just beneath the surface are filled with fresh ground water; from these deposits El Paso gets most of its city water.[5]

Archaeological investigation has divided the culture history of the area into the following periods: Paleoindian, Archaic, and Formative. The Paleoindian, or Early Man, which dates roughly from ten thousand to eight thousand years ago, featured people who subsisted primarily by hunting large game animals in the Hueco bolson, as indicated by artifactual evidence consisting of projectile points and other chipped stone tools. With climatic changes, the extinction of many large animals, and the establishment of cave sites, there emerged around 6000 B.C. the Desert Culture, or Archaic period, which extended to the Christian era. Horticulture became more important, and there was a greater dependence on plant foods, with rabbits, deer, and antelope providing the bulk of the meat diet. For the most part, the Archaic period featured a culture of hunters and gatherers inhabiting caves and mountain shelters, using projectile points and stone tools, but remaining nonceramic until the later phases of the period.[6]

The Archaic period is followed by the Formative, which dates from the beginning of the Christian era to about A.D. 1400. As archaeologist Thomas C. O'Laughlin points out, it differs from the Archaic in the addition of new traits such as pottery, the bow and arrow, and sedentary agricultural villages featuring pit houses, or partially subterranean structures. In turn the Formative is divided into three phases — Mesilla (100-1100), Doña Ana (1100-1200), and El Paso (1200-1400). By 1200 pit house structures had given way to large pueblos of contiguous blocks of east-west aligned surface rooms, a social organization, ceremonial activities, the cultivation of corn, beans, and squash, food storage facilities, and the importation of items from trade centers such as Casas Grandes in Chihuahua.[7]

The El Paso phase came to an abrupt end sometime after 1400 when the area apparently was abandoned. Possible explanations of this reduction or dispersal of population resulted from a too heavy reliance on agriculture, or the decline of the trade center of Casas Grandes about this time, or perhaps a combination of the two. At any rate, the first Europeans to arrive found nonsedentary hunting and gathering tribes known variously as Suma, Manso, Jocome, and Jumano, who were living in *rancherías*, or small villages of a hundred people or so, using extremely primitive agricultural methods. The first Spaniards who arrived in the area were not particularly impressed.[8]

In the fifty-year period that followed the discovery of America, Spanish conquistadores explored and colonized considerable portions of North and South America. The explanation for this spectacular achievement was the search for riches by ambitious Spaniards, a desire for fame and fortune, and a love of adventure. Of the numerous conquistadores who participated in the search, Hernando Cortez, who overthrew the Aztecs of Mexico, and the Pizarro brothers, who conquered the Incas of Peru, were the most successful. Most of the others, who never doubted they could duplicate the feats of Cortez and the Pizarros in their quest for a Fountain of Youth, an El Dorado, the Seven Cities of Cíbola, or a Grand Quivira, were doomed to failure and disappointment. But it was such a search for one of these mythical kingdoms that set the stage for the beginning of Spanish explorations in what is now called the American Southwest.[9]

In all probability the first Spaniards came to the El Paso area in late 1535, less than fifteen years after Hernando Cortez overthrew the Aztec empire. They were survivors of an ill-fated expedition to Florida in 1528 who, in their attempt to return to Cuba, were blown by a storm upon the coast of Texas. In 1534 Alvar Núñez Cabeza de Vaca and his three companions escaped from their captors, set out to the southwest, and for nearly two years continued their wanderings across what is now southern and western Texas. Although the exact route of their travels is debated by historians, they apparently struck the Rio Grande above its juncture with the Conchos, forded it, and followed it to the northwest. Two women guides led them up "the river which ran between some ridges" to a town where the inhabitants lived in

*Alvar Núñez Cabeza de Vaca and his
companions explore the El Paso del Norte
region, 1535. (José Cisneros, 1980)*

5

houses and grew corn, beans, and squashes, suggesting one of the
rancherías in the El Paso area. They continued in a westerly direction, and at an Indian village in the present Mexican state of
Sonora they feasted on deer hearts; thus, the place became known
as Los Corazones. The Indians showed them turquoises and what
were believed to be precious stones; they told the travelers about
the existence of rich cities to the north. Naturally, this was ex-
citing news. It was easy for the travelers to imagine that these
reports confirmed the location of the mythical Seven Cities of
Cíbola, seven rich cities which, according to legend, had been
established by seven bishops in the eighth century.[10]

After Cabeza de Vaca returned to Mexico City, his story of
reputed rich cities to the north so stirred the imagination and
interest of Spanish officials that the viceroy commissioned the
Franciscan Fray Marcos de Niza to lead a small expedition to
verify the Cabeza de Vaca report. The party proceeded northward
from Culiacán in March 1539 and at length arrived at a site
probably in present-day southeastern Arizona. According to the
friar's written report, he ascended a hill and sighted Cíbola, stating
that it had a fine appearance, that the houses were built of stone
with terraces and flat roofs, and that the city was larger than
Mexico City. The existence of the legendary Seven Cities had thus
been confirmed![11]

The task of conquering the Seven Cities was assigned to
Francisco Vásquez de Coronado early in 1540, but his two years
of effort in what is now the American Southwest resulted only in
a series of disappointments, frustrations, and failures. In present-
day western New Mexico Coronado located Fray Marcos' Cíbola,
but it proved to be only adobe structures two to three stories high
housing hostile Indians. An enormous expanse of territory was
subsequently explored, including the Grand Canyon, a route to
the Gulf of California, northern New Mexico, the Texas Panhandle, and southern Kansas, but the great riches the Spaniards
sought remained elusive. While Cabeza de Vaca, Fray Marcos,
and Francisco Vásquez de Coronado had no direct impact on the
El Paso area, they were the first Europeans to probe the mysteries
of the American Southwest, and it is therefore indeed appropriate
that the name Coronado has been memorialized in El Paso's
Westside.[12]

For almost half a century Spain took but little interest in the
American Southwest following Coronado's extensive explorations
and failure to find great riches. Meanwhile, the conquest and
colonization of the northern frontier of the Viceroyalty of New
Spain, as Mexico was officially called in the colonial period, advanced by gradual stages in the sixteenth century with the discovery of mineral deposits in Zacatecas, Durango, and present-day
Chihuahua. The rich silver veins found in southern Chihuahua
led to the establishment of Santa Bárbara in 1567, located on a
tributary of the Conchos River, which flowed northward to the
Rio Grande. Here was a new route to New Mexico that would
make possible the colonization of the upper Rio Grande valley by
the end of the century. The founding of Santa Bárbara, therefore,
was a significant event in El Paso history, as it brought within fifteen years the first Spanish expeditions to the Pass of the North.[13]

In June 1581 three Franciscans—Fray Agustín Rodríguez, Fray
Francisco López, and Fray Juan de Santa María—left Santa Bárbara to explore missionary possibilities in New Mexico. They were
accompanied by an armed escort under the command of Francisco
Sánchez Chamuscado. Descending the Conchos to its juncture
with the Rio Grande, they encountered, according to the account
of Pedro de Bustamante, wild, primitive, and naked Indians who
told the Spaniards there were more settlements upstream. This information is confirmed in the account of Hernán Gallegos, who
also mentioned that the Indians told the Spaniards that some
years before four Christians had passed through the area—no
doubt Cabeza de Vaca and his companions. This was an indication that the Rodríguez-Chamuscado expedition was approaching
the El Paso area. Continuing upstream the Spaniards encountered
an Indian group—apparently the Sumas—who reported that
further up the river there was a clothed, settled people living in
multi-storied houses. They were very warlike and had given the
Sumas a great deal of trouble.[14]

The Rodríguez-Chamuscado expedition of 1581, the first party
of Spaniards to arrive at the Pass of the North, marks the beginning of four hundred years of history in the El Paso area. Apparently the expedition reached the Pass early in August 1581. In
New Mexico the party explored to both the east and west of the
Rio Grande, thus covering much of the same territory viewed by

The Rodríguez-Chamuscado expedition reached the
El Paso area in 1581. (José Cisneros, 1980)

Coronado. In the meantime Fray Santa María had ill-advisedly set out on his own to report to the viceroy and was killed by Indians on 10 September 1581. His companions, however, did not learn of his fate until sometime later.[15]

Early in 1582 Chamuscado and his men discussed the desirability of returning to Santa Bárbara and reporting to the viceroy, but the two Franciscans, Fray Agustín Rodríguez and Fray Francisco López, announced their intention of continuing their missionary endeavors in New Mexico. Chamuscado's warnings of the great dangers involved went unheeded, and on 31 January 1582 the little band took leave of the two missionaries and returned by way of the Pass of the North to Santa Bárbara. The aged Chamuscado fell ill and had to be carried on a stretcher. He died before reaching Santa Bárbara, but the remainder of the party reached this northern outpost on 15 April 1582, after an absence of almost eleven months. In its opening up of a new route to New Mexico by way of the Pass of the North, the Rodríguez-Chamuscado expedition laid the foundations for the introduction of European civilization in what is now the American Southwest.[16]

The glowing accounts of the new discoveries made by the Rodríguez-Chamuscado expedition spread rapidly throughout the northern frontier and fired imaginations. Moreover, in Santa Bárbara there was the greatest concern for the safety of Fray Rodríguez and Fray López, who had remained in New Mexico. As a result, a second expedition was organized under the leadership of Antonio de Espejo, a wealthy Spaniard, and Fray Bernardino Beltrán. Leaving Santa Bárbara in November 1582, this expedition, like its predecessor, followed the Conchos and the Rio Grande through the Pass of the North to New Mexico.[17]

The Conchos nation, wrote Espejo, numbered more than 1,000. They went about naked, lived in grass huts, used bows and arrows, and obeyed their caciques. They lived on deer and rabbits, and grew corn, gourds, melons, beans, and made a sweet jam from a plant called *lechuguilla*. Up the river another nation, which Espejo called Pozaguantes, lived in *rancherías*, built huts, and grew food like the Conchos. Another nation, which Espejo called Jobosos, lived on the same things as the Pozaguantes, used bows and arrows, and went about naked. The next nation, the Jumanos, lived in large pueblos with flat roofs and grew corn, gourds, and beans.

The caciques gave the Spaniards food and hides, and told them that some years before three Christians and a Negro had passed through the area. Continuing up the Rio Grande, the Espejo party entered what appears to be the El Paso area.[18]

According to the account of Diego Pérez de Luxán, the expedition entered the El Paso area in early January 1583 and encountered an Indian group thought to be the Sumas, who met the Spaniards peacefully, performed impressive dances, and offered gifts. Espejo wrote that the Indians brought many articles made of feathers of different colors, and cotton shawls, striped blue and white, resembling some that are imported from China. People of another nation had brought these articles, Espejo was told, for purposes of trade. This nation lay to the west, the Indians said, and contained an abundance of shiny minerals. Continuing upstream, the expedition then encountered a group living in *rancherías*, thought to be Mansos, who brought the Spaniards a large quantity of mesquite, corn, and fish. On beyond the El Paso area, Espejo wrote, "We always followed the river upstream, with a mountain chain on each side of it, both of which were without timber throughout the entire distance until we came near the settlements which they call New Mexico."[19]

On the upper Rio Grande Espejo learned that both Fray Rodríguez and Fray López had been killed. The sole remaining objective of the expedition then was to verify the presence of mineral wealth. Espejo pushed westward into present-day Arizona and continued to receive reports of the existence of rich mines. Convinced that the stories were true, he decided to return to Santa Bárbara to organize a larger expedition for the conquest and occupation of the area which he had just explored. Espejo, however, was to be denied the opportunity to become the founder of New Mexico; instead, the authorization of a military and colonizing expedition by the crown and the viceroy was to go to another.[20]

During the 1580s and 1590s the monarchy of Philip II of Spain became extremely interested in the conquest and colonization of New Mexico. To be sure, the mining and missionary possibilities in that frontier territory stimulated interest, but there was an additional factor — namely, the intense international rivalry between Spain and England, with its dynastic, religious, and commercial overtones. Like the monarchy of Philip II of Spain, that of Elizabeth I of England in the last quarter of the sixteenth century was

The Antonio de Espejo expedition came north
through the Pass in 1582. (José Cisneros, 1980)

actively engaged in a program of overseas and imperial expansion. During these years, one of the greatest English sea captains of all time, Sir Francis Drake, achieved fame and fortune with his raids on Spanish colonial ports and his capture of Spanish treasure ships. In the 1590s reports of English activity on the California coast were received by Philip II with great concern, as it was rumored that Drake had discovered a transcontinental strait that cut eastward through North America – a serious threat to Spain's plans for New Mexico with its reported riches. No such strait, of course, existed, but in view of the limited knowledge of North American geography by the Europeans of that day, this was not known.[21]

For more than a decade the viceroy of New Spain searched for a suitable candidate to implement Philip's plans for New Mexico. Individual fame and fortune were essential ingredients in the selection process since the Spanish crown had decreed that no royal funds would be forthcoming, and that the candidate himself would have to bear all the costs of the expedition. At length, in 1595 the viceroy awarded the contract to Don Juan de Oñate, whose father had made a fortune from the silver mines of Zacatecas, and whose wife was the granddaughter of Cortez and the great-granddaughter of Montezuma. The contract gave Oñate the title of governor and captain-general, while religious duties were assigned to the Franciscans. There were countless delays in getting the expedition assembled, but at length in January 1598 the colony of 400 men, of whom 130 brought families, began the march northward from Santa Bárbara along the Conchos. Thus, the Oñate enterprise was to be involved in colonization as well as conquest, as one-third of its membership enlisted for the purpose of settling the new land and starting a new life on the northern frontier. In addition, there were eighty-three wagons and carts to carry the baggage and provisions, and more than 7,000 head of stock.[22]

"No expedition before that of Don Juan de Oñate, and none after it," observes an El Paso scholar, "has so sharply focused the attention of historians on the El Paso Valley." Unlike previous expeditions, which followed the Conchos to the Rio Grande, this one headed straight north across the sand dunes of the Chihuahua desert. On 19 April the expedition divided, the vanguard reaching the river the next day. The Spaniards named it the Río del Norte.

The chronicler of the expedition, Gaspar Pérez de Villagrá, captured the spirit and drama of the moment:

> Our faith was finally rewarded. That Providence which never deserted us at length crowned our efforts with success! After journeying, as stated, for four days without water, on the morning of the fifth we joyfully viewed in the distance the long sought waters of the Río del Norte.
> The gaunt horses approached the rolling stream and plunged headlong into it. Two of them drank so much that they burst their sides and died. Two others, blinded by their raving thirst, plunged so far into the stream that they were caught in its swift current and drowned.
> Our men, consumed by the burning thirst, their tongues swollen and their throats parched, threw themselves into the water and drank as though the entire river did not carry enough to quench their terrible thirst. Then satisfied, they threw themselves upon the cool sands.... Joyfully we tarried beneath the pleasant shade of the wide spreading trees which grew along the river banks.[23]

On 26 April the expedition was reunited. As Villagrá noted:

> To make our happiness complete, we saw our general and the rest of the expedition approaching in the distance. They had followed us, and it had now been several days since we had seen them. It was, indeed, a happy meeting. We built a great bonfire and roasted the meat and fish, and then all sat down to a repast the like of which we had never enjoyed before. We were happy that our trials were over; as happy as were the passengers in the Ark when they saw the dove returning with the olive branch in his beak, bringing tidings that the deluge had subsided.[24]

Oñate addressed the assembled group, praised them for their courage and endurance, proclaimed a day of rest for all, and sent out an exploring party with orders to find the best place for fording the river. A few days later the expedition moved three leagues up the river. Oñate ordered the construction of a small chapel under the trees, and on 30 April there was held a solemn High Mass, a sermon, and the enactment of a drama written by one of the officers. Then after the army had been drawn up in formation there took place an event of great significance in the history of the El Paso Southwest. On that day, 30 April 1598, Oñate in a formal ceremony issued a proclamation in which he took official possession

13

of the entire territory drained by the Río del Norte for his monarch, Philip II of Spain. This act, which took place at a site near present-day San Elizario (the river at that time ran several miles north of its present channel), is called La Toma, or the taking possession of, and is significant because it brought European civilization to the Pass of the North in 1598 and laid the foundations of more than two centuries of Spanish rule in the American Southwest. Oñate's La Toma, therefore, preceded by a decade or more the colonizing activities of the English on the Atlantic seaboard, the French in Canada, and the Dutch on the Hudson River. An imposing monument in the plaza of San Elizario commemorates this historic event and summarizes the contribution made by the Spanish pioneers of the late sixteenth century.[25]

During the next several days the expedition ascended the river, and on 4 May 1598, at a site just west of present-day downtown El Paso, it crossed the river to the east side. Oñate called this operation "El Paso del Río del Norte," meaning the fording or crossing of the river – and one of the early uses of the name "El Paso."[26]

Subsequently, the Oñate party moved up the Rio Grande and established headquarters near the upper reaches of the river, north of present-day Santa Fe. A church was constructed, and in a formal ceremony the province of New Mexico was founded. It failed to yield the wealth that Oñate expected, and in 1608 he resigned his command and retired from the scene. The Spanish crown after some hesitation decided to hold on to its frontier province and organized it as a royal colony. In 1609 Don Pedro de Peralta was appointed governor. With the founding of Santa Fe that year, the Pass of the North became the principal gateway to New Mexico, and so it remained for more than two centuries.[27]

A caravan service through the Pass was soon organized to supply New Mexico, and in 1630 Fray Alonso de Benavides recommended the establishment of a mission to minister to the Manso Indians in the El Paso area. It would also serve as a way station on the caravan route known as the Camino Real (Royal Road). The friar wrote in 1630, "The last time when I passed by these Mansos they said that they would be glad to have Religious there to instruct them and baptize them," adding that the establishment of a mission with friars and soldiers would make safe the passage of the two hundred leagues from southern Chihuahua to Santa Fe.

The friar later wrote that "if anyone should wish to found at his own cost a town at the Pass of the Río del Norte, which is midway to New Mexico, royal authorities and powers should be sent to the viceroy of Mexico regarding the privileges that might be granted to him and that he might demand.... That pass is extremely important," he added, "both for keeping open that trail and for the conversion of the many savage nations in that region. Your Majesty would be greatly benefited by the foundation of such a town and by the production of the mines and farms that may be established there."[28]

Benavides's suggestion was at length honored in 1656 when two friars, Francisco Pérez and Juan Cabal, congregated some Mansos in a mission at the Pass and built a little church. Two years later, however, when a quarrel broke out between the governor of New Mexico and the procurator-general of the New Mexico missions, a number of friars including Pérez and Cabal fled to Mexico, and the abandoned Manso mission at the Pass fell into ruin.[29]

The traditional date for the founding on a permanent basis of Mission Nuestra Señora de Guadalupe de los Mansos del Paso del Norte is 8 December 1659. According to ecclesiastical records, Fray García de San Francisco served as the mission's first minister, using a small adobe church as a temporary structure until a permanent church was completed. He performed the first baptism in 1662, the first marriage, uniting Francisco Mutarama and Juana Mata, on 3 February 1662, and the first burial on 28 March 1663, when María, daughter of Tomás Fiscal, was laid to rest.[30]

The permanent church, completed on 15 January 1668, was the most beautiful in the entire Custodia of New Mexico, according to an account written by Fray Salvador de Guerra. The nave was 99 feet long and 33 feet wide; the transept measured 28 feet by 45 feet; and the chancel was 20 feet long and 21 feet wide on the side of the transept. The interior of the temple was decorated with statues, canvases, and landscapes. Under the spacious choir loft was a 15-foot-square baptistry. The sacristy measured 24 feet long and 18 feet wide, with an attached closet holding a handsome chest of drawers where ornaments, chalices, candlesticks, and wine vessels were kept. The convent provided ample quarters for the friars, and an irrigation ditch supplied water for the orchards and vineyards which surrounded the church and convent. Four hundred people

The Mission Nuestra Señora de Guadalupe became a
landmark in El Paso del Norte. (José Cisneros, 1980)

attended the dedication ceremony, concluded with native dances and fireworks. Fray Juan Talabán, later a martyr during the Pueblo Revolt of 1680, presided over the impressive affair.[31]

During the 1670s the Guadalupe mission attracted, in addition to Mansos and some Spanish settlers, Jumanos, Sumas, Tanos, and Apaches. It became the largest way station for all travelers between Parral and Santa Fe, and between Casas Grandes and Santa Fe. By 1680 a civil Spanish community had been established under the jurisdiction of Nueva Vizcaya, and the mission itself was administered by the Custodia of New Mexico. Today, this little church still stands after more than three hundred years of continuous service, a part of the cathedral complex in downtown Ciudad Juárez.[32]

By the time the Guadalupe mission was completed in 1668, work had begun among the Sumas, and in 1665 at a site twelve leagues to the southeast about where Oñate had taken formal possession of the area in 1598, a mission named San Francisco de los Sumas was built. Moreover, another mission, called Nuestra Señora de la Soledad, was built at Janos, near Casas Grandes. These three missions—Guadalupe, San Francisco, and La Soledad—were the only permanent settlements in the El Paso area when the refugees from the Pueblo Revolt in New Mexico arrived in September 1680.[33]

On 10 August 1680 Indian discontent with Spanish rule in New Mexico erupted in open revolt in what Bancroft describes as "the greatest disaster that ever befell Spain on the northern frontier, if not indeed in any part of America." From Taos to Santa Fe and from Isleta to Zuñi there were murder, pillage, devastation, and desecration. For a short time Santa Fe under the leadership of Gov. Antonio de Otermín held out, as did Isleta under Capt. Alonso García. But when communication between these two groups became impossible, the two commanders decided independently to flee southward to the comparative safety of the Pass of the North.[34]

The two groups of refugees met at Fray Cristóbal, New Mexico, on 13 September, some five weeks after the initial outbreak. Here they rested for a few days before continuing their retreat southward. On 18 September they reached La Salineta, about four leagues north of the Mission Nuestra Señora de Guadalupe, where their spirits were greatly bolstered with the arrival of a large supply expedition of some twenty-four wagons of provisions led by Father Francisco de Ayeta coming from the south. Here at La Salineta the refugees remained through the first week of October.[35]

Several important decisions were made during the three weeks the refugees were camped at La Salineta. First, a muster was taken, which indicated that the total number of soldiers, servants, women, children, and Indians amounted to 1,946. Of this number, 317 were Indian groups, inhabitants of the four Piro pueblos of Senecú, Socorro, Alamillo, and Sevilleta, and Tiguas from Isleta, who to this day insist that they fled because they sought the safety of the Pass rather than because of any special loyalty to the Spaniards. A second important decision made by Otermín at La Salineta was that the reconquest of New Mexico should be delayed until further aid could be obtained from the viceroy. Thirdly, Otermín decided that in view of the many dangers and inconveniences that confronted the refugees at La Salineta, the whole camp should be moved across the river near the Guadalupe mission where pasture was available for the livestock and wood for building shelters.[36]

By 9 October the refugees were moved to the new site, and were settled in three camps at intervals of two leagues downriver from the Guadalupe mission – Real del Santísimo Sacramento, Real de San Pedro de Alcántara, and San Lorenzo, apparently located near the site of Oñate's La Toma of 30 April 1598, where the governor and the *cabildo* established residence. At Real del Santísimo Sacramento on 12 October 1680 the first Catholic Mass was celebrated near present-day Ysleta. Placed on the Texas side by the shifting river in 1829, Ysleta thus stoutly defends its claim to being the oldest European settlement within the present boundaries of Texas. By 1682 five settlements had been founded in a chain along the right bank of the Rio Grande – El Paso del Norte, San Lorenzo, Senecú, Ysleta, and Socorro. Since that day in October 1680, there has been a concentration of population at the Pass of the North.[37]

In preparation for an expedition to New Mexico for the restoration of Spanish rule Otermín, in the fall of 1681, established a presidio and ordered a muster of all the soldiers and settlers in the area. The resulting *entrada*, however, produced only negative results, but in his retreat to the El Paso area in January 1682 Otermín brought 385 more Tiguas from Isleta, New Mexico,

and settled them with other Tiguas at the mission of Corpus
Christi de la Ysleta del Sur, near the site of Santísimo Sacra-
mento. Piros and Tompiros who came with the initial refugees
were settled at the mission of San Antonio de Senecú, while more
Piros and some Tanos were settled at the mission of Nuestra
Señora de Socorro. Thus, in a letter written by Fray Francisco de
Ayeta probably in February 1682, three Spanish settlements –
San Lorenzo, San Pedro de Alcántara, and the Presidio of San
José – were listed, along with five Indian missions – Guadalupe,
Santísimo Sacramento de la Ysleta, Senecú, Santa Gertrudis de
los Sumas, and San Francisco de los Sumas, as well as Nuestra
Señora de la Soledad, located at Janos to the southwest.[38]

Don Domingo Jironza Petriz de Cruzate, who replaced Otermín as governor in August 1683, planned to establish a presidio
named Nuestra Señora del Pilar y Glorioso San José in a location
midway between the Guadalupe mission and San Lorenzo, probably near the present site of San Elizario. Whether the presidio
was ever constructed in this location, however, is doubtful in view
of the opposition of soldiers and citizens who complained of the
insufficient wood and pasture. Moreover, the threat of prolonged
Indian warfare by the Mansos and Sumas made imperative the
concentration of the Spanish and Indian settlers closer to the
Guadalupe mission.[39]

Since the time of the first expeditions that had visited the
Jumanos at La Junta de los Rios, where the Conchos joins the Rio
Grande, the Spanish had shifted to a more direct route to New
Mexico through the Pass of the North. The Jumanos were thus left
isolated and neglected until 1683 when they seized the initiative
themselves and surprised the Spanish officials at the Pass by sending the Jumano chief, Juan de Sabeata, with a request for missionaries. Gov. Jironza de Cruzate responded by ordering Juan
Domínguez de Mendoza and Fray Nicolás López to Jumano country to found missions, explore the area for any products of value
such as pearls, and establish trade relations with the Indians.[40]

The small party arrived at La Junta and then pushed eastward
to about the present location of San Angelo. Mendoza built a fort
and a chapel, baptized Indians, killed several thousand head of
buffalo, and promised to return within a year. Memorials were
drafted calling for the occupation of the entire Jumano country

with missionaries and soldiers, but they were rejected by the viceroy in Mexico City. Quite possibly the viceroy's action, as a number of scholars have suggested, was based upon the receipt of reports of French activities on the Gulf Coast of Texas, a threat which Spanish officials had decided to give the highest priority. Had it not been for this new factor on the Spanish horizon, one can only speculate about what the history of West Texas would otherwise have been.[41]

The year 1684 was a precarious one for Spanish officials on the El Paso frontier with the outbreak of Indian hostilities along the Rio Grande and in the Janos-Casas Grandes area in what historian Jack D. Forbes has labeled "The Great Southwestern Revolt." Manso, Suma, Piro, and Tigua conspiracies and hostilities kept meager Spanish forces on the defensive for the entire year, resulting in the murder of priests, the burning of convents, the destruction of grain and livestock, and the public execution of captured Indian leaders.[42]

Not until March 1685 was peace restored, leaving a legacy of food and clothing shortages, drought, and famine. So scarce was food that many resorted to eating wild herbs, and great numbers refused to go to mass because they did not have sufficient clothing to hide their nakedness. Dissension spread through the ranks of Spanish officialdom, but Governor Jironza held firm against the cabildo's insistence that the area ought to be abandoned. His determination to preserve the El Paso district as the key to all of Spain's northern provinces, as Vina Walz has noted, was a major factor in bringing about the decline of the cabildo's influence.[43]

The Indian hostilities of 1684 emphasized the need for a more compact arrangement of the Spanish settlements for purposes of their own defense. There followed, therefore, a concentrated effort to consolidate the settlements at the Pass. Moved to a new site close to the Guadalupe mission was the presidio, soon to be known as El Paso del Norte; two leagues east of the mission was Real de San Lorenzo; three leagues to the east was Senecú; four leagues to the east was Socorro. Also mentioned in a census of 1684 were San Pedro de Alcántara, and the Suma settlements of San Francisco, Santa Gertrudis, and La Soledad. Of these, San Francisco and Santa Gertrudis were destroyed during the Manso revolt, and several other settlements were abandoned. Thus, by the eighteenth century, the following five remained: El Paso del Norte, San Lorenzo, Senecú, Ysleta, and Socorro.[44]

In the census of 1684 a population of 1,051 persons is indicated, a decline of about 50 percent since October 1680, a stark reminder that Indian wars, desertions, and starvation had taken their toll. By this time varying degrees of mixtures of Spaniards and Christianized Indians had taken place despite Spain's official policy of keeping the two groups segregated, and thus a significant mestizo population was taking shape at the Pass of the North. Moreover, about this time these settlements were declared officially to be within the jurisdiction of New Mexico rather than Nueva Vizcaya, a decision no doubt dictated by Spain's interest in the reconquest of the northern province.[45]

The price the Spanish crown had to pay to maintain the settlement on the El Paso frontier far exceeded any expected return on the investment, but the dream of reconquering the lost province of New Mexico never died. Moreover, fear of possible French intrusion in New Mexico made the abandonment of the El Paso area unthinkable in spite of all the problems. In 1685, therefore, the Spanish government granted 2,500 pesos to Governor Jironza to help him improve conditions in the area; even so, many continued to flee, defying official and ecclesiastical opposition.[46]

In 1688 and 1689 Governors Reneros de Posada and Jironza de Cruzate led forces northward, and in bloody fighting destroyed the pueblos of Santa Ana and Zía. In the following year the Spanish crown, having decided on permanent reconquest, appointed as governor of New Mexico Don Diego de Vargas Zapata y Luján Ponce de León, of distinguished Spanish ancestry. Arriving in the El Paso area on 22 February 1691, Don Diego found conditions that would have overwhelmed a less determined official. The settlements were decimated by disease, deaths, desertions, and famine. Nevertheless, the enterprising Vargas obtained peace with the Mansos and some of the Sumas, asked only for fifty more soldiers for a preliminary *entrada* into New Mexico, and said that he would bear the expenses of the expedition himself.[47]

In addition, in May 1692 Vargas worked out an arrangement involving mission lands at the pueblos of San Lorenzo, Senecú, Ysleta, and Socorro. To Fray Joaquín de Hinojosa, father pastor of El Paso del Norte, reverend father vice custodian, and lieutenant governor and captain general of New Mexico, Vargas granted *autos* of possession for each of the churches and convents, together with enough land to support the padre at each mission. He carefully omitted any reference to lands for the Indians, and in spite of a threat of excommunication Vargas held firm and continued to refuse to allow the pueblo Indians to be placed under the mission system.[48]

After Vargas's failure to receive the fifty soldiers he had requested, he recruited a hundred picked Indian warriors from Ysleta, Socorro, and Senecú. According to Vargas's plans, this first *entrada*, which left the El Paso area for Santa Fe on 16 August 1692, was to reconnoiter and determine the state of affairs in New Mexico, and was to be followed within a year with a colonizing expedition, more completely organized and equipped. The Vargas party, which remained in New Mexico for four months, returning to the El Paso area in December, was a complete success. Twenty-three Indian pueblos were restored to Spanish rule without a fight; more than 2,000 Indians were baptized. Moreover, they reported the Spanish language was still being used in a number of communities.[49]

Conditions in the El Paso area on Vargas's return were as bad as ever. A census taken during December 1692 reveals that the total population in the district was about 1,000, less than half the number who had come to the area in 1680. Moreover, only one-fourth of the New Mexico exiles of 1680 were still living in the El Paso district in 1692. Nevertheless, on 12 January 1693, Vargas in a report to the viceroy outlined his plans for the reconquest of New Mexico in which settlers were to be recruited so that the Piros of Socorro and the Tiguas of Ysleta could be reestablished up the river in the pueblos where they had lived prior to their flight in 1680.[50]

After many delays, the colonizing expedition of more than 800 persons, including soldiers and Indian auxiliaries from the El Paso jurisdiction, 900 cattle, 2,000 horses, and 1,000 mules began the march northward on 4 October 1693. Vargas was apparently unaware that the Indian situation in New Mexico had changed considerably since his first *entrada*. The natives had come to believe that they were going to be punished for their rebellious activities of 1680. As a result, Vargas encountered resistance at Santa Fe. The Spaniards countered with an assault on the community on 29 December, and by the following day Santa Fe had

been restored to Spanish control. Even so, two more years of warfare were necessary before the entire province was subjugated. In
this campaign of reconquest and colonization, the military
assistance, information, food, and other supplies provided by some
of the Pueblo Indian auxiliaries played a role of major significance.
Without this support, the Spanish effort in New Mexico would
have been a complete failure.[51]

According to the census of 1692 the population of the El Paso
district was about 1,000 – 73 married couples, 115 single men and
women, 448 boys and girls, and 250 domestic servants – living in
112 houses located in five settlements along the right bank of the
Rio Grande – El Paso del Norte; Real de San Lorenzo, Senecú,
Ysleta, and Socorro, the last four situated to the east of the El
Paso del Norte, two, three, four, and five leagues respectively. In
all probability the El Paso district lost some population after 1692
as a number of El Paso residents moved north to establish new
homes in and around Santa Fe.[52]

Thus, five settlements with a population of something fewer
than 1,000 survived those turbulent and difficult years beginning
with the arrival of the refugees of the Pueblo Revolt in 1680 and
culminating in the reconquest of New Mexico, 1693-1695. According to a report on these El Paso settlements made by Fray Juan
Alvarez in January 1706, the mission of Nuestra Señora del Paso
was ministering to the Mansos and Piros, together with some
Spanish settlers and the presidio of fifty soldiers. The Real de San
Lorenzo had become an incorporated *villa* of Spaniards and was
administered by the mission of San Antonio de Senecú, composed
of Piro Indians. The Tigua Indians lived at the mission of San Antonio de la Ysleta, and the mission of Nuestra Señora del Socorro
ministered to the Piros and Sumas. The friar also mentioned in his
1706 report a new mission of Santa María Magdalena, composed
of Sumas.[53]

Anne Hughes has summed up the significance of these
seventeenth-century El Paso settlements in this way:

> The importance of El Paso in the frontier history of
> New Spain can scarcely be overestimated. At the most
> critical period in the early history of New Mexico, El Paso
> became the bulwark of the New Mexican colonists against
> the ravages of the Pueblo Indians, and made it possible

eventually for Spanish arms to reposess the abandoned province. And, as El Paso was the bulwark of New Mexico, it was also the safeguard of the frontier settlements of Nueva Viscaya. Nor is the relation of El Paso to early Texas history the least important part that place plays in the frontier history of New Spain. Though the beginning of Texas is commonly associated with the small group of missions established by Massanet in 1690 on the Neches River in Eastern Texas, as a matter of fact, the true beginnings of what is now Texas are to be found in the settlements grouped along the Rio Grande del Norte in the El Paso district.[54]

CHAPTER TWO

The El Paso Area
in the 18th Century

FOLLOWING the establishment of the Guadalupe mission there was significant agricultural development in the El Paso area with the introduction by the Spaniards of advanced European farming techniques. At the dedication ceremonies for the mission held on 15 January 1668, Fray Salvador de Guerra made reference to the nearby orchards and vineyards. Most likely the first irrigation canal had been dug by this time by the Indians under Spanish guidance. Naturally, there was little agricultural development during the period of confusion, 1680-1684, but after the suppression of the Manso revolt and the reconquest of New Mexico, dams, gates, and *acequias* were constructed to stimulate agriculture and stock raising, thus giving the El Paso settlements a greater degree of self sufficiency. Farms and ranches grew in size and number along both sides of the Rio Grande.[1]

The *acequia* (canal or irrigation ditch) was the technological device that made it possible for Spaniards to establish settlements and support a population in the arid El Paso area. The system had been used in Spain for centuries, having been introduced by the Moors. Dams were used to divert water from the Rio Grande into ditches which averaged about four feet in depth and five feet in width. In the early part of the eighteenth century each community in the El Paso valley was fed by a diversion dam and ditch, but later the *acequia madre* (mother ditch) was constructed, connecting the various towns to a diversion dam built a short distance north of El Paso del Norte. "The *acequia madre*," wrote Carey McWilliams, the noted authority on the Hispanic American Southwest, "had almost a personality of its own, becoming the most intimate friend of every inhabitant. With dancing and ceremony the *acequias* were opened in the spring and scraped with scrupulous care. To these life-giving main canals the word 'ditches' would minimize their importance in a desert environment."[2]

While the capricious Rio Grande would frequently overflow its banks during the spring months, it often dried up in the summer. The renowned Prussian scientist, Baron Alexander von Humboldt, records that in 1752 the whole bed of the river became dry for more than thirty leagues above and twenty leagues below El Paso. He continues:

> This loss of the Río del Norte remained for a considerable time; the fine plains which surround El Paso and which are intersected with small canals of irrigation, remained without water; and the inhabitants dug wells in the sand, with which the bed of the river was filled. At length, after the lapse of several weeks, the water resumed its ancient course, no doubt because the chasm and the subterraneous conductors had filled up.[3]

No agricultural product, says an El Paso authority, caught the imagination of visitors to the area like the grape and wine industry. Arising out of a need by the missions for a dependable supply of sacramental wine, El Paso's vineyards quickly became the principal agricultural activity. They gave the area a monopoly on wine, vinegar, brandy, and raisin production, all of which was shipped in great volume during the eighteenth century over the Camino Real to Chihuahua and Santa Fe. A list of the total number of barrels of wine and *aguardiente* (brandy) shipped to Chihuahua in the period from 1788 to 1796 ran to some twenty-two pages of manuscript. As to the quality the El Paso valley produced, it ranked, according to any number of Spanish officials,

William M. Pierson, United States vice consul to Ciudad Juárez in 1872, made sketches of farming and the wine-making process in the El Paso valley in his 1872 Report to the Secretary of State. On the opposite page a farmer plows, upper left, with an ox cart at lower left. Above is an El Paso del Norte farmer sowing his field. (Pierson's Report no. 101, 30 November 1872, UTEP Library Microfilm M184R2)

Pierson's report included sketches of the grape processing for making wine.
(Report no. 101, 30 November 1872, UTEP Library Microfilm M184R2)

with the best to be found anywhere in the Viceroyalty of New
Spain. "The environs of El Paso are delicious," wrote von Humboldt,

and resemble the finest parts of Andalusia. The fields are
cultivated with maize and wheat; and the vineyards produce such excellent sweet wines that they are even preferred to the wines of Parras in New Biscay. The gardens
contain in abundance all the fruits of Europe, figs, peaches,
apples and pears.[4]

No better description can be found of the wine-making process, developed over the centuries, than that of William M. Pierson, United States consul in El Paso del Norte from 1871 to 1883.

The wine maker, he reported, first provided himself with a sufficient quantity of rawhide sacks, formed by fastening the outer edge of a large green hide to a sack form. The hide sack was allowed to dry in the sun until it was of ironlike solidity. A set of leather tramping pans, eight inches deep and large enough to fit over the mouth of the rawhide sacks, was made. These pans were made by drawing a piece of green hide over a square box. The outer edge of the hide was lashed to a square frame made of round poles. After the tramping pan dried, it was removed from the box, and the bottom was perforated with holes to allow the juice of mashed grapes to drain into the main hide sack hanging below the tramping pan.[5]

The wine house was constructed in a barn or any open space where the main hide wine sack could be suspended. Four forked poles were placed upright and stuck in the ground. Across these, horizontal poles hung, forming a frame for suspension of the hide wine sack. The tramping pan was then placed over the mouth of the wine sack after it was filled with grapes. To extract the juice from the grapes, said Pierson, "a stalwart Mexican performs the office of wine pressing by virtue of vigorous tramps from a pair of remarkable brawny feet."[6]

The juice, fresh from the press, was poured into barrels. It was allowed to remain ten days for "hot fermentation." The juice was then drawn off, leaving the sediment in the bottom of the barrel. The next step was to allow the juice to remain in barrels for sixty days. Then it was drained again "in a cool state." Thirty days from the second draining, the wine was considered to be ready for use.[7]

In addition to agriculture and stock raising, the El Paso area, strategically located roughly midway between Chihuahua and Santa Fe, became a flourishing commercial center on the Camino Real in the eighteenth century. For more than two centuries, the Camino Real from Mexico City to Santa Fe and Taos, New Mexico, was the lifeline of the Spanish northern frontier. It had its beginnings in the seventeenth century as a supply system for the missions, and the wagon trains and caravans were initially controlled by the friars. The 1,500-mile trip from Mexico City to Santa Fe took about six months, with an equal time to distribute the cargo, and another six months for the return. Gradually, especially after the founding of Chihuahua in the early eighteenth century, merchant interests supplanted those of the religious, and the El Paso area became not only a way station on the Camino Real, but an important trade center supplying both Santa Fe and Chihuahua with products.[8]

Lightweight freight wagons, after leaving the Salinas de Samalayuca, would approach El Paso del Norte directly and ford the river just north of town. The heavier freight wagons, in order to avoid the sand dunes between the Salinas de Samalayuca and El Paso del Norte, would follow an alternate route to the northeast approximating that taken by the Juan de Oñate expedition in 1598, passing through the settlements in the El Paso valley before fording the river. Ordinarily, caravans would try to avoid arrivals in the late spring months when the river would be at its all-time seasonal high. Otherwise the wagons would have to be unloaded, dismantled, and packed on rafts with the cargo, animals, and personnel.[9]

In 1752 the governor of New Mexico, Don Tomás Vélez Cachupín, after an inspection trip of his province, summarized the vital importance of the Camino Real as follows:

> The territory of New Mexico has an annual trade with that of Nueva Vizcaya through the mining towns of San Felipe de Chihuahua. In the month of November after completing their harvests, representatives from the settlements rendezvous and depart together, convoyed by soldiers from the presidio of Santa Fe to El Paso del Norte one hundred leagues to the south. There the convoy returns and is replaced by another from El Paso that serves as escort until they reach San Felipe de Chihuahua itself, another ninety-five or one hundred leagues to the south. They proceed in close order, camping at the water holes and areas that offer sufficient pasture for the horses and livestock being transported, and that are defensible against the ambushes and attacks made throughout this long journey by the enemy tribes of Gilas, Faraones, and Sumas, all three of whom live like nomads in rough and rugged places in the intervening area. Sometimes coming and going to New Mexico they lose many lives and are ruined commercially by the loss of their chief items of trade.... By the middle of April they are home to start planting. Representatives of the settlements must make these annual trips because in their province there is no way to obtain the necessary garments since merchants do

not go there, being only attracted to places where there is mining of silver, which New Mexico lacks.[10]

Because this vital commercial artery which supplied the northern frontier was being seriously threatened by the barbaric tribes, the governor strongly recommended the establishment of settlements in the intervening areas. He continued:

For the security, conservation, and well-being of the province it would be desirable if the route to the presidio of El Paso were settled; the land would permit it, being of good quality and located all along the banks of the famous Río del Norte. Likewise, the regions previously settled from the El Paso presidio itself to the boundary of Nueva Vizcaya should be repopulated. With those settlements we would succeed in keeping the enemies away from the indispensable highway, and it would not be easy for them to assault and interrupt the trade. Even though it is a project involving great expense for the royal treasury, if the plan is not carried out one fears the depopulation and ruin of New Mexico.[11]

With the beginning of the eighteenth century a new and far greater problem than any yet experienced by the El Paso frontier had emerged—a nomadic and predatory group known as the Apaches. The land they inhabited—the Gran Apachería, as the Spaniards sometimes called it, stretched from the Texas Panhandle to the Rio Grande valley, and westward to the Arizona desert. But while their main range was what is now the desert Southwest, they could extend their murderous raids, for either plunder or revenge, deep into what is now northern Mexico. Hostilities between Apache and Spaniard became a major theme in the area for a century and a half, and the hardy settlers of El Paso del Norte time and time again became the victims of the relentless and destructive Apache raids and depredations.[12]

Although many tribes and sub-tribes were affiliated with the Apaches, by far the most troublesome for the El Paso settlers were the Gilénos west of the Rio Grande, the Mescaleros in southern New Mexico, and the Natagés in the Pecos River region. These groups traditionally had lived off the buffalo, but during the eighteenth century as they came under increasing Comanche pressure, they became a far greater threat to settlements everywhere on the northern frontier. Their principal target was livestock, since they

considered the flesh of horses and mules the sweetest and tastiest
of meats, and they would go to any length to obtain it, destroying
anyone who stood in their way. They chose the highest lookout
points to appraise a situation but rarely attacked if they suspected
superior numbers. Their style of fighting was to raid and plunder
small towns and ranches, murder the inhabitants, carry off the
children, and drive off the horses and cattle. Mounted on fleet
ponies, capable of performing incredible feats of marksmanship
with the bow and arrow and the lance, the Apaches learned to
strike fast, stay out of range of Spanish muzzle-loaders, burn,
pillage, ambush, retreat, and scatter, thus making them a formidable foe, virtually impossible to control. They used smoke signals
to warn their tribes of the approach of Spanish soldiers, then
would retreat to mountainous areas the Spanish forces found
impossible to penetrate. For an entire century and a half the
Apaches kept the residents of frontier communities in a continual
state of terror, since it was difficult to predict when these "Mongols
of the desert" would strike, or in what numbers. "Ay Chihuahua...
cuanto Apache!"[13]

In 1723 Viceroy Marqués de Casafuerte, concerned not only
with Indian raids and uprisings but also with possible encroach-
ments on Spanish territory by the French, Russians, and English,
decided to conduct a complete investigation and inspection of
Spain's frontier defense system. For this assignment Casafuerte
appointed Col. Pedro de Rivera, elevated him to the rank of brigadier general, and instructed him to visit each of the twenty-three
garrisons and submit recommendations with regard to the need for
increasing or reducing the existing number, the suitability of their
present locations, the matter of salaries, supplies, and equipment,
and possible fraud and abuses involving military personnel. On 21
November 1724 Brigadier Rivera left Mexico City, traveled more
than three thousand leagues, and spent three and a half years in
his inspection of the twenty-three scattered garrisons.[14]

Arriving in the El Paso area in May 1726, Brigadier Rivera
wrote:

> I arrived in the Presidio de Nuestra Señora del Pilar y
> Señor San José del Paso del Norte, which is located on the
> south bank of this river. Next to it there is a sizable town
> of Spaniards, mestizos, and mulattoes, with two pueblos or

wards inhabited by the Mansos and Piros, who are administered by the Franciscans.

On the east bank opposite the town at a distance of four leagues are located the towns of Socorro, Ysleta, Senecú, and San Lorenzo, small settlements similar to those of El Paso. In this same direction there is a spacious valley dotted with farms where they plant wheat, corn, beans, and all kinds of vegetables, as well as a quantity of vineyards which yield fruit of superior quality to that of Parras. The natural fertility of the land is improved by the number of irrigation ditches which carry water from the Río del Norte so that the farms are free from droughts.

The pueblos of Socorro, Ysleta, and San Lorenzo are inhabited by Indians of the following nations: Tiguas, Sumas, and Piros, and they are under the care of the Franciscan order.[15]

Pursuant to Brigadier Rivera's inspection and recommendations, the Spanish crown enacted the celebrated Reglamento of 1729, the first general ordinance, notes historian Max Moorhead, for a uniform regulation of all the frontier presidios:

> In effect, the Reglamento of 1729 did little or nothing to strengthen the defenses of the northern frontier, either quantitatively or qualitatively. Rather it merely cut military costs, and even this saving to the royal treasury was not to last. In all, reforms reduced the number of frontier posts from twenty-three to nineteen, lowered their combined strength from 1,006 to 734 officers and men, and slashed the total salary budget from 444,883 to 381,930 pesos.... Forty-three years after its promulgation it was necessary to adopt another general regulation to solve the same problems.[16]

Specifically, despite the general policies of retrenchment and economy recommended by Brigadier Rivera, the presidio of El Paso del Norte fared rather well. Forty-nine soldiers were stationed in the presidio, each receiving 450 pesos a year. The soldiers were all fit, well drilled, and properly equipped. The captain was commended for instilling discipline and for his zeal in keeping the Indians under control. In spite of the viceroy's suggestion that the force be reduced to thirty men, Brigadier Rivera emphatically declared that the entire force was needed, in view of the presence of 5,000 Apaches only sixty leagues to the north. The salary of each soldier was, however, reduced to four hundred pesos, inasmuch as a price ceiling was to be placed on all the supplies and equipment they needed. The captain's salary remained at six hundred pesos a year. At length, the viceroy approved the recommendations; the proposal to reduce the garrison was not included.[17]

In general, the Reglamento of 1729 failed to provide the northern frontier with an adequate system of defense. By the 1740s the Apaches were continuing their southward surge and were attacking the interior sections of Nueva Vizcaya. The dangers to that province, as historian Elizabeth John points out, exceeded any immediate damages that the raiders might inflict, for the disturbances posed a grave danger of uprising by Indians native to the area. Although most were nominally reduced to mission life, the stress of war could possibly excite them to try to overthrow Spanish rule. During the 1750s, according to Spanish estimates, Apache marauders killed more than eight hundred people and destroyed approximately four million pesos' worth of property, all within a two-hundred-mile radius of Chihuahua. Cattle ranches, farms, and missions were being abandoned, and many silver mines were being shut down because the roads were no longer safe for transporting the ore and supplies. To a limited degree, the El Paso settlements, which had borne the brunt of the Apaches' southward surge in the early years of the eighteenth century, were given something of a respite under the protection of the local presidio, thus permitting them a limited amount of social and economic progress in the mid-century years.[18]

In May 1744 Fray Miguel de Menchero submitted a report of his visitation of the missions of New Mexico. While his population figures for the El Paso area appear to be somewhat on the high side in comparison with the computations made by Alicia V. Tjarks in 1978, they do nevertheless indicate the relative size of the settlements. Fray Menchero's figures are given in Table 1.[19]

Fray Menchero also noted that the Guadalupe mission was situated half a league from the Río del Norte and three quarters of a league from the river ditches that had been constructed for irrigating wheat and grapevines, which he said "yield abundantly and produce fruit of a good flavor and a rich wine in no way inferior to that of our Spain." A new capacious church, the friar wrote, was under construction in Ysleta. Mention was also made

T A B L E   1

Population of El Paso Communities — 1744

Settlements	Spanish Families	Indian Families	Total Families
Mission of Nuestra Señora de Guadalupe del Paso	180 *(plus 40 presidial soldiers)*	40	220
San Lorenzo	12	50 *(Sumas)*	62
San Antonio Senecú	5	70	75
San Antonio de la Ysleta		90	90
Nuestra Señora del Socorro	6	60	66
Nuestra Señora de las Caldas and Hacienda El Capitán		60	
Ranches of Ojo Caliente and El Carrizal	20 *(mixed with Indians)*		20
Hacienda de la Ranchería	20	"some"	20
Totals	243	370	613

T A B L E   2

Population of El Paso Communities — 1750

Missions	Whites	Indians	Language Groups
El Paso	1,090	200	Tigua-Piro
San Lorenzo	150	150	Suma
Senecú	102	384	Piro
Ysleta	54	500	Tigua
Socorro	250	250	
Totals	1,646	1,484	
Grand Total	3,130		

of the Mission of Nuestra Señora de las Caldas, which had been
founded north of the river by the year 1733, and the haciendas of
El Capitán and La Ranchería. Although the Hacienda de Tiburcios, the property of Diego Tiburcios de Ortega and the future
location of the presidio of San Elizario, is not mentioned in Menchero's report, it appears on his map and extends to both sides of
the river.[20]

By 1750 the population of the El Paso settlements had reached
more than 3,000, according to a census report made by Fray Andrés Varo, whose figures are given in Table 2.[21]

Quarreling between civil and religious authorities was frequent
on the northern frontier of New Spain. In 1749 Fray Andrés Varo
sent a secret letter to the viceroy that was so critical of the civil
government of New Mexico, he was prompted to dispatch Juan
Antonio de Ordenal to New Mexico to investigate and report.
Varo's charges that the Indians were oppressed and exploited by
the friars brought forth a formal denial from Fray José Ximeno,
reverend father provincial of the Province of El Santo Evangelio,
who pointed to the industriousness of the Indians and their contribution to the agricultural development of the area. The missionaries, he continued, are not only instructing the Indians in the
holy Catholic faith and the spiritual life, but also in practical matters for maintaining their corporal life, teaching them to cultivate
the land, to plant fruits, and to harvest their crops. Much good
comes to the Indians as the result of the work they do, said the
Father Provincial, because they are removed from idleness and the
many sins that they would commit. Without work to divert them,
Ximeno argued, they would soon return to their pagan ways.[22]

The civil authorities, however, refused to accept Fray Ximeno's
passionate defense of Franciscan policy toward the Indians and his
denial of the charges made by Juan Antonio de Ordenal. On 17
February 1751 Don Tomás Vélez Capuchín, governor of New
Mexico, decreed that land was to be assigned in perpetuity to the
Mansos, Piros, Tiguas, and all others who were affiliated with
them or who should join them in the future, in compliance with a
petition submitted by these Indians. They were authorized to plant
whatever seeds they wished, and their lands were to remain free of
orchards, houses, and structures. Each Indian group was to receive
a four-league tract — one league in each direction from the church

Vineyards on both sides of the Rio Grande over the centuries appeared much the same as this one near Ciudad Juárez in the late nineteenth century. (Souvenir of El Paso, Texas and Paso del Norte, Mexico, Ward Bros., Columbus, Ohio, 1887)

entrance – and they were prohibited from selling or transferring their lands. This important decree was a drastic reversal of the decision made in 1692 that left the mission lands in the hands of the Franciscans, and forms the basis for the establishment of the communally-owned *ejido* lands belonging to the Indians of San Lorenzo, Senecú, Ysleta, and Socorro. The missionaries would administer their jurisdiction, but the mission lands belonged to the Indians.[23]

The assignment of lands to the Indians was soon followed by the registration of individually owned haciendas and ranches in the area by Don Diego Tiburcios de Ortega, whose family had lived in the area for more than half a century. The property the Tiburcios family had acquired was among the largest in the area, and extended to both sides of the river.[24]

A comprehensive report on the El Paso missions was provided by Father Manuel de San Juan Nepomuceno y Trigo, who visited the area in 1754 under orders from the procurator general of the Franciscans. The Guadalupe mission he described as being

> the flower of them all, both on account of its fruits and garden products and of its climate. Although the region is cold, it is not so cold as that of the interior missions, for, while some snow falls, the average weather is like that of summer. At a distance of half a league to the east, the residents have their vineyards and fruit trees – peaches, apples, plums, and several kinds of pears. In the same

Map by Don Bernardo de Miera y Pacheco of the El Paso
area in 1758. (Reprinted with permission of University of
New Mexico Press from The Missions of New Mexico, 1776
edited by Eleanor B. Adams and Fray Angélico Chávez.)

neighborhood they have their garden, in the midst of the settlement, and a vineyard which is cultivated and pruned by a horticulturist furnished each week by the Indians, whose wines defray the necessary expenses of the celebration of the bell-ringer, a cook, two sacristans and two women to bring *fanegas* of wheat, from which their minister obtains sufficient bread for a year, and they themselves enough to meet their own needs. For this sowing the father gives them half a *fanega* of corn, oxen, and all the tools necessary for cultivation. But as we do not live by bread alone, the minister is always obliged to concern himself about the other things needed for sustenance, for, as the Indians pay no obventions, the necessary expenses for current needs are barely met from the fees which the presidials and residents pay.[25]

"The great Río del Norte," the friar continued, "is a beautiful image of the celebrated Nile, for if mortals, urged by necessity, are enlisted under the banner of the waters of the Nile, so also are other mortals for the same reason settled along the banks of the Río del Norte." The Indians of Senecú, Ysleta, and Socorro in particular had vineyards, orchards, gardens, grew corn and wheat, and performed a variety of services for the father. The Socorro Indians were the foremost in Christian fidelity and lived in an orderly and Christian manner. By contrast, the Sumas of San Lorenzo had revolted, as they had in 1745 at Nuestra Señora de las Caldas, and returned to their heathenism and their mountains. Thus, a map made by Don Bernardo de Miera y Pacheco in 1758 designates five Indian pueblos along the banks of the river with a total population of 1,065, and the district of El Paso del Río del Norte, including the presidio, with a population of 2,568, making a total of 3,633 in the area. In addition, Miera places a small settlement on the Hacienda de Tiburcios south of the river, and inserts the name Las Caldas (but without a settlement) north of the river. The name Suma appears far downriver from the El Paso settlements.[26]

In April 1760 Pedro Tamarón y Romeral, bishop of Durango, arrived in the El Paso area on an episcopal visitation of New Mexico. Despite a decade of friction in the relations between the Franciscans and the secular authorities on the frontier, the seculars joined the friars in giving him a warm welcome and in receiving the sixty-three-year-old prelate with due solemnity. He was met by a party that included Capt. San Juan de Santa Cruz, the *custos*, or superior, of New Mexico, and a large number of settlers and mission Indians in the El Paso area who met him three leagues south of town and ushered him to his destination with all pomp and ceremony. The bishop wrote that the El Paso establishment included a presidio with a captain and fifty soldiers and a large settlement of Spaniards, mestizos, and Indians. Spiritual administration was under the care of two Franciscans, one being the *custos* of New Mexico, the other the curate of the settlement. He was assisted by two secular priests, one of whom was vicar and ecclesiastical judge. The bishop had appointed the *custos* to this office during his visitation in an effort to improve relations between the two branches.[27]

A population census of the area conducted by the bishop indicated a total of 4,790 persons. A breakdown of the bishop's census is given in Table 3.[28]

T A B L E   3
El Paso Area Population — 1760

| | GENTE DE RAZÓN | | INDIOS | |
	Families	Persons	Families	Persons
El Paso del Norte	354	2,479	72	249
San Lorenzo del Real	32	192	21	58
Senecú	29	141		
a. Piros	–	–	111	425
b. Sumas	–	–	18	52
c. Sumas infieles	–	–	–	28
El Socorro (incl. gente de razón at the Hacienda de Tiburcios)	82	424	46	182
La Isleta	18	131	80	429
Totals	515	3,367	348	1,423
Grand Totals	863 Families; 4,790 Persons			

The river was a matter of great concern to the bishop, who noted that it flooded and overran its banks in the late spring months each year. A dam and a large irrigation ditch (the *acequia madre*), he wrote, diverted half of the river's waters through a network of ditches which irrigated the fields, vineyards, and orchards.

Every year, however, the flooding carried away the dam, and it had to be rebuilt. This was done by making large cylindrical baskets out of willow and slender twigs. These were filled with small stones and gravel, and when the flood subsided they were rolled into position. Thus, the bishop had touched upon a crucial problem which would demand the attention and test the ingenuity of Spanish officials for some time to come.[29]

Documentary evidence indicates that for some years during the late 1750s and early 1760s Spanish officials earnestly desired the construction of a dam strong enough to withstand the seasonal floods. The project was to be funded by a special tax on the owners of the vineyards, there being an estimated 250,000 vines in the area. Although the owners stood to benefit most from such a project, they stoutly resisted, declaring they could not afford the tax in either money or labor. The result was a stern letter from Tomás Vélez Capuchín, governor of New Mexico, to Manuel Antonio San Juan de Santa Cruz, captain of the presidio of El Paso del Norte. The governor stated in no uncertain terms his displeasure with the lack of progress on the dam project and with the engineer who was its director.[30]

After two years without progress on the dam, the governor decided on a personal visit to the area. His anger was understandable and is evident in his letter of 16 October 1764, written from El Paso del Norte. He pointed to the distinct possibility of the total flooding of Ysleta, Socorro, and the Hacienda de Tiburcios, and the loss of churches, convents, houses, wheat, and corn fields in the coming year unless immediate action was taken to control the river. Apparently deciding there was not enough time to construct a dam, he wrote that he had given orders to Don Joseph Sobrado y Horcasitas, *teniente de justicia mayor* of Senecú, Ysleta, and Socorro, to organize all Indians and residents in November to dig a large ditch and line it with branches so the river could be channeled to the fields and the settlements protected. The governor concluded by saying that he would accept no excuses for any delays and that he was depending on the fullest cooperation of all residents in order to bring the project to a swift and complete conclusion.[31]

By 1766 the dam had been completed, according to the map drawn by Joseph de Urrutia in that year. It shows the presidio of El Paso del Norte, the Guadalupe mission, an *acequia para regadio* (the *acequia madre*), a branch *acequia* labeled *Acequia de los Indios*, and a *Camino de la Presa y del Nuevo México* (Highway of the Dam and New Mexico). A description of the area written in 1773 essentially agrees with the chief features of the Urrutia sketch, pointing out that the Indians had their farms and a branch irrigation ditch, while the Spaniards had the main ditch, containing two floodgates from which the Indians' water came. The upkeep of the dam, said this writer, was obligatory upon all.[32]

Meanwhile, the population of the El Paso settlements, according to a census of 1765, remained the same as in 1760, with a total of 1,060 families and 4,750 persons for the six settlements, including the Hacienda de Tiburcios. See Table 4 for a breakdown of the 1765 population figures.[33]

These figures invite several observations. In the first place, El Paso del Norte was the largest of the six settlements, with a greater population than that of other settlements combined. Together with San Lorenzo and the Hacienda de Tiburcios, its population was largely *criollo* (Spanish born in the colonies) and mestizo. Senecú was a Piro settlement; Ysleta was Tigua; and Socorro was mixed Spanish and Piro. The Sumas were not concentrated in any one of the six settlements. El Paso del Norte had a sizable population of *genízaros* – detribalized Indians who had become a part of Spanish society. Finally, the *gente de razón* outnumbered the *Indios* by a four-to-one-margin.[34]

In addition to the perennial problem of Apache raids in the 1750s and 1760s, a second factor arose in 1763 – the international situation, which demanded the immediate attention of the Spanish monarchy. In the Treaty of Paris of 1763, at the close of the Seven Years' War, Spain was forced to cede Florida to Great Britain in return for Havana and Manila which she had lost to British forces during the war. Moreover, the treaty removed Spain's ally France from North America. While Spain received all French territory west of the Mississippi, Great Britain, Spain's foremost rival, received all territory east of that river. Such a development, in addition to the intensification of Indian hostilities, necessitated a reevaluation of Spanish policy along the entire northern frontier of the Viceroyalty of New Spain.[35]

The monarchy of Charles III, who ascended the Spanish throne in 1759, was the most empire-minded since the reign of

T A B L E 4

El Paso Area Population — 1765

Settlement	Families	Persons
El Paso del Río del Norte		
Indians	55	222
Genízaros	87	309
Citizens	420	2,068
Genízaros with status of citizens	10	36
Presidial company	49	230
San Lorenzo el Real		
Sumas	20	62
Citizens	36	202
Senecú		
Piros	95	382
Sumas	9	25
Citizens	23	115
Ysleta		
Tiguas	91	339
Sumas	3	10
Citizens	26	126
Socorro		
Piros	40	123
Sumas	15	58
Citizens	50	242
Hacienda de Tiburcios		
Citizens	21	157
Genízaros	10	44
Total	1,060	4,750

Philip II in the latter half of the sixteenth century. In 1765 the king sent the brilliant José de Gálvez to New Spain with the title of *visitador-general* and authority to institute sweeping reforms in the administrative and financial functions of the viceroyalty. In that same year, and as part of the same reorganization, the king appointed the Marqués de Rubí to inspect all the presidios on the northern frontier and to submit whatever recommendations he thought necessary for the improvement of the system. Assigned to accompany Rubí was Nicolás de Lafora, captain of the Spanish Royal Engineers, for the purpose of mapping and describing the regions visited. The result was a day-by-day narrative of the journey which lasted twenty-three months and covered almost 3,000 leagues, or more than 7,600 miles. Lawrence Kinnaird has summarized Lafora's contribution as follows:

> In the preparation of his report, Lafora used documents obtained from governmental archives in Mexico and from the presidios visited in the course of his tour with the Marqués de Rubí. Frontier officials and local guides or escorts pointed out geographical features en route. A prodigious amount of detail is contained in the report. Even the most insignificant settlements and the smallest arroyos are specifically named. Meticulous information is given about geographical features, population statistics, and frontier conditions. His knowledge of Indians in the borderlands was also extensive. Practically every tribe known to modern anthropologists and many others whose history is still obscure are mentioned. Everywhere along the northern frontier he heard stories about the savage Apaches and their audacious exploits—how they raided ranches and even immobilized whole presidial garrisons by stampeding their horses. He concluded his report by recommending improvement in methods of warfare against the Apaches.[36]

In March 1766 the Rubí party, including Lafora and the cartographer José Urrutia, left Mexico City. Over the next two years Rubí conducted his inspection in three principal areas—the regions on the route to Santa Fe, a western tour through Sonora, and the long journey to eastern Texas. In general, everywhere he went, he found the presidios in deplorable condition—little discipline, no training, soldiers in debt, and a complete lack of uniformity in weapons, uniforms, and even in the caliber of the firearms. On his return to Mexico City in February 1768, Rubí completed his celebrated *Dictamen,* or general assessment of the situation on the frontier. His basic assumption was that Spain could not and should not attempt to control regions beyond what she effectively occupied. In his opinion, the true royal dominions, with the exception of New Mexico and Texas, lay to the south of the thirtieth parallel. His recommendation, therefore, was a single cordon of presidios – possibly fifteen spaced about forty leagues (a hundred miles) apart, that could halt any invasion of the interior. Beyond the cordon of fifteen presidios would be two – Santa Fe in New Mexico and San Antonio in Texas – which would necessitate reinforcements so that they could maintain themselves in isolation.[37]

With regard to El Paso del Norte specifically, Lafora wrote:

> We arrived at the presidio of Nuestra Señora del Pilar del Paso del Río del Norte, where there is a cavalry company composed of forty-six men, one sergeant, and three officers. The annual cost of the company is 20,265 pesos.
>
> The map I drew shows the arrangements of what they call a presidio and part of Guadalupe pueblo. Following the river to the east along its right bank one comes to the pueblos of San Lorenzo del Real, San Antonio de Senecú, San Antonio de la Isleta, La Purísima Concepción del Socorro, and the hacienda Los Tiburcios. These places constitute a continuous settlement seven leagues long. The inhabitants of Nuestra Señora de Guadalupe are Spaniards, mestizos, mulattoes, and Indians of the Tigua and Piro nations, and some Genízaros. At San Lorenzo are the Sumas Indians; at Senecú the Piros, and La Isleta the Tiguas: at Socorro more Piros. In each one there are a few civilized people. Those who live in Los Tiburcios hacienda belong to this class. The total is 5,000 souls.
>
> All this stretch of land is very well cultivated, producing everything that is planted, particularly very good grapes which are in no way inferior to those of Spain. There are many European fruits which are produced in such abundance that they are allowed to rot on the trees. The inhabitants make passable wine and better brandy, but at times they do not harvest enough maize for their support, because the ground is devoted to vines and other crops.
>
> The captain of the company is also the alcalde mayor, and the people are administered by five Franciscan friars who attend the five missions, each with a stipend of four hundred pesos annually, paid by his Majesty. These stipends could be saved by placing there one or two curates with assistants. This saving would be by no means small considering that the fertility of the country brings the missionary of Guadalupe alone an annual income of four hundred pesos.[38]

Rubí noted in his *Dictamen* that the El Paso del Norte garrison, situated at latitude 33°6N, was more than three degrees above his recommended line; moreover, since the El Paso complex with its 5,000 souls was the largest in the Interior Provinces, it could provide its own defense. The El Paso garrison should then be removed from the jurisdiction of New Mexico to Carrizal, in the jurisdiction of Nueva Vizcaya. To protect the approaches to the El Paso settlements a garrison of one officer and thirty militia should be established at Robledo, on the banks of the Río del Norte, some thirty leagues, or seventy miles, to the north. Subsequently, the Rubí recommendations, including those for El Paso del Norte, were incorporated by the Spanish crown into one of the most significant documents in Spanish Borderlands history – The Royal Regulations of 1772.[39]

In 1772 Don Hugh O'Connor, or Hugo Oconor, a red-headed Spanish official of Irish extraction with seven years' experience in Texas, was named to the post of inspector general of the Interior Provinces. His task was twofold – to relocate the presidios in keeping with the Rubí recommendations, and to organize an all-out campaign against the Apaches. During the next three years Oconor traveled ten thousand miles in an attempt to carry out his assigned tasks. Some of the older sites, particularly in East Texas, were abandoned; others, such as San Buenaventura, were established; several were transferred, for example, El Paso del Norte to Carrizal. On the other hand, his efforts to launch an attack against the Apaches in the Bolsón de Mapimí, in which he hoped to utilize forces to be supplied by the governors of Texas, Coahuila, and New Mexico, fell short of desired objectives. His failure was largely due to inadequate planning, faulty coordination, and shortage of supplies, personnel, firearms, and mounts. A disappointed, frustrated Oconor asked to be relieved of his position, citing declining health as the reason, and late in 1776 his request was granted. He died three years later at the age of forty-five.[40]

The task of implementing the provisions of the Royal Regulations relating to the El Paso area was entrusted to Don Antonio María Sánchez de Daroca, lieutenant governor of New Mexico, headquartered in El Paso del Norte. On 19 November 1773 Daroca issued a proclamation ordering all residents between eighteen and sixty years of age to report to his office on Sunday, 5 December, with their firearms. All persons would then draw lots assigning them to companies. Failure to comply would result in a prison sentence, fine, and the loss of most of their personal possessions. Daroca also stated that all orders issued by any public official under his jurisdiction must first be cleared and approved by him. Failure to comply would result in imprisonment and a fine. Persons of color who violated the order—Negroes, mulattoes, and those of mixed Negro and Indian blood—would receive fifty lashes.[41]

On 7 December 1773 Daroca submitted his plan for the establishment of the El Paso militia. Six companies were to be organized —four for El Paso del Norte, one for Senecú and Ysleta, and one for Socorro and the Tiburcios property. Each company was to have one captain, two lieutenants, one ensign, four sergeants, and six corporals. Of the total of 857, only 179 were to be armed. Salaries would be paid by the Spanish crown, but most of the armament and equipment would have to be supplied by the local citizenry.[42]

Daroca's correspondence for late 1773 and early 1774 indicates that he experienced great difficulty in organizing the six companies. Although he calculated that 371 persons were available for duty in the El Paso area, he had succeeded in organizing only two companies by August 1774, and was forced to resort to a system of special guards to protect the settlements. He was working on the completion of the third and fourth companies when he was struck down by a Suma arrow. Four companies of fifty-three men each were eventually organized by his successor, Don Antonio de Arrieta, with the assistance of Don Hugo Oconor, but the Rubí recommendation of a military detachment at Robledo had not as yet been implemented.[43]

Although Oconor worked with great energy and determination to bring the Apache problem under control, the situation on the northern frontier failed to improve. The governor of Nueva Vizcaya, for example, was reporting enormous casualties. Between 1771 and 1776 in that province, where Oconor had been concentrating his efforts, Apache raiders had killed 1,963 persons, captured 155 others, made off with 68,873 head of cattle, sheep, and goats, and caused the abandonment of 116 haciendas and ranches. Moreover, as Max Moorhead points out, these alarming figures did not include the losses of military personnel or of passengers on the road whose deaths had not been reported, nor did they include the large number of horses and mules the Apaches had taken from the presidios and haciendas.[44]

The future of Spanish rule in New Mexico remained in great doubt. Fray Francisco Atanasio Domínguez, who arrived at the Guadalupe mission on 4 September 1775, wrote that he had received a letter from his superior dated 28 July 1775, citing information about the situation in New Mexico which he had received from the *custos*, Fray Juan de Hinojosa. "Its contents sorely grieved me," wrote Father Domínguez. He continued:

> The sweeping terms in which this father writes and by which he fears the ultimate extermination of this Custody arise from a justifiable concern which worries him greatly and keeps him like all those who live in these regions in a state of panic because of the repeated assaults the barbarous Apache Indians are making on this whole New Kingdom. In addition to the outrages and hostilities they commit against every kind of traveler on the roads, they enter the pueblos, steal from them all the horses and mules they find, make captives of the little ones who fall into their hands, and leave their parents, if not completely dead, without the better half of their lives, which is their children.[45]

It was readily apparent that the Rubí recommendations and the resulting Royal Regulations of 1772 had not yet solved the problem. What was most lacking was a frontier military commander with the imagination to evaluate changing situations, with the ability to implement reforms, and with the authority to deal with crises as they arose. Such an independent command was created when the Spanish crown in 1776 established the office of commandant general of the Provincias Internas, or Interior Provinces, with powers virtually equal to those of a viceroy. To this new frontier office was appointed an officer of exceptional intelligence, energy, and competence — the Caballero Teodoro de Croix.[46]

Croix went about his assigned task of crushing the Apaches with great vigor. In a series of war councils, with a number of provincial governors in attendance, a general strategy was agreed upon — a campaign against the eastern Apaches (Natagé, Mescalero, Lipan) involving a force of 3,000 men; an investigation of the possibility of a Spanish-Comanche alliance; an increase in presidial complement by some 1,800 or more; and the creation of provincial militias and *compañías volantes* (flying companies), quick-striking, hard-hitting mobile units.[47]

In July 1779, however, just as Croix's offense was beginning to gain momentum, the announcement was made by the crown of a startling new development – Spain was about to declare war on Great Britain. Croix was therefore ordered to reduce his own expenditures, cease all offensive operations against the hostiles, make an attempt to conciliate them by peaceful persuasion, and to confine his own activities to purely defensive measures. Thus, the aggressive Indian policy first recommended by Rubí, which had been consistently pursued since 1768, had now been drastically reversed by the Spanish crown. Croix's dream of a war of extermination from the Gulf of California to the Gulf of Mexico had been completely shattered.[48]

A disappointed Croix nevertheless decided that he must carry on. Obviously, he would have to revise his thinking and adopt a defensive pattern. He first moved his headquarters to Arizpe, Sonora, an indication that California was gaining importance in Spanish frontier strategy. During the next four years he was able to achieve some degree of success in stabilizing the Indian problem. He relocated some presidios and established several new ones, made his system of *compañías volantes* more effective, built a second line of defense with such organizations as the Provincial Corps of Nueva Vizcaya, reorganized a number of local militias, and brought the Comanches of New Mexico to peace terms. As a result, for services rendered to the Spanish crown he was rewarded in 1783 with the prestigious title of viceroy of Peru.[49]

Several matters relating to the El Paso area were handled by Juan Bautista de Anza, a third generation frontiersman with a distinguished record, who had been appointed governor of New Mexico by Croix in 1778. On his way to Santa Fe in the latter part of that year, Anza reviewed the El Paso militia and reduced the four companies of fifty-three men each to two companies of forty-six Spaniards and thirty Indians, and forty-seven Spaniards and thirty Indians, respectively. Anza added that the two companies would be supplied with horses and arms and would be required to make two annual expeditions of fifteen or twenty days against the Apaches, one at the beginning of the rains and the other at the onset of winter. Campaigns of three or four months could be organized anytime except during the harvest months of September and October. Finally, on Croix's order in 1780 the El Paso militia was again reorganized into one squadron with three auxiliary squads of twenty Indians each.[50]

It will be recalled that the Marqués de Rubí had recommended that a military detachment be established at Robledo on the Rio Grande, about thirty leagues north of the El Paso settlements, utilizing one officer and thirty men from the presidio of Santa Fe. Although Anza suggested in 1778 that the old pueblo of Socorro would be a better site, Croix decided to leave the Santa Fe presidio unimpaired and use the funds which had been set aside for the Robledo auxiliaries to improve the militia at El Paso. The provision relating to a detachment at Robledo was never carried out.[51]

On assuming his post as governor of New Mexico, Anza, under orders from Croix, explained to the New Mexicans that they must bow to strategic necessities inasmuch as there was an empire at stake as well as their own scalps. In Santa Fe, Albuquerque, and Taos, he placed the populace in walled towns with towers, at least fifty families in each town. Apparently the experiment worked well enough in New Mexico as a means of bringing the Comanches under control that Spanish officials decided to try it in the El Paso area.[52]

The proposal to place the population inside a walled town brought forth a loud outcry from the aroused citizenry of El Paso del Norte, who drafted a fervent protest to their superior authorities. Should this proposal be placed into effect, they argued, all residents of the area would be obliged to abandon their homes, most of which were situated on or near their *ranchos* and haciendas. As a result, the fields, crops, vineyards, and livestock would be neglected; commerce would be stifled, and the local residents, all of whom were loyal and obedient, would be unable to pay the *diezmos* (tithe) to the church or the *alcabala* (sales tax) on needed commodities. Obviously the proposal would result in great damage to the homes and possessions of all the residents. They pointed out that since the presidio of San Elizario was too far away to provide effective protection for El Paso del Norte, an increase in the number of mounts for the local militia would help a great deal in defending the settlers against the Apache attacks. The protest concluded with an expression of hope that the superior authorities would give it serious consideration and that the proposal would not be put into effect, lest it cause great damage, even the total ruin of all property and all means of subsistence.[53]

The citizens' protest had the desired effect. The lieutenant governor of New Mexico, in a letter to the commandant general, recommended that the position of the citizens be supported. What action, if any, the commandant general took is not known, but as yet no evidence has come to light to indicate that a wall was ever constructed for El Paso del Norte.[54]

By 1783 despite the rough and rugged elements of a desert environment — the inadequate rainfall, the relentless winds, the ravaging river, and the destructive Apache attacks — the hardy residents of the El Paso area not only survived but sustained an increase in population and developed a flourishing agricultural economy as well as a thriving trade with Chihuahua and New Mexico. Fray Juan Agustín de Morfi, renowned historian of Spanish Texas, commented in 1782 on a century of progress the El Paso area had made. Beginning with eleven settlements, some of Spaniards and others of Indians who had fled the Pueblo Revolt of 1680, Morfi wrote, only five remained in 1782, but each had showed gains in population and in the development of the economy. To be sure, the residents must have often wondered about their future in a period when survival required courage, fortitude, and determination. Baron von Humboldt noted their strength of character while in a state of perpetual warfare with the hostile Indians, and said that they bore a great resemblance to the Europeans of the Middle Ages, who lived and survived in a period of great insecurity.[55]

CHAPTER THREE

Spain's Last Years, 1783-1821

D U R I N G the period of the American Revolution the Spanish monarchy became heavily involved in European international affairs. Regarding the struggle of the American Patriots against Great Britain as an unparalleled opportunity to recover Florida, lost by Spain in 1763, the Spanish monarchy declared war on Great Britain in 1779. Under the effective leadership of Bernardo de Gálvez, governor of Spanish Louisiana, the entire Mississippi River valley was brought under Spanish control. Then followed the defeat of British forces in 1780 at Mobile Bay, and at Pensacola Bay a year later. Soon after the victory of American forces at Yorktown in October 1781, however, American and Spanish interests suddenly came into sharp conflict. Both sought to obtain the vast and important trans-Appalachian region lying between the mountains and the Mississippi. In the

Treaty of Paris of 1783 this disputed area went to the United States, with Spain retaining the Louisiana territory west of the river. Potential rivals and enemies thus met at the Mississippi, a threatening and alarming situation for the Spanish monarchy in addition to its perennial problem of maintaining an adequate defense system against the hostile Indians of the northern frontier.[1]

Under the successors of Teodoro de Croix in the 1780s the situation on the El Paso frontier saw some improvement. Juan Bautista de Anza, governor of New Mexico, late in 1783 forced the Navajos to give up their alliance with the Gileño Apaches, thus stabilizing the situation in New Mexico. In the following year the Provincias Internas were put once more under the direct authority of the viceroy, and in 1785 one of the most dynamic and brilliant frontier officials of the century took over the viceregal office – Bernardo de Gálvez, nephew of the great José de Gálvez, former governor of Spanish Louisiana and hero of Pensacola Bay. The able and experienced Jacobo Ugarte y Loyola was named commandant general under the direct authority of Viceroy Gálvez.[2]

The viceroy, who had mastered Indian psychology while serving as governor of Spanish Louisiana, set forth his new Indian policy in a document known as the *Instrucción* of 1786. It assumed that converting the Apaches to Christianity, for the time being at least, was impossible, and that the civil authorities would have to take over the Apache problem from the missionaries. The Indians were to be persuaded to settle near the presidios, where they would be given rations of food, liquor, and firearms (of poor quality), and opportunities to trade among themselves and with the Spaniards. They would thus become more and more dependent and would gradually give up their hostility. Should antagonisms persist, however, the Indians should be encouraged to fight among themselves. This plan, which Max Moorhead has described as "a highly sophisticated, brutal, and deceptive policy of divide and conquer, of peace by purchase, of studied debilitation of those who accepted peace and extermination of those who rejected it," was retained for the rest of the Spanish period. Although Gálvez died within three months after the document was published, its principles were effectively implemented by outstanding commanders such as Jacobo Ugarte y Loyola and Pedro de Nava, who brought a large measure of stability to the northern frontier.[3]

In the early 1780s the El Paso settlements suffered a decline in population, no doubt the result of what has been called "the greatest smallpox epidemic in the history of the Southwest." This decline is reflected in a *padrón general*, or registration, of 1784, in the Juárez Archives, one of the most comprehensive yet to come to light. A total population of 4,091 for the five settlements is indicated, or about a thousand less than the figure for the 1760s. A breakdown of the population of the five towns is as follows:[4]

Town	Men	Women	Boys	Girls	Totals
El Paso	816	845	521	549	2,731
San Lorenzo	68	74	60	41	243
Senecú	106	105	70	71	352
Ysleta	115	95	74	79	363
Socorro	115	104	95	88	402
Totals	1,220	1,223	820	828	4,091
Grand Total	4,091				

The names listed in the *padrón* are given in two separate groups: (1) Spanish citizens, residents, or *vecinos*, including *españoles*, mestizos, mulattoes, Indians (genízaros), *coyotes* (mixed Indian and Negro), and Negroes; and (2) Indians. *Españoles* outnumber Indians, the second largest group, by more than two to one, and slightly outnumber all other groups combined, including Indians. The document indicates that El Paso del Norte and San Lorenzo were predominately Spanish, while Senecú and Ysleta were largely Indian; Socorro was Spanish and mestizo. Ten slaves (four males and six females – probably Indian) are listed, as well as three Negro servants. The term *color quebrado*, or brown-skinned, is used to group mulattoes, *coyotes*, and Negroes. A breakdown of the racial classification is given as follows and represents heads of households:[5]

Town	Españoles	Mestizos	Indios(G)	Mulattoes	Coyotes	Negroes	Indios
El Paso	395	46	23	68	20	2	51
San Lorenzo	41	6			3		22
Senecú	8	17	5	1	2		70
Ysleta	24	3	7				64
Socorro	48	45	7		9	1	18
Totals	516	117	42	69	34	3	225
Grand Total	1,006						

The occupation of the vast majority of the male population, the document indicates, was that of *labrador*, whether farm owner or farm worker, reflecting the agricultural character of the area's economy. Yet El Paso del Norte had six tailors, five carpenters, three barbers, three muleteers, three shopkeepers, two merchants, two foremen, two bricklayers, two silversmiths, and one each of the following—notary, clerk, miner, painter, ironsmith, musician, beggar, and an Indian town crier.[6]

For four years, 1784 to 1788, the population of the El Paso area remained at slightly more than the 4,100 level. El Paso del Norte continued to number more than the other settlements combined; the number of *españoles* continued to equal the number of Indians, mestizos, and *colores quebrados* combined; the occupation of the vast majority of adult males remained that of farm worker. But in 1788 the area's population increased to 4,782, to 5,314 in 1789, and to 5,471 in 1795, a possible indication that Apache depredations had been brought under a measure of control. El Paso del Norte continued to be the largest of the five settlements; *españoles* remained the largest group, but there was a significant increase in the size of the mestizo population. On the other hand, the number of Indians declined significantly during the 1790s. By 1800 the El Paso settlements reached a population figure of 6,000, and thus, as Oakah Jones has noted, "there were more people in the El Paso del Norte area by this time than there were in the whole of Texas, in Baja and Alta California combined, or in the Pimería Alta region of Sonora."[7]

One major development about this time involved the presidio of San Elizario. From 1753 to 1774 a presidial force was stationed at Guajoquilla, near present-day Jiménez, Chihuahua. but in accordance with a Rubí recommendation, it was moved to the Valle of San Elzeario (as it is spelled in Spanish documents), on the banks of the Rio Grande. Here it remained for more than fifteen years, when an order dated 14 February 1789 called for its removal thirty-seven miles up the river to the pueblo of Tiburcios, near the present site of San Elizario, Texas. Several documents in the Juárez Archives dated 1790, which concern the construction of a *fábrica*, or materials plant, the making of adobes, and the recruiting of workers, suggest that the presidio of San Elizario may have been completed by 1792. Located some twenty miles downriver from El

The Presidio of San Elizario, moved to the El Paso
area in 1789, The spelling "San Elzeario" on the
soldier's uniform is correct; Americans spelled the
name "Elizario." (José Cisneros, 1980)

Paso del Norte, the presidio offered the area enough protection, in the opinion of Spanish officials, that the squadron of El Paso militia could be suppressed.[8]

During the first decade of the nineteenth century there was a significant population increase in the El Paso area from 6,190 in 1804, to 6,209 in 1805, to 6,945 in 1806. Not only had the Apache problem been brought under a measure of control, but there was the additional factor of the introduction of vaccine for smallpox and measles in 1805. Five years after Edward Jenner had published the results of his cowpox vaccination process, the Spanish government dispatched an official expedition to introduce the vaccine in the Americas. By November 1805 more than 3,600 children in New Mexico had been vaccinated at a cost of one *real* per person, and the results exceeded all expectations.[9]

A public school system was established by Nemesio Salcedo, commandant general in Chihuahua, in 1803, with thirteen schools in the El Paso area—nine in El Paso del Norte, and one each in San Lorenzo, Senecú, Ysleta, and Socorro, involving a total enrollment of 856 children. Within a year, however, the number had dropped to 584, of whom only 111 knew how to write, 96 could read a book, and 31 could say their prayers. By 1807 the number had dropped to 460, the decrease at least partially caused by children who were forced to drop out of school to help their parents support the family. The valiant effort made by Spanish officials to curb illiteracy on the frontier had met with only a limited degree of success at best.[10]

The royal postal system of New Spain had been extended to include the northern frontier in the 1770s and eventually reached the El Paso area in 1783. Santa Fe, however, remained outside the service and continued to depend upon the annual caravan for carrying both ordinary and official mail. Spanish officials therefore soon perceived the need for linking the provincial capital of New Mexico with the postal service of the Provincias Internas. A branch post office was established at the presidio of San Elizario, and by 1805 the mail service between Santa Fe and Chihuahua was operating on a fairly regular schedule. Four times a year mail left Santa Fe with the annual caravan and a military escort. The mail pouches were transported to the campsite of Fray Cristóbal north of El Paso del Norte, where a contingent from San Elizario was waiting. The bags were then exchanged and the party from upriver returned to deliver the mail from the south. Some years later a monthly postal service was organized to carry both public and official mail from Santa Fe to El Paso. By that time the transporting of mail and merchandise had been greatly facilitated with the building of a bridge at El Paso del Norte. It was over five hundred feet long and seventeen feet wide, supported by eight caissons and a bed of crosspoles. Like so many other bridges which had been built there in the past, this one washed away in 1815, but was replaced with a new one in the following year.[11]

Although the Apache problem had been stabilized by the early years of the nineteenth century, a new development had emerged on the northern frontier that gave Spanish officials great concern. Specifically, the Louisiana territory, which was ceded by France to Spain in 1763, was retroceded to France in 1800. When Napoleon Bonaparte's attempt to colonize Louisiana failed, he sold it to the United States in 1803. Thus, the United States touched upon Spanish territory at the Rocky Mountains, though the exact boundary, including the status of Texas, remained uncertain until resolved by treaty in 1819. Exploring vast portions of the new acquisition was the Lewis and Clark expedition of 1804-1806, which wintered on the Columbia River in territory claimed by Spain. By that time American merchants from St. Louis who had begun to arrive in Santa Fe, New Mexico, were seized and imprisoned by suspicious Spanish officials.[12]

In 1807 Zebulon Montgomery Pike, a United States army captain, was arrested by Spanish officials on the headwaters of the Rio Grande above Santa Fe and charged with entering Spanish territory illegally. Although Pike insisted that he was not aware that he was in Spanish territory, he was held for a time in Santa Fe and was then brought downriver under heavy guard. He arrived in El Paso del Norte on 21 March 1807, spent two days in the home of Don Francisco García, a wealthy merchant, and then was taken to the presidio of San Elizario. He remained there for three days, was greatly impressed with the hospitality of the people and the productivity of the area, and was then taken to Chihuahua for questioning. Although Pike's papers were confiscated, he managed to hide his journal, so that after his release he returned to Philadelphia, where in 1810 he published a narrative of his explorations.[13]

Other Anglo-Americans had been reported in the area by Spanish officials even before Pike was brought there in March 1807. A Dimas Procell (possibly James Purcell or James Pursley) and a Francis Lorenzo Duroret (Lawrence Durocher) were reported in the El Paso area in late 1806. No doubt the presence of the Anglo-American the Spaniards called Dimas caused them great concern, inasmuch as Nemesio Salcedo, the commandant general in Chihuahua, wrote in early 1808 that the Anglo-American was not to be allowed to volunteer for military campaigns since this would provide him with an opportunity to become familiar with the terrain in the region. In August 1807 Spanish authorities reported that an Anglo-American named Elías Bean – no doubt Ellis Bean, the one survivor of the ill-fated Philip Nolan filibustering expedition into East Texas in 1800 – was being held at the presidio of San Elizario, that his personal effects had been seized, and that he was going to be escorted to Chihuahua.[14]

Future events would prove that the appearances of these Anglo-Americans in the Spanish territory of New Mexico were not isolated cases; rather, they represented the beginning of a significant trend – the Anglo-American advance into the area. Spanish officials, finding themselves faced with a new threat, became so thoroughly aroused that those Anglo-American traders who arrived in Santa Fe in increasing numbers by 1810 would face arrest, imprisonment, and confiscation of their merchandise. Such was the prevailing situation in New Mexico on the eve of the Mexican independence movement.[15]

The invasion of Spain by the French legions of Napoleon Bonaparte in 1808 provided the spark that set into motion a vast revolutionary movement which led ultimately to the overthrow of the Spanish colonial empire and the establishment of independent republics throughout Spanish America. The Spanish monarch Ferdinand VII was taken prisoner by Napoleon, who then proclaimed his brother Joseph king of Spain. The ensuing protestation on a national scale involved denunciations of Joseph as a usurper and expressions of sympathy for the dethroned Ferdinand. A Spanish government of national resistance, first organized under the Junta of Sevilla in 1808, and then under the Cádiz Regency a year later, at length decided to call into session the Spanish Cortes, a traditional elective, representative institution, to rule Spain during Ferdinand's absence.[16]

By mid-1810 Nemesio Salcedo y Salcedo, commandant general at Chihuahua, had been informed of the establishment of the Cádiz Regency, and had received from that body a call for elections of deputies to the Spanish Cortes, to be composed of representatives from both Spain and America. The American deputies were to be selected by the *ayuntamientos*, or municipal councils, in the provincial capitals. Each council was to select three men, natives of the province, their names to be placed in a container from which one would be drawn who was to be the deputy to the Cortes. Once his election had been certified, he was to proceed to the island of Mayorca where all deputies would assemble prior to the first meeting of the Cortes.[17]

In New Mexico, Gov. José Manrrique decided that the province should be represented even though there was no *ayuntamiento* in Santa Fe to elect one. He therefore substituted prominent provincial officials, who in a meeting in Santa Fe on 11 August 1810 with the governor serving as presiding officer, selected Pedro Bautista Pino deputy to the Spanish Cortes. There were so many delays, however, that Pino did not leave New Mexico until the middle of October 1811 and did not arrive in Cádiz until August 1812, too late to participate in the debates and drafting of the Spanish Constitution of 1812, which was proclaimed in March of that year. In addition, the province of Coahuila elected Miguel Ramos Arizpe, but in Chihuahua, which had an *ayuntamiento*, the election of a deputy apparently never took place. One can only conclude that in 1811 Salcedo was much more concerned about defense measures against the spread of revolutionary activity within his jurisdiction than the election of a Chihuahua deputy to the Spanish Cortes.[18]

In Mexico City during the period from 1808 to 1810 protestations of loyalty were made to the imprisoned Ferdinand, but a power struggle developed between the *peninsulares*, or Spaniards born in Spain, and the *criollos*, or Spaniards born in America. By the end of 1810 the *peninsulares* had emerged as the dominant political force in Mexico City, even to the extent of maintaining their control over the viceregal office. By that time, however, this ruling group found itself faced with the most formidable revolt that Spanish authority had yet encountered – the revolutionary flames ignited by the parish priest of Dolores, Miguel Hidalgo.[19]

Miguel Hidalgo y Costilla, a *criollo*, in addition to the customary resentment of the Spanish-born *peninsulares* (*gachupines*
they were called in Mexico), had developed an acute sense of social
concern for the underprivileged that was not shared by the bulk of
his fellow *criollos*. He thus came to favor social as well as political
revolution – contradictory objectives as viewed by most members of
his social class. By 1810 Hidalgo was in communication with the
leaders of a conspiracy in Querétaro which sought the destruction
of *gachupín* power in Mexico and the establishment of a revolutionary government of *criollos*, mestizos, and Indians. It would rule
Mexico in the name of Ferdinand VII, otherwise ignoring all
allegiance to Spain. Late in August 1810 the Querétaro con-
spirators discovered their plans had become known to the Spanish
officials, information relayed to Hidalgo on the evening of 15
September through the medium of a midnight ride to Dolores. On
receipt of the news as daybreak was approaching, Hidalgo decided
in favor of immediate action. The townspeople were awakened and
as the crowd gathered, Hidalgo gave the battle cry that is proclaimed each year throughout Mexico at midnight of 15-16
September and which forever will be celebrated as the Grito de
Dolores. The church bells were rung, the crowd entered the sanctuary, and Hidalgo in an impassioned speech exhorted his
parishioners to recover the lands of their forefathers which the
hated Spaniards had stolen three hundred years before, and to
overthrow their treacherous Spanish masters who were about to
deliver their country and religion to the French. "Long live Ferdinand VII, and death to the *gachupines!*"[20]

Setting out across the countryside, Hidalgo's poorly armed rab-
ble gathered numbers, hoisted a picture of the Virgin of
Guadalupe, the patron saint of the Indians, as the symbol of the
revolution, took several towns in quick succession, and shortly
became an unmanageable, undisciplined mob. As the racial aspects
of the movement, Indians versus Spaniards, became more pronounced, protestations of loyalty to Ferdinand VII became far less
meaningful, while "death to the *gachupines*" was understood only as
an opportunity to plunder and pillage. At Guadalajara Hidalgo
proclaimed several reforms and undertook the organization of a
revolutionary government in late 1810. By that time, however, the
viceroy's forces had recoiled from their early losses, and in January

1811 at Guadalajara, the revolutionary army suffered a disastrous defeat from which it never recovered. Hidalgo and the remnants retreated northward, until just above Saltillo on 21 March 1811, he and the other revolutionary leaders were captured. Led over the long, dusty trail across the barren Bolsón de Mapimí to Chihuahua, Hidalgo faced the ecclesiastical and civil authorities with dignity and fortitude, assumed full responsibility for initiating the insurrection, and even confessed that the bloodshed and destruction he had caused was a mistake. Unfrocked, he was given the death sentence by a military court. On 31 July 1811 a firing squad carried out the order.[21]

In 1804 a royal order had called for the division of the Provincias Internas into two jurisdictions of equal rank, dependent upon the viceroy and designated Eastern and Western. It was at length implemented in May 1811, when Brigadier Nemesio Salcedo was named commandant of the Western jurisdiction with headquarters in Chihuahua. Having been informed of the Hidalgo movement within two weeks after its inception, and deeply disturbed by its cries of "down with bad government and death to the *gachupines*," Salcedo began immediate preparations for the defense and security of his commandancy. The Ayuntamiento (municipal council) of Chihuahua was entrusted with the task of organizing militias, raising revenues, and taking appropriate action against those whose loyalty and patriotism was suspect. As a result, during 1811 three companies of infantry and one of cavalry were organized in the city, and the other towns within the jurisdiction, such as El Paso del Norte and San Elizario, were ordered to do likewise. Officially called the Patriots of Ferdinand VII, they came to be popularly referred to as "the fernandinos." New taxes were imposed on incoming merchandise, cattle, *aguardiente*, cockfights, and dances; forced loans and contributions were ordered; and raffles and lotteries were organized. A Junta de Seguridad, or committee of surveillance, was established, its mission to bring charges against any person or organization suspected of harboring insurgent sympathies.[22]

Of the more than forty cases in the files of the junta only a relatively few dealt with insurgency or sedition, and most of these were based largely on hearsay evidence. The majority of cases involved such matters as vagrancy, drunkenness, petty thievery, forged passports, and desertion, and the usual sentence was several months of hard labor in the *obraje*. The most important case in Chihuahua involving alleged insurgency concerned Don Salvador Porras, a captain of the infantry and member of the *ayuntamiento*. Even though sufficient proof to condemn him was lacking, he was removed from both positions and fined the sum of three hundred pesos. Significantly, in two years of the Junta's operation, from 1811 to 1813, charges were brought against only two persons from the El Paso area.[23]

One case concerned Don Luciano de Torres García, a forty-year-old merchant of El Paso del Norte, who was charged with selling merchandise to an insurgent group near Monclova, Coahuila. In addition, he allegedly disseminated seditious literature, and was said to have been offered a captaincy in an insurgent military force. This information was forwarded to Francisco Xavier Bernal, lieutenant governor of New Mexico with headquarters in El Paso del Norte. Conceding that many of the stories were fabrications, Bernal nevertheless, in view of García's dealings with the insurgents, ordered him to appear before the Junta de Seguridad in Chihuahua. García was questioned by the junta in September 1811, but largely because of the collapse of the Hidalgo movement in the meantime, he was released and allowed to return to El Paso del Norte.[24]

A second case from the El Paso area, of much greater importance, involved a resident of Ysleta named Felipe Montoya. In February 1811 Commandant Salcedo wrote both the governor of New Mexico and the lieutenant governor at El Paso del Norte to be on the alert for Montoya. Montoya's correspondence, which had fallen into the hands of Spanish authorities, indicated that he sympathized with the objectives of the Hidalgo movement and was in communication with its leaders. Montoya was at length arrested in Chihuahua, interrogated by the Junta de Seguridad, convicted, and sentenced to be executed. But with the collapse of the Hidalgo movement about that time, Montoya's sentence was later commuted by the governor of New Mexico to four months of hard labor and a fine. By the fall of 1811 revolutionary activity throughout the Chihuahua-New Mexico area had subsided. From that time forward during the remainder of the era of Mexican independence, El Paso del Norte took the path of constitutional government and an elective, representative system in preference to the revolutionary movement under the effective leadership of José María Morelos, a mestizo priest.[25]

In the meantime, the Spanish Cortes, which had been convoked in September 1810, after eighteen months of deliberation produced the Spanish Constitution of 1812. A typical product of the political liberalism in the era of the French Revolution, this constitution established a representative parliamentary monarchy for Spain and its overseas dominions. Citizenship and voting rights were bestowed upon all subjects except those of African descent. Each province with a population of 60,000 or more was accorded one deputy, but two provinces with a common boundary and with less than 60,000 might be joined, giving them one deputy in common. Elections were to be held on three levels – parish, district, and provincial. Delegates from the various parishes would meet at the district level and select one district delegate to the provincial meeting. There deputies would then be elected to both the Spanish Cortes and the provincial deputation, an assembly of some nine members established by the constitution to administer provincial affairs. At the local level the constitution provided that an *ayuntamiento* was to be established for each town with a population of a thousand or more. The constitution was proclaimed in Spain in March 1812 but a copy of the document was not received in El Paso del Norte until January 1814.[26]

In July 1813 Nemesio Salcedo, commandant general of the western provinces, was succeeded by Bernardo Bonavía y Zapata, who moved the capital to Durango, much to the displeasure of Chihuahua. At a *junta preparatoria* in Durango called by Bonavía in January 1814, details concerning the elections prescribed by the constitution were discussed. It was decided that since New Mexico did not have sufficient population, northern Nueva Vizcaya was to be joined to it, thus placing El Paso del Norte near the geographical center of the area. This jurisdiction was allowed one deputy and one alternate to the Cortes, and two delegates and one alternate to the provincial deputation. Parish and district elections were to be held as soon as possible, and El Paso del Norte was designated by Gov. José Manrrique of New Mexico as the site of the provincial meeting, which was to begin on the second Sunday of March.[27]

From 11 to 14 March twelve district electors met in El Paso del Norte to select their national and provincial representatives. In accordance with the Constitution of 1812, the first act of the delegates was to hear a Mass of the Holy Spirit. This was followed by a brief address reminding the delegates of their responsibilities. Then they retired to the *casa consistorial,* or town hall, to begin the selection process. Rafael Montes, lieutenant governor at El Paso del Norte, presided, and a secretary and two *escrutadores,* or poll watchers, were elected. These were formed into a credentials committee, which then certified the delegates and the legality of their election. On the morning of 13 March the delegates elected by majority vote Francisco José de Jaúregui of Chihuahua to serve as deputy to the Cortes and Simón de Ochoa, also from Chihuahua, as his *suplente* or alternate. On the next day Juan Rafael Ortiz of Santa Fe and Mateo Sánchez Albares of Chihuahua were elected delegates to the provincial deputation, and Francisco Xavier Chaves of Albuquerque was selected as an alternate. In July an *ayuntamiento* was established in El Paso del Norte with a president, two *alcaldes,* five *regidores,* two *síndicos,* and a secretary.[28]

This experience in a representative system, the electoral process, and local self-government was, however, of short duration. With the return of Ferdinand VII in 1814 constitutional government was suspended, the Cortes was dissolved, and the Ayuntamiento of El Paso del Norte was abolished. Francisco José de Jaúregui, deputy-elect to the Spanish Cortes, apparently never left Chihuahua. An oath of allegiance to Ferdinand VII and a public demonstration of loyalty to the Spanish king were required of all subjects; anyone who continued to support constitutional government would be charged with treason. Accordingly, in El Paso del Norte an oath of allegiance to the king was taken by the citizens on 15 October 1815.[29]

In Chihuahua significant opposition to the suspension of constitutional government was expressed. José Félix Trespalacios, a prominent Chihuahua *criollo* and member of the military tribunal of 1811 which had condemned Hidalgo, was greatly disturbed by the suspension of the Constitution of 1812. In late April 1814, as he stood before the members of the Ayuntamiento of Chihuahua just before it was abolished, he declared that the constitution had guaranteed that all men were free and equal before the law, but that the doors of freedom had been closed by the king's arbitrary action. His plans to seize the military garrison in Chihuahua as a prelude to restoring local self-government were detected, and Tres-palacios was sentenced to ten years' imprisonment "beyond the seas" and perpetual exile from the Interior Provinces. His public career, however, had not yet come to an end, as he later escaped from prison, joined the James Long movement to liberate east Texas from Spanish rule in 1819, and at length became the first Mexican governor of Texas in 1822.[30]

At the beginning of the Mexican independence period the population of the El Paso area (not including San Elizario) was about 7,000, and by 1815 had almost reached 8,000. In a census taken that year the figure for the eight districts in which El Paso del Norte had been divided was 5,854, of whom 4,839 were Spanish (that is, *criollos* and mestizos), and 1,015 were Indians. The 206 members of the company of volunteers brought the total to 6,060. In addition, the population of San Lorenzo was 263, most of whom were Spanish; Ysleta had a population of 453, half of whom were Indian; Senecú had a population of 462, two thirds of whom were Indian; and Socorro had a population of 700, most of whom were Spanish, bringing the total figure in the area to 7,938. Although there was some decline in the area population in the years immediately following 1815, the 8,000 figure was reached again shortly after Mexican independence was established in 1821.[31]

A significant development during the Mexican independence period, and one which has received but little attention until recent years, was the movement to secularize the frontier missions. Although the bishop of Durango in 1767 had recommended the secularization of the Franciscan missions in Santa Fe, Santa Cruz de la Cañada, Albuquerque, and El Paso del Norte, little had been done to implement the order until after the outbreak of the Hidalgo movement. Revolutionary activity in Mexico, therefore, brought action on the part of Spanish officials to tighten their control over the mission system.[32]

An important first step in the secularization of the frontier missions was taken in September 1812 when José Miguel de Irigoyen, bishop of Durango, named Don Juan Tomás Terrazas of the secular clergy as *cura interino* of the Guadalupe mission in El Paso del Norte. Then in July 1813 a closer relationship between civil and ecclesiastical authority was enabled when Bernardo Bonavía, commandant of the Western Interior Provinces, moved his headquarters from Chihuahua to Durango, the residence of the bishop. In April 1814 the bishop named Juan Rafael Rascón *cura propietario vicario* of El Paso del Norte, and shortly after named Cura Terrazas the *capellán* of San Elizario. Rascón was then named *capellán castrense* de la Compañía de Realistas Fieles, that is, chaplain of the Company of Faithful Royalists, in addition to his title of *cura propietario vicario*.[33]

In 1817 Marqués de Juan Francisco de Castañiza, bishop of Durango, commissioned as *visitador* to the missions of New Mexico Juan Bautista Ladrón del Niño de Guevara. His visitation report contained an inventory of the Guadalupe del Paso parish, including church, sacristy, *fábrica*, and archive, as well as a description of the church and rectory. Don Juan Rafael Rascón is listed as pastor. In addition, Fray Isodoro Barcenilla, *custos*, is mentioned as the Franciscan missionary in charge of San Lorenzo del Real and San Antonio de Senecú. He was also serving temporarily at San Antonio de Ysleta and Purísima Concepción del Socorro during the illness of Fray José González. A secular thus was serving at Guadalupe del Paso while two Franciscans remained in charge of the other four missions, insisting that those which were essentially Indian in character were exempt from secular jurisdiction.[34]

Guevara's final report, written at the conclusion of his visitation, was, as might be expected, a tremendous indictment of Franciscan administration of the missions of New Mexico, including those in the El Paso area. He pointed out that the Indians were living in ignorance and refusing to comply with their Christian obligations, the schools were not cared for, the attendance of the children was irregular, their parents were neglectful and indifferent, the people were sacrilegious, and the churches were filthy and lacking in essential utensils and ornaments. He added that while the church at El Paso del Norte was the best cared for in the whole province, it was dirtier than any *pulquería* warehouse in Mexico City. So infested was it with bats and bird's nests, droppings fell on the altar cloth and in the baptismal font, and the swallows provided accompaniment for the organ. The frightful conditions in the El Paso missions prevailed, said Guevara, because of the negligence of Fray Barcenilla. To the east about twenty leagues from El Paso del Norte the heathen and perverted Apaches went to a place called El Hueco for their bacchanalian fiestas

A Mexican hacendado *(large landowner) about 1800. (José Cisneros, 1971)*

where they performed lewd dances before their children, evidence of their barbaric and idolatrous nature.[35]

Guevara concluded his report by pointing out that of the twenty-eight ministers in the province of New Mexico, twenty-three were friars, none of whom had learned the language of the Indian. Since New Mexico was so isolated and underdeveloped, he recommended a program of public education, where the Indians would be taught Castilian, Christian piety and moral virtues, and respect for the civil authorities. The arts, industry, commerce, agriculture, and mining must be developed, a provincial militia of 7,000 maintained, and needed revenues collected so that the work of the church would be supported. In view of his familiarity with New Mexico's problems, said Guevara in closing, he was ready and willing to offer his service and assistance should his superior approve.[36]

The return of autocratic rule in Spain under Ferdinand VII was followed by the restoration of Spanish authority throughout the Viceroyalty of New Spain. Although the revolutionary program under the leadership of Morelos made significant gains from 1811 to 1814, his movement had collapsed by 1815 with the defeat of his forces and his subsequent capture and execution. For the next five years the independence movement consisted of little more than sporadic guerrilla bands lacking supplies and coordination. In 1819 the viceroy in Mexico City reported to his king that the situation was under control, that there was no further need for reinforcements, and that he was issuing a pardon for all those who would lay down their arms.[37]

In Spain, however, Ferdinand's autocratic rule was suddenly and surprisingly interrupted in March 1820 by a military revolt which forced the king to restore the Constitution of 1812, the liberal document he had set aside in 1814. Celebrations were held in Chihuahua and El Paso del Norte, followed by steps to restore the *ayuntamientos* and to elect deputies to the Spanish Cortes once again.[38]

Instructions for holding elections were issued from Durango early in July 1820. As in 1814, northern Nueva Vizcaya and New Mexico were joined, this jurisdiction to be allowed one deputy and one alternate to the Cortes and two delegates and one alternate to the provincial deputation. Parish and district elections were to be held as soon as possible so that the deputy-elect might take his seat in the Cortes before the end of the year.[39]

On 24-25 September 1820 about a dozen delegates met in El
Paso del Norte, as they had in 1814, and elected as deputy to the
Cortes Pedro Bautista Pino, the same New Mexican chosen in Santa Fe in 1810. Pino set out for Spain, but never reached his
destination. He was able to collect only about half of the six thousand pesos authorized for his travel expenses, and after a long wait
in Veracruz, he decided to return home. *Pino fué y Pino vino* (Pino
left and Pino returned)![40]

In addition, the El Paso del Norte meeting of delegates also
selected Francisco Xavier Chaves of Albuquerque as alternate to
the Cortes. Juan José Ruiz de Bustamante and Lorenzo Gutiérrez
were chosen as delegates to the provincial deputation, and Santiago Baca y Ortiz was elected as alternate.[41]

Another electoral meeting, held in El Paso del Norte in September 1821, selected José Antonio Chávez deputy to the
1822-1823 session of the Cortes. All became academic, however,
when news was received about this time of the progress of the
movement for Mexican independence under the leadership of
Agustín de Iturbide.[42]

Born in Valladolid of conservative Spanish parents, Iturbide
pursued a military career and fought the Mexican insurgents for
almost a decade, at times serving the viceroy with distinction.
With the support of Mexican conservatives, who were deeply
disturbed over the restoration of the Spanish Constitution of 1812,
the clever Iturbide planned to liberate Mexico from liberal Spain.
He then obtained the viceroy's permission to march an army
southward ostensibly to crush an insurgent force under Vicente
Guerrero. Instead, after a few skirmishes, they agreed to join
forces, and together they issued the Plan of Iguala of 24 February
1821. The plan contained three major guarantees – an independent
Mexico under a constitutional monarchy; the Roman Catholic
religion and the protection of clerical privileges; and the equality
of Spaniards and Mexicans. Within the next few months Iturbide's
brilliant plan swept the country. The viceroy could do little but
accept it. Iturbide and his army entered Mexico City in triumph
in September 1821.[43]

Recent research by David Weber reveals that frontier governors at first opposed the Iturbide movement, and that local celebrations of independence did not generate much enthusiasm. In

New Mexico, for example, celebrations occurred only in response to instructions requiring the citizenry to take an oath of allegiance to the new government. Alejo García Conde, commandant general in Chihuahua, contemplating the establishment of the Western Interior Provinces as an independent jurisdiction, dispatched a military force to Durango to intercept the Iturbidists. When Durango fell to Iturbide's army, García Conde's detachment joined in support of it, thus leaving Chihuahua without defenses. On 27 August 1821 the commandant general and the Ayuntamiento of Chihuahua approved Iturbide's plan of independence and called upon all subjects to proclaim their loyalty to it. El Paso del Norte thus became a part of the independent Mexican nation.[44]

The success of the Iturbide movement in September 1821 brought to an end three hundred years of Spanish rule in Mexico, dating from the time of Hernando Cortez's conquest of Tenochtitlán in 1521. The conservative basis for Iturbide's plan of independence, of course, was vastly different from the social revolution envisaged by Hidalgo and Morelos, a Mexico ruled by all those born in Mexico, regardless of race or class, whether *criollos*, mestizos, or Indios. For that reason Mexican Independence is celebrated on 16 September, the anniversary of Hidalgo's Grito de Dolores of 1810, rather than commemorating any particular event in 1821 associated with the victorious Iturbide.[45]

CHAPTER FOUR

The Mexican Period, 1821-1848

W I T H the establishment of Mexican independence from Spain in 1821, what is now called the American Southwest became a part of the Mexican nation. After a brief rule by Agustín de Iturbide, the liberator of Mexico, a new constitution, adopted in 1824, created a federal republic roughly patterned after that of the United States. The six El Paso settlements – the five older ones that had been under New Mexico juridsidiction, plus San Elizario, formerly a part of Nueva Vizcaya – were incorporated into the state of Chihuahua. El Paso del Norte was designated *cabecera*, or capital, of the Partido del Paso, and was accorded *villa* status with its own *ayuntamiento*, consisting of a president and six members. Each of the downriver settlements was governed by an *alcalde* appointed by the *ayuntamiento*. Although elections were regularly held, the landowning and mercantile aristocracy of El Paso del Norte dominated the local political structure.[1]

After 1835 there was a strong centralizing trend, largely the result of the influence of Gen. Antonio López de Santa Anna in Mexican political affairs. States became departments and the state governors, named by the national executive, appointed local officials called *prefectos*, or *jefes políticos*, who in turn selected three-man *juntas municipales* for the larger communities and *jueces de paz*, or justices of the peace, for the smaller ones. The *ayuntamiento* was retained, but the prefect, a position largely dominated by the aristocracy of El Paso del Norte, became the real political power at the local level after 1835.[2]

With the population of the area being about 8,000 at the beginning of the Mexican period, El Paso del Norte was the largest of the six settlements with a greater number of residents than the others combined. The traditional economic activities, agriculture, stock raising, and commerce, continued to flourish in the Mexican period, providing a large degree of self-sufficiency, with the river serving as a spinal cord unifying the region. It frequently overflowed its banks, particularly in late spring, resulting in untold damage to fields, crops, livestock, and adobe structures. In the 1829 to 1831 period the rampaging river formed a new channel that ran south of the towns of Ysleta, Socorro, and San Elizario, thus placing them on an island some twenty miles in length and two to four miles in width, which the residents called "the Island," for the remainder of the Mexican period. The flooding washed away the Ysleta and Socorro missions, but in time they were replaced on higher ground by the present structures, the main part of the Socorro mission in 1843 and that of Ysleta in late 1851.[3]

A census in the Juárez Archives for the Lower Valley settlements of Ysleta, Socorro, and San Elizario for the year 1841, much more comprehensive than most, reveals a total population of 2,850. Socorro was the largest, with 1,101; San Elizario was second, with 1,018; and Ysleta had 731, involving 456 Spanish and 275 Indians, who continued to be listed separately. There were 229 heads of families for Socorro, 195 for San Elizario, and 157 for Ysleta (100 Spanish and 57 Indian). The average size of the Indian family was five, not as large as might be expected, possibly because of infant mortality and disease. No noticeable difference is found between the size of the Indian family and that of the others. The two-room adobe structure was the general pattern for all homes. The vast

*A landmark of the Ysleta area is the mission of
Our Lady of Mount Carmel, successor to the earlier
eighteenth-century building which was destroyed by a
Rio Grande flood. (Courtesy El Paso Public Library)*

majority of heads of families were farm workers, reflecting the agricultural character of the area, with servants running second. Each
settlement had a silversmith, an iron worker, several foremen, a
hat maker, a shoemaker, several carpenters, and muledrivers.
Indicators of poverty were listings in each settlement for beggars,
or the poor and needy.[4]

Interest in establishing colonies to the north along both sides
of 'the river had developed even before the area became a part of
Mexico. The earliest was the Santa Teresa grant, a four-league
tract of land assigned sometime prior to 1790 by the lieutenant
governor of Nueva Vizcaya to Don Francisco García, the military
commandant of El Paso del Norte. Situated on the west bank
about seven miles northwest of El Paso del Norte, Santa Teresa in
time became one of the wealthiest ranches in the area. Its twenty
thousand sheep and thousand head of cattle became a certain
target of increasing Apache raids and depredations in the 1830s.[5]

75

Lying thirty-three miles to the north of El Paso del Norte was El Brazito (Little Arm), a sandy tract of land within a horseshoe bend of the Rio Grande, used for centuries as a campsite by the merchant caravans traveling the Camino Real. Although El Brazito was granted to Juan Antonio García de Noriega, a retired lieutenant of the provincial militia of El Paso del Norte, and was approved by both the governor of New Mexico in 1805 and the commandant-general of Durango in 1816, several prominent citizens of El Paso del Norte voiced their opposition to García's claim to the site, since it provided Paseños pasturage for their livestock and furnished most of the area's lumber and fuel requirements. Before García could take any action, Apache attacks on the site forced him to return to El Paso del Norte.[6]

In the meantime, an Anglo-American from Missouri named John G. Heath had entered the picture. An enterprising businessman who was well acquainted with Stephen F. Austin and the Santa Fe traders from Missouri, Heath had become interested in developing the El Brazito site, and on 3 April 1823 petitioned the Ayuntamiento of El Paso del Norte for a grant. Offering to establish a colony of thirty Catholic families representing various trades and professions, Heath further agreed to provide all necessary equipment for the cultivation of the land and to build a hospital, drug store, warehouse, powder factory, and a textile mill. As a result, the Ayuntamiento, perceiving that Heath's proposal offered more benefits to the welfare of the area than did Garcia's, in accordance with the provisions of the National Colonization Law of 3 January 1823, granted Heath the El Brazito tract on 3 April 1823, subject to approval by the governor of New Mexico.[7]

Early in 1824 Heath returned to Missouri and organized a party of 150 colonists. He sold his extensive holdings and bought agricultural implements, machinery, and supplies. In April he and his colonists descended the Missouri and Mississippi in flatboats to New Orleans, chartered a boat to transport them to the Mexican port of Soto la Marina, then made their way westward across the Bolsón de Mapimí to Chihuahua and El Paso del Norte. He had no sooner settled his colonists on his land, however, when he was informed by Mexican authorities that the Iturbide regime, which had sponsored the National Colonization Law of 3 January 1823, had been overthrown by a revolution, that its colonization law

The Socorro mission was first built on a site southeast of the present one. This church replaced one that was washed away in a flood. (Courtesy El Paso Public Library)

had been repealed, and that the governor of New Mexico had therefore repudiated Heath's grant. With the rejection by Mexican authorities of Heath's numerous protests, the colonists returned to Missouri in 1825, and Heath was ordered to leave the area. He was now financially ruined, the enterprise having cost him more than $75,000, a fortune for that day. Juan Antonio García returned to El Brazito for a short time, but because of incessant Apache attacks, the property was vacated after his death in 1828. J. J. Bowden, in his excellent study of land grants in the El Paso area, writes of the Heath enterprise:

> It is interesting to speculate as to what role this Anglo-American Colony would have played in the history of the southwest if it had been permitted to remain in Mexico. The living standards of this poverty stricken area undoubtedly would have been raised as a result of the introduction of scientific farming practices, industry and skilled artisans. The new colonists and their modern firearms also would have been of avail to help check the frequent Indian uprisings. Alas, it is indeed disconcerting to learn that after the colonists withdrew from the country, Juan María Ponce de León, the Secretary of the Ayuntamiento of El Paso del

Missions of the El Paso area typically were built of adobe with decorated ceiling beams. (José Cisneros, 1987)

Norte at the time of the colony's expulsion, stated that he and other officials at El Paso del Norte subsequently regretted not allowing Heath and his associates to remain at Bracito.[8]

In addition to the Santa Teresa and El Brazito grants, there was the Canutillo grant, located on the east bank of the Rio Grande about sixteen miles northwest of El Paso del Norte. In June 1823 it was assigned by the Ayuntamiento to Juan María Ponce de León and twenty-nine other citizens of El Paso del Norte. A small settlement was established in 1824 and an effort was made to cultivate the land until 1833, when Apache raids forced the owners to leave. The property, like the other grants along the river north of El Paso del Norte, remained vacant until after the coming of the Anglo-Americans.[9]

The best known and most significant of the various land grants of the Mexican period was the Ponce de León grant located just across the river from El Paso del Norte on what is now the downtown business district of El Paso, Texas. Following a survey made on 25 September 1827, the Ayuntamiento of El Paso del Norte granted Juan María Ponce de León, a wealthy influential Paseño, a *caballería* of land, roughly about 106 acres. On his property Ponce built an adobe house, which the river washed away several years later. Then on 4 May 1830, Ponce received a second *caballería* from the Ayuntamiento, and in time developed his property into a thriving agricultural and ranching enterprise. A ranch house was constructed, together with quarters for a hundred workers, all of whom were employed in the cultivation of the fields and the care of the livestock. Ponce's Rancho was by far the most successful of the various enterprises established by Paseños prior to the arrival of the Anglo-Americans.[10]

As has been noted, Apache raids continued to be a vexing problem for Mexican officials as they had been for the Spanish, and thus constituted a major factor in the failure of the Santa Teresa, El Brazito, and Canutillo colonizing projects. As these raids increased in the late 1830s, particularly in the mining area to the west around Janos and Corralitos, a desperate Chihuahua government formed in 1839 La Sociedad de Guerra contra los Bárbaros (The Society for War Against the Barbarians). Irish-born James Kirker was placed in charge of the project and was offered

100,000 pesos to bring the Indian problem under control. Kirker, soon to become known as "the king of New Mexico," could match the Apaches in marksmanship, horsemanship, treachery, and torture. The party of scalp hunters he gathered would collect huge bounty in New Mexico and Chihuahua during the next two years. George Ruxton, the English traveler, was impressed with the fruits of Kirker's campaigns – namely the trophies he saw "dangling in front of the cathedral." But in 1841 the "king of New Mexico" retired from the project to join his former adversaries and become known as "the chief of the Apache nation." Because of the activities of the scalp hunters, Apache raids had intensified, and the destruction of life and property was probably greater during the 1840s than in any other decade of the century. As a result, Chihuahua's resources were depleted, and her capacity to defend herself was significantly compromised.[11]

Another major development in the El Paso area in the 1830s was the Chihuahua trade along the Camino Real, a natural extension of the Santa Fe trade with Missouri that began a decade earlier. In view of Chihuahua's population, twice that of Santa Fe, its extensive mining operations, and a mint that annually issued over half a million pesos in coin, Chihuahua held promise of eventually replacing Santa Fe as "the principal emporium of the overland trade." In 1822, for example, seventy men, supplied with pack animals and three wagons, carried $15,000 worth of goods, mainly of American manufacture, to Santa Fe, of which about $9,000 went on to Chihuahua. In 1846 the volume of trade was such that 750 men and 363 wagons took $1,000,000 worth of goods to Santa Fe and "sold all but a very small amount of it in Chihuahua and other interior cities." Profits generally were about 50 percent and sometimes as much as 100 percent, but the risk was always great.[12]

Edward J. Glasgow, a veteran of the Chihuahua trade in the 1840s, described the details of that trade in a letter as follows:

The goods dealt in were largely of brown and bleached cotton manufactures and printed cottons or calico – some few silk goods and woolen cloth and cassimires were included and the usual assortment of articles sold in dry goods stores, but the great bulk of the trade was in cotton goods. – Up to the time of our war with Mexico those goods were sent in steamboats to Independence, Mo. and there loaded

in wagons of large size and generally drawn by eight or
Ten [sic] mules—oxen were occasionally used but mules
were preferred, being faster and better able to live on the
short grass of the plains, to endure fatigue and the long
stretches where water was not obtainable. No white people
lived on the road between Independence and Las Vegas,
—the plains were occupied by many tribes of Indians,
Pawnees, Cheyennes, Arapahoes, Comanches, Kiowas, &
Utes—buffalo and antelopes were plentiful and the chief
subsistence for the traders and Indians—In New Mexico
and Chihuahua the Apaches roamed and constant vigilance was necessary to protect the trader's mules, there
and on the plains from Indian thieving.[13]

Josiah Gregg's statistics, while perhaps lacking in reliability in
certain details, can be used to underscore the volume of trade that
passed through El Paso del Norte. They reveal that in the years
1734 to 1843, inclusive, an annual average of $90,000 worth of
merchandise destined for Chihuahua came through El Paso del
Norte, involving 87 wagons and 157 men. The town became a
commercial center of such importance the Mexican government
authorized an annual trade fair in 1842, beginning each 8 December and lasting for eight days, with the privileges and exemptions
enjoyed by the great fair of San Juan de los Lagos in the interior.[14]

In 1835 the Mexican government established a customhouse in
El Paso del Norte for the inspection of cargoes, seizure of contraband goods, enforcement of prescribed procedures and regulations,
and collection of customs duties. Judging from an examination of
local archival material, it appears that the customhouse in El Paso
del Norte was managed fairly efficiently, and that there was far less
corruption there than at Santa Fe, for example. Basic in the Mexican system of trade regulation was the *guía* or mercantile passport,
listing pertinent information such as the name of the merchant,
number of packages, value of the merchandise, place of destination,
and the name of the person to whom it was consigned. Failure to
obtain a *guía* or any attempt to falsify information, might lead to
confiscation of the merchandise, a fine, or both.[15]

Another regulation involved the *fierro*, or brand, which determined the ownership of horses or mules. Unmarked livestock, of
course, was subject to confiscation. On numerous occasions American merchants, unfamiliar with Mexican procedures, would purchase

*One of the most impressive landmarks on the
Mission Trail is the San Elizario church facing
the plaza. (Courtesy El Paso Public Library)*

at Santa Fe horses or mules which had been stolen in Chihuahua
by Indians, only to have them claimed at El Paso del Norte by
their legal owners. The number of animals that had strayed from
their owners, or that had been stolen by Indians or sold without
the sale brand, reportedly made a "large portion of the mules in
New Mexico rather insecure property," especially if they were used
in the Chihuahua trade.[16]

Documents from state and local archives in Chihuahua reveal
that during the 1840s some fifty Americans were engaged in mining and/or merchandising activities, and that they were largely
concentrated in three localities. Perhaps half of them were in
Chihuahua, the capital city; a dozen or more were in Corralitos,
while the remainder were in El Paso del Norte. The names of four
of these Americans – James W. Magoffin, Stephen Courcier, Robert
McKnight, and Hugh Stephenson – appear in the documents with
considerable frequency, an indication of the significant role they
played in Chihuahua affairs. Two of these – Magoffin and Stephenson – later became prominent El Paso pioneers.[17]

Kentucky-born James Wiley Magoffin entered the Mexican
trade as a young man and served as United States consul in
Saltillo from 1825 to 1831. He married Doña María Gertrudis

Valdez de Veramendí of Saltillo and San Antonio in 1830. Magoffin's tenure in Saltillo coincided with the period of Coahuila's liberal colonization policy, with its far-reaching implications for Texas, but whether he had any part in shaping this policy is not known. Again, whether the Mexican Law of 6 April 1830, prohibiting any further Anglo-American immigration to Texas, had any effect on Magoffin's decision to leave Saltillo is also unknown. At any rate, by 1832 he was in Chihuahua. A letter written in December of that year to his brother Samuel indicates that he was planning a trip to Mazatlán by way of Jesús María and Alamos to purchase goods, from which he fully expected to realize a profit of $10,000. By 1835 Magoffin was supplementing his merchandising activities with a copper mining operation. Because of the great demand for copper, not only for coinage purposes but also for making household utensils, he was able to build a lucrative trade. Convivial by nature, full of Irish wit, a master story-teller, and a lavish dispenser of hospitality, Magoffin soon became "Don Santiago" to his many Mexican friends.[18]

Magoffin, like a number of other Americans, became heavily involved in the Santa Fe-Chihuahua trade. Their presence caused the Mexican officials the greatest concern, particularly because they suspected the Americans of violating a Chihuahua circular which prohibited "the sale or arms, ammunition, and alcohol" to the Apaches. The *jefe político* of El Paso del Norte reported to his superior in Chihuahua that Americans in great numbers had entered the Territory of New Mexico with mule trains, that they had been trading with the Apaches on the Mimbres River, had caused at least one stampede near Fray Cristóbal, had violated and ridiculed Mexican laws and regulations, and had stolen livestock and manipulated the brands. One of these Americans, the *jefe político* said, was named Don Santiago. He had an extensive copper trade in Chihuahua, the official continued, and encouraged his American friends to give gunpowder to the Apaches and arms and munitions to the Comanches so that the trade between Santa Fe and Chihuahua would not be disturbed.[19]

Magoffin continued his mining and merchandising operations during the late 1830s, spending considerable time on the Pacific coast. He became a member of the Ayuntamiento of Chihuahua during part of 1841 and 1842, and on several occasions served as president of that body. Presumably he acquired his Mexican citizenship about this time. Late in 1841 he led a caravan back to St. Louis, returning by way of Santa Fe with forty wagons of merchandise. South of Santa Fe he provided coffee and tobacco to the prisoners of the ill-fated Texan-Santa Fe expedition, and in Chihuahua Señora Magoffin gave them a variety of Mexican dishes and champagne. In 1844 Magoffin moved his family back to Missouri, although what prompted the action is not clear. It may have been his concern over the increasing number of Mexican regulations, the growing tensions between Mexican officials and American merchants, the lack of a United States consul in Chihuahua to represent American interests, a desire to educate his children in the United States, or perhaps a combination of factors. At any rate, the next time he would see Chihuahua it would be as a prisoner of Mexican forces in September 1846, several months after war had broken out between the United States and Mexico.[20]

It is difficult to chart the career of Hugh Stephenson prior to 1835, when his name begins to appear in the Juárez Archives. Like Magoffin, he was born in Kentucky, and he appears to have entered the Chihuahua trade by 1828. In that year he married Juana María Ascárate, daughter of a wealthy Paseño family who had extensive mining interests in the Corralitos area. At about this time Stephenson brought to Chihuahua Dr. Henry Connelly, who became well known in Chihuahua circles as a business partner of Edward J. Glasgow.[21]

Documents in the Juárez Archives indicate that by 1835 Hugh Stephenson, or "Don Hugo," was the owner of a mercantile store in El Paso del Norte in partnership with Archibald Stevenson (or Stephenson?), possibly a brother. In 1836 Hugh Stephenson was brought before the customs officials in El Paso del Norte on a charge of importing contraband gunpowder, for which he was assessed a fine, and Archibald Stephenson was fined about that same time for trading merchandise without authorization, or *sin guía*. In 1843 Hugh Stephenson moved to Corralitos to manage the family interests, but apparently he never applied for Mexican citizenship. Whether he was interned after the outbreak of war in 1845, as well as Archibald Stevenson, is not clear.[22]

Certain general observations may be made with regard to the Americans who were engaged in business activities in Chihuahua in the 1840s. Many of them amassed great wealth, particularly those who arrived before 1840; many married Mexican women from prominent and influential families, conveniently providing them social and economic advantages; some acquired Mexican citizenship, probably in most cases because it was simpler to do business as citizens rather than try to cope with all the regulations governing foreign traders; some held offices in state and local government — which required Mexican citizenship, particularly at the state level — presumably because it placed them in a better position to protect and advance their own interests. None of the American merchants in Chihuahua wanted a war between the United States and Mexico, simply because it would disrupt business, reduce profits, strain family relations, and force everyone to declare his national loyalties. On the other hand, those who arrived after 1840, men generally in their twenties, in most cases retained their American citizenship and remained single. With the outbreak of war, American merchants in the Chihuahua area were confined and imprisoned; all of them hoped for peace at the earliest possible time, not just because it would secure their release, but because it would normalize their business conditions and bring profits once again.[23]

The archival records of El Paso del Norte in the 1830s and 1840s reveal that the residents were all well informed of events in Mexico, particularly those in Mexico City, as well happenings in Texas and New Mexico. The official newspaper of the state government of Chihuahua was received regularly in El Paso del Norte, and handwritten copies were often made for the downriver settlements. Naturally, a time lag existed in the receipt of information, but the isolation and remoteness of these frontier settlements has been exaggerated.[24]

In early January 1836 officials in El Paso del Norte received a printed proclamation from Chihuahua concerning the outbreak of hostilities in October 1835 between the Texas colonists and Mexicans. All Mexicans were urged to follow the lead of Chihuahua in resisting this movement to the fullest by subscribing to a voluntary contribution to sustain the Mexican troops fighting on the Texas frontier. By 1 April 1836 El Paso del Norte had received news of the fall of the Alamo, causing Mexican newspapers to editorialize that 6 March would forever remain a memorable date in Mexican history. Mexican jubilation over the fall of the Alamo, however, was short lived. News came of General Santa Anna's defeat at the battle of San Jacinto, his capture, and his signing of the Treaty of Velasco of 14 May 1836 that called for a cessation of hostilities and a withdrawal of all Mexican forces from Texas beyond the Rio Grande.[25]

Mutual fears and suspicions between Texans and Mexicans grew in intensity after the establishment of the Republic of Texas in 1836. Texans were convinced that the Mexicans intended to reconquer the Republic; Mexicans were just as convinced that the Texans intended to conquer New Mexico. The language of the proclamations became more emotional and bellicose. In El Paso del Norte, there was no denying the conviction that New Mexico was the next target. As a result, Mexican officials made frequent calls for personal sacrifices – for contributions of men and money to help defend the national territory against the "perfidious machinations of the Texans, who have been busy forming alliances with certain disloyal elements in the Department of New Mexico."[26]

The Texan-Santa Fe expedition of 1841 was a project initiated by Pres. Mirabeau B. Lamar, who dreamed of extending the Republic of Texas to the Pacific. Having received reports that Mexican rule in New Mexico was weak and unpopular, Lamar was led to believe that the residents there would welcome a Texas commercial-military expedition that would establish profitable trade relations with Santa Fe merchants and set up a government under the authority of Texas. This would then realize Texas's ambitious claim to the Rio Grande as its southern and western boundary, as established by the Texas Congress in an act of 19 December 1836.[27]

The expedition of fifty merchants and 270 troops which left Austin in June 1841 was a disaster. The heat, hunger, thirst, wild Indians, poor leadership, and lack of discipline they experienced are all vividly told in the narrative by George Wilkins Kendall, editor of the *New Orleans Picayune*, who had accompanied the group in anticipation of a vacation. Instead of the welcome they expected in New Mexico, the men encountered determined resistance under the leadership of the governor, Manuel Armijo. The exhausted Texans were in no condition to fight, and the 172 surviving members of the expedition were taken prisoner. On the next day, 7 October 1841, they began the long march to Mexico City.[28]

From the Mexican point of view the Texan-Santa Fe expedition was regarded as a foreign invasion of Mexican soil, and its members were therefore enemies of the Mexican nation. The Mexican historian Carlos María Bustamante insisted that the affair had been instigated by Anglo-Americans in New Mexico, and urged Governor Armijo to organize an expedition for the reconquest of Texas in the interest of justice, national honor, and humanity. Otherwise, he said, New Mexico would undoubtedly be invaded again, if not by the Texans then by the Anglo-Americans, who were intent upon making New Mexico a part of the United States. Bustamante's statements proved to be highly prophetic.[29]

In New Mexico, where Mexican anger was extremely intense, the Texas prisoners were manacled, tortured, and starved, and there was considerable suffering across the Jornada del Muerto. But much needed relief came when they reached El Paso del Norte, largely because of the many kindnesses extended by the town's *cura*, Ramón Ortiz. Kendall wrote that the priest gave him a dinner with wine, a bath, clean clothes, money, and a horse and saddle. "Nor did the liberality of the incomparable *cura* end here," said Kendall. He continued:

> He ordered his domestics to bake two or three cart loads of excellent bread for the use of the prisoners on the road, and sent his own teams of oxen to transport it. To those who were most in need he gave articles of comfortable clothing, and imitating the charitable example of their pastor, the citizens were very liberal in their gifts. Mrs. Stephenson, the wife of an American merchant who was absent at the time, was indefatigable in her exertions to procure clothing, provisions, and necessities for our comfort and subsistence on the road.[30]

Kendall's description of the prisoner's departure from El Paso del Norte was touching:

> Seldom have I parted from a friend with more real regret than with Ortiz, and as I shook him by the hand for the last time and bade him perhaps an eternal adieu, I thought if ever a noble heart beat in a man it was in the breast of this young, generous, and liberal priest.[31]

Finally, as to his impression of El Paso del Norte, Kendall wrote:

> Almost the only place in Mexico I turned my back upon with anything like regret was the lovely town or city of El

87

Paso. Its delightful situation in a quiet and secluded valley, its rippling artificial brooks, its shady streets, its teeming and luxurious vineyards, its dry, pure air and mild climate, and above all, its kind and hospitable inhabitants, all held me to the spot by their endearing ties.[32]

The growth of friction during the 1840s between American merchants and Mexican officials in New Mexico and Chihuahua brought the enactment of strong measures against foreigners. Required of all foreigners engaged in business in Mexico was the *carta de seguridad*, a safe-conduct pass. This document listed the holder's physical features in great detail, was valid for one year, cost three dollars, and could only be obtained from the authorities in Mexico City. Obviously, this last requirement alone presented considerable inconvenience and numerous practical difficulties, but the failure of a foreigner to produce a *carta* would subject him to a fine or imprisonment.[33]

From time to time the Mexican government would impose a forced contribution on foreign merchants. One such levy, from which Mexican merchants were generally exempt, was enacted in 1839 in order to raise funds for the conflict with France known as the Pastry War. In addition, an 1843 decree closed the frontier customhouses and ordered a halt in the overland trade with the United States. So great was the opposition from New Mexico, Chihuahua, and the United States that Josiah Gregg predicted the outbreak of a revolution in New Mexico. As it turned out, the decree was repealed the following spring. But in 1844 came another law "which prohibited foreigners from exercising the retail trade unless they were naturalized citizens, married to Mexicans, or residents in Mexico with their own families." Obviously this law directly affected most American merchants in Chihuahua – those who had arrived only a short time before, retained their American citizenship, and remained single. Many American merchants, caught with a great amount of goods on hand, were eventually forced to sell their entire stock at a tremendous loss. The law was apparently repealed by a new revolutionary government in Mexico City in 1845.[34]

In sum, revolutionary activities in Texas in the 1830s and Texas attempts to take New Mexico in the 1840s caused Mexican officials great concern, and brought forth new laws and regulations designed to control and circumscribe the activities of foreigners operating in Mexico. An impressive number of lists of foreigners, including pertinent information about each one, appeared in the local archives for the years 1844 and 1845. Naturally, Americans complained that they were being victimized by capricious and tyrannical Mexican officials, interested only in obtaining bribes. Many Americans, argued one of their number, were being forced to accept Mexican citizenship against their will, and all of them must have felt increasingly frustrated without an American consul in Chihuahua to articulate their grievances effectively. Yet in spite of the inconveniences, the growing tensions, and the strained relations between the United States and Mexico, what the merchants feared most was a war between the two countries. Possible losses of more than a million dollars would be involved, for example, for a merchant caravan of three hundred wagons and its aggregate cargo.[35]

As the threat of war between the United States and Mexico became more imminent, and the possibilities of an American invasion of the Mexican frontier became more real, it was significant that in August of 1845, Angel Trías, whose anti-American sentiments were well known, was named governor of Chihuahua. Trías was a well educated and wealthy *hacendado* who enjoyed great popularity because of his dedication to the interests of his state. His selection, according to one historian, represented "the first time in Chihuahua history that public opinion intervened in the appointment of a governor." Learning of the annexation of Texas by the United States, Trías called for a registration of all males eighteen years and above and their organization into military battalions. He urged towns to take all steps possible for the defense of the nation. The El Paso settlements responded that they had 1,796 men ready for duty, with 677 firearms, 575 bows and arrows, and 193 lances. Presumably, they planned to fight the Americans in the same way they had fought the Apaches.[36]

After the election of James K. Polk in November 1844, but prior to his inauguration in March, Texas was annexed by joint resolution, leading to the breaking of diplomatic relations between the United States and Mexico. Desirous of restoring relations so that matters such as unpaid claims, boundaries, and the purchase of Mexican territory could be discussed, Polk was informed by the government of José Joaquín Herrera that it would be willing to receive a commissioner to negotiate a settlement. Polk promptly appointed John C. Slidell as minister to Mexico, demonstrating his failure to understand the Mexican distinction between the two terms. Word was soon received in Mexico City that Polk had appointed a minister with instructions to assume the claims in return for Mexico's acceptance of the Rio Grande boundary, and to purchase Mexican territory, particularly California. Overnight Herrera was accused of compromising the national honor, so in the hope of saving his government, he refused to receive Slidell, using the technicality that he had agreed only to receive a commissioner. Even so, he was overthrown by a military revolt led by Gen. Mariano Paredes y Arrillaga, and Slidell was given his passports and ordered to leave the country. In Polk's mind there was already sufficient justification for a declaration of war, but he was restrained by his cabinet's argument that he should wait until Mexico struck the first blow. It came in April 1846 when Mexican cavalry attacked some American dragoons commanded by Gen. Zachary Taylor, who had taken a position on the Rio Grande in territory in dispute between the United States and Mexico. Polk then drafted his war message, stating that American blood had been shed on American soil, and that war existed by an act of Mexico. Congress declared war on 13 May 1846.[37]

Governor Trías was overthrown in Chihuahua early in 1846 when he refused to support the revolt of Gen. Mariano Paredes y Arrillaga in Mexico City. Trías was succeeded by Col. Cayetano Justiniani, whose interim government attempted to inform the people of the deterioration of relations between Mexico and the United States and to rally them in defense of the nation. The prefect of El Paso del Norte, advised of the mission of John C. Slidell to Mexico, was warned of the unlikelihood of a satisfactory settlement between the two countries. The protection of Mexican territory had become an urgent matter, said the governor, and force should be met with force. It was necessary for the people to be armed and the resources found to repel the enemy; the authorities must do everything possible to protect the lives of the Chihuahuenses. The note from Chihuahua concluded by recalling the strategy employed by aggressors of the past, who had used hordes of savages to destroy property and decimate the people, and suggested that additional forces would have to be found if this should happen. Indispensable to the defense of the nation, the governor concluded, was the patriotism of the people and their determination to resist.[38]

In spite of Justiniani's leadership and strong measures, General Paredes, on 4 May 1846, named as governor of Chihuahua José María de Irigoyen, an elderly man of moderate views. Since hostilities by that time had begun on the lower Rio Grande, Irigoyen notified the prefect of El Paso del Norte that Mexican territory had been invaded and promised two armed companies of infantry to help defend the frontier. Americans in Chihuahua were arrested and imprisoned. All towns were ordered to compile lists of individuals aged sixteen through forty who could help defend the country. But by the latter part of August 1846, the Irigoyen government had received word that Santa Fe was in American hands and that an army of six thousand was marching on Chihuahua.[39]

The role of James Magoffin in the bloodless conquest of Santa Fe by American forces under Gen. Stephen W. Kearny was undoubtedly significant despite the insistence of some historians that his own account of his accomplishment was an exaggeration. Magoffin was engaged in a profitable trade between Independence, Missouri, and Santa Fe when war broke out between the United States and Mexico. Sen. Thomas Hart Benton then brought Magoffin to Washington, D.C., and introduced him to President Polk as a man of considerable expertise on northern Mexico, with a facility in Spanish and with numerous influential friends in Chihuahua and New Mexico. Polk was extremely impressed with Magoffin, wrote letters of recommendation in his behalf, and ordered him to join General Kearny's Army of the West on its way to New Mexico in the hope that Magoffin could persuade the governor of New Mexico to give up without a fight.[40]

Magoffin joined Kearny late in July and began negotiations with Gov. Manuel Armijo, who had 3,000 troops under his command. Yet during the next two weeks, Magoffin apparently was able to convince Armijo that armed resistance to the American occupation would be both unwise and futile. Col. Diego Archuleta, Armijo's second in command, had 1,000 troops prepared to resist until Magoffin informed him that the United States was claiming territory only to the Rio Grande, and that if Archuleta should lay down his arms, he might well seize the territory west of the river for himself! On 18 August General Kearny's army of 1,700 men entered Santa Fe unopposed without the firing of a shot or the spilling of a drop of blood.[41]

With the overthrow of the Paredes government in Mexico City in August 1846, Angel Trías returned to the Chihuahua governorship, replacing Irigoyen, who had failed to provide the necessary leadership. Trías knew that the news was ominous and that the situation was desperate, but he went about his task with zeal and determination. A Mexican wrote:

> [Governor Trías] has displayed the energy and activity which might be expected from his genius and patriotism. He takes not a moment's repose. He has reanimated public spirit. All is action and movement among the citizens, who hurry to enrol themselves on the registers. But we want everything, everything. There is no powder – there are not arms enough, and the few that we have are out of order – there is no lead; there is no copper, nor pieces of artillery; there is no money, and finally, no time to create resources and prepare for a regular resistance, for men cannot perform miracles. Notwithstanding this, I do not believe that the same thing will happen here, which has happened in New Mexico.[42]

Sebastián Bermúdez, the prefect of El Paso del Norte, advised the governor of Chihuahua that, despite the loss of Santa Fe, the residents of the area were enthusiastic, patriotic, loyal, and determined to prevent the soil of Chihuahua from being trampled on by American forces. He lacked weapons and gunpowder, however, and he expressed the hope that the governor could provide some help. Obviously, Governor Trías was in no position to do that, but on 26 September 1846 he did forward to the prefect of El Paso del Norte a note outlining a defensive strategy which had been approved by the Chihuahua authorities. A squadron of two hundred cavalry was to be sent to El Paso del Norte to reinforce the local militia, thus preventing the Americans from erecting a strong barricade in that area to impede the advance of Mexican forces northward. Should the Americans take El Paso del Norte, he added, the Mexicans would be prevented from sending expeditions to recover Santa Fe; it was therefore of the greatest importance that El Paso del Norte be defended, as well as the town of Doña Ana, some forty miles to the north. Mexican strategy was thus clearly defined – the highest priority was the defense of El Paso del Norte.[43]

James Magoffin, who had played such an important role in the bloodless conquest of Santa Fe, could logically assume that he could win Chihuahua in the same manner – through negotiation and persuasion rather than by force of arms. If satisfactory arrangements could be made with the Chihuahua officials, American merchants could be released and business conditions would return to normal. Magoffin thus hoped to convince his many influential friends in Chihuahua that they had as much to gain by negotiating a peaceful settlement as did the Americans.[44]

In early September 1846 James Magoffin and party began their march down the Rio Grande in the hope that a settlement with the Mexican officials could be negotiated and peace restored. But on 27 September 1846 Sebastián Bermúdez, the prefect of El Paso del Norte, reported that Don Santiago Magoffin, a naturalized Mexican citizen, and four others had been detained by the *juez de paz* of Doña Ana and ordered under escort to El Paso del Norte, where they were to be placed under arrest, their final disposition to be decided by the *juez* of El Paso del Norte. All of Magoffin's wagons, equipment, and papers, said Bermúdez, had been carried off by the Apaches at Brazito. Finally, the prefect said that he was greatly concerned about the possibility that Kearny and his army of 2,000 might proceed to California by way of the Pass.[45]

Documents in the Juárez Archives indicate that all of Magoffin's personal effects were recovered and inventoried in El Paso del Norte. The documents also reveal that Henry Connelly and Francis McManus were captured with Magoffin, and that all of them, highly suspect in the eyes of Mexican officials, were to be sent under heavy guard to be confined at the presidio of Carrizal.[46]

Juárez historian Armando Chávez has published a document, dated 12 October 1846, which indicates that on at least one occasion the higher authorities in Chihuahua, doubting the ability of Mexican forces to resist successfully the coming invasion for lack of arms, horses, and munitions, decided on a systematic retreat, the employment of guerrilla-style warfare, and the destruction of all resources that could be utilized by the invader. Such strategy, however, even if seriously considered, was discarded in favor of making a stand north of El Paso del Norte in an effort to halt the advance of a force of Missouri volunteers under the command of Col. Alexander Doniphan. "The sacrilegious invaders of Mexico

A United States sergeant in the U.S.-Mexico War. (José Cisneros, 1982)

are approaching the city of El Paso," Governor Trías told some soldiers he had assembled in Chihuahua, and "it is necessary that you go – you defenders of the honor and glory of the Republic, that you may give a lesson to those pirates." Then, after alluding to a report he had received of dissension and insubordination in the local militia of El Paso del Norte, he exhorted the troops: "You go to reestablish the character of those Mexicans, and to chastise the enemy if he should dare to touch the soil of the State: the State ennobled by the blood of the fathers of Independence."[47]

A Mexican force under the command of Capt. Antonio Ponce de León met Doniphan's rough-and-ready volunteers on 25 December 1846 at the Battle of Brazito (which the Mexicans call Temascalitos), twenty-eight miles northwest of El Paso del Norte. The Mexican troops, who had been confident of victory, were routed in a clash lasting about thirty minutes. Reportedly, the Mexicans misinterpreted a bugle call, which left them in a confused, demoralized condition and at the mercy of a strong American charge. On 27 December American forces entered El Paso del Norte and, as the American standard was raised in the plaza, one old Mexican patriot was moved to comment, "This sad event was the last important occurrence of the mournful year 1846."[48]

In the meantime, the old scalp hunter James Kirker, erstwhile "king of New Mexico" and "chief of the Apache nation," had joined Doniphan's forces. Kirker during the summer of 1846 once again had worked for the Chihuahua government, but when the hard-pressed Trías was no longer able to pay for Apache scalps, Kirker was offered the rank of colonel in the Mexican army. This he refused, so with a ten-thousand-peso price on his head as an enemy of the state, he headed north to join Doniphan's volunteers as they entered El Paso del Norte.[49]

Shortly after the American occupation, a junta of Mexican officials voted overwhelmingly to continue the resistance and to carry the war to the enemy insofar as possible. Meanwhile, Doniphan's troops arrested several Mexicans for anti-American activities, including the prefect Sebastián Bermúdez and the priest Ramón Ortiz, who had been so hospitable toward the prisoners of the Texan-Santa Fe expedition. Somewhat later, eighteen-year-old Susan Magoffin, sister-in-law of James Magoffin, recorded the opinions of José Ignacio Ronquillo, a Paseño aristocrat:

Don Ygnacio is a second George Washington in his *appearance*, and is altogether a great admirer of the man whose name is ever dear to the hearts of the American; he said the course Mr. Polk is persuing [sic] in regard to this war, is entirely against the principals [sic] of Washington, which were to remain at home, encourage all home improvements, to defend our rights *there* against the incroachments [sic] of others, and never to invade the territory of another nation.[50]

But for the most part the general populace seemed to accept the reality of the occupation and apparently decided to make the best of an unenviable situation. Doniphan's men took over the mills, assuring them of a food supply, and the people gave the soldiers fruits, wine, and provisions. The Americans found the women and fandangos to their liking; several romances developed. In spite of the wind and the sand, one American wrote, after he had been in El Paso del Norte for more than a month, it appeared "to be the garden spot of Mexico."[51]

In the opinion of John T. Hughes, who accompanied the Doniphan expedition and wrote its history, the conquest of the El Paso area was an extremely significant development in the "westward march of civilization and republican government." Commenting on the superior quality of the wine and the revenue it produced, Hughes then added:

If this valley were cultivated by an energetic American population, it would yield, perhaps, ten times the quantity of wine and fruits at present produced. Were the wholesome influences and protection of our Republican Institutions extended to the Río del Norte, an American population, possessing American feelings, and speaking the American language, would soon spring up here.

Hughes then pointed out that with the opening of a communication between this rich valley and the western states of our union by a turnpike, railroad, or canal, this area would soon become the "seat of wealth, influence, and refinement, and one of the richest and most fashionable parts of the continent."[52]

The American army remained in El Paso del Norte during the entire month of January 1847, since Doniphan was still not clear about his next assignment, and was in need of reinforcements and artillery. With all the inactivity the men became restless and roving, leading to depression, drunkenness, dissipation, and rioting.

There was an outbreak of scurvy. But the greatest tragedy of the American occupation of El Paso del Norte in 1846-1847 was the destruction of a portion of the municipal archives by soldiers quartered in government buildings, who used the manuscripts to light their candles.[53]

Doniphan's problems were immensely complicated by the arrival from Santa Fe of some 150 merchants and 315 wagons of merchandise valued at $2,000 to $3,000 per wagon. Since the war was obviously interfering with sales and profits, the merchants pressured Doniphan to provide a vanguard and sufficient protection so that the goods could be sold, rather than allowed to fall into the hands of the Mexican army. At length, after receiving additional artillery from Santa Fe and concluding that Gen. John Wool's army in Coahuila, for unknown reasons, was not going to invade Chihuahua, Doniphan, his army, and the merchants departed for the capital of the state on 8 February 1847. A few days later Doniphan organized the merchants into two infantry companies, in the hope that they might become a military asset rather than just a liability.[54]

The Americans could see that the Mexicans were making feverish preparations to resist, staking everything on a crushing defeat over the invading army deep in the interior of Chihuahua. Measures included the forcible enlistment of "volunteers," the casting and mounting of cannons, the manufacturing of clothing and ammunition, and the levying of a forced loan. The story was circulated that in the event of an American victory, Doniphan had promised his soldiers "two hours to ravish the women, two hours to sack the city, and two hours to burn it." The Mexican commander, José Heredia, ordered a stand to be made at the Sacramento River, about fifteen miles north of the capital, where he camped on 27 February. Expecting the American army to arrive on the following day, Mexican soldiers celebrated the coming encounter.

> In every tent, in every friendly group, cheerful toasts were drunk to the liberty of the country, the young men abandoning themselves to the illusive delirium of expected triumph, and thinking more of their expedition to New Mexico, to assist their brethren, and to cast off the American yoke, than of the approaching encounter, which they looked upon as less important than it was.[55]

The battle of Sacramento began the next afternoon, lasted about three hours, and resulted in a complete rout of Heredia's forces, many of whom had never before "heard the whisperings of a cannon ball." Mexican historians generally agree that the defeat at the Sacramento River was due to the lack of leadership, organization, discipline, and experience. Bustamante adds that the demand for American merchandise undermined the Mexican will to resist. The news of the defeat caused such panic in Chihuahua, says historian Ponce de León, that the people fled to the countryside, preferring the ferocity of the Apaches to the rapacity of the American soldiers.[56]

Doniphan's army entered Chihuahua on 2 March 1847. Feelings between Americans and Mexicans ran much higher than they had in El Paso del Norte, and there was a greater amount of destruction of property by the invading forces. According to Almada, Doniphan's men profaned the cathedral, sacked some homes, including that of Governor Trías, seized the flour in the alhóndiga (granary), cut the trees on the alamedas for firewood, and destroyed part of an archive. The Americans published a newspaper called The Anglo Saxon, a title with obvious racial overtones. Although Doniphan and Trías could never agree to armistice terms, twenty American merchants who had been held at Cusihuiriachic were released. James Magoffin, however, still regarded as an enemy alien, remained in custody in Durango until the end of the war. American forces at length occupied Galeana, Barranco, and Corralitos for a time, but all forces were evacuated when Doniphan and his army left for Saltillo on 28 April 1847. Most of the merchants left with Doniphan. Some returned to New Mexico and a few remained in Chihuahua, one of them, Alfonso C. Anderson, being named United States vice consul.[57]

The final phase of the war came with the landing of Gen. Winfield Scott's army at Veracruz in March 1847. During the next six months American forces fought their way into Mexico's heartland, and by August they had penetrated the outskirts of Mexico City. The final battle was fought when Chapultepec Castle was taken by storm on 13 September 1847, and was followed by negotiations leading to the signing of a peace treaty.[58]

The Treaty of Guadalupe Hidalgo, signed on 2 February 1848, officially ended the war between the United States and Mexico. It provided that the new international boundary was to be "the Rio Grande...following the deepest channel...to the point where it strikes the southern boundary of New Mexico; thence, westwardly, along the whole southern boundary of New Mexico (which runs north of the town called Paso) to its western termination," north to the Gila River, then following the Gila until it empties into the Colorado River, and westward to the Pacific. Thus, all the territory north of that line, known as the Mexican Cession and comprising half of Mexico's national domain, became a part of the United States, which was to pay Mexico the sum of $15 million.[59]

Three days later, on 5 February, a Chihuahua delegation submitted to the Mexican government a formal protest specifically outlining the official Chihuahua position regarding the northern boundary. Undoubtedly they understood that their efforts would amount only to an exercise in futility, but their thinking on the matter of making the Rio Grande an international boundary is of interest. The delegation argued:

> It can be seen clearly how much this state would lose if the Río Bravo becomes the eastern boundary of the republic between Chihuahua and the United States. Since 1845 the Chihuahua government has made clear not only the value of what it is losing, but also the very serious problems involved in the dismemberment of a portion of the territory of this state.... Lost will be the fertile river banks, the mountains, the salt deposits, and finally, all the lands that the inhabitants of El Paso del Norte possess on the left bank of the Rio Bravo from 31°57' to 32°57' 43" north latitude, and thus all the elements they need for their subsistence will have disappeared.... If they have to move to the other bank of the river, they will have to abandon their *ejidos* on the east side, and they will have to apply to a foreign country for firewood, charcoal, and the palisade they need to construct the dam to bring water to the center of town. Such could be the dilemma of a district of 15,000 inhabitants....
>
> Another problem concerns the savage tribes living between the Bravo and the Pecos rivers. If these lands are lost to Chihuahua and the Americans begin to colonize them, the barbarians will be driven by the settlers into Chihuahua and the ruin of the state is inevitable since the citizens who do not leave will no doubt perish at the hands of these savages, commerce and agriculture will suffer, lives

will be lost, cattle will be stolen, and property will be
destroyed. Furthermore, our salt supply from the mines of
El Paso will fall under foreign control.... Thus, the question is one of life or death for the state, and we do not
believe it is obligated to commit suicide in consenting to
the sale of part of its territory.

May we point out that Chihuahua, in spite of her sad
situation, organized her own defenses against the invaders
and fought them at El Paso del Norte without any
assistance from the national government, and when Mexico abandoned her, Chihuahua made a formal declaration
of her adherence and loyalty to the republic.... But now if
it is dismembered, it will never feel sufficiently assured that
the Mexican government might not some day transfer the
rest of this country and its inhabitants, and we do not
want to be turned over to a foreign government at the
price of the liberty of the other states.[60]

In February 1848 Gen. Sterling Price, commander of an American army in New Mexico, descended the Rio Grande and invaded
Chihuahua. Price had not yet learned that a treaty had been
signed and apparently believed that a Mexican force was about to
reconquer Chihuahua. Mexican efforts to negotiate an agreement
with Price were rejected as a Mexican subterfuge, and at Santa
Cruz de Rosales a force commanded by Gov. Angel Trías was
assaulted and forced to surrender. With the receipt of word that
peace had been signed, Price withdrew his force to New Mexico in
July 1848, but left one company of dragoons stationed at Socorro
on the new boundary between the United States and Mexico.[61]

Momentous changes took place in the El Paso area during the
Mexican period, reaching a climax in the year 1848. Before that
date there had been six settlements in a chain along the right
bank of the Rio Grande – El Paso del Norte with its haciendas and
ranchos, and the five downriver towns with their *ejidos* and forests
on both sides of the river. But in 1848 the river became an international boundary, and El Paso del Norte became a border town.
Within a short time five settlements were established by Anglo-
Americans, joining the three Mexican settlements of Ysleta,
Socorro, and San Elizario, which the shifting river placed on the
United States side. The nucleus of a bicultural community across
the river from El Paso del Norte was in the process of formation.[62]

II. The Legacy of the American Southwest

Coming of the Railroad, 1881.
(José Cisneros, 1980)

CHAPTER FIVE

American El Paso, 1848-1854

I N late January 1848, less than two weeks before the signing of the Treaty of Guadalupe Hidalgo that gave the American Southwest to the United States, gold was discovered in California. Within a short time this brought into the El Paso area hordes of adventurers, opportunists, characters larger than life, discharged soldiers, outlaws, wife deserters, debtors, and the first Anglo female resident, a six-foot amazon known as "the Great Western." Overnight the quiet little adobe town of El Paso del Norte was transformed into a bustling, brawling frontier crossroads, described as "the last place to rest, pur-chase supplies, ask directions, secure passports," and refresh dehy-drated bodies with generous allotments of "Pass Whiskey."[1]

To the California emigrants of 1849 who braved hundreds of miles of vast dry plain of western Texas, a region virtually without

The mission of Our Lady of Guadalupe in El Paso
del Norte has been a landmark since the late seventeenth
century. (Courtesy El Paso Public Library)

timber, grassland, or water, El Paso del Norte, with its cottonwood
trees, gardens, vineyards, town plaza, adobe structures with thick
walls and shaded entrances, must have seemed like a true oasis.
"The sight of this little place," wrote one,

> is truly refreshing to the weary traveller of the plains –
> indeed, the cool shady avenues, fragrant breezes, delicious
> fruits and luxuriant appearance of everything around,
> makes one almost feel that he is transported to the bowers
> of Eden. The productions of this place are corn, wheat,
> beans, vegetables, and fruits of every variety. Great care
> and attention is paid to the culture of the grape and con-
> siderable wine is manufactured. The houses are built of
> adobe, flat roofed and one story high. They are comfort-
> able both in summer and winter and said to be very dur-
> able. The church which is the largest building in the place
> is about forty by one hundred feet in dimension and two
> stories high. The interior is very handsomely carved and
> ornamented, and the church is situated in the Grand Plaza
> and about the center of town. The whole valley is irrigated
> by means of an aqueduct which leads from the falls of the
> river one mile above the town. There is but little to sell
> here and everything commands a high price.[2]

Contemporary sources report that by mid-1849 four thousand emigrants and from twelve to fifteen hundred wagons were encamped north of the river across from El Paso del Norte. The price of mules, wagons, and provisions soared to such a degree that the native Mexican population, alarmed at the prospects of a famine, began to hoard provisions, causing strained relations between the emigrants and the Mexicans and a considerable amount of disorder. Yet some of the new arrivals decided to remain in the area, with the result that by late 1849 five settlements had been founded by Anglo-Americans, roughly a mile or two apart, along the left bank of the Rio Grande. These were: Frontera, established in 1848 by T. Frank White; El Molino, the flour mill of Mexican War veteran Simeon Hart; the mercantile store of Benjamin Franklin Coons, located on the ranch that he purchased from Juan María Ponce de León; Magoffinsville, east of Coons's property, where James Wiley Magoffin entertained in his traditional elegant manner; and the property of Hugh Stephenson, later called Concordia.[3]

Moreover, the old Mexican settlements of Ysleta, Socorro, and San Elizario on "the Island" were declared to be within the jurisdiction of the United States. In accordance with the Treaty of Guadalupe Hidalgo, which stated that the international boundary should follow "the deepest channel," American officials in 1848 ruled that the southern channel was the deepest one and that therefore Ysleta, Socorro, and San Elizario were in United States territory. Mexican protests proved futile.[4]

In 1848 T. Frank White of Frontera was appointed prefect by Col. John M. Washington, military governor of New Mexico, and in November of that year White was directed to extend his jurisdiction over the territory north and east of the river, formerly a part of Chihuahua. In early 1849 White removed local Mexican officials, made his own appointments, and warned Mexicans south of the river not to trespass on American territory. In February 1849 the prefect of El Paso del Norte reported that an armed force of the United States had occupied Ysleta, Socorro, and San Elizario, and had taken possession of the *ejidos*, or communal land holdings, and the woods belonging to the three towns. In vain Mexican officials, both state and local, protested the seizures and the unilateral action taken by the United States in determining the boundary. Thus, by the end of 1849 eight settlements were

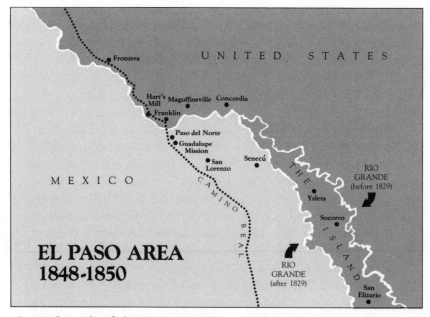

located north of the river—the five established by White, Hart, Coons, Magoffin, and Stephenson, together with the three Mexican settlements that the shifting river had placed on the American side. A bilingual, bicultural, binational complex was taking shape at the Pass of the North.[5]

By late 1848 there were a number of compelling reasons for establishing a U.S. military post on the Rio Grande—the defense of the new boundary, the protection of settlers against Apache attacks, and the maintenance of law and order, made increasingly difficult by the arrival of hordes of California emigrants. Secretary of War William L. Marcy's recommendation in July 1848 that a post ought to be established on the north side of the Rio Grande opposite El Paso del Norte, was at length implemented with the arrival of six companies of infantry from San Antonio on 8 September 1849 under the command of Maj. Jefferson Van Horne. Two companies were stationed at San Elizario and four were quartered across the river from El Paso del Norte on Benjamin F. Coons's ranch, called the Post Opposite El Paso.[6]

Van Horne and his superior officer in Santa Fe, Bvt. Col. John Munroe, agreed that the boundary between the eighth and ninth military districts was the thirty-second degree of north latitude, running in an east-west direction on both sides of the Rio Grande about twenty miles north of El Paso del Norte. But on the matter of whether the civil jurisdiction of New Mexico or that of Texas should prevail in the area between the thirty-second parallel and the Rio Grande, Van Horne said he needed clarification, since he had been called upon to sustain the laws of both states by different individuals. At length, on 28 December 1849, Van Horne was ordered to sustain the civil jurisdiction of the Territory of New Mexico "until such time as Texas shall officially assume civil jurisdiction, or the Congress of the United States finally settle the boundary between Texas and New Mexico."[7]

As to the establishment of a permanent site for the military post in the area, both Van Horne and his commander at San Elizario, Capt. William S. Henry, favored the old presidio. Benjamin F. Coons, described by Van Horne as a "shrewd, enterprising man," was charging the army $250 per month, soon to be increased to $350 on the completion of certain additions and improvements. On the other hand, said Van Horne, the rent for the hospital and officers' quarters at the Presidio of San Elizario was much less. Van Horne believed that the old presidio established by Spanish officials in 1789 could be repaired partially and rebuilt with little expense. With the purchase of a few adjacent buildings on moderate terms, he said, the presidio could quarter four or even six companies much better than existing facilities on Coons's property. Wood was plentiful, grazing was good around San Elizario, and the people there were orderly and well behaved. Finally, Van Horne pointed out that if the troops were stationed at the old presidio, they would be "removed from the wretched hordes of gamblers, drunkards, and desperadoes in El Paso del Norte."[8]

Van Horne's plan to locate the permanent post at San Elizario encountered opposition from several quarters. Capt. Thomas L. Brent of the quartermaster corps said that the site was low and subject to overflow water, at that time standing in numerous stagnant pools. He noted that the old barracks were in a most dilapidated state; even if they were repaired, they would accommodate only two companies. Finally, Captain Brent said he could see no military advantages in the San Elizario site.[9]

Strong opposition to Van Horne's plan came also from the merchants of the area. Under the leadership of James W. Magoffin, they drew up a petition pointing out that any removal of troops from Coons's property would leave the major routes through the Pass of the North completely unprotected, expose United States citizens to Indian depredations, and endanger property valued at $300,000. All law and order would break down, the merchants argued, and the area would soon be victimized by the large band of outlaws of all nations at that time infesting El Paso del Norte. This point in particular was emphasized by Col. Emilio Langberg, the commander of the El Paso del Norte garrison, who said it would be impossible for the small number of troops under his command to protect the settlers from the Indians and the marauders. As a result, for the time being at least, the four companies of infantry remained on the property of Benjamin F. Coons, and the two companies at San Elizario were left at the old presidio.[10]

Capt. William S. Henry, the commanding officer of San Elizario, strongly urged that it be established as a permanent post, pointing out that the presence of troops there had given the residents a feeling of security and had served as a tremendous impetus in increasing agricultural production and stockraising. "The inhabitants are nervously anxious to know whether this protection is to be continued," he said, adding that many were refusing to make any improvements owing to the uncertainty, while others were leaving and settling on the Mexican side of the river. The old presidio, he pointed out, offered numerous advantages for the construction of a permanent garrison for two companies of infantry. But the authorization that Captain Henry sought never came.[11]

In the 1849-1851 period the four American settlements of Hart's Mill, Coons's Ranch, Magoffinsville, and Stephenson's Ranch endured, their proprietors playing roles of great importance in the development of the area. Frontera, located about eight miles above El Paso del Norte, did not survive. Although White established a customhouse there and collected duties on merchandise and livestock coming from Mexico, his hope that a military post would be established at Frontera failed to materialize. As a result, when United States Boundary Commissioner John R. Bartlett arrived in the area in November 1850, White offered him the option of buying Frontera for three thousand dollars, or title to two acres of land for one dollar and the buildings for a rental fee of sixty-five dollars a month so that an observatory for the commission could be erected there. Bartlett accepted the second option and built an observatory which the commission used during 1851. By that time White had ceased to be the political influence in the area that he had been in the 1848-1850 period.[12]

Simeon Hart came to the Pass with Sterling Price in the spring of 1848, was wounded in the battle of Santa Cruz de Rosales, and was nursed back to health in the home of Don Leandro Siqueiros, wealthy flour miller. Hart fell in love with his daughter Jesusita, whom he married and brought back to the Rio Grande in late 1849. He established his flour mill, El Molino, and several years later built his residence, now the Hacienda Cafe. It has been described as in the Mexican style, large and convenient, with every luxury and comfort, its principal attraction being the private library. It served as a welcome haven for weary travelers for years.[13]

Hart signed his first contract with the army on 28 March 1850. He agreed to furnish flour in an unspecified quantity for one year to the posts of Doña Ana, Coons's Ranch, and San Elizario for eleven cents a pound. Much of Hart's flour had to be imported from his father-in-law's mill at Santa Cruz de Rosales, since the mill on the Rio Grande remained a comparatively small operation for some time. Hart was not satisfied with the agreement and asked to have his contract extended to three years and expanded to include all military posts in Texas as far east as Eagle Pass, pointing out that he had spent $25,000 for machinery, a wheat crop, and the purchase of teams. In 1851 Hart got another contract to furnish flour to the same three posts, plus the escort to the United States-Mexico Boundary Commission, at twelve and a half cents per pound. Here again Hart wanted more, even though he always received better terms for his flour than any of the other major producers. Hart strongly protested the removal of troops from the Post Opposite El Paso and San Elizario to Fort Fillmore, eliciting the comment from an officer, "It is not unreasonable to suppose that the removal of the troops interfered very much with his interests and expectations."[14]

To the east of Hart's Mill lay the property of Benjamin Franklin Coons, who had purchased it from Juan María Ponce de León of El Paso del Norte, probably in the summer of 1849. Known as Coons's Ranch, it contained an adobe house and several other buildings. Maj. Jefferson Van Horne, commander of the six companies of the Third Infantry that arrived on 8 September 1849, found the existing facilities on Coons's Ranch to be the most suitable in the area. Coons leased the main buildings and six acres of land to the army as a military post. Shortly after, Coons erected new buildings, including a tavern, warehouse, stables, and corrals just west of the army post to house his mercantile enterprises.[15]

Early in 1850 Coons went to San Antonio, where he immediately impressed the merchants with the advantages of a trade route across Texas in comparison with the road to Missouri to Santa Fe and El Paso del Norte. The trip from Independence, Missouri, to El Paso del Norte, he pointed out, took eighty days, while the trip from San Antonio could be done in fifty. The annual trade with Chihuahua, he emphasized, amounted to 625 tons of freight worth $625,000. Coons then entered into partnership with Lewis and Groesbeeck of San Antonio, well-known commission merchants, with the object of obtaining a major part of the freight business between San Antonio and El Paso del Norte in the transportation of military supplies to the Post Opposite El Paso.[16]

Coons ran into all sorts of problems toward the end of the summer of 1850, resulting in tremendous financial losses. A train of 300 teams left San Antonio around the middle of April, but four months later it was still 250 miles short of its destination. As it entered the trans-Pecos region water became scarce, the grass was parched, and the teamsters, many of whom were rogues, fugitives, and footloose ex-soldiers of the U.S.-Mexico War, became extremely troublesome. Learning of these details, Major Van Horne on 1 September wrote his superior that while part of the train might reach its destination by 10 September, "the remainder God knows when." "The oxen are perishing," he continued, "and Coons' train is in wretched condition, he himself doubtful whether it will ever reach here." One month later Van Horne wrote that the whole system of transporting supplies seemed very defective. Much of the merchandise had been damaged, and the teamsters had used government supplies for their own subsistence.[17]

The last segments of Coons's train finally arrived late in November, but Van Horne reported that the shipment was of very inferior quality, and that the hard bread, bacon, and pork were unfit for use. So much had been consumed by the command escort, combined with the demands likely to be made by starving Indians, Van Horne added, that the supply was very short and would not last long. Adding to Coons's problems was a transaction he had made with a notorious adventurer named Parker H. French. On 18 August Coons sold 18 wagons, 176 mules, and 2 horses to French for the tidy sum of $17,720.95, but the bills of credit Coons received, drawn on Aspinwall and Howland of New York, turned out to be forgeries.[18]

Realizing that the whole enterprise had been a complete failure, Coons sold twelve wagons to George Wentworth for $3,000 in October to stave off his creditors, then left for California. Here he was able to repair his fortunes somewhat, possibly with the help of a loan from his brother, and in early 1851 he returned to the El Paso area. By this time Coons's Ranch was occasionally called Franklin, presumably after his middle name, and it was usually called this for another decade or so, even though a post office was established in 1852 naming the settlement El Paso, Texas.[19]

Coons had been back in the El Paso area only a short time before he began to run into more hard luck. On 12 July 1851 Maj. Electus Backus recommended the removal of troops from the Coons's Ranch site, which he had found objectionable for a number of reasons. He wrote:

> The unusual expenditures to which the government has been subjected at this post have induced me to inquire into some of the most prominent causes which have produced them and to search for an appropriate remedy. A brief examination has satisfied me that the position occupied by the troops tends greatly to augment these expenditures, and that by removing them up or down the river a few miles only, you will add to the safety, health, and comfort of the troops, and seriously diminish the unnecessary ,outlay of funds.[20]

The major then proceeded to list his objections to the location: (1) it was not defensible even against musketry; (2) it afforded no appropriate accommodations for troops, and the annual rent, which had been increased to $4,900, he called "an exorbitant charge"; (3) it afforded neither fuel nor grazing, and the army was paying $6,160 a year for wood and $7,000 for hay; (4) it afforded no timber; and (5) it afforded no opportunities for farming. The

major concluded by saying that adequate protection of officials
and settlers in the area could be accomplished by one officer, fifteen men, a good guardhouse, an acre or two of land, and some
fast horses.[21]

Word of the possible withdrawal of troops spread rapidly
around the area, causing conditions bordering on panic. Under
the leadership of Charles W. Ogden and Simeon Hart, a petition
was prepared protesting the move and signed by twenty-one of the
local citizenry. Furthermore, Coons, in a document dated 26
August 1851, proposed to furnish the quarters and grounds then
occupied by the troops free of rent for one year. He said he would
also provide space for the erection of barracks and storehouses,
and 250 acres of farmland to be selected by the commanding officer, to be occupied by the troops free of all charges and rents for
twenty years. At the end of that period of time the property was
to revert to Coons or his heirs, with the United States having the
privilege of purchasing the property at a valuation agreeable to
both parties. Coons was thus making every effort to cooperate
with the local merchants, even at a great personal sacrifice.
Although the local commander, Maj. Gouverneur Morris, recommended that the proposal be accepted, his superior in Santa Fe rejected it, and the troops were moved in September 1851 to Fort
Fillmore, some forty miles to the north.[22]

With the loss of income from the army, Coons was unable to
make the payments on his property. Juan María Ponce de León
promptly repossessed it, and on his death in 1852 it passed to his
wife and daughter, who sold it within a year to William T. Smith
for $10,000. By that time Coons had once again returned to
California.[23]

To the east of Coons's Ranch, or Franklin, was Magoffinsville,
established in 1849 by the veteran Chihuahua trader James W.
Magoffin. Known as "the American El Paso," it consisted of a
group of large, well-built adobe structures erected around an open
square. The buildings were used as stores and warehouses and
were filled with merchandise. The property was well situated about
half a mile from the river and was watered by an *acequia* which
ran through the square. Here Magoffin built a mansion of hacienda proportions where he frequently hosted army officers and
government officials, entertaining them in the grand manner.

"With 'delicacies prepared in New York and Paris for the foreign markets,' he could serve 'a cold collation...that would have done credit to the caterer of a metropolitan hotel.'" John R. Bartlett, the boundary commissioner, stayed at Magoffinsville for a while, and on one occasion gave a party there which lasted all night. "It was a success, even to four great 'new-fashioned chandeliers improvised for the occasion' out of sardine tins fixed to a hoop off a pork barrel, wrapped with Apache calicoes and supplied with a 'dozen burners each,' that 'shed such a ray of light upon the festal hall, as rendered the charms of the fair señoritas doubly captivating.'" Bartlett predicted that Magoffinsville would remain the center of American settlements in the El Paso area.[24]

Magoffin's merchandising and livestock activities, supplemented by income from a ranch known as Canutillo about fifteen miles to the north, brought him a fortune. He furnished Bartlett's commission with food, clothing, and supplies for a sum totaling more than $5,500, and deposited it in his account with the firm of Wood, Bacon, and Co. in Philadelphia. On the other hand, Magoffin's efforts to levy a toll on the salt deposits on the eastern slopes of the San Andrés range met with armed resistance. Moreover, he suffered great losses of livestock because of Indian depredations. Apaches raided his corrals at Magoffinsville, and on one occasion he wrote that he had lost, over a period of seven months, sixty mules taken within 150 yards of his house; Indians in two raids had taken all his cattle and farm animals. This naturally gave rise to the formation of citizens' committees and the drafting of petitions to state and national authorities demanding relief and protection. But none would be forthcoming for another two years.[25]

To the east of Magoffinsville was the property of Hugh Stephenson, of Chihuahua mining fame. His ranch was situated on that part of an estate belonging to his wife's family that the shifting Rio Grande had placed on the north side. Stephenson, who had extensive silver mining and livestock interests, was the first to prospect in New Mexico and systematically develop its mineral resources, particularly in the Organ Mountains. On his property in the El Paso area, which by 1852 had come to be known as Concordia, he erected a number of buildings. His home was large and comfortable, though perhaps not as pretentious as

Magoffin's or Hart's. Like Magoffin, Stephenson suffered heavy losses from Indian hostilities and depredations after the army troops were withdrawn from the El Paso area. He took a leading role in organizing the citizenry and drafting petitions to relieve a situation that was completely out of hand. His own livestock losses, as he indicated in a letter to the local committee, came to more than three thousand dollars.[26]

The creation of an international boundary at the Pass of the North necessitated the establishment of consulates and custom-houses by the United States and Mexico. In May 1849 John S. Lucas was named United States consul at El Paso del Norte, and about a year later Manuel Armendáriz was appointed Mexican consul at Franklin. Numerous problems arose concerning pass-ports, *cartas de seguridad* (safe-conduct passes), and rights of foreigners living in Mexico, causing frequent misunderstandings and strained relations most of the time. Failure to comply with the many and varied Mexican regulations would result in a fine, or imprisonment, or forcible expulsion from the country.[27]

On one occasion in 1850 the *jefe político* of El Paso del Norte stated that no passports would be honored in Mexico unless issued by the Mexican consul in Franklin. A response in strong language came from James A. Lucas, who was serving as acting consul while his brother John was on leave. "You are denying me the right as Consul of the United States to grant passports to American citizens," he warned the *jefe político*, adding, "I would ask of you what purpose the President of the United States has placed a con-sul in El Paso del Norte if it is not to assist his countrymen and to see that their rights are protected." At length, an arrangement was worked out whereby the Mexican consul in Franklin would issue passports, but they would be required only of Americans traveling into the interior of Mexico. While passports thus would not be re-quired of Americans in El Paso del Norte, they would be expected to register with the Mexican authorities.[28]

Consul John Lucas served until mid-1851, when he was re-placed by David R. Diffenderffer. About the same time, Juan N. Zubirán was named consul at Franklin. Diffenderffer's correspon-dence indicates that he found the position difficult and frustrating. For one thing, he wrote Secretary of State Daniel Webster that he had received the seal and press, but that the consulate was entirely destitute of the necessary flag, coat of arms, and pertinent documents such as laws and treaties. After more than a year had passed, Diffenderffer was still writing that he had never received any communication from the Department of State and that the consulate in El Paso del Norte had never received the requisite papers and documents necessary to conduct business. "On many subjects," he said, "I am left completely in the dark." When after two years on the job, Diffenderffer's situation still had not improved, in desperation he wrote Secretary of State William Marcy, stating that the consulship in El Paso del Norte was not a sinecure, that it involved a great deal of work and responsibility, and that unless the new administration took steps to help him protect American citizens, he would have to tender his resignation.[29]

Because of the prevailing frontier conditions during the 1850s, the lack of an effective civil authority, and the clash of cultural and legal traditions in this border environment, it was rare indeed when there was not an incident of some sort, usually featuring mob action and a generous display of pistols and knives. A considerable number of cases involved army deserters and criminals from either country attempting to escape to the other.[30]

One of the most serious incidents concerned an American citizen named James Magee, whose cattle were stolen and taken across the Rio Grande. While attempting to recover the stolen livestock on the Mexican side of the river, Magee was arrested and thrown in jail. All attempts to secure his release failed, and the *jefe político* of El Paso del Norte, after first promising to free Magee for $100, changed his mind. With that, an armed band of Americans crossed the river and laid siege to the jail. They were repulsed and driven back across the river, having lost one killed and another mortally wounded. Magee was carried off to Chihuahua, and Diffenderffer came under considerable fire for failing to obtain Magee's release. A Dr. James Tucker charged the consul with being a weak and "illiterate man, [a] man destitute of moral worth or character, whose counsel [is] his wife and whose wife has been a public prostitute in El Paso for 15 or 20 years past. It is a fine thing indeed that a greaser woman should be consul for Americans." But Diffenderffer stayed at his post; early in 1855 he again wrote the Department of State saying that the consulate still had not received the flag, the coat of arms, or the necessary documents.[31]

During the Mexican period, 1821-1848, El Paso del Norte had become an important commercial center in the Santa Fe-Chihuahua trade along the historic Camino Real. The volume of the United States trade had significantly increased during the period, from $22,000 worth of goods in 1822 to approximately $1,000,000 in 1846. Because of this, a customhouse had been established in El Paso del Norte in 1835, charged with the inspection of cargoes, seizure of contraband goods, enforcement of prescribed procedures and regulations, and the collection of duties on merchandise brought from the United States.[32]

The establishment of the Rio Grande as a boundary, followed by high protective tariff duties levied on American goods by Mexican officials, brought a significant decline in commercial activity in the El Paso area and marked the end of an era. Although T. Frank White of Frontera had established a customhouse and collected duties on goods from Mexico, as has been noted, an American customs collector for the El Paso area was not appointed until 1854. In that year Caleb Sherman became the first collector of customs in the El Paso district and received authorization to appoint mounted inspectors to patrol the border. That the volume of trade continued to impair American interests was noted by Consul Diffenderffer, who wrote in March 1854 that while American imports of Mexican wine, brandy, sugar, soap, rebozos, fruits, leather goods, and cigars amounted to between $60,000 and $70,000 annually, American goods attempting to enter Mexico encountered prohibitively high duties. In the same dispatch Diffenderffer said that the volume of goods entering Mexico during 1852 and 1853 amounted to less than 50 percent of the amount for 1850 and 1851. The following year he wrote in a dispatch that the aggregate value of American exports into El Paso del Norte during 1851-1853 was about $150,000, the duty amounting to $60,000, evidence that a commercial revolution had taken place on the Rio Grande.[33]

The appointment of T. F. White of Frontera as prefect over the area north and east of the river by Col. John M. Washington, military governor of New Mexico, placed that territory in a favorable position to extend its jurisdiction there. On the other hand, Texas since 1836 had claimed all territory east of the Rio Grande. But when Maj. Jefferson Van Horne on 23 September 1849 wrote for instructions on the matter of civil jurisdiction in the area, he was told by Col. John Munroe, who had replaced Colonel Washington in Santa Fe as commander and ex-officio governor, that the military authority should sustain the civil jurisdiction of the Territory of New Mexico until such a time as Texas should assume civil jurisdiction, or until the boundary between Texas and New Mexico should be finally settled.[34]

Playing a leading role in the establishment of American political and legal institutions in the El Paso area were several whose names should be remembered along with the Harts, Magoffins, and Stephensons. One of these was Rhode Island-born Charles A. Hoppin, who arrived in 1849, establishing residence at San Elizario. Impressed with the beauty and potential of the Lower Valley, though concerned about the conflicting and confusing political jurisdictions, Hoppin took the lead in appealing to Gov. Peter H. Bell of Texas to extend the civil jurisdiction of the state and organize a county in the El Paso area. He wrote as follows from San Elizario on 3 January 1850:

> We are here[,] sir[,] situated in a beautiful valley containing from 1,000 to 1,500 inhabitants—the majority of whom are Mexicans but Americans are daily coming in, and but a few years will elapse before this island will become an important point from its position[,] fertility of soil[,] & abundant production. It will teem with inhabitants—To whom does it belong[?] If to Texas, then[,] sir[,] Texas ought to give its citizens dwelling her [sic] the protection of her laws. Now we are in a region without law. Tis true there is a prefect residing some miles above El Paso & there [are] in each of the small towns up on the island Alcaldes appointed by him. The Prefect rec[eive]d his appointment from the Governor of the Territory of New Mexico, but what laws govern the decisions of the Alcaldes I know not. I presume each one selects such a code as best suits him. Here the Alcalde[,] a very worthy Mexican[,] is governed by Laws enacted by the state of Chihuahua. We have no Magistrates[,] no exhibits[?] so clearly the situation in which we are placed that I have felt it a duty I owe to Law abiding citizens to present it to you. An American has been arrested and now is in the Guard House here charged with the revolting crime of rape. How can he be tried[?] If he is brought before an Alcalde has he the power of punishing if the charge is not proven[?] An American citizen is entitled to a jury trial. Who can summons [sic]

117

the jury[?] Who gives sentence[?] Who is authorized to execute the sentence if given[?] You see[,] sir[,] the necessity of organizing Courts for this part of the state[.] The people wish it and it is their right to ask it. If this is not a part of Texas[,] then from New Mexico they must ask the protection of Civil Laws.

The organization of a county with the appointment of Magistrates and Judges would have a highly beneficial effect upon the population here[.]

Let me ask you to confer upon me a great favor. I would be glad to receive a copy of the Laws of Texas. I do not think there is a copy this side of San Antonio[,] & important questions will arise requiring reference to the statutes. If you see fit to send it[,] direct it to the care of the "Officer Commanding[,] Post Opposite El Paso."[35]

By the time Hoppin presented the case of the early Anglo-American settlers, Texas had already decided to renew its old claim to everything east of the Rio Grande and to make its bid for the El Paso area. In his message of 26 December 1849 Governor Bell called for the organization of western counties and the immediate extension of Texas's jurisdiction there, pointing out that many of the inhabitants had already made known their desire to be brought under the protection of the state. The legislature quickly responded, and on 31 December 1849 it designated new boundaries for Santa Fe County, reducing its size, while creating the three new counties of Presidio, El Paso, and Worth.[36]

On 3 January 1850 Governor Bell appointed Maj. Robert S. Neighbors commissioner to organize the counties and to hold elections for county officers. Neighbors, who was familiar with the El Paso area, having visited it a year before as a member of an exploratory expedition, left Austin on 8 January 1850 and reached San Elizario in early February. He circulated a proclamation by Governor Bell explaining the history of Texas's claim to the region, and he called upon all citizens to assist him in organizing the county. On 23 February 1850 Neighbors wrote Col. John Munroe at Santa Fe of his arrival in the El Paso area for the purpose of extending the civil jurisdiction of Texas, and announced his intention to come to Santa Fe after he had organized El Paso County. He added that he had encountered no opposition, had issued writs of election, and was proceeding with the organization of the county, which extended from sixty miles below El Paso to twenty miles above San Diego, and east to the Pecos River.[37]

In elections held on 4 March 1850, 765 votes were cast for county officers. Charles A. Hoppin was elected chief justice of the county, later called county judge. Austin was the overwhelming choice for the state capital, and San Elizario, with a Mexican population of 1,200, became the county seat of El Paso County. Just how this happened remains unclear since Neighbors did not provide details, but presumably Hoppin's influence on the Mexican population was decisive. At any rate, on 23 March 1850 Neighbors reported to Governor Bell that El Paso County was fully organized, and elected officials were discharging their duties.[38]

Hoppin served until 20 August 1850, when he was replaced by Connecticut-born Archibald C. Hyde. Establishing residence at San Elizario in the summer of 1850, he served two terms as county judge. His successor was Henry L. Dexter, one of the first Anglo-Americans to reside in Ysleta. Here Dexter eventually held a number of local offices and operated a chain of profitable mercantile stores extending from Ysleta to Mesilla. As district judge of the Eleventh Judicial District, the Texas Legislature selected Joel L. Ankrim, a resident of San Elizario, who served from 1850 to 1856. Judge Ankrim brought to El Paso for his health Josiah Fraser Crosby, one of the great names in the history of the El Paso legal profession. He succeeded Ankrim as district judge and remained in that position until 1861.[39]

The organization of El Paso County, however, proved to be Neighbors's only success on this assignment. He could not organize Presidio County without an escort because the Indians were so hostile, and United States troops in the region were insufficient for coping with the problem. The organization of Worth County, Neighbors believed, would follow the establishment of county government in the Santa Fe region, but here he encountered strong resistance. Opposition to the organization of Santa Fe County came not only from Col. John Munroe, who refused to support the Texas cause, but also from Pres. Zachary Taylor, who argued that New Mexico was a United States territory, that it should remain so until its boundaries were determined by some competent authority, and that Texas therefore should not attempt to interfere with the possession of the territory by the United States. Neighbors's report of his activities on his return to Austin caused such great excitement that the state legislature adopted unanimously a resolution that "Texas will maintain the integrity of her territory at all hazards and to the last extremity." Both Texas and Millard Fillmore, who had succeeded to the presidency on the death of Zachary Taylor, threatened to use force; unless a settlement could be reached within a short time, armed conflict remained a distinct possibility.[40]

With the organization of El Paso County in March 1850, the civil jurisdiction of Texas was extended into the area north of the Rio Grande, but the boundary between Texas and New Mexico remained unresolved. Topographically, the county had much more in common with New Mexico than Texas; historically, in the Spanish period it had been administered by the governor of New Mexico, while during the Mexican period it had been a part of the state of Chihuahua; commercially, the old Camino Real had linked Santa Fe, El Paso del Norte, and Chihuahua for more than a century. In June, however, the voters in New Mexico overwhelmingly approved a state constitution that drew a southern boundary north of El Paso del Norte, extending eastward to the 100th meridian, then north to the Arkansas River. New Mexico thus was relinquishing any claim to El Paso County, but whether Texas would accept the New Mexico line was entirely another matter. The question of the boundary between New Mexico and Texas ultimately was to be determined by the Senate after deliberations lasting most of the year, with no fewer than five different proposals offered before one was finally accepted.[41]

The Senate of the United States in 1850 had a brilliant array of talent among its membership, constituting one of the most distinguished groups in the history of that body. Older men such as Thomas Hart Benton and Lewis Cass were there, along with Henry Clay, John C. Calhoun, and Daniel Webster, all serving their last term; newer members included Stephen A. Douglas, William H. Seward, John Bell, and Jefferson Davis.[42]

On 16 January 1850 Sen. Thomas Hart Benton of Missouri presented a boundary proposal, the only one of the five submitted that left the El Paso settlements, not yet a part of Texas, in New Mexico. Benton was primarily interested in reducing Texas's size. "Texas is too large," he argued, "either for her own convenience or for the proper quality and well-being of the other states…. She is large enough to make seven states of the first class and ought...to be reduced to a reasonable size. The proper time for the reduction was the time of her admission to the union, and I proposed it at that time.... That proposition was overruled.... What might have been done easily then becomes difficult now."[43]

Benton fixed the western boundary of Texas at the 102d meridian, leaving everything to the west as part of New Mexico. Texas's northern boundary was to remain at the Red River. Then he proposed that when the population of Texas reached 100,000, the state should be divided at the Colorado River and the 98th meridian, making two states instead of one. The territory west of the 102d meridian was to be ceded to the United States, and Texas was to renounce all claims to the territory east of the Rio Grande. For this, the state was to receive $15 million. Benton concluded by saying that he had informed the Texas senators of his proposal, and it was referred to the Committee on the Judiciary.[44]

On the same day Benton submitted his proposal, Sen. Henry S. Foote of Mississippi submitted another. It called for the creation, with Texas's consent, of the state of Jacinto, its western boundary to be fixed at the Brazos River. The state of Texas, supported here in its claim to the Rio Grande, would extend from that river on the west to the Brazos on the east. The El Paso settlements would become a part of Texas. The remaining territory acquired by the United States in the Treaty of Guadalupe Hidalgo would be organized into three territories—California, Deseret, and New Mexico. Foote concluded with a bitter attack on Benton for deliberately attempting to decrease the amount of slave territory by setting Texas's western boundary at the 102d longitude. Clearly the slavery question had become the nation's paramount issue.[45]

On 29 January Henry Clay introduced a series of resolutions, among them one concerning the boundary between Texas and New Mexico. He proposed to start the line on the Rio Grande just above the El Paso settlements, then run it in a northeasterly direction to a point where the Red River intersected the 100th meridian. Texas was to relinquish claim to any part of New Mexico, but in return for this Clay suggested that the United States should pay the debt contracted by Texas prior to annexation.[46]

Clay's proposals brought an immediate reply from Sen. Thomas J. Rusk of Texas, causing prolonged and heated debate that lasted for

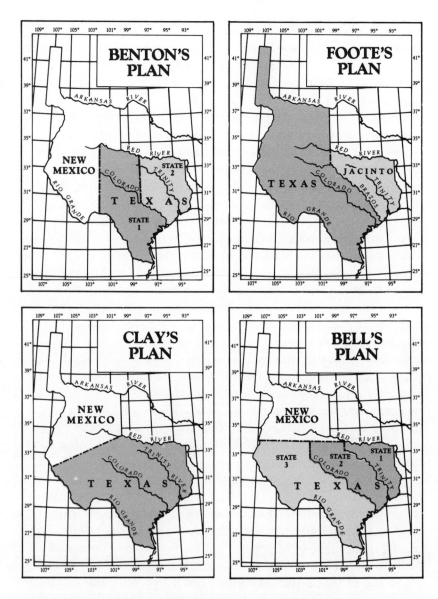

Five boundary proposals were submitted to the United States Senate in 1850. Among them were those of Senator Benton, upper left; Senator Foote, upper right; Senator Clay, lower left; and Senator Bell, lower right.

more than a month. "I regret extremely," said the senator from Texas, "that the distinguished Senator from Kentucky...should have seen proper, rather unceremoniously as I think, to take one-half of the territory of the State I have the honor in part here to represent, to make a peace-offering to a spirit of encroachment on the constitutional rights of one-half of this Union." Equally critical of Clay's proposal was Thomas Hart Benton, who said it would "cut New Mexico in two just below the hips, and give the lower half to Texas, leaving New Mexico to stump it about as she can, without feet or legs."[47]

Debate on Clay's proposals continued through February, and on the last day of the month still another boundary proposal was submitted, this one by John Bell of Tennessee. It called for the eventual organization of three states extending westward to the Rio Grande, the northern boundary of each to be fixed at the Red River and the thirty-fourth parallel. The Trinity River was to be the boundary between the first two states, while the Colorado River was to divide the second and third. All territory north of the thirty-fourth parallel would become a part of the Territory of New Mexico, which eventually was to be admitted as a fourth state. The El Paso settlements would be a part of Bell's third state. The senator expressed the hope that a balance of free and slave states could be maintained, apparently assuming that the two eastern states would be slave, the two western states, free.[48]

During the next month or so, the Senate listened to the great oratory of Webster, Calhoun, and Seward, but the matter of the Texas boundary remained unresolved. Finally, on 19 April the Senate appointed a committee of thirteen members, chaired by Clay, to work out a compromise that would adjust all questions involving the slavery issue, including the matter of the Texas boundary. At length, on 8 May the committee offered a series of recommendations that came to be known as the Compromise of 1850. Regarding the boundary question, the committee upheld Clay's proposal that the line should run in a northeasterly direction from a point twenty miles above El Paso del Norte to a point where the Red River and the 100th meridian intersect. Clay was also upheld in his recommendation that the United States should pay the debt owed by Texas.[49]

Meanwhile, in the El Paso area, since Commissioner Robert S. Neighbors had organized El Paso County and extended the civil

The fifth boundary proposal submitted to the Senate in 1850 and accepted was that of Senator Pearce.

jurisdiction of Texas there, the approval of the Benton plan, which placed the El Paso settlements in New Mexico, would have resulted in serious complications. Moreover, Neighbors's report of the opposition he had received from both the Santa Fe officials and the federal government in his attempt to organize Santa Fe County for Texas brought matters between Texas and the United States to a critical stage in July, making it imperative that the Texas-New Mexico boundary problem be resolved as soon as possible.[50]

On 5 August Senator James A. Pearce of Maryland called for the removal from Clay's proposals of everything relating to Texas and New Mexico. He then introduced a bill providing that the boundary should follow the 100th meridian from the Red River northward to latitude 36°30′, west on that parallel to the 103d meridian, south to the 32d parallel, and west to the Rio Grande. The Texas Panhandle was being born! In consideration of her acceptance of this boundary, Texas was to receive $10 million.[51]

Pearce's bill had a number of commendable features, as historian William C. Binkley has pointed out: "This boundary was one degree farther west than that proposed by Benton, in order to conciliate the Texans; two degrees farther north than the one suggested by Bell, in order to appease the demands of the slavery interests; far enough east to please the advocates of New Mexican rights; and the sum offered to Texas was almost the exact amount needed to cancel her debt." The bill passed the Senate on 9 August by a vote of 30 to 20, the House (with an amendment providing for the organization of New Mexico as a territory) on 6 September by a vote of 108 to 97, and received President Fillmore's signature on 9 September 1850. Although some heated opposition greeted the bill in Texas, voters approved it by almost a three-to-one margin. El Paso County was listed in the final tabulation, but no vote was specified. The Texas Legislature then officially accepted the mandate of the people, and Governor Bell approved its action on 25 November 1850. The El Paso settlements were now officially a part of Texas insofar as the federal government was concerned. Some twenty miles to their north, along the thirty-second parallel, ran the boundary line between Texas and New Mexico.[52]

The final settlement of the Texas-New Mexico boundary question became the object of sharp criticism, particularly from New Mexico. For example, historian Percy M. Baldwin observed:

> Of all the various boundary proposals put forward in 1850, this one which was finally adopted drew the most inconvenient and illogical line. It gave Texas a shape as peculiar as a gerrymandered country. Northward, the "panhandle" projected nearly, but not quite, to the southern boundary of Kansas, leaving room for the "no man's land" that later became the grotesque elongation of Oklahoma. The triangular extension westward, with El Paso at its furthest limit, belongs to the region of the high plains and is geographically, economically, and historically connected with southern New Mexico, yet the parallel of 32°, for no particular reason, throws this natural area into two political jurisdictions.[53]

The validity of Baldwin's points was demonstrated when William Wallace Mills, the El Paso delegate to the Texas Constitutional Convention in 1868, submitted a plan calling for the creation of a Montezuma Territory, comprising El Paso and Doña Ana counties. Although the plan had some support in El Paso, it was rejected by the convention. Another effort to detach El Paso County from Texas came in 1899 with a short-lived movement to create a separate state of "West Texas," or "Sacramento." It was voted down, however, because of strong opposition to the inclusion of New Mexico in the project.[54]

With the settlement of the Texas-New Mexico problem in 1850, yet another boundary remained to be surveyed and determined – the one between the United States and Mexico. Article 5 of the Treaty of Guadalupe Hidalgo had delineated the new international boundary and had provided that a joint survey commission of officials from both nations should draw the line. Heading the American party was the scholarly John Russell Bartlett, who came to the El Paso area on 13 November 1850; his Mexican counterpart was Gen. Pedro García Conde, who arrived in early December. Bartlett stayed at the home of James Magoffin, and subsequently met Major Van Horne, Charles A. Hoppin, T. F. White, Padre Ramón Ortiz, Col. Emilio Langberg, and the bishop of Durango. The prelate took this opportunity to tell Bartlett that several Bartolomé Esteban Murillo paintings in the Guadalupe Mission had been plundered by Alexander W. Doniphan's soldiers during the recent war.[55]

Bartlett and García Conde soon discovered through astronomical observations two errors in the Disturnell map used by the Guadalupe Hidalgo treaty negotiators. As drawn on the treaty map, the southern boundary of New Mexico was to begin on the Rio Grande eight miles north of El Paso del Norte and run westward three degrees of longitude or 175.28 miles, before turning north to strike the Gila River. But the map showed El Paso del Norte at 32°15′ north latitude, whereas the true position was 31°45′. Moreover, the map placed the Rio Grande at 104°39′ west longitude, whereas the true position was 106°29′. The latitude error placed El Paso del Norte thirty-four miles too far north, while the longitude error put the Rio Grande more than a hundred miles too far east. The area in question involved the status of the Santa Rita copper mines, a transcontinental railroad route, and the Mexican settlement of Mesilla and the fertile valley nearby.[56]

Mesilla had been founded in 1850 by Rafael Ruelas across the river from Doña Ana and was settled primarily by Mexicans of New Mexico who were fearful of losing their lands to the Americans. Padre Ramón Ortiz of El Paso del Norte, serving as commissioner of *colonias*, issued land grants to the settlers. Mesilla's population was about 2,000 by 1853. Yet when Bartlett visited the town in 1851, he saw it as only mud-and-stick houses, and expressed serious doubts that the population would accept American jurisdiction.[57]

Negotiations between Bartlett and García Conde resulted in a compromise in which Bartlett "traded Conde latitude for longitude." The agreement, reached on Christmas Day, 1850, fixed the boundary, known as the Bartlett-García Conde line, on the Rio

Grande at 32°22' north latitude, or forty-two miles north of El Paso del Norte. The line was then to extend westward three degrees, or 175.28 miles, from the river's true longitude. Bartlett was pleased with the arrangement, and defended the compromise by stating that American jurisdiction over the copper mines had been confirmed, while at the same time nothing of importance south of the line had been yielded.[58]

The Bartlett-García Conde compromise encountered strong opposition from the first. Members of Bartlett's own survey team criticized him for not obtaining the fertile Mesilla Valley and for bargaining away a prime railroad route. Secretary of the Interior A. H. H. Stuart ordered Andrew B. Gray, the commissioner's surveyor, to sign the agreement, but before Gray could refuse, Stuart removed him from office. Expansionist Democrats in Washington and elsewhere were in no mood for a compromise solution, a position that caused the Whig administration of Millard Fillmore no little distress. The commission's surveying activities were drastically reduced, whereupon Bartlett, "the adventure-loving bookman," set out on a year-long peregrination that took him to Mazatlán, San Diego, and California before he returned overland to the El Paso area in August 1852.[59]

In the meantime, William H. Emory, an experienced surveyor and an expert on the American Southwest, had arrived in the El Paso area. In spite of his desperate attempt to keep the commission alive, expansionist Democrats in Congress scuttled the commission's appropriation and repudiated the Bartlett-García Conde compromise. Bartlett, whose leadership throughout had been ineffective, then retired to Providence, Rhode Island, to write what has become one of the great classics on the American Southwest, his *Personal Narrative*.[60]

As has been noted, the Eleventh Judicial District, organized early in 1850, originally included the counties of Presidio, El Paso, Worth, and Santa Fe. By the end of the year, however, the district involved only El Paso County since Worth and Santa Fe counties became a part of Third Judicial District of New Mexico; Presidio remained unorganized until 1875. Joel L. Ankrim, district judge, established the first district court, but judging from Bartlett's description of a trial he observed, a distinctly frontier style of justice prevailed. He wrote:

It is doubtful whether in the whole history of trial by jury a more remarkable scene than the one here presented was ever exhibited. The trial took place in one of the adobe...houses peculiar to the country, which was dimly lighted from a single small window. Scarcely an individual was present who had not the appearance and garb of men who spend their lives on the frontier, far from civilization and its softening influences. Surrounded as we had been, and now were, by hostile Indians, and constantly mingling with half civilized and renegade men, it was necessary to go constantly armed.... In the court room, therefore, where one of the most solemn scenes of human experience was enacting, all were armed save the prisoners. There sat the judge, with a pistol lying on the table before him; the clerks and attorneys wore revolvers at their sides; and the jurors were either armed with similar weapons, or carried with them the unerring rifle. The members of the Commission and citizens, who were either guarding the prisoners or protecting the court, carried by their sides a revolver, a rifle, or a fowling piece, this presenting a scene more characteristic of feudal times than of the nineteenth century.[61]

The removal of troops from the El Paso area in September 1851, as the settlers had predicted, left the frontier completely exposed and at the mercy of raiding Apaches, who murdered and plundered almost at will. The result was the formation of local committees, letters of complaint enumerating the losses of lives and property, and petitions to the governor and the president demanding relief and protection. The deplorable conditions, as one committee pointed out, has resulted in the flight of hundreds of Mexican families across the river to Mexico seeking refuge and safety and the establishment of the new towns of Guadalupe Bravos and San Ignacio. Many respectable citizens of Mexico, said the petition, were induced by the guarantees offered by the Treaty of Guadalupe Hidalgo to abandon their original homes, to become American citizens, and to make the County of El Paso their place of residence. Although many have been found worthy of the protection of our government and the benefit of our laws, the petition stated, they have been forced to sacrifice their property and compelled to leave our country.[62]

The repudiation of the Bartlett-García Conde line had left in limbo a tract of territory situated between the Disturnell treaty

line at 31°45′ north latitude and the compromise line at 32°22′–
an area some 6,000 miles in extent that included the fertile Mesilla
Valley. The region became the object of a bitter dispute between
New Mexico and Chihuahua in 1853, with both sides threatening
the use of military force. Soon after the repudiation of the compromise line, Gov. William Carr Lane of New Mexico issued a
proclamation in March 1853, claiming authority over the disputed
tract. As a result, Gov. Angel Trías of Chihuahua, who had
fought the American invaders of his state during the Mexican
War, ordered soldiers into the Mesilla Valley. Governor Lane then
threatened to send troops into the disputed area, but was effectively restrained when Col. Edwin V. Sumner, commander at Fort
Fillmore, refused to cooperate.[63]

James Magoffin, in a letter of 24 April 1853 to Bartlett, summarized the situation:

> Governor Carr Lane of New Mexico paid us a visit a
> few weeks since and issued a proclamation to the author-
> ities of El Paso del Norte that he intended to take posses-
> sion of Mesilla, which created great excitement throughout
> the territory and in fact as far as the City of Mexico.
> General Trillas [sic] arrived here today with 750 soldiers in
> order to defend the soil, but the Governor had returned
> home, not being supported by the citizens and getting no
> military aid, and so this matter rests. General Trillas will
> no doubt make his headquarters at El Paso del Norte for
> some time.[64]

Since relations between the United States and Mexico were near-
ing the breaking point, the Franklin Pierce administration, in an
attempt to resolve differences through negotiation, replaced Governor Lane with David W. Meriwether and instructed him to "ab-
stain from taking forcible possession of the tract."[65]

In May 1853 President Pierce appointed as minister to Mexico
James Gadsden, a South Carolina railroad executive and champion of a southern transcontinental route to the Pacific. In Mexico
Gadsden found the dictatorial regime of Antonio López de Santa
Anna on the verge of bankruptcy and, as was its custom, in need
of money to stave off collapse. On 30 December 1853 Santa Anna
agreed to a Treaty of Boundary and Cession of Territory, usually
called the Gadsden Purchase treaty. For a purchase price of $15

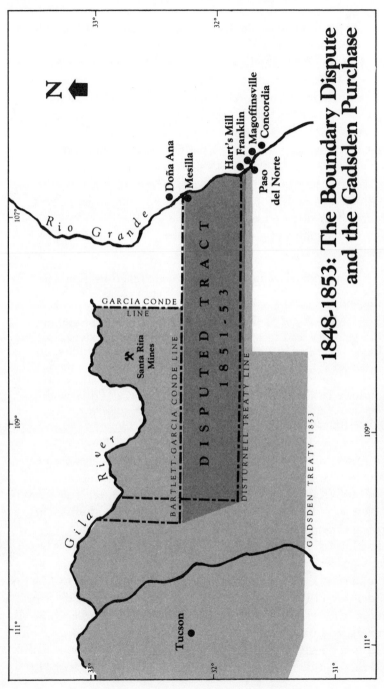

1848-1853: The Boundary Dispute and the Gadsden Purchase

The Gadsden Purchase of 1848-1853 settled the United States-Mexico boundary dispute.

million, the United States would acquire 29,760 square miles of territory south of the Gila River, including the railroad route and the Mesilla Valley. After several months of bitter debate in both the Senate and the House of Representatives, the acquired territory was reduced by 9,000 square miles and the purchase price to $10 million. The treaty was ratified by the Senate on 25 April 1854, and proclaimed on 30 June. At a later date El Paso historian Owen White took note of the significance of the purchase when he wrote: "That sixty mile drop in the boundary line gave the United States the control of the richest copper deposits in the world and made El Paso what it is today."[66]

Meanwhile, important developments had been taking place at the Pass of the North. From the time of the removal of troops from Coons's Ranch in September 1851, the settlers had continued to complain about their losses from Indian depredations and to urge the reestablishment of a military post. Joel L. Ankrim, district judge, listed the losses suffered during the past two years in a letter to the military authorities; twenty-three attacks from Indians had resulted in the loss of lives and property, disruption of business, and a general feeling of insecurity. A copy of Ankrim's letter was enclosed in a report submitted by Col. Joseph K. F. Mansfield, who had inspected western military posts and had recommended that a post be established opposite the town of El Paso del Norte either at Magoffinsville or at Smith's Ranch, preferably the former. As a result, a post was established at Magoffinsville in January 1854, four companies of the Eighth Infantry under the command of Maj. Edmund B. Alexander being quartered in buildings owned by James Magoffin. In March the name was officially designated Fort Bliss, in honor of Maj. William W. S. Bliss, chief of staff for Zachary Taylor during the U.S.-Mexico War and later his son-in-law.[67]

Gov. Angel Trías had remained in El Paso del Norte with his forces since his arrival there in April 1853, as tension over the Mesilla problem mounted. But with the ratification of the Gadsden Purchase treaty by the United States, Santa Anna's government ordered Governor Trías to relinquish the disputed area to the United States. At length, when this information reached Gov. David Meriwether of New Mexico, he decided that he and Gen. John Garland, commander of the Ninth Military District of New Mexico, should meet with Governor Trías and make arrangements for the formal transfer of the Mesilla territory. The meeting took place at Fort Bliss, sometime in October 1854. Governor Meriwether later wrote that he and Governor Trías agreed that Mexican forces should cross the river above Hart's mill to the west bank and that the Mexicans, on seeing the American flag approach, would pull down the Mexican flag, march their troops out of the fort, and leave the gates open for the Americans. Although warned of the possibility of a Mexican ruse, Meriwether said he had no fears. "On reaching within a few hundred yards of the fort," he wrote,

> I saw the Mexican flag come down, the Mexican troops march out, and our troops march in. Then the American flag was at once hoisted to the flagstaff so recently occupied by the Mexican flag. Our flag was saluted with two pieces of artillery which we had taken across the river with us. The band played "Hail, Columbia," "Yankee Doodle," and several other national airs, at the close of which I arose to make a speech to the large crowd of Mexicans who had gathered to witness the transfer. I told the Mexicans, through an interpreter, that by peaceful negotiations the disputed territory had been transferred to the United States; that I hoped they would prove themselves loyal and law-abiding citizens, but if they did not, I would feel it my duty at all hazards to see that the laws were executed; that any citizen who preferred the Mexican to the American government was at liberty to sell his possessions and move to the Mexican side of the line. But I hoped they would give the American government an opportunity of showing its advantages before doing so. I then caused a large number of proclamations which had been printed in the Spanish language...and which [were] of the same import as my speech, to be distributed among those present. The Mexicans appeared to be satisfied with what I had said to them and applauded lustily, many coming to be introduced to me, and to whom I gave a cordial shake of the hand.[68]

This ceremony was followed by another held in the plaza of Mesilla on 16 November 1854. Apparently the Mexican residents of Mesilla were now more willing to accept American jurisdiction than before. Their benefactor, Padre Ramón Ortiz, had been replaced as commissioner of *colonias* in 1853, and Consul Diffenderffer reported that El Paso del Norte authorities had been seizing Mesilla's municipal funds and redividing the land, much to the displeasure of the settlers.[69]

In sum, events of the greatest significance had taken place along the Rio Grande in the period from 1848 to 1854. With the establishment of that river as the international boundary between the United States and Mexico in 1848, the two cultural traditions — the Spanish-Mexican North and the Anglo-American Southwest — converged, thus producing a distinctive bicultural area which has remained to the present day. The year 1848, therefore, must be regarded as the single most important date in El Paso's four-hundred-year history. Before that date six Mexican settlements lay in a chain along the right bank of the Rio Grande; shortly after that date five new settlements had been established by Americans along the left bank, to be joined by three more Mexican towns the shifting river had placed on the American side. One of these settlements, known as Franklin, became the nucleus of El Paso, Texas, and thus by 1854 the foundations of a bilingual and bicultural community had been laid.[70]

CHAPTER SIX

The Continental Crossroads, 1849-1881

I N the decade following the close of the war with Mexico the United
States government inaugurated and conducted an extensive program of exploration in West Texas, one phase of a general policy of
developing the entire trans-Mississippi country in the interest of the
immigrant, the settler, the soldier, and the merchant. A significant
aspect of the program was the exploration and survey of the most
suitable routes for the construction of transcontinental railroads
across the trans-Mississippi West to the Pacific Ocean. One of these
considered throughout the 1850s was the southern route, extending
from central Texas westward through the Pass of the North, then
along the thirty-second parallel south of the Gila River to southern
California. W. H. Emory, the United States boundary surveyor-
commissioner, had noted in 1846 that the Sierra Madre and Rocky

Mountains lose their continuous character at about the thirty-second parallel. "It is possible," he wrote,

> to pass through these mountains near the 32nd parallel almost on the level of the plateau; so that if the sea were to rise 4,000 feet above its present level, the navigator could cross the continent near the 32nd parallel of latitude. He would be on soundings of uniform depth, from the Gulf of California to the Pecos River. He would see to the north and the south prominent peaks and sierras, and at times his passage would be narrow and intricate. At El Paso he would be within gunshot of both shores.[1]

Interest in determining the most suitable route from San Antonio to the El Paso area resulted in the organization of two exploring expeditions early in 1849. The first of these was commanded by William H. C. Whiting of the Army Engineering Corps and Lt. William F. Smith of the Topographical Engineers. Leaving San Antonio on 12 February, the expedition moved northwestward to the German settlement of Fredericksburg, on to the San Saba River, crossed the Pecos River, then traveled to Presidio del Norte, and arrived at Ponce's Ranch on 12 April. On the return trip the expedition followed a more southerly course, which in time came to be referred to as "the lower route." Its practicality was tested with the arrival from San Antonio in September 1849, as was noted in the previous chapter, of six companies of the Third Infantry under the command of Maj. Jefferson Van Horne. Capt. Samuel G. French, assistant quartermaster of the expedition, commented as follows:

> El Paso, from its geographical position, presents itself as a resting place on one of the great overland routes between the seaports of the Atlantic on one side and those of the Pacific on the other.... A little further to the north and west are the head-waters of the Gila; and should the route from El Paso to the seaboard on the west present no more difficulties than that from the east, there can easily be established between the Atlantic states and those that have so suddenly sprung into existence in the West—and which are destined to change, perhaps, the political institutions and commercial relations of half the world—a connexion that will strengthen the bonds of union by free and constant intercourse. The government has been a pioneer in the enterprise and the little labor bestowed may not be lost to the public weal.[2]

In the meantime, a second expedition, partially sponsored by the Army and commanded by Maj. Robert S. Neighbors of the Texas Rangers and by John S. "Rip" Ford, the federal Indian agent for Texas, had taken a more northerly route along the upper Colorado, then west to the Pecos, arriving at Ponce's Ranch on 2 May. The return trip was through the Guadalupe Mountains to the Pecos, then across the San Saba to San Antonio, which came to be known as "the upper route." In July it was resurveyed by Lt. Francis T. Bryan and pronounced fit for the easy passage of wagons. "Grass and water," he reported,

> may be had every day within marches of twenty-five miles, except from the head of the Conchos to the Pecos—a distance of sixty-eight miles, which is entirely without permanent water at present. The character of the country is such, however, as to leave no doubt of the success of attempts to find water by means of wells, sunk at proper intervals.[3]

Within a few months two new important roads from San Antonio to El Paso had been opened. Government trains, troops, and supplies, and emigrants could now travel between those points with greater ease and safety. "These routes," notes Goetzmann in his excellent study of Army explorations in the West, "remained for years the main lines of communication for soldier, settler, and gold seeker alike. When the railroads were built through Texas, the Texas and Pacific followed generally Bryan's trail and the Southern Pacific followed part way along the lower road."[4]

Simultaneous with the expeditions from San Antonio to the El Paso area during 1849 was one commanded by Capt. Randolph B. Marcy from Fort Smith, Arkansas, to Santa Fe, then down the Rio Grande to Doña Ana, and eastward through the Organ, Sacramento, and Guadalupe Mountains to the Pecos, Brazos, and Red rivers, and return. This route from Doña Ana to Fort Smith, Marcy wrote, should be given serious consideration by the emigrants to California. Flour, corn, vegetables, beef cattle, and many articles of merchandise that travelers require such as clothing and shoes, said Marcy, could be obtained for moderate prices at Doña Ana or El Paso. He added:

> From Doña Ana or El Paso to near where we crossed Red River there are probably as few difficulties to encounter as

upon any other road that can be found in our country....
For a great portion of the distance, the surface of the earth
is so perfectly firm and smooth that it would appear to
have been designed by the Great Architect of the Universe
for a railroad.[5]

Possibly the most enthusiastic champion of the thirty-second
parallel as the best one for the construction of a transcontinental
railroad was Capt. John Pope, who in early 1854 conducted the
most comprehensive survey yet undertaken of the thirty-second
parallel from the Rio Grande east to the Red. Specifically, with
regard to the El Paso area, he wrote:

> The next settlements along the river below Doña Ana,
> with the exception of the abandoned ranch of Frontera,
> are the town of Molino at the rapids of the Rio Grande,
> about two miles above El Paso, and the town of Franklin,
> about two miles below.
>
> Molino has been but recently laid out into lots, but
> occupying the point at which a railroad must intersect the
> Rio Grande; and presenting by far the most practicable
> point for crossing the river within many miles, it bids fair
> to become a place of much consequence. Franklin, opposite
> El Paso, is at present occupied by four companies of the
> 8th infantry, and is almost entirely the property of Mr.
> James McGoffin [sic], a wealthy and enterprising citizen
> of El Paso county.
>
> The small villages of Isletta [sic] and San Elizario are
> twelve and twenty-five miles, respectively, below El Paso.
>
> At Frontera, about five miles above El Paso, the Rio
> Grande commences to make its passage through the chain
> of mountains which intersect its course, and to a point im-
> mediately in the neighborhood of Molino it is bordered
> closely on both sides by a range of high and rugged moun-
> tains. Between Frontera and Molino the river cuts through
> them by a succession of rapids, and at one place a perpen-
> dicular fall of two or three feet; this passage has from the
> period of its discovery by the Spaniards been known as
> El Paso.[6]

Following in the wake of the initial survey and exploration expeditions seeking the best wagon roads and railroad routes came
the inauguration of mail service from San Antonio through El Paso
to Santa Fe. First to carry the mail was a big, broad-shouldered
frontiersman named Henry Skillman. He had long sandy hair and

beard, stood six feet tall, and packed two hundred pounds of hard muscle and bone on his tough frame. He signed a contract with the Post Office Department in late 1851 and established a monthly passenger service using four horse coaches. The fare from San Antonio to El Paso was fixed at $100, and through fare to Santa Fe at $125. Passengers were allowed forty pounds of baggage. Joining Skillman as stage driver was another frontier character, the fabled William Alexander Wallace, named "Bigfoot" for his longstanding feud with a Lipan Apache who left huge moccasin tracks in his path. The purchase of a new improved carbine produced by the Sharps Rifle Manufacturing Company gave the drivers and guards a needed and welcome advantage in dealing with the Apaches. By early 1853 the entire trip from Santa Fe to San Antonio was completed in twenty-four days, only sixteen of them for the El Paso-San Antonio leg.[7]

The increased volume of mail necessitated the establishment of a post office in 1852 for El Paso, Texas. The name Franklin, however (spelled Franquilín in the Mexican documents), continued to be used by officials on both sides of the border for a number of years, probably to avoid confusion with the name El Paso del Norte. Skillman continued his service until 1854, when he lost his federal subsidy, and all efforts during the next three years to keep the line going failed. At length, a contract to establish a semimonthly mail service between San Antonio and San Diego, California, was obtained in 1857 by George H. Giddings, who began a mail and passenger service in May 1858. Often called the "Jackass Line" because of its use of mules over most of the route, the service left from both ends twice a month, the fare being $200, with a baggage allowance of thirty pounds. Eighty-seven stage stations were erected, known as "the longest uninterrupted route in the United States if not in the world," but with the exception of El Paso, most stations were merely mud huts. Unquestionably, the through passenger on this bimonthly operation could expect an unforgettable experience.[8]

One other means of transportation attempted in the Southwest prior to the Civil War was the testing of camels as beasts of burden. The experiment should come as no surprise when one recalls that the West in the textbooks of the period was labeled "The Great American Desert." Although the idea had been advanced on

Fort Bliss was established in 1854 at Magoffinsville,
a settlement started by trader James Wiley Magoffin.
(Courtesy National Archives, neg. no. 88047)

a number of occasions, it failed to gain acceptance until 1854
when Lt. Edward Fitzgerald Beale, a veteran of the Mexican War
who thought camels might prove useful in the Southwest, found
support from Jefferson Davis, secretary of war in the Franklin
Pierce administration. Necessary funds were appropriated, and by
February 1857, seventy-seven animals had been imported and
stabled at a camp sixty miles northwest of San Antonio. Late in
June 1857 a wagon train and a caravan of twenty-five camels, each
carrying about five hundred pounds, left camp. Commanded by
Lieutenant Beale, they arrived in San Elizario on 26 July. The
wagon train continued on through the town, but the camels were
detained in San Elizario for all to see. "Our train arrived this
morning of July 26," wrote Lieutenant Beale,

> and the whole Mexican population, which since our ar-
> rival, had been in a perfectly feverish state of excitement
> in relation to the camels, had their curiosity gratified. The
> street was crowded, and when we went on to camp the
> whole town followed. I drove to Franklin in the evening,
> and spent the next day at Fort Bliss, where I was kindly
> received by the officers. I dined with Mr. McGoffin [sic]
> and attended a pleasant party at his house afterwards.[9]

Capt. John Pope's endorsement of the thirty-second parallel for a transcontinental railroad route greatly interested Southerners such as John C. Reid of Selma, Alabama, who visited the El Paso area late in 1857. He was impressed with the productivity of the valleys; of the Lower Valley settlements he liked San Elizario the best. He preferred Magoffinsville to Stephenson's Ranch, and he thought the facilities and strong adobe structures at Fort Bliss displayed good planning. Most impressive was the town of Franklin, said Reid, with its half dozen dry goods stores, customhouse, and post office. With the completion of an interoceanic railroad, he predicted, it would occupy an important midway position and could become the most important inland city in America. While there was much in El Paso del Norte that he liked—the fandangos, the fiesta of Our Lady of Guadalupe, the friendliness of the people, and the beautiful ladies—there was much that he found distasteful—poverty, peonage, deteriorated buildings, the tariff, beggars, and thieves. On the whole, however, Reid was highly impressed with the El Paso area, and remained fully convinced that the thirty-second parallel offered advantages for a railroad that far exceeded all the other routes. The South, he insisted, must shake off its lethargy, assert itself in defense of its interests, and build "that commercial empire which is ours by manifest and inevitable destiny."[10]

In September 1858 a new transportation service was established between St. Louis and San Francisco, exerting a far greater impact on the El Paso area than any other until the arrival of the railroad. This was John Butterfield's Overland Mail, a company which had contracted one year earlier to carry the mail and passengers by stage from Tipton, Missouri, where the railroad came to an end, to San Francisco, the entire trip to be completed in no more than twenty-five days. The Butterfield system thus would span the longest distance over which coach service had ever been attempted, involving 2,700 miles of mud, dust, and rock-covered trail. Granted the difficulties were enormous, but the experience and determination of John Butterfield proved equal to the task. Each stage was to be pulled by four or six horses or mules, and could carry six to eight passengers together with the mail. Stations were constructed on the average about twenty miles apart, where the passengers could get water and a simple meal while a fresh

*This stagecoach, typical of those that served El Paso for
many years, was photographed in 1916 when it was still
in use between Chihuahua City and Presidio, Texas.*

team of horses or mules was hitched to the coach. Fare for the entire distance was $200, with all meals extra. Baggage allowance was
forty pounds. Sleep and relaxation were not guaranteed.[11]

Accompanying the Butterfield's first stage out of Tipton was
Waterman L. Ormsby, special correspondent of the New York
Herald, who was commissioned by his newspaper to record this
dramatic new chapter in transportation history. Some two weeks
after Ormsby's stage left Tipton, Missouri, he survived the throat-
parching ride from Hueco Tanks, and arrived at Franklin in the
early morning hours of 30 September 1858. "As we neared the
river," Ormsby wrote,

> the delightful aroma of the fruit and herbs was most grate-
> ful after so long and dreary a ride over the desert, and at
> that moment I could have endorsed all the encomiums on
> "the fertile valley of the Rio Grande." We passed many
> vineyards and comfortable ranches built of adobe and
> looking extremely neat. About two miles from Franklin is
> Fort Bliss, now occupied by a small garrison of United
> States troops. The fort is built of adobe.
> The city of Franklin, on the American side of the
> river, contains a few hundred inhabitants, and is in the
> midst of a fine agricultural district. The onions as well as
> the grapes of this locality are of world-wide celebrity, and
> El Paso wines are universally appreciated.... We left

Franklin at 5:40 A.M. on Thursday, the 30th, for Messilla [Mesilla], our route leading through the valley of the Rio Grande.[12]

Ten days later the Butterfield stage galloped into San Francisco, twenty-three days, twenty-three and a half hours from the time it had left Tipton. A mail bag dispatched from St. Louis on 16 September 1858, the same day the Butterfield stage left Tipton, was carried by train to New York, then by ship around the Horn; it reached San Francisco six days after the stage had arrived. Thus the overland route to California had become a reality, and Franklin, Texas, had become the continental crossroads with twice-weekly contact with the outside world. "Bounding along Overland Street," as Professor Joseph Leach puts it, "the east and west bound stages could eat each other's dust."[13]

Arriving on a stage on 8 May 1858, several months before the first Butterfield stage reached the El Paso area, was Anson Mills, who, like Magoffin, Hart, and Stephenson, was one of El Paso's foremost pioneers. He had attended West Point, learned some surveying, taught school in Texas for a year, and decided that the El Paso area was a land of promise that would eventually become a place of importance. "After seven days' and nights' travel," Mills writes in *My Story*,

> when I arrived at the bluffs overlooking the valley of the Rio Grande, I thought it was the most pleasant sight I had ever seen. When we drove into the town, which consisted of a ranch of some hundred and fifty acres in cultivation in beautiful grape, apple, pear, and peach orchards, watermelons, grain, wheat and corn, it seemed still more beautiful, especially when, under the shade of the large cottonwood trees along the acequias, ...we saw Mexican girls selling fruits of all kinds grown on the opposite side of the river at what was known as Paso del Norte.[14]

Shortly after Mills arrived in El Paso, he was contracted by the Butterfield company to build its station. Completed in September 1858, about the time the first stage arrived, the building and corrals were constructed on two acres bounded by Oregon, Overland, and El Paso streets, making the station the largest and best equipped on the Butterfield route. Occupying half a city block, it was the most imposing structure in town. Across the street on the

corner where the Westin Paso del Norte Hotel now stands was
another adobe structure that housed the post office, store, bar,
and tables for billiards, cards, and dice – the property of Post-
master Ben Dowell, and the favorite meeting place in town. Out of
a population of 300, most of whom were Mexicans, writes Owen
White in his classic, *Out of the Desert*, there were twenty professional gamblers. "Nobody worked," he continues,

> that is, nobody except Mexicans worked regularly. The
> "white men" in the community did practically nothing for
> the very simple reason that there was nothing to do, and
> the very natural result of this pleasing state of affairs was
> that Uncle Ben Dowell's saloon sheltered the entire Ameri-
> can male population of the town for the greater part of
> every day and for nearly all of every night.[15]

Early in 1859 Mills completed his survey and plat of the Town
of El Paso, a sketch which looks very much like the present downtown, with its public square (now San Jacinto Plaza), plaza (now
Pioneer Plaza), and principal streets named for the stage lines – St.
Louis (now Mills) and San Antonio, which headed eastward; San
Francisco to the west; Santa Fe to the north; Overland, the site of
the stage station; and El Paso, which ran south to the ferry to El
Paso del Norte. The main *acequia*, which ran in an easterly direction by the plaza, was lined with cottonwood trees, and most of
the area south of San Antonio and San Francisco streets had vineyards, fruit trees, and fields of wheat and corn in cultivation. A
second *acequia* carried water to the valley settlements. Nailed to a
tree in the plaza was a plank which served as a bulletin board
where announcements were posted and where anyone could and
did voice his opinions about one or more of his fellow citizens.[16]

William Wallace Mills, who had arrived in El Paso in December 1858 some six months after his elder brother Anson, appraised
the forty-odd Americans in the community as follows:

> The men who, for whatever reasons, had made their way
> to this distant frontier, were nearly all men of character;
> not all of good character, certainly, but of positive, asser-
> tive individual character, with strong personality and self-
> reliance. (The weaklings remained at home.) Many of them
> were well bred and of more than ordinary intelligence, and
> maintaining the manners of gentlemen. Even the worst
> of these men are not to be classed with the professional

Since the early days when it was known as Franklin,
El Paso has been a meeting place for diverse cultures.
This drawing depicts Anglo Americans being welcomed
by Mexican Americans. (José Cisneros, 1981)

145

"toughs" and "thugs" who came later with the railroads. They were neither assassins nor thieves nor robbers. Vices? Plenty; but they were not of the concealed or most degrading kinds. Violence? Yes, but such acts were usually the result of sudden anger or of a feeling that under the conditions then existing each man must right his own wrongs or they would never be righted. Their ideas of right and wrong were peculiar, but they *had* such ideas nevertheless.

With regard to Mexican relations, he wrote:

Common trials and dangers united the two races as one family, and the fact that one man was a Mexican and another an American was seldom mentioned, and I believe as seldom thought about. Each man was esteemed at his real worth, and I think our estimates of each other's characters were generally more correct than in more artificial societies. Spanish was the language of the country, but many of our Mexican friends spoke English well, and often conversations, and even sentences, were amusingly and expressively made up of words or phrases of both languages.[17]

The decade of the 1850s had been one of growth and development for the El Paso community, and by 1861 the outlook was bright. As El Paso historian Nancy Hammons has noted, the county had been organized, economic conditions were good, a railroad was in prospect, the population had increased to 428 according to the 1860 census, and the Pass of the North had become nationally known as an important way station on the southern route to California. But the period of the Civil War and Reconstruction which was to follow stunted growth and development for more than a decade. "From the first I foresaw the prospective importance of the place," noted W. W. Mills in his *Forty Years at El Paso*,

and many a still, lonesome night have I listened to the roaring of the waters over the dam at Hart's Mill, a mile above the village, and tried to fancy it the rumbling of railroad trains, which were then fifteen hundred miles away. No, I do not claim to have foreseen that El Paso would be the center of so many railroads, but I felt sure that the first road to the Pacific Ocean would pass through El Paso, and *so it would*, had it not been for the Rebellion.[18]

News of the election of Abraham Lincoln in 1860, the candidate of the party opposing the extension of slavery into the territories of the United States, brought forth immediate action on the part of the Southern states, including Texas. Even before Lincoln's inaugural on 4 March 1861, seven Southern states had held conventions that adopted ordinances of secession from the Union. On 1 February 1861 a state convention in Austin voted overwhelmingly in favor of secession. In El Paso, only limited interest was shown by the Mexican-American population, which made up the vast majority, but the Anglo-Americans were almost unanimously pro-Southern. Although a few such as Simeon Hart owned slaves, the issue of slavery locally was hardly the burning issue it had become nationally. A more significant factor explaining the overwhelming pro-Southern sentiment was the identification of Jefferson Davis, president of the Confederate States, with the southern transcontinental railroad route and its obvious implications for El Paso's strategic importance.[19]

On receipt of the news of the action of the state convention, a local election on the question of Texas's secession was held in Ben Dowell's saloon. Two opposition votes were cast, and everyone in town knew whose they were – the Mills brothers, Anson and W. W. "Champagne for the secessionists," shouted Simeon Hart when he saw W. W. Mills enter the saloon, "the noose for all Unionists." Although the Mills brothers charged that the election was a fraud since the nine hundred votes cast included several hundred by Mexicans from El Paso del Norte, there was little doubt of the decisive influence of the pro-Southerners such as Simeon Hart, James Magoffin, and Josiah Crosby.[20]

In compliance with an order of the Union commander in Texas to surrender all posts to Confederate authority, Bvt. Lt. Col. Isaac V. D. Brown, commander at Fort Bliss, evacuated his troops under parole to San Antonio. According to Magoffin, most of the federal property at Fort Bliss was eventually seized, but only after an attempt by a "party of rascals" was thwarted in an effort to carry some of it across the river and bury the rest. Magoffin then ran up the Confederate flag, while Anson Mills left for Washington, D.C., to serve the Union cause, and his brother went to New Mexico to work for Lt. Col. E. R. S. Canby, Union commander in the area.[21]

In July 1861 three companies of the Texas Mounted Rifles occupied Fort Bliss, to be followed a few days later by two other

companies commanded by Lt. Col. John R. Baylor. On one occasion while Baylor's men were stationed at Fort Bliss, they caught
W. W. Mills in El Paso del Norte, accused him of spying on Confederate activities, and imprisoned him at Fort Bliss, part of the
time in chains. Mills eventually escaped and returned to New
Mexico, but he never forgot nor forgave Simeon Hart, whom he
continued to hold responsible for his humiliation. Similarly, Consul David Diffenderffer, while on private business in Franklin, was
arrested, charged with harboring spies and using his influence to
undermine the Confederate cause, and was confined at Fort Bliss.[22]

Late in July Baylor advanced northward, occupied the Mesilla
Valley, and forced the surrender of Col. Isaac Lynde and seven
hundred men at Fort Fillmore. Lynde was found guilty of coward-
ice and treason and was discharged from the army, although he
was exonerated and reinstated after the war. The defeat at Fort
Fillmore cleared southern New Mexico and West Texas of Union
forces. Unquestionably, one explanation for the success of Confederate arms in the early months of the war in the El Paso area
was the supply of flour provided by Simeon Hart. Late in 1861 he
said he had on hand 40,000 to 50,000 pounds stored across the
river for safekeeping in El Paso del Norte.[23]

With southern New Mexico in Confederate hands, Jefferson
Davis late in 1861 decided on an offensive designed to bring New
Mexico and Arizona under Confederate control. Col. Henry H.
Sibley, who had been stationed with the United States Army in
Santa Fe, "went South" at the opening of the war, and assisted
Baylor in raising the Confederate banner over the El Paso area.
Commissioned a brigadier general, Sibley was ordered to Fort Bliss
with a regiment of Texas Rangers and was placed in command of
the Army of New Mexico.[24]

Early in 1862 Sibley launched an offensive into New Mexico.
He engaged Canby at Valverde, near Socorro, New Mexico, and
won a victory, capturing six Union cannons. Confederate forces
then occupied Albuquerque and Santa Fe, but Canby, with rein-
forcements just received, retaliated and defeated a detachment of
Sibley's forces at Glorieta Pass, 26-29 March 1862. As historian C.
L. Sonnichsen puts it, "Glorieta was the Gettysburg of the West."
Their supplies cut off, Sibley's men made their way back to Fort
Bliss after having suffered a 50 percent loss in dead, wounded, sick,

and prisoners of war. Gov. Henry Connelly of New Mexico explained in a letter to Secretary of State W. H. Seward: "The Texans ...arrived with about one half of their original number in a perfectly disorganized condition at Mesilla on the west bank of the river where they hurriedly crossed it and continued their flight without delay to El Paso, driving before them every quadruped that was upon the borders of the river or in the possession of the inhabitants of that valley."[25]

Confederate plans for the conquest of the West also involved diplomatic agreements with the Mexican states of Chihuahua and Sonora to give the Confederacy access to the mineral resources of the area and a seaport on the Gulf of California. To this end, early in 1862 Sibley sent Col. James Reily on a mission to the governors of Chihuahua and Sonora. Luis Terrazas, governor of Chihuahua, was willing to recognize the Confederacy as an official government, but offered little else, while Ignacio Pesqueira, governor of Sonora, refused to make any deal with the Confederates, stating that he was sympathetic with the Union cause.[26]

During May and June 1862, there occurred the famous march of California Volunteers, or California Column – some 1,400 troops commanded by Gen. James H. Carleton, whose assignment was to restore Union control over Arizona and New Mexico. On 20 May 1862 one advance column took Tucson, and another reached the Rio Grande near the present town of Hatch. The Confederates abandoned Mesilla and Las Cruces, and for the first time since the surrender of Fort Fillmore by Colonel Lynde, the Stars and Stripes floated again on the lower Rio Grande. Col. William Steele, the Confederate commander at Fort Fillmore, wrote on 12 July 1862 about the desperate situation that compelled him to abandon New Mexico for Fort Bliss. He stated that he had incurred the hostility of the native population when he was forced to seize their supplies. His own troops were demoralized and on the verge of open mutiny, he said, while the enemy at that time was in a position to bring 3,000 troops against him. He continued:

The sale was ordered of all public property at Fort Bliss which was too bulky for transporting or was of no value. This sale was held for specie and breadstuffs. The specie was turned over to the general hospital which I was compelled to leave at Franklin. There was besides a considerable quantity of stores that could not be sold and which were too weighty for transportation. To conclude, I am now about to start for San Antonio with very limited means of transportation, and an insufficient supply of breadstuff and beef and with troops in many instances almost naked. This I submit as a true representation of the condition of affairs in this country.[27]

In August 1862, following Sibley's orders to abandon Fort Bliss, the long, dreary retreat eastward began. Some like Magoffin left with the Confederate forces; others crossed the river to El Paso del Norte. Union forces took possession of the post which the Confederates had left in a shambles on 20 August 1862, and the Union flag was again raised, the first time in a year and a half. The California Column remained in occupation of the area until February 1865, when the United States Army took over.[28]

After the California Column occupied New Mexico and El Paso, many citizens in the area were indicted for treason. A congressional law, passed 17 July 1862, provided for seizure and confiscation of property of any person engaged in armed rebellion or aiding rebellion against the United States. Proceedings soon were begun leading to the seizure of property of those El Pasoans known for their Southern sympathies. Most cases were brought against Texans in the federal district court at Mesilla in Doña Ana County, Territory of New Mexico. Charges of treason were supported by unreliable testimony, and the proceedings were frequently irregular. A United States marshal for the district, Abraham Cutler, supervised the seizure and sale of properties, which went for ridiculously low prices. Simeon Hart's property, including flour mills, dwelling houses, corrals, ranch houses, machinery, and stables, sold for $3,000; other properties sold for as little as five dollars. Two years later, Cutler was charged with embezzlement, and although it was established that he had received more than $13,000 for services rendered in handling the sales, the jury brought in a verdict of not guilty. Historian Larry D. Ball notes that W. W. Mills, the United States collector of customs at El Paso during the Civil War, many years later admitted that he supported the subordination of his district to Marshal Cutler and the New Mexico courts. But he "did not then even dream of the confiscation of anyone's real estate." Mills thought the New Mexican courts, Ball adds, would "enable me to condemn and sell goods smuggled into El Paso County."[29]

In time, El Paso County residents who had lost properties appealed to the New Mexico Supreme Court on grounds that the Mesilla district had no jurisdiction. The appeal was sustained, the decision of the district court was reversed, and the forfeiture suits were dismissed. In 1868 the United States Supreme Court upheld the decision of the New Mexico Supreme Court in the case of United States vs. S. Hart, which paved the way for all those who had sympathized with the Confederacy eventually to recover their properties. Even though Hart received a presidential pardon, he still had to battle W. W. Mills for the recovery of his property, a long struggle which finally came to an end in May 1873 when W. W. and his brother Anson accepted a payment of ten dollars. Worn out by all the tension and anxiety, Hart died early the following year.[30]

James Magoffin, after an effort lasting more than a year, received a presidential pardon, but the *carte blanche* he was given by A. J. Hamilton, provisional governor of Texas, to reorganize county government in El Paso was blocked by the Union commander at Fort Bliss. Magoffin then returned to San Antonio, where he spent most of his remaining years until his death in 1868. Title to his property was returned to his son, Joseph Magoffin, on 6 January 1869, but was subsequently challenged by Alejandro Ramírez of El Paso del Norte, the original grantee of the title when the property was part of Mexico. Ramírez built a log cabin and other small houses on the property but failed to establish residence there despite warnings by El Paso county officials that his title would be nullified if he did not occupy and live on the land. In 1872 John S. Watts, chief justice of the Supreme Court of New Mexico, ruled that title to the land formerly known as Ponce's Ranch belonged to James W. Magoffin, who occupied the land in 1849, built a log house, and lived on the property, rather than to Ramírez, who did not. With Joseph Magoffin's title to his father's property upheld, it became in 1875 the site of the Magoffin Homestead, one of El Paso's most historic treasures.[31]

Fort Bliss, located on Magoffin's property since 1854, suffered considerable flood damage, and was moved in 1868 to Concordia, Hugh Stephenson's property. Lydia Spencer Lane, a soldier's wife who had spend some time at the post in 1857, wrote at a later date that "the Fort Bliss of 1869 was not the one we knew and enjoyed so much." Some of the buildings had been washed away by the river, she said, while the others were "masses of crumbling adobe." After Stephenson's death in 1870, the property passed to his heirs. The post remained at Concordia until 1877 when it was closed down for lack of funds.[32]

Mail and stage service from San Antonio to El Paso, largely suspended during the Civil War, was renewed in April 1866, when Bethel Coopwood received a mail contract for his United States Mail Stage Line. The first mail left San Antonio on 24 April with James Magoffin and Simeon Hart as passengers and arrived in El Paso on 6 May, as the local citizenry celebrated their first regular communication with the eastern settlements in nearly four years. Coopwood, like Skillman and Giddings, struggled valiantly to keep the operation going, but at length transferred the line to Frederick A. Sawyer late in 1866. Apache and Comanche hostilities in the Pecos River valley continued to interrupt service during most of 1867, depriving San Antonio of any regular connection with the recent gold discoveries in Arizona. "If the El Paso mail was making regular trips between this city and Mesilla," complained a San Antonio newspaper, "all the gold produced in that section would find remittance to this place for exchange, and thousands of dollars worth of business could be made between the two points. Our city is suffering from the withdrawal of this service."[33]

The town of San Antonio, however, would not have to wait long for the mails to start moving again, as about that time there arrived on the scene a man of proven business ability whose name became synonymous with staging in West Texas, Benjamin Franklin Ficklin. With extensive experience gained as manager of several western lines in the late 1850s, including the celebrated Pony Express, Ficklin initiated his mail service from San Antonio to El Paso in late 1867. Despite Indian hostilities, clashes with the army, and the enmity of W. W. Mills, Republican political boss of El Paso, Ficklin kept his operation going until his untimely death in 1871. His partner, Frederick A. Sawyer, continued the service until his death in 1875; it was taken over in the late 1870s by Francis C. Taylor and Charles Bain.[34]

Sawyer's death, as historian Austerman has noted, marked a turning point for the El Paso Mail.

The organization survived his passing, but it was less of an empire than an appendage to the rapidly expanding railroads. Even though it still served the vital function of uniting El Paso and the country to the west with the settled portions of Texas, it was obvious by the fall of 1875 that there was no longer any question that the railroads would span the state; the only unanswered question was when the task would be completed.... The El Paso Mail had moved far beyond the role of a simple courier to act as a colonizing force on the frontier.... Change and progress may have brought a pang of remorse to many of the people who could yet remember the start of it all a quarter of a century before with Henry Skillman, but their passing remained as gallant as their coming.[35]

While the United States was enduring the tragedy of war, Mexico was also ravaged by civil strife, known as the War of the Reform, 1858-1861, followed by the French Intervention and the imposition of a foreign monarch on a Mexican throne, 1864-1867. Under the leadership of Benito Juárez, a Zapotec Indian from Oaxaca, the Liberal Party had formulated a program favoring constitutional government, a federal republic, individual rights and guarantees, public education, the civil registration of births, marriages, and deaths, and the breaking of the political and economic power of the Catholic Church in Mexico. Ordinarily such a program would be regarded as mid-nineteenth-century European liberalism, but in Mexico at that time it amounted to revolution. Compromise was impossible, and the result was civil war in 1858.[36]

David Diffenderffer, the United States consul in El Paso del Norte with seven years of service in the position, wrote early in April 1858 that the situation in Mexico was deplorable. Trade had come to a standstill, he said; the country was still being run by unprincipled men interested only in enriching themselves in office, and there was little hope for Mexico, whose problems could only be overcome through the education of the coming generation. Early in 1860 Diffenderffer said that he full expected the Conservatives to win in Chihuahua; should that happen, the *Zona Libre*, established by the Chihuahua Liberals in 1858 following the example of the Mexican state of Tamaulipas, would be removed and the protective system restored. James Magoffin, in a letter of 24 May

1860 to Gov. Sam Houston of Texas, said that he was in full ac-
cord with the governor's suggestion that a United States protectorate should be established in Mexico. "That fine country," wrote
Magoffin, "has totally gone to ruin for want of protection – too
bad, but so it is. I hope to see the day myself when Mexico will
be freed from oppression. Texas has to be first as the single best
hope that makes tyranny and oppression tremble throughout that
noble country."[37]

By that time, the tide had turned in favor of the Liberal cause,
whose victorious forces entered Mexico City on New Year's Day,
1861. Benito Juárez, whose leadership was now unchallenged, arrived ten days later to take over the reins of government. Although
Mexico desperately needed a breathing spell to rebuild a war-torn
nation, Juárez now found himself with an even more formidable
foe – military intervention by France under Emperor Napoleon III.[38]

The crafty French emperor, who loved to dazzle his subjects
with grandiose imperial projects, planned to establish, with the
encouragement and support of Mexican conservatives, a puppet
monarchy in Mexico to repeal the Juárez reforms and erect a
strong Catholic state. With the hands of the United States tied by
its own Civil War, an unparalleled opportunity thus presented
itself to France to intervene militarily in Mexico, disguising its
action as a means of forcing the Juárez administration to pay its
debts. The Mexicans resisted, and their victory over the French in
Puebla on 5 May 1862 (Cinco de Mayo in Mexican history) set
back the French for almost a year. Ultimately, however, with the
arrival of French reinforcements, most of Mexico was occupied,
forcing Juárez to flee and take refuge with his cabinet in El Paso
del Norte in August 1865. He remained there nearly a year.[39]

The French-sponsored monarchy in Mexico was entrusted to
the celebrated couple, Maximilian and Carlota, who arrived in
Mexico in June 1864. While Maximilian was a well-meaning
moderate who sought to rise above faction and unite the country,
his policies alienated both the Juaristas and the Mexican conservatives. Moreover, the United States, as the Civil War drew to a
close, began to take a much harder line toward France for its
violations of the Monroe Doctrine. Napoleon III meanwhile had
become increasingly exasperated with Maximilian's extravagance
and incompetence, and in July 1866 took the first steps toward

liquidating his imperial project by announcing that all French troops would be withdrawn from Mexico within eighteen months.[40]

In El Paso del Norte Consul Diffenderffer, arrested and confined by the Confederate forces of Lt. Col. John R. Baylor, was compelled to resign his position in order to obtain his release. In 1863, following the occupation of Fort Bliss by Union forces, Irish-born Henry J. Cuniffe became consul. His prediction that the Liberal cause in Mexico would collapse underestimated the tenacity of its leadership. Benito Juárez, upon entering El Paso del Norte, stated that he was establishing the national government there so that he could remain in touch with states along the border as well as with the interior of Mexico, utilizing California and New York as his means of communication. He politely but firmly declined an offer from Gen. James Carleton to use Simeon Hart's El Molino as his headquarters, and steadfastly refused to leave Mexican soil while it was being occupied by foreign troops. Significantly, a reception in Juárez's honor which was to be held at Fort Bliss was moved to El Paso del Norte. Other social affairs held on the American side were attended by his son and his cabinet, but not by Juárez, in accordance with his policy.[41]

While in El Paso del Norte on 8 November 1865, Juárez issued a decree extending his presidential powers beyond the four-year constitutional term in view of the national emergency, an indication of his determination to see the republican cause through to final victory. In the United States the Civil War had come to an end, thus permitting Secretary of State William H. Seward to abandon his policy of strict neutrality in favor of one that made it possible for the Juárez republicans to purchase American arms and munitions. The tide began to turn in Juárez's favor. On 31 March 1866 Consul Cuniffe wrote Seward that he had received the welcome news that the Liberal Army under the command of Luis Terrazas had taken Chihuahua City, that the state was in the possession of the national troops, and that President Juárez and his cabinet would be departing for the Chihuahua capital within a few days.[42]

Immediately following Napoleon III's announcement of the withdrawal of all French troops, Carlota left Mexico to seek help for Maximilian, who had decided that abdicating his Mexican throne was beneath the Hapsburg dignity. In June 1867 his army was defeated at the Hill of the Bells outside Querétaro, and when "the lucky bullet" failed to appear, Maximilian was captured and taken before a firing squad. The indomitable Benito Juárez meanwhile had returned to Mexico City in triumph to rule the nation until his death in 1872.[43]

By the 1860s the settlements south of the river, which included El Paso del Norte and its nine districts, together with Real de San Lorenzo, Senecú, Guadalupe, and San Ignacio, had a total population of more than 6,000. Late in 1862 the town of Zaragosa was founded, named for the hero of the battle of Puebla on 5 May 1862. It was settled by Mexicans from the Lower Valley who were discontented with the rule of American officials. In 1868 the nine districts in El Paso del Norte were renamed for the leaders of the republican movement – Juárez, Mejía, Romero, Díaz, Doblado, La Fuente, Escobedo, Lerdo, and Iglesias.[44]

In the United States the Civil War was followed by a period equally as painful and acrimonious: Reconstruction. With the South in ruins and the Democratic party splintered and broken, the leadership of the Republican party remained unchallenged for a decade or more. Significant change occurred in political leadership in El Paso as many of those who had served as officers and soldiers with the California Column, such as Albert H. French, James A. Zabriskie, and Albert J. Fountain, took over positions of power and influence. This new group looked to W. W. Mills, collector of customs from 1863 to 1869 and principal organizer of the local Republican party. With assistance from French and Zabriskie, Mills formed the "customhouse ring," a vehicle for giving favors to local merchants, controlling appointments to office, and manipulating elections. During the late sixties and early seventies, therefore, it was rare indeed in El Paso when a local election was not characterized by fraud, vote purchasing, ballot stuffing, bribery, intimidation, or tampering by corrupt election officials.[45]

The Mexican population in Ysleta found the new Republican leadership under Mills to be oppressive and complained to Gov. J. W. Throckmorton. "We were forcibly seized and kidnapped by one French," it began,

> and we were imprisoned and afterwards sent into the town of El Paso del Norte, Mexico, where, without being informed of the offense or the charges against us, we were

immediately thrown into jail.... We have been separated from our businesses and families, a particularly cruel treatment since we are small farmers and poor, dependent upon our daily labor for our support. No comforts or food are allowed us unless from our own homes some 12 or 15 miles distant.... We are not the first who have suffered in the same way within the last three years, and unless some remedy is found for this gross injustice and growing evil, we will not be the last victims of oppression and tyranny supported by bayonets, where none save martial law is respected and anarchy reigns supreme, although on Texas soil.[46]

A List of Registered Voters in El Paso compiled from 1867 to 1869 indicates a total of 741 in the county's four precincts. Of these, all but eighty-two were Mexican-Americans, the vast majority illiterate, who cast their votes by making a mark. Of the eighty-two, eleven had come from Europe, two were designated "colored," and the remainder were from the United States, particularly New England and the Middle West. Of the sixty-nine from the United States, only nineteen had been in the El Paso area for three years or more. On the other hand, 145 Mexican-American voters had lived in the Lower Valley for forty years or more. Quick to perceive the importance of the Mexican-American vote, the Mills group soon found ways to bring it under control. It was necessary to speak and conduct county business in Spanish, to establish alliances with key local Mexican-American leaders, and to elect a few of them to some of the lesser important offices.[47]

By 1867 the Republican Party had come under the control of the Radical wing, whose program called for an iron-clad oath to the United States Constitution for office holders, Negro suffrage, disfranchisement of the ex-Confederates, ratification of the Thirteenth, Fourteenth, and Fifteenth amendments, and military rule to insure these objectives. The labels "rebel" and "Democrat" became synonymous, as Radical Republicans took a solemn vow that neither the South nor the Democratic party should ever rise again. Bitter but powerless ex-Confederates could only label the Radicals "Carpetbaggers" and "Black Republicans."[48]

In El Paso W. W. Mills was named delegate to a constitutional convention in June 1868 in Austin where the Radical majority selected Edmund J. Davis as president. Opposition from those favoring a more moderate policy on Reconstruction was led by A.

J. Hamilton, Mills's father-in-law. He was appointed provisional governor by Pres. Andrew Johnson but was defeated by J. W. Throckmorton in the gubernatorial election of 1866. Although Mills had maintained a neutral position on Reconstruction in El Paso, he increasingly gave his support in Austin to the moderate views of his father-in-law.[49]

As a diversionary attempt to weaken Radical strength in the convention, Mills proposed the creation of the Montezuma Territory, consisting of the County of El Paso and the adjacent County of Doña Ana, on the condition that the United States grant it territorial government. Claiming that almost everyone in El Paso favored the proposal, Mills proceeded at length in the convention to give reasons why it should be supported. After a week of debate, however, the proposal was rejected, largely the result of the influence of Hamilton, who had come to the conclusion that a division of the state would strengthen the hand of Davis and the Radicals.[50]

During Mills's year in Austin, El Paso Republican party leadership fell upon Albert J. Fountain, who in contrast with Mills, gave his full support to the Radical Republican program. By early 1869 it was clear that the Mills-Fountain relationship was heading for a showdown. Moderate Republicans in their convention in Austin nominated Hamilton for governor and Mills for legislative representative from El Paso. A Radical convention in Corpus Christi then nominated Edmund J. Davis for governor and Fountain for El Paso representative. Davis's influence with the national Republican party leaders was decisive, and Mills was removed from his post as collector of customs, thus sharply curtailing his local power and influence.[51]

One hundred miles to the east of El Paso were the Guadalupe salt beds, where historically the salt had been free for the taking by the Mexican population in the Lower Valley. Word had leaked out, however, that Mills and a group had attempted to secure title for the purpose of collecting a fee for extracted salt, and that they had rejected Fountain's suggestion to abandon the enterprise. Although the title obtained by the Mills group was found defective and the salt beds remained public land, Fountain cleverly exploited the issue politically by attacking the Mills crowd for attempting to appropriate from the Mexican-Americans what he claimed was rightfully theirs. The state election began on 30 November 1869 and lasted for four days. A detachment of soldiers at San Elizario checked credentials and counted the ballots. Within a week it was evident that the Davis Radicals had swept all state offices, and that Albert Fountain had won a major political victory over the once-powerful Mills.[52]

The intensity and bitterness of the campaign left tragedy and bloodshed in its wake. In an attempt to win over the opposition and unite the El Paso Republicans under his leadership, Fountain gave important appointments to two of Mills's friends, Gaylord Clarke and A. H. French, and in so doing bypassed his own principal supporter, Benjamin F. Williams. Becoming more bitter and belligerent each day, Williams spent most of his time at Ben Dowell's saloon cursing Fountain, Clarke, and French, and threatening to even the score at the first opportunity. On the morning of 7 December 1870 Fountain and Williams met in Ben Dowell's saloon and had an angry exchange of words. Williams, who had been drinking heavily, fired and wounded Fountain, who then ran to Judge Clarke's home nearby. A hurriedly formed posse went to Williams's quarters and battered down the door. Williams came out and blasted Judge Clarke at close range with his shotgun, killing him instantly. Albert French, a member of the posse, then ran Williams down and shot him twice with his pistol; Williams died about twenty minutes later. Fountain eventually recovered from the two wounds he had received, and returned to Austin in January.[53]

By 1872 Carpetbag rule in Texas had run its course with the defeat of Gov. Edmund J. Davis by a combination of conservative Republicans and Democrats. In El Paso the Republican organization was in ruins, shattered by the Fountain-Mills feud and the gun blasts that killed Clarke and Williams. The need for a major political realignment had become all too evident to Charles Howard, a strong-willed Democrat and a shrewd politician. He wasted no time in enlisting the support of Luis Cardis, an Italian immigrant, whose polished Spanish brought him a large following from the Mexican-American population. Moreover, Cardis had a staunch ally in Father Antonio Borrajo, the parish priest of San Elizario, who threatened to excommunicate any Catholic who voted the Republican ticket.[54]

Early in 1873 Howard and Cardis confidently concluded that the political breezes were beginning to blow their way. They drew up a petition to the Texas Legislature, dated 19 February 1873, which carried more than 350 signatures, mostly those of Mexicans, and many written in the same hand. "For more than three years," it began,

> the voice of the legal voters of this country has been sup-
> pressed by fraud on the part of those whose duty it was
> under the law to see that all elections were fairly con-
> ducted—we have been misrepresented and calumniated by
> men who have thrust themselves into office against our
> wishes and consent, most of whom were strangers to us,
> and who by their oppressive, insolent, and arbitrary con-
> duct in office have forfeited all claims to our confidence
> and respect.... These frauds [of the past three years] were
> in a great measure planned and executed through the in-
> strumentality of A. J. Fountain, at present a member of
> Your Honorable Body, into which position he crept by a
> fraud and trick perpetrated by him on the people of this
> county. We have never considered him as our represen-
> tative, and we declare him a disgrace to our county and a
> blemish upon Your Honorable Body.

The petition then focused on Simon Bolivar Newcomb, district judge of El Paso County. "He was appointed by the influence of A. J. Fountain," it stated,

> and has ever since been his willing and superserviceable
> tool, and he has prostituted his office to the obtaining of
> partisan ends, and has brought odium and contempt upon
> his court.... We believe that he renders his judgments
> through favoritism and for money, and that he has leagued
> himself with our enemies and oppressors. We therefore
> most earnestly beg of Your Honorable Body that he may
> be removed from his position, and that some capable and
> honest man be placed in his stead.[55]

Howard and Cardis had appraised the political situation cor-
rectly. In 1874 Cardis was elected to the legislature. District Judge
Simon B. Newcomb was removed from office, Charles Howard
receiving the appointment to the district judgeship on the following day. Thus far, the alliance between Howard and Cardis had
served them well, but whether the existing relationship would continue in view of the ambitious and aggressive nature of each man,
soon became a matter of conjecture.[56]

In May 1873 El Paso, with a population of about 800, was incorporated as a city, and the following August the 105 qualified voters chose Ben Dowell as mayor. Six aldermen, representing three wards, were also elected. The first ordinances concerned the care and cleanliness of the *acequias* – there was to be no bathing in the ditches, no throwing of trash, or watering of dogs or livestock in them, and every man eighteen years or older must devote one day to cleaning and maintaining the ditches. Violators could be fined up to $100. Other ordinances dealt with the town's morals – it became illegal to swear in a saloon, to carry firearms, to become intoxicated, to pitch pennies, to play marbles for keeps, to steal, to conceal stolen property, to create a disturbance, or to start a riot. Violations of any of these called for the payment of a fine, but in a six-month period from August 1873 to February 1874 only three dollars was collected in fines, a commentary on the efficiency of the law enforcement system. The principal issue in the mayor's election of 1874 was whether dogs should be restrained or allowed to go free. As the result of the limited interest in city government and the unwillingness of the citizenry to pay taxes and obey the regulations, the charter was set aside for several years, to be extricated from the files with the approach of the railroads in 1880.[57]

In the meantime, in an election held 7 December 1873, by a vote of 259 to 222, the county seat was moved from San Elizario to Ysleta, even though San Elizario, with a population of 1,120, had 300 more residents than Ysleta. Then on 15 February 1876 the voters overwhelmingly approved the new state Constitution of 1876 and elected Joseph Magoffin county judge. A Commissioners Court, composed of four county commissioners, all of whom were Mexican-Americans, was also elected, and at the first meeting they took the oath of office, appointed election judges, selected polling places, and selected a committee to provide a courthouse and a jail.[58]

Dominating the political, social, and economic life of El Paso after the Civil War was a tough breed of strong-willed, individualistic, and ambitious Anglo-American males. They sought wealth and power, and while they were intent on survival, they were not afraid to die by the gun if personal honor or a principle were involved. Most of them were engaged in merchandising, freighting, mining, or the law. They brought to the frontier the mechanisms

161

of local government which they had learned east of the Mississippi, making it possible for them to manipulate elections and control local officials. They hired the new arrivals in town to work in their commercial operations, thus producing a frontier, writes Rex Strickland, in distinct contrast to Frederick Jackson Turner's twin gods of free land and democracy. They fraternized with their brothers in the local Masonic lodge, socialized in two languages with the Paseño aristocrats across the river, and married native Mexican women of the upper classes. As for the confirmed Anglo bachelors, most kept Mexican mistresses. Strickland concludes:

> There seems to be little of the Turnerian pattern in the settlement of the arid border: It was not a small farming frontier; ...it attracted wage earners rather than landless poor in search of land; it was essentially an exploitative frontier in which self-seeking and highly individualistic men sought to acquire wealth by merchandising, freighting or mining.[59]

On the other hand, the poor Mexican-Americans, who constituted the vast majority of the population and provided the manual labor for ten to thirty cents a day, were regarded with the utmost contempt. In this clash of cultures the Anglo commercial elite looked down on the Mexican-American as a mixed breed, an inferior whose principal traits were ignorance, indolence, and backwardness. By nature he was lazy, irresponsible, untrustworthy, and dirty – in a word, he was labeled "a greaser."[60]

Across the river in El Paso del Norte a powerful and influential elite dominated the political, social, and economic life of the town in much the same fashion as the Anglo commercial counterparts on the American side. Best known of the town's influentials was Ramón Ortiz, who was born in Santa Fe, New Mexico in 1813, and became *cura* of Nuestra Señora de Guadalupe in 1839, serving in that position until his death in 1896. Literate, erudite, wealthy, and aristocratic, Cura Ortiz was El Paso del Norte's Renaissance man, long remembered for his acts of kindness to the Texans captured in the Santa Fe Expedition, his opposition to the American invasion of 1846 and the Treaty of Guadalupe Hidalgo, and his colonizing efforts in the early 1850s while serving as commissioner of colonias. His home in El Paso del Norte was the center of the town's social life, and it was here that he reared the children of his niece, Josefa Delgado de Samaniego, in particular the eminent Dr. Mariano Samaniego.[61]

The family of Florentino Samaniego lived in Bavispe, Sonora, until 1838 when he was killed in an Apache raid while serving as presidio commander. The widow, Josefa Delgado, Cura Ortiz's niece, then brought her five children to El Paso del Norte, where they were reared and educated in the padre's home. Born in 1831, Mariano, the youngest of the five, was educated in the seminary at Durango and at the University of Paris, where he received a degree in medicine. Among his teachers was Louis Pasteur. Returning to Mexico, he served as surgeon with the republican forces of Luis Terrazas. By 1870 his reputation was well established on both sides of the river not only for his medical practice, but also for his financial interests and political influence, serving in a number of the offices at the local, state, and national levels, and accumulating one of the largest fortunes in the El Paso area. One of his sisters married Alexandre Daguerre, of French extraction, who made a fortune in the freighting business; another sister married Ynocente Ochoa, who also became one of the area's wealthiest individuals.[62]

Born in Aldama, Chihuahua, in 1832, Ochoa came to El Paso del Norte after the Mexican War, started a freight business, and worked his way to a fortune that involved cattle ranches and mercantile activities. With Mariano Samaniego and Luis Terrazas, Ochoa founded the Banco Minero of Chihuahua and soon became the richest man in town. His political influence soon took on added significance as Terrazas expanded his economic and political empire in Chihuahua, gaining control of the state. Ochoa's Paso del Norte residence on what is now 16th of September Street was the showplace of the entire area. There parties for the best families in the two towns were staged, and there Porfirio Díaz made his headquarters when he visited the border in 1909. In all probability, relations between the social set of the two border communities have never been so close and cordial as they were in the 1870s.[63]

The two elites, who so completely dominated the political, social, and economic life of the area, comprised less than 5 percent of the total population of some 3,700 on the American side and about 10,000 on the Mexican side. The remaining 95 percent or more were the *pobres*, who, like their ancestors over the centuries, lived in the patchwork of tiny fields and squat houses of straw and river clay, always with the fervent hope that they could eke out an existence from the land. They remained chained to a routine closely circumscribed by the valley, the river, and the cycle of the seasons. Their interests naturally were insular, confined largely to the concerns of home and family and the cultivation of the field lest they become victims of the rugged, uncertain, and precarious north Mexican frontier. In short, writes historian Frank Halla, these two kinds of Paseño were often at odds. The bulk of the valley people were forced to weigh duty and devotion on the one hand against possible starvation and destitution on the other. Caught in the middle of the two alternatives, they usually chose a third course, which was to straddle the fence between them.[64]

Although the commercial and freighting operations of the Americans together with the banking and ranching enterprises of the Mexicans were important in the region's economy, agriculture remained the dominant activity. It supported, as it had for centuries, the vast majority of the Mexican population on both sides of the river. The American consul in El Paso del Norte, William M. Pierson, found the productivity of the area and its potential impressive. The country was beautiful but isolated, he wrote, the climate was salubrious but arid, and the soil was sandy intermixed with a black loam. On the American side of the valley about fifteen square miles were under cultivation, mostly farmed by Mexicans, while on the Mexican side there was a solid mass under cultivation stretching down the river for sixteen miles and varying in width from six to ten miles. This, he added, represented only one fiftieth of the potential. Limited rainfall made extensive irrigation necessary, and while timber was insufficient for fencing, adobe walls for centuries had proved satisfactory. The quality of the cereals produced, especially wheat, was excellent, as well as the vegetables, particularly the onion, which often reached three to four pounds in weight. Fruits such as the grape far surpassed in flavor those in the United States, and the wine had been given first rank in North America by competent judges. The wine yield of a healthy vineyard, said Pierson, was 250 gallons to the acre, and sold for one dollar a gallon. Thus, in view of the area's unlimited potential, it is not surprising that on one occasion the consul recommended that the United States annex Chihuahua and Sonora.[65]

In 1877 the peace and tranquility of the Rio Grande valley came to an abrupt halt with the outbreak of the bloodiest civil disorder in the county's history. Known as the Salt War, it contained all the ingredients of a vicious and violent border dispute, which set Anglo-American against Mexican-American, strong man against strong man, faction against faction, and the United States against Mexico. Bad blood, personal rivalries, and racial hostilities characterized this ugly affair, resulting in mob violence, rape, looting, and murder, most of which took place in and around San Elizario, the former county seat and still at that time the largest settlement in the county.[66]

The Salt War began as a personal struggle between former allies, Judge Charles Howard and Luis Cardis, the Italian immigrant who had won a seat in the Texas Legislature. When Howard announced that the hundreds of acres of salt beds east of El Paso were now his private property and that a fee would be charged for salt, Cardis saw an opportunity to champion Mexican interests and increase his own political following. Raising his voice in protest to Howard's action, Cardis found support in the Mexican population of San Elizario and a valuable ally in the Reverend Antonio Borrajo, the parish priest. Several fist fights occurred between the two antagonists before Howard, armed with a shotgun, found Cardis in Solomon Schutz's store on San Francisco street in El Paso on 10 October 1877 and killed him with a blast into his chest.[67]

News of the killing spread like wildfire. Howard was captured in San Elizario by a mob made up of Mexicans from both sides of the river. There a firing squad cut him down. Two of Howard's bondsmen were killed; their personal effects were taken to Mexico. The homes of Howard's supporters were pillaged. An untrained group of Texas Rangers was forced to surrender after two of their number were killed. With Fort Bliss closed for lack of funds all law and order broke down. On both sides of the border there was talk of war between the United States and Mexico. Before a semblance of order was finally restored, a posse of thirty volunteers from Silver City, New Mexico, ravaged the Lower Valley towns, killing people and destroying property. A congressional investigation early in 1878 collected evidence, but no one was arrested, tried, or convicted. Fort Bliss was reestablished in El Paso, where it has remained ever since, and the Mexican families of the Lower Valley were allowed once again to haul salt free of charge under the watchful eye of a Texas Ranger. The railroad which came to El Paso three years later bypassed San Elizario. It is now a quiet, peaceful, picturesque farm community in marked contrast with the bloody days of yesteryear.[68]

For a decade prior to the Civil War, the residents of El Paso had eagerly awaited the arrival of a transcontinental railroad, convinced that the route through the Pass of the North at the thirty-second parallel offered so many advantages that its selection seemed almost a foregone conclusion. Its most vigorous champion was Jefferson Davis, who became secretary of war in 1853, but as Goetzmann points out, his inflexible advocacy of the southern route at a time when sectional interests had become paramount in the thinking of the nation's leaders, was doomed to failure. Not until 1869 was the first transcontinental completed. The utilization of the central route rather than the southern was the direct result of Southern secession.[69]

Even so, the construction of a transcontinental railroad through the Pass of the North did not lie too far in the future. By the late 1870s a race had developed between the Southern Pacific, which was building eastward from southern California, and the Texas and Pacific, controlled by the powerful Jay Gould. The Southern Pacific, with the help of 1,600 Chinese laborers, reached Tucson in March 1880, Lordsburg in October, and Deming in December. By that time Gould's Texas and Pacific, building west from Fort Worth, was only 130 miles from El Paso. The Southern Pacific reached El Paso first, on 19 May 1881, an event generally considered to be the most significant in the city's history. It continued to lay track east of El Paso, but faced the possibility of meeting the Texas and Pacific before it could join with the Southern Pacific-controlled Galveston, Harrisburg, and San Antonio building westward. Gould, however, realizing that he had lost the transcontinental race, agreed to halt construction of his line at Sierra Blanca, providing that his trains could use Southern Pacific tracks westward to El Paso. On 16 December 1881 the rails of the two rival lines were joined.[70]

Undoubtedly the primary local champion of a railroad through El Paso was James P. Hague, who was appointed district attorney in 1871. He had been so unnerved by the trip to El Paso on the stagecoach that he arrived imbued with the angry conviction that there was a need for a better way to travel. Having acquired a considerable amount of property as payment for his legal services, Hague deeded a sizeable strip of land through the middle of the town to the Southern Pacific for its tracks, depot, roundhouse, and freight yards. During the 1870s Hague's reputation as a brilliant attorney was well established, and he was named district judge before he was thirty years old. His home, which occupied a square block on Santa Fe and San Francisco streets, contained his law office and furnishings, among them the first piano in El Paso.[71]

The coming of the railroad had a profound and revolutionary effect on the little town. Before its arrival El Paso was a sleepy, dusty village of about 800 souls, but as soon as it became known that the Southern Pacific was approaching, a floating element arrived on the scene during the winter of 1880-1881 that doubled the size of the town. As lawman James B. Gillett described it:

> Bankers, merchants, capitalists, real estate dealers, cattlemen, miners, railroad men, gamblers, saloon-keepers, and sporting people of both sexes flocked to town. They came in buggies, hacks, wagons, horseback, and even afoot. There was not half enough hotel accommodations to go around, so people just slept and ate at any old place.... A saloon was opened on almost every corner of the town with many in between, but if one wished a seat at the gaming tables he had to come early or he could not get within thirty feet of them.

Lots jumped from $100 an acre to $200 per front foot, reported the *Lone Star*, and room rents rose to unheard-of prices. Tents were pitched along both sides of the streets and hundreds slept in the saloons.[72]

The great day came on 26 May 1881. The El Paso *Herald* of 1 June 1881 covered the ceremonies and the drama of that historic occasion, with its abundance of color, noise, oratory, and spirits. The train arrived an hour early; there was some delay before the Fort Bliss cannons began to roar. The town was resplendent with banners, bunting, and flags in red, white, and green as well as red, white, and blue. A welcoming committee of local dignitaries boarded the train to join the Southern Pacific officials and took a short ride to a pavilion erected for the occasion. Many for the first time, with some degree of apprehension, heard the whistle and saw the black smoke coming from the locomotive's stack.[73]

Judge Allan Blacker, who made the first speech, in commenting on the significance of the event, told the Southern Pacific officials that they had brought the "iron bands that bring us together in the pleasantest place in which God in his providence has cast our lots. Here cities will spring up on both sides of the river, and together with the railroads they will, to a considerable extent, handle the commerce of the world." He added that the governor of Texas had told him on one occasion that El Paso was the best and last place in the United States to make a fortune in a single lifetime. Blacker was followed by Don Espiridón Provencio, representing El Paso del Norte, who also offered his appreciation for the memorable welcome.[74]

After these speeches, the party adjourned to a tent where wine was served, then proceeded to Schutz's Hall. Judge J. P. Hague gave the major address of the day. "The Lone Star," he declared, "shall now enter the portals of the Golden Gate. California and Texas have struck hands and today they stand united. The coming of the railroads has today spread out a prospect before us, beautiful as a landscape." In the evening a formal banquet was held, followed by dancing until midnight. Music was furnished by a band from El Paso del Norte; refreshments included seventeen gallons of wine, a dozen bottles of champagne, four hundred glasses of lemonade, and three and a half gallons of other bottled refreshments.[75]

Everyone sensed that the arrival of the railroad had ushered in a new era of history. Merchants, bankers, and businessmen could point with pride to the area's economic potential, the varied business opportunities, the rich soil of the valleys, and the future of the mining and transportation industries. A population of 25,000 by 1900 was confidently predicted. El Paso, it was argued, would be the most important city between Kansas City and the Pacific Coast, with the possible exception of Denver. Not only had the railroads wrought a transportation revolution; they had assured El Paso's destiny as a continental crossroads in the future.[76]

CHAPTER SEVEN

Frontier Town to Western Community, 1881-1917

D U R I N G the four decades following the coming of the railroads to El Paso, a frontier town of fewer than 1,000 people was transformed into a modern western city with a total population of 80,000. A combination of factors made this remarkable development possible. El Paso's geographical location as a gateway to Mexico and as the lowest of the various east-west routes through the Rockies assured the area's future as a transportation center of importance. Added to this was proximity to the mining areas of northern Mexico, New Mexico, and Arizona. Then there were factors such as the mild year-round climate, unlimited natural resources, an enterprising livestock industry, and an abundance of cheap labor. Plans announced in 1906 for the construction of Elephant Butte dam, which promised to make

El Paso Street, upper left, and the Merrick Building, upper
right, were in the heart of El Paso's business district in the
1880s. The downtown skyline is dominated by the county
courthouse, near the center, in a bird's-eye view from Mesa
Garden. (Souvenir of El Paso, Texas and Paso del Norte,
Mexico, Ward Bros., Columbus, Ohio, 1887)

El Paso's valleys green, convinced businessmen, investors, farmers,
and ranchers that the area had a future.[1]

At the time of the arrival of the Southern Pacific in May 1881,
the town of El Paso consisted of eight land divisions. Some were
owned by local proprietors; others had been purchased by eastern
capitalists. The first was the original Anson Mills survey, the future
central business district, largely owned by a group of pioneer proprietors. Surrounding this was the Campbell Addition, the property
of a wealthy St. Louis fur trader. To the east was the Magoffin
Addition, where Joseph Magoffin built the historic Magoffin
Homestead in 1875, followed by residences built by El Paso's elite
in the 1880s. East of the Magoffin Addition was the property of

MERRICK BUILDING.

the Boston capitalist Frank B. Cotton. To two newly arrived mid-
western businessmen, C. R. Morehead and O. T. Bassett, Magoffin
sold properties, one north of the Magoffin Addition and the other
east of the Cotton Addition. Northwest of the downtown business
district was the property of J. Fisher Satterthwaite, a New York
capitalist. This became the nucleus of the historic residential area
known as Sunset Heights. Finally there was the Mundy Addition
to the northwest of Satterthwaite's property, owned by Simeon
Hart's heirs. Thus, most of the downtown area and the properties
of the Magoffin and Hart families were owned by local pioneers.
Two other tracts were acquired by recent arrivals, and the remaining four were in the hands of easterners.[2]

The central business district was bounded on the south by
First and Second streets, on the west by Durango, on the north by
Missouri, and on the east by Campbell and Kansas. Because the
valuable properties in this area were owned by local pioneers who
were more interested in the town's progress than in large profits for
themselves, these sites underwent rapid development, particularly

along both sides of El Paso Street south of San Francisco Street and along San Antonio east of El Paso Street. Overnight the corner of El Paso and San Antonio streets became the center of town, and there the State National Bank, El Paso's first financial institution, was built. Then came the First National Bank, a post office, and three newspapers, together with offices, stores, and shops lining El Paso, San Antonio, St. Louis (now Mills), and San Francisco streets. Gradually, frame and brick structures, some of them two stories high, replaced the old one-story adobes.[3]

Typical of the frontier boom towns of the Old West, El Paso was a "Sin City," with its saloons, dance halls, and gambling halls. Nearly every corner was occupied by a saloon, and in between were at least three other drinking establishments. Each saloon had its own gambling hall, offering roulette, faro, sweat, craps, and keno. Then there was the tenderloin on Utah Street (now South Mesa) where the madams and ladies of easy virtue, some living in palatial mansions, sold their charms. The Chinese who came with the railroads built restaurants and laundries in each block that intermingled with American shops and stores in an area extending from St. Louis Street (now Mills) to Fourth Street and from Stanton west to El Paso Street. While the Chinese did much to keep the town's population well fed and clean, most residents found their opium traffic to be offensive.[4]

The problems faced by Mayor Joseph Magoffin and his council, elected in August 1881, were overwhelming—law enforcement, health and sanitation, public transportation, flood control and drainage, utilities, and the like. Not to be ignored by any means was the self-appointed watchdog over community affairs, local newspaper editor S. H. Newman, founder of the Lone Star. Although genuinely concerned about the progress and welfare of the town, Newman nevertheless was relentless in his outspoken criticism and biting attacks on local government and the town's leadership. While vice and crime—prostitution, the opium dens, gambling, drunkenness, or gun toting—were his main targets, little escaped his watchful eye and his verbal blows. Yet all in all Newman was a positive good for the town, and contributed immeasurably to its growth and development.[5]

The Magoffin administration made substantial progress, particularly in the areas of public transportation, water system, fire protection, and utilities in supplying services to the town's population. A streetcar service was provided, consisting of two mule-drawn lines. One went down San Antonio Street, looped around the car barns, and returned on Magoffin. The second connected El Paso with its sister city across the river, running down El Paso Street to Seventh, along Seventh to Stanton, then across a flimsy wooden bridge constructed for that purpose. A franchise for a water system was granted to Sylvester Watts of St. Louis. Its completion, however, was soon followed by a number of complaints of its muddy and unsanitary condition, leaky pipes, and high rates charged for the service. Naturally, the *Lone Star* joined in the attack. Pressure from the *Lone Star* on the need for fire protection brought positive results – the organization of a volunteer fire department consisting of two hose companies and a hook and ladder company. Telephone service was introduced in 1883, followed shortly by franchises for a gas works and an electric plant.[6]

Until 1881 El Paso was without a church building of any kind. Those of the Catholic faith either crossed the river and worshiped in El Paso del Norte or attended one of the missions in the Lower Valley. The few Protestants held services in private homes. Although a Methodist preacher named Harper had spent a year in El Paso in 1859, and the Reverend Joseph W. Tays, an Episcopalian minister, had arrived in 1870 and organized a congregation, no church buildings had been constructed prior to the coming of the railroads. By 1882 the Methodists, Episcopalians, Presbyterians, and Baptists had organized their congregations. They shared a "preachin'" tent that year to conduct services pending the completion of their church buildings. The Catholics completed their church, St. Mary's Chapel, in 1883. Each congregation ranged in numbers from 150 to 300, and injected a strong moral and stabilizing influence into the community. They challenged the views of the business interests that the town's "Sin City" reputation was one of its principal assets.[7]

By the end of 1882 El Paso had a street railway, two banks, three newspapers, four churches, an established city government, and the largest hotel in the state, the Grand Central. A school board, elected in December 1882, opened the first public school in March 1883, purchased a site at the corner of Myrtle and Campbell streets, and found temporary quarters until Central School was

The first public school in El Paso was a small adobe building opened in 1884. Mrs. Ada Brennand executed this painting of it in the 1950s and presented it to the El Paso Independent School District. (Courtesy El Paso ISD)

completed in September 1884, at a cost of $17,500. By that time a school for blacks had been established, the forerunner of Douglass, and in 1887 a dedicated and remarkable man named Olivas V. Aoy had organized a school for the Mexican-American children. He taught, fed, and clothed them without any thought of compensation. At length the school board paid him seventy-five dollars a month to teach the Mexican children English so they could enter the public schools. He died in 1895, loved and respected by all the community, and five hundred people attended his funeral.[8]

In 1878, after the Salt War, the county seat had been moved from San Elizario to Ysleta, which had a population of about 1,400. There local politics for years had been under the firm control of the Alderete family, father Martín and son Benigno. Texas Ranger headquarters were established in Ysleta in 1879 under the command of Capt. G. W. Baylor to keep the peace and protect the residents from Apache raids. With the coming of the railroads, however, El Paso's population began to approach that of Ysleta. This resulted in a movement by El Paso's business leaders to move the county seat from Ysleta to El Paso. The citizens of Ysleta, confident that they had a better chance in 1883 of keeping the county seat than by waiting until later, petitioned for an election. They did not, however, take seriously enough the political techniques that El Paso civic leaders had learned over the years. In accordance with the familiar pattern of elections held on the border, a battalion of Mexicans was imported to vote in favor of El Paso, receiving, of course, some kind of compensation for services rendered. Moreover, a number of El Pasoans voted several times. One in particular, according to Owen P. White, cast twelve votes during the day. He first voted in each of the three precincts just as he was, then with whiskers trimmed, then with just a moustache, and finally, as a smooth-shaven individual wearing a new suit of clothes. Although the total registered voting strength of El Paso was known to be about 300, as many as 2,000 votes were cast by midafternoon. Ysleta's protest proved futile, and the county seat was moved to El Paso in early 1884. Plans for a new county courthouse and jail were soon under way.[9]

The transfer of the county seat was a significant event in the area's history. During the 1860s and 1870s the Mexican-American population of some 3,000 in the Lower Valley was able to exercise a controlling influence over county politics; a number of them held major positions in county government. But by 1883 their political power had come to an end, and El Paso's Anglo business and professional establishment now had the control. Because the Anglo establishment understood the importance of the Mexican-American vote, a reciprocal relationship was developed, assigning minor city and county positions to certain safe, cooperative, and dependable Mexican-American leaders. They would be expected to organize and deliver the vote in return for a certain degree of ethnic protection in order to insure their continued loyalty. A significant statistic dramatizes this transfer of political power: while five Mexican-Americans held the office of county judge prior to 1883, none have held the position since that time.[10]

In July 1884 the *Lone Star*, in a more positive mood than usual, devoted an entire issue to local progress. Five major trunk lines provided direct communication with San Francisco, Kansas City, New Orleans, Galveston, and Mexico City. The town was assured a future as an important transportation center. The

175

population was approaching 5,000, and for the first time, would soon pass that of the sister community across the river. Banks and businesses had been established; municipal services and cultural facilities had been provided. Considering the town's favorable geographic position, mild climate, economic potential, and tourist attractions, the *Lone Star* predicted a bullish future. Significantly, the following year El Paso's first city directory appeared, and in 1886 the El Paso Bureau of Information published an eighty-four-page pamphlet appropriately entitled *The City and County of El Paso, Texas, the Future Great Metropolis of the Southwest.*[11]

That El Paso should become an important mining center was dictated by its ample transportation facilities and by its strategic location near the mining operations of Arizona, New Mexico, Texas, and Chihuahua. In 1887 a custom smelter was built by Robert Stafford Towne three miles west of the downtown area. Later it became ASARCO, the most important custom smelter in the Southwest. One year later, Charles Longuemare of Socorro, New Mexico, moved his publication, *The Bullion*, to El Paso. He became the town's greatest promoter of the mining industry, insisting that it had contributed more to the progress of the Pass than everything else combined. Two of his favorite projects were periodic miners' conventions and the establishment of a school for the training of miners.[12]

During the 1880s cultural development accompanied economic growth, and interest in a theatre developed soon after the coming of the railroads. The arrival of the Nellie Boyd Dramatic Company late in 1881 led to the construction of Hills' Hall, barely completed in time for the first performance. Then came the Coliseum in 1882, more of a honky-tonk dance hall than a theatre. Samuel Schutz, a German immigrant who had become mayor in 1880, opened what he called "an opera house," the word "theatre" having fallen into disrepute. The Schutz Opera House staged performances from 1883 to 1885, then was turned into a ballroom and dancing academy. The Pictorial and Gem Theatres were essentially variety houses, while the National Theatre managed to have a couple of successful seasons during 1886-1887 before it closed its doors. By that time the site of the National on El Paso Street had been purchased by Henry W. Myar, a German immigrant who made a fortune in cotton in Camden, Arkansas. He erected a

Myar's Opera House was a cultural center from its opening in 1887 until it burned in 1905. (Souvenir of El Paso, Texas and Paso del Norte, Mexico, Ward Bros., Columbus, Ohio, 1887).

structure which became the pride of El Paso theatre-goers for almost two decades – the Myar Opera House.[13]

Built in the Renaissance style and designed to accommodate 1,200 people, Myar's theatre featured six boxes curtained with tapestries, a polished brass chandelier, blue dome with white metallic stars, ornamental iron work, and panel paintings and frescoes. Total cost of the structure was $80,000. On opening night, 15 December 1887, Dumas's *Monte Cristo* played before a capacity audience. The editor of the *Times* commented favorably on El Paso's beautiful cultural facility and the quality of the production, adding:

> At last we have a first class opera house.... In the most unbounded terms we must publicly endorse the action of the managers of our new opera house in excluding public prostitutes from the choice parts of the theatre and limiting their attendance only to the balcony.... This is customary throughout the country and there is no reason to make an exception in El Paso.[14]

After El Paso won a hotly disputed election to become county seat in 1883, this courthouse was built on the site of the present City-County Building which replaced it in 1913. (Souvenir of El Paso, Texas and Paso del Norte, Mexico, *Ward Bros., Columbus, Ohio, 1887)*

Other impressive features completed by the time the opera house opened its doors were the county courthouse, a smelter with four furnaces, and the El Paso National Bank. Plans for a custom-house and post office were under way, and the Sheldon Hotel, featuring hot and cold running water throughout, was under construction. The town caught the eye of the Ward Brothers of Columbus, Ohio, described as "dealers in View Albums of All American Cities." Their attractive booklet on El Paso with its delightful etchings of street scenes, buildings, and residences, is entitled *Souvenir of El Paso, Texas and Paso del Norte, Mexico.*[15]

Reflecting the pride of the community in its growth and development in the 1880s and its confidence in the future was the McGinty Club, a musical, merry-making group that included several hundred leading citizens. Long on conviviality and short on sobriety, the group took its name from a popular song of that day,

"Down Went McGinty," and featured a marching band, parades, picnics, fireworks, speeches, and promotions of every description. Its headquarters was a pavilion known as Mesa Garden, located on the highest hill in the Satterthwaite Addition. Its activities, writes Conrey Bryson, the historian of the group, covered everything imaginable — parades, concerts, performances at the Myar Opera House, the acquisition of a Civil War cannon, a Cardiff Giant display (which was a fake), a rain-making experiment, and the promotion of such sports events as local baseball, a heavyweight championship fight, and bicycle racing. But the most important McGinty event of the year was the St. Patrick's Day parade. The celebration featured the brass band in green hats and coats, a procession of dignitaries, refreshments at the White House Saloon, and a banquet in the evening based on a recipe of one part food and five parts drink.[16]

Fort Bliss, first located at Magoffinsville, following the flood of 1868 was moved to Concordia, a site that proved to be no more healthful than the previous one. In 1877 the post was abolished, but after the tragic Salt War, it was relocated in present downtown El Paso. Known as "Garrison Town," it was to serve only as a temporary arrangement until a permanent and more suitable site could be found. In April 1879 John F. Finerty, correspondent for the *Chicago Times*, returning from four months' travel in Mexico, referred to the post by its traditional name, and wrote that "Fort Bliss seemed to be the very antithesis of its name. I met with several Army officers who looked worn and melancholy." He added:

> There was not the slightest suggestion of the "loved soldier boy" in their manners or their movements. They yawned and complained of the station, damned the eternal heat and flies, cursed the bad water and inveighed against the sandstorms. They longed for action and would much prefer the roughest kind of frontier service to the torrid tranquility of Fort Bliss.[17]

The new site chosen for the post was on the Rio Grande near Simeon Hart's residence (today La Hacienda Cafe). Two tracts of about sixty acres each were purchased from his son, Juan Hart. At this site, occupied late in 1880, conditions generally seemed to be no better than at the previous one, an officer describing the place as dismal, dirty, hot, crowded, and full of rattlesnakes. The place would only accommodate four companies. The crowning blow came

FORT BLISS TWO MILES FROM EL PASO.

OFFICERS QUARTERS.

Construction started in late 1890 on a new
Fort Bliss on La Noria Mesa east of the city.
Officers' quarters and dress parade are pictured in
an 1887 souvenir booklet published in Ohio.

when the Santa Fe railroad laid its track through the middle of
the parade ground. Obviously, another site had to be found.[18]
    Largely because of the influence of such community leaders as
Joseph Magoffin, Anson Mills, and J. F. Crosby, and efforts of W.
T. Lanham, El Paso's representative in Congress, legislation was
passed in 1890 authorizing construction of a new and expanded
Fort Bliss. It was to occupy no fewer than 1,000 acres at La Noria
Mesa, northeast of Concordia, at a cost not to exceed $150,000.
Capt. George Ruhlen was assigned the responsibility for construction. An extremely effective leader, Ruhlen completed the negotiations for securing the land, contracted the work for the post's construction, and supervised all the details until its completion in 1893.
The largest post on the border, Fort Bliss remained primarily an infantry garrison until the Mexican Revolution. El Paso's well known
reputation as the "mother-in-law of the army" began at this time

with the development of social relationships resulting in marriage between young officers and daughters of prominent El Paso families. The most celebrated social event of the 1890s was the marriage in 1896 of Lt. William Jefferson Glasgow and Josephine Richardson Magoffin, granddaughter of pioneer James Magoffin.[19]

The Tigua Pueblo of Ysleta del Sur was about two hundred years old when Lt. John G. Bourke, who had cultivated an interest in Indian pueblos, visited it in November 1881. The Tiguas, he reported, had essentially become Mexicanized, judging from their one-story adobe houses without ladders, their dress and manner, and use of the Spanish language. There had been considerable intermarriage, Bourke said, the infusion of foreign blood betrayed by the lighter complexions, softer features, and ruddier cheeks. On the other hand, when Bourke entered one of the houses, he wrote that he saw a shield, bows and arrows, guns, a bundle of eagle feathers, and a pair of wooden spurs. One Tigua told Bourke that there were still thirty-six heads of families, and that the pueblo had always furnished scouts and guided the soldiers in the campaigns against the Apaches. The acting governor of the pueblo, Juan Severiano González, gave as his principal complaint the crowding of Americans and Mexicans into their valley and taking the Indians' land without recompense. In spite of the trend toward Mexicanization in the 1890s, Tigua determination to preserve language, customs, and traditions remained strong. This resulted in the adoption in 1895 of a constitution and by-laws to insure the survival of the ancient tribal organization.[20]

The most imposing structure in Ysleta is the church with its silver dome, a symbolic reminder of the area's religious tradition that dates from the seventeenth century. Built in 1851, the church remained under secular authority until 1881. Then the Jesuits took control and renamed the church Misión de Nuestra Señora del Monte Carmelo, or Our Lady of Mount Carmel, the name by which it is known today. But to the Tiguas it remains the Church of Saint Anthony, named for their patron saint. In 1907 a disastrous fire destroyed the tower and roof, but within little more than a year the dedicated parishioners completely restored the church, which remains one of El Paso's most cherished historic treasures.[21]

The general appearance of the town across the river, El Paso del Norte, was in marked contrast to the impressive structures

From 1881 until 1973, trolley cars transported passengers across international bridges linking El Paso and Ciudad Juarez. (Souvenir of El Paso, Texas and Paso del Norte, Mexico, Ward Bros., Columbus, Ohio, 1887)

being built on the Texas side. According to Frederick Ober, who visited the area in the early 1880s, El Paso del Norte was "an unpretentious mud village, which was content to remain so, if those restless Americanos from over the border will only allow it to. But they will not, and the Yankee 'City of the Pass,' like Laredo, is pushing its apathetic Mexican sister into prominence." He continued:

> About the only buildings not of adobe are those compos-
> ing the offices of the Mexican Central, while the other
> conspicuous and native structures are the old church and
> the mud fort. Both are ancient, but the church is of great
> age.... Amongst a heap of old church registers thrown
> carelessly into a corner of the chapel, I saw one of the year
> 1682. The sexton who displays them is a curiosity of the
> border, and will for a small fee eagerly conduct visitors
> through the little church.

Obviously fascinated with "this lonely church on the Mexican border," Ober wrote as follows:

> It was far more interesting to me than that of the great
> cathedral in Mexico City, since its ornaments and para-
> phernalia are reduced to the simplest requirements for con-
> fessional and pulpit service, and the requisite decoration of
> the Virgin and altar piece. Add in imagination a group of
> kneeling figures before each altar rail, and you had all the
> characteristic features of a church interior throughout
> Mexico. Farther into the republic, the houses of worship
> are more lavishly adorned, but here, doubtless, the clergy

feared to make the usual display of gilded carving and
paste ornaments, lest the cupidity of the border ruffian
should excite him to lay sacrilegious hands thereon. A
grateful coolness, even in hottest weather, always pervades
the churches, owing to the thickness of their walls,
whether of stone or adobe. Great beams, ornately carved
in lilies and roses, support the tiled roof of this particular
structure, which is not so high as some sanctuaries I have
seen in Indian pueblos.[22]

On one occasion a newspaper correspondent visiting the El
Paso area discovered a direct connection between the Guadalupe
church and one of the best known of the southwestern legends –
the Lost Padre Mine. "Those visitors who are permitted to ascend
a stairway of logs leading to the church's tower," wrote Walter B.
Stevens of the St. Louis Globe-Democrat,

will see in the distance the Franklin Mountains, and there
is the lost mine. According to the tradition one must stand
in a certain position and look through a certain window in
the tower and in a line with certain landmarks. If the conditions are fully complied with, the vision will rest on the
exact location of the lost mine. But where is the place to
stand, which is the window, and what are the landmarks?
The padre shakes his head. He would like to know himself![23]

On 16 September 1888 the name of El Paso del Norte was
changed to Ciudad Juárez at the suggestion of Lauro Carrillo,
governor of Chihuahua, and its status was elevated from "villa" to
"ciudad." "It was a fitting tribute to one of Mexico's heroes," notes
a writer of the period, "and the governor's constituents, in their
desire to honor the memory of Benito Juárez, did not deem it a
small undertaking to change a name of three hundred years' standing." It was a great day for the border town, which featured Rafael
Calderón de la Barca, Mexico's greatest banderillero, and a new
$10,000 monte game, as well as roulette, faro, and chuck-a-luck.
More importantly, the confusion over the two El Pasos which had
existed for thirty years or more had at long last been eliminated.[24]

In 1893 an observant New Yorker named Rudolf Eickemeyer
visited El Paso and wrote that he was impressed with the attractive
central plaza with its fountain, basin with two alligators, government buildings, businesses, banks, newspapers, churches, and
schools. El Paso was part Mexican and part American, wrote

Eickemeyer, and Second Street was the dividing line. To the south were hundreds of adobe houses one story high with one or two rooms where the Mexicans, Negroes, and Chinese lived, and where Spanish was the dominant language. To the north was the English-speaking, Anglo-American population who lived in structures of brick and stone in fashionable residential areas such as the Magoffin and Morehead Additions to the east of the downtown business district and the Satterthwaite Addition to the northwest. Eickemeyer was highly impressed with the two distinct cultures existing side by side, and the considerable social and economic disparity between the two groups.[25]

On several occasions Eickemeyer visited Juárez during his stay in El Paso, and wrote that he was favorably impressed with the Guadalupe mission and its carved ceiling beams, as well as the main plaza with its bust of Benito Juárez and the Plaza de Toros. The cockfight he attended was, in his opinion, a disgusting and brutal affair, but he conceded that the half-dollar bet he lost may have affected his judgment. On another occasion Eickemeyer crossed to Juárez by way of a "two-legged ferryboat," on the back of a broad-shouldered Mexican who carried him across the shallow river for a little more than a penny. Expressing his delight with the gardens and vineyards on the Mexican side, Eickemeyer wrote:

> The whole country around Juárez shows that it has been under cultivation for many years, yet the soil is as fruitful as ever. The waters of the Rio Grande, like the waters of the Nile in old Egypt, carry the top soil of the mountains in which they had their source, and deposit it year after year upon the land, keeping it up to its full bearing power.
> The grapevines and gardens are generally surrounded by adobe walls connecting with the adobe houses of the inhabitants, and it is a singular sight to see a landscape where all there is has but one color. Everything is the color of the soil.[26]

On a third trip to Juárez he went over "as dry-shod as the Jews did when Moses led them across the Red Sea, and it did not cost a cent." It was an Easter Sunday, and the people were in a festive mood. Hiring a buggy, Eickemeyer toured the presidio, the plaza, two churches, and the countryside. "Some time ago," he wrote, "I looked through some books illustrating the Egypt of the present day, and the villages of the peasantry, with their flat-roofed dwellings, were just like those of the Mexican peasantry."[27]

Returning to El Paso, he told of a visit to a Negro school, a ranch — "Water is the last thing these cowboys seem to hanker after" — a jury trial, burros, the wind — "I think I have a good conception of what a simoon in the Sahara may be like" — an election — "out of sixteen hundred voters, about five hundred were Mexicans, and of course they were all bought by the 'straights'" — and a trip his son Carl made to Hueco Tanks. "On leaving El Paso," Eickemeyer wrote on 19 April, "I can conscientiously recommend it to any one who, like myself wants rest and sunshine in the winter, a dry atmosphere, and pure, clean air. Should I ever want to emigrate again and bask in the sunshine of health-giving climate, I will make a beeline for the Pass of the North, knowing that I shall not be disappointed."[28]

During the 1880s and 1890s, with the development of El Paso as an important transportation, mining, trade, and cattle center, population increased to more than 8,000 in 1890 and almost 16,000 in 1900. While most of the newcomers in the 1880s were Anglo-Americans, a wave of Mexican immigration to El Paso beginning in the 1890s gave the Mexican-Americans a majority of the city's population by the turn of the century. Mexicans migrated to the United States, says Mario García in his excellent study, *Desert Immigrants*, because of opportunities for employment coupled with serious dislocations in their own country. With the integration of the El Paso Southwest into the American system of industrial capitalism in the late nineteenth century, El Paso, aided by its geographic and border location, became a significant railroad, smelting, ranching, and commercial center, as well as the main arrival terminal for Mexican immigrants. These four economic sectors, by stimulating various additional enterprises such as the wholesale and retail trade, manufacturing, tourism, and construction, brought boom times to the El Paso Southwest. This would not have been possible without the availability of Mexican labor. The Anglos provided the initiative and the capital, but the Mexican immigrants supplied the muscle.[29]

A basic policy of the Porfirio Díaz regime favored the *hacendados*, or large landowners, at the expense of the *campesinos*, or farm workers. This resulted in the seizure of *ejidos* throughout

185

central and northern Mexico and the creation of a large class of landless rural workers without any means of support. They looked to the booming economic conditions north of the border for work with the railroads, smelters, or ranches — jobs that would pay up to a dollar a day. They planned to remain in the United States only long enough to save a little money so they could return to their native Mexico and buy some land. The abolition of the duty-free Zona Libre (Free Zone) in 1905 resulted in economic depression in Ciudad Juárez. These adverse economic factors, plus climatic conditions throughout the north central Mexican states, produced a tide of immigration to the United States of some 2,000 per month. By 1910 El Paso, with more than 10,000 people of Mexican birth or parentage, was the largest Mexican center in the United States. Then during the Mexican Revolution hundreds of political refugees, both rich and poor, fled to El Paso to escape the violence, destruction, and persecution left in the wake of that conflagration.[30]

Until 1917 Mexican immigration was unrestricted — the only Mexicans who could not enter the United States were the physically and mentally handicapped, paupers, beggars, persons incapable of earning a living, criminals, polygamists, anarchists, and prostitutes. But as the result of "hordes of Mexicans pouring over the border," as the Bureau of Immigration phrased it on one occasion, great concern was expressed by El Paso officials about the possibilities of an epidemic. Border authorities required the passing of a physical examination on entering the United States, and local health officials initiated a vaccination program for Mexican-American residents in El Paso, particularly in Chihuahuita near the border, where most of the poor and hungry had found shelter. Yet a new immigration law passed in 1917 requiring a head tax and a literacy test was suspended in part because the demand for Mexican workers was so great. As a result, twice as many Mexicans entered the United States during 1919 than in any previous year since 1900, a trend that continued during the 1920s. While the population of El Paso doubled each decade after 1900, the percentage of new residents from Mexico was more than half the total. Until 1940 most Mexican-Americans in El Paso were born in Mexico; after that date, most of them were born in El Paso.[31]

Arriving in El Paso, the Mexican immigrants, most of whom after 1900 brought their families, found employment and better

U.S. Consulate in Paso del Norte. (Souvenir of El Paso, Texas and Paso del Norte, Mexico, *Ward Bros., Columbus, Ohio, 1887*)

economic opportunities than they had known in Mexico. Yet, never completely abandoning the possibility of returning to their homeland, they did little to integrate with American society. As a result, they remained extremely vulnerable to exploitation and, as Mario García points out, soon became the victims of economic discrimination, racial and cultural prejudice, political pressures, and residential segregation in slums featuring overcrowded conditions, little or no sanitation, high infant mortality rates, disease, and crime. They tolerated such conditions because they believed that their existence in the United States was only temporary, and because they feared reprisals if they complained or protested too loudly. They stayed in the United States, though their loyalties remained with their native land.[32]

Of the 1,200 Chinese laborers who helped bring the Southern Pacific to El Paso in 1881, many returned to China; those who remained in El Paso numbered about 300 in the 1890s. They engaged in a variety of occupations, particularly the laundry business, which they practically monopolized for more than three decades. They also owned a sizable share of the restaurants, essentially chop houses serving meat-and-potato dishes, as American tastes had not yet taken to Chinese cooking. Other Chinese worked as train wipers and truck farmers. A few made fortunes, among them Sam Hing, labor contractor, tong organizer, merchant, and businessman. He built one of the magnificent residences in town in the Magoffin Addition, and fathered a son—"probably the first Chinaman ever born in Texas." Because his wife, a New Orleans creole, felt ostracized by the women of El Paso, she moved to Mexico. Hing soon followed, and reportedly made another fortune there.[33]

El Paso's Chinese population, largely urban in character, was overwhelmingly adult male, since the exclusion laws prohibited Chinese from bringing their wives to the United States. Most El Paso Chinese lived on South Oregon Street between Overland and Second Street. Here were the boarding houses, the mercantile stores, and the lodge hall of the local tong, to which half of the town's Chinese population belonged. For the most part the Chinese remained apart from the rest of the community, consulted their own herbalist doctors, held their own festivals, and maintained their own burial ground in Concordia Cemetery, the only Chinese burial plot in Texas.[34]

Because the Chinese population remained apart, monopolized the laundry business, operated opium dens and gambling halls, and smuggled alien Chinese through Mexico in violation of the Chinese Exclusion Act of 1882, they quickly incurred the wrath and resentment of the El Paso community. American immigration officials became convinced that the entire Chinese population "banded together as one man" in support of these illegal activities, and that "Chinese buildings were linked by a honeycomb of underground passages in the area of South Oregon Street in the heart of Chinatown, which made it possible for Chinese to enter one house and exit through another house several doors or blocks away." The Immigration Service, determined to stop the illegal entry of Chinese into the United States, increased its surveillance so that it became extremely difficult for Chinese to cross from Juárez to El Paso. After the turn of the century, as El Paso's population grew significantly, the Chinese population remained stationary. As the relative number of Chinese declined, so inevitably did Chinatown, its demise simply a matter of time.[35]

A Negro population had resided in El Paso since the Civil War, but their number had never been large. There were 361 living in El Paso in 1890. The first Negro school, founded in 1883, was named after the famous Negro leader, Frederick Douglass. In 1886 it was incorporated into the public school system, though it remained segregated until 1954. A Baptist and a Methodist church were organized by Negroes in 1884. Because El Paso is more western than southern, and because the number of Negroes did not pose a threat to the economic or political life of the community as it did in many areas of the South, they could achieve a greater degree of political and economic freedom than elsewhere throughout the South. Thus a number of of El Paso Negroes were able to amass varying degrees of wealth. Opposition from whites remained, and the Negro was never allowed to forget his race. "His social standing," as one writer has noted, "never equalled his financial status." Details about one particular family are deserving of note.[36]

Virginia-born John Woods came to the El Paso area during the Civil War, married an ex-slave from Missouri, and became a registered voter in 1867. He began to accumulate property in downtown El Paso, and became the owner of a blacksmith shop, a bar, a boarding house, a stage line, a grocery store, and a saloon in Juárez. W. W. Mills mentions Woods as his one-time landlord, and his blacksmith shop cast the first bell for St. Clement's Episcopal Church. On the other hand, Woods, never too discreet about the payment of his debts and taxes, began to come under a considerable amount of criticism from the newspapers for all the sordid things that took place in his saloon, and for suspected crimes for which he had not been convicted. In a war of words between two newspapers, one said that its rival planned to hire "John Woods, the colored blacksmith, as editor."[37]

Woods was eventually killed by a policeman in a shooting incident that had no witnesses. One newspaper said Woods was heavily armed and drunk, and that he had threatened the policeman who fired in self-defense. Some wondered why Woods had been shot in the back of the head. The policeman was bound over by the grand jury, but was soon released. Mary Woods inherited an estate which she skillfully managed through leases on property at the corner of Mesa and Mills, so that at the time of her death her estate was valued at $160,000. As an illiterate Negro couple, both of whom may have been ex-slaves, they had prospered in El Paso.[38]

Among other prominent Negroes who came to the El Paso Southwest mention should be made of Lt. Henry O. Flipper, the first Negro graduate of West Point. He served with the Army for four years, until a highly questionable court martial ended his military career. He then worked for thirty-seven years in northern Mexico as a mining engineer with such well-known promoters and

189

speculators as Col. William C. "Bill" Greene and Albert B. Fall. He became assistant to Secretary of the Interior Fall from 1921 to 1923, a noteworthy accomplishment for a Negro at that time. Also in El Paso there was Florida J. Wolfe, the devoted black companion of British aristocrat Lord Delaval Beresford. She was known to El Pasoans as "Lady Flo."[39]

In 1899 Company A of the Twenty-Fifth Infantry arrived at Fort Bliss. Although the unit had an enviable record, the community clearly harbored reservations about this presence of a Negro army in its midst. Many whites regarded the black man in uniform as a symbol of authority, a threat to white supremacy. This attitude resulted in considerable racial strife in the early 1900s. Every evidence of military misconduct was carefully catalogued, and each transgression was publicized as certification of the Negro soldier's racial instability. A military report in 1900 cited racial bias against Negro troops in the border city:

> Soldiers from the post are arrested for infractions of the police regulations, or when intoxicated, or in the least degree noisy or disorderly, when white men committing the same offenses are not interfered with.... A Negro soldier in uniform is frequently subjected to insult though behaving with perfect propriety for no other reason than his color.[40]

Of the various immigrant groups who came to El Paso in the 1880s and 1890s by far the most significant and influential in the life of the business community were the Jews from Germany and Austria-Hungary. Motivated by a desire to escape the militaristic regimes of their European homelands, coupled with the promise of rich rewards and opportunities on the Southwest frontier, the Jewish pioneers came by the scores. Their names, accomplishments, and contributions have been etched in the memories of El Pasoans for a century or more – Blaugrund, Blumenthal, Calisher, Freudenthal, Goodman, Kahn, Kohlberg, Krakauer, Krupp, Levy, Lapowski, Lesinski, Mathias, Rosenfield, Schuster, Schutz, Schwartz, Solomon, Zork, and so on. Some started their businesses in Ciudad Juárez before moving to El Paso to take advantage of the *Zona Libre*, the duty-free trading zone which the Mexican government had established along the border in 1885; others, such as the Oppenheims, remained in Juárez. A few, such as the Schutzes and

Schusters, accepted the Christian faith, but most remained with the faith of their forefathers. In 1898 a Jewish congregation was organized, a rabbi was secured, and the following year Temple Mount Sinai was completed. Whether in business, medicine, or public office, the Jewish contribution to the building of the El Paso community has been a significant one.[41]

The first two decades of the twentieth century witnessed the arrival of a significant number of immigrants from Syria. Because Syrians were regarded as undesirable on the East Coast of the United States, were viewed with alarm and denied entry at New York and other Atlantic seaports, they came to the Southwest through Mexico – America's "Back Door." Soon after arriving in a Mexican seaport, the Syrian immigrant bought a *sombrero* and learned how to say he was a Mexican in Spanish. Many settled on South El Paso Street where their dry goods, grocery, and clothing stores were located, and gained facility in Spanish and English. Some became Catholics; others, Episcopalians and Orthodox. Thus, the names Ayoub, Azar, Dipp, Farah, Haddad, Malooly, Shamaley, and Wardy have been familiar to El Pasoans for generations.[42]

The mayor's race in 1889 was between the Democratic candidate, C. R. Morehead, and the Republican nominee, Adolph Krakauer. Like most of El Paso's past elections, this one featured a lavish expenditure of funds and the importation of voters from across the river by both parties. They were entertained by dance hall girls from El Paso and Juárez, the festivities beginning in the afternoon of the day before the election and lasting all night. The doors of the dance hall were kept locked until the next morning when everyone was marched to the polls and handed a prepared ballot, each voter receiving three dollars. German-born Krakauer was the apparent victor, but was disqualified from holding office when the Democrats disclosed that he had not completed his citizenship papers. Political chaos resulted until a special election was called in which Irish-born Richard Caples, a Democrat, was chosen mayor just minutes after he became an American citizen! The election marked the beginning of a decade of political control by the regular or stalwart faction of the Democratic party in El Paso usually referred to as "the Ring," or "the Morehead gang." Composed of businessmen, lawyers, and politicians who knew El Paso well, they understood the importance of the Mexican vote in winning elections, and perceived the town's "Sin City" reputation as a needed asset to finance projects and balance the budget.[43]

On the other hand, during the 1890s a growing concern developed that the town's "Sin City" image could become a distinct liability. Under the leadership of Waters Davis, William H. and Richard F. Burges, brothers and eminent lawyers, and Dr. William Yandell, city health officer, the Law and Order League was organized. The league called for a general cleanup of vice and crime, with big-time gambling as its initial target. In spite of their determined effort, little was accomplished with the Democratic machine in control of local politics. Yet the reformers stood firm, refused to give up, and continued to apply pressure for the rest of the decade.[44]

The issue of "the sporting element" versus the reformers surfaced in the race for mayor in 1903. The Democratic machine nominated C. R. Morehead, who since his defeat in 1889 had been content to direct political affairs from his office at the State National Bank. The reformers gained control of the Republican party but nominated a staunch Democrat, former sheriff James H. White, who had an enviable record in the community. Supporting Morehead was Juan Hart, editor of the *Times* and son of pioneer Simeon Hart, while the reform ticket received its support from the Burges brothers and the former New Mexican businessman, Félix Martínez. It was a noisy campaign with no holds barred. Morehead was portrayed as the defender of all the vice and villainy on the border. Both sides, as usual, imported hundreds of Mexicans, provided them with beer and whisky, handed them the marked ballots to drop in the box, and paid them three dollars for doing so. More of them voted for Morehead than White, the Morehead ticket sweeping every office.[45]

Although the reformers once again had tasted defeat, they still refused to surrender. They organized the Citizens' Reform League with Waters Davis at its head to educate the public about the prevalence of gambling and its influence on the community. They kept pressure on the Morehead administration by holding rallies and obtaining 1,500 signatures on a petition to end gambling. In November 1904 Morehead gave in, closing all the dance halls, saloons, and brothels. This forced the gamblers and the girls, for the time being at least, to move to Juárez and elsewhere. In time many would return and simply go into hiding. Since Morehead made it clear that his action would result in a $65,000 deficit in city funds, he may have taken the action to prove a point in the hope that the whole effort of the reformers would backfire.[46]

Even so, the reform issue played a fundamental role in the transforming of El Paso from a wide-open frontier town into a respectable western community. As Jack Vowell has noted in his excellent study of El Paso politics, the basic social unit from 1880 to 1905 had remained, as it had on the frontier, the individual, whereas by 1905, the social microcosm became the family, thus altering the demands and tastes of society. The saloon, dance hall, and gambling casino, he continues, offered no positive threat to a social structure based upon the individual frontiersman. However, once the family became the basic unit, the old wide-open vices were unstabilizing in a society becoming more firmly rooted with the passage of time. The reform period, says Vowell, stands as a bridge between the frontier town and the urban, metropolitan community.[47]

In the meantime, a program of civic improvements and expansion of city services had already been started. The beginning of electric streetcar service was proclaimed in an impressive ceremony in 1902, and Mandy the mule was retired after twenty years of dedicated service. During the administration of Charles Davis, "a mayor without equal in the history of El Paso," in the opinion of Owen White, assessed valuations were doubled and the tax rate was slightly decreased, making it possible for the city to initiate a street paving program. Henry Ford's famous Model T soon made its appearance, gradually replacing the wagons, buggies, hitching posts, and saddle horses. The fire and police departments attained a more professional status. In a local election in 1910 involving only 25 percent of the electorate, voters approved the municipal ownership of the water works. Other public utilities remained under private ownership.[48]

More signs of progress included the construction in 1906 of the Union Depot at a cost of $260,000. As the result of the reputation which El Paso had established as a health center, Hotel Dieu Hospital was completed in 1894, Providence Memorial in 1902, and the Albert Baldwin Health Resort, the largest of several sanatoriums, in 1907. The Baldwin property became the Homan Sanatorium in 1910 and was subsequently relocated in a new building later remodeled and reopened in 1937 as Southwestern

This 1899 photo looks northward from the Sheldon Hotel
(on the site now occupied by the Plaza Hotel), across San
Jacinto Plaza toward the Franklin Mountains. At right is
the Orndorff Hotel. Facing the railroad tracks at left is the
Angelus Hotel. In the distance at left center are the gables
of Hotel Dieu, the city's first major hospital.

General Hospital. The first separate high school, El Paso High, was
built in 1902 on Arizona Street. Municipal progress and development were aggressively championed by the Woman's Club of El
Paso, organized in 1894, and the El Paso Chamber of Commerce,
begun in 1899. The El Paso Public Library was founded in 1895 by
Mary I. Stanton, who began its enduring tradition of dedicated
public service. Recreation and socializing for the city's affluent and
influential were provided by the elegant Toltec Club and the impressive El Paso Country Club with its nine-hole golf course.[49]

The discovery of rich coal deposits about 140 miles northeast
of El Paso near White Oaks, New Mexico, led to the organization
by Charles Bishop Eddy in 1897 of the El Paso and Northeastern
Railroad Company. By June 1898 rails had been laid to the new
town of Alamogordo, and soon reached Tularosa and Carrizozo.

But because the residents of White Oaks drastically raised the prices of their land, the builders bypassed the town, and it soon withered and died. Eddy's need for timber, coupled with his in-terest in building a mountain resort for El Pasoans, led to the organization of the Alamogordo and Sacramento Railroad and the establishment of Cloudcroft as a summer retreat. With the comple-tion of the Cloudcroft Lodge in 1901, El Pasoans could take the excursion train for the weekend at a cost of three dollars per per-son, or they could spend an entire summer in a cabin which cost three to four hundred dollars, including lot.[50]

The availability of an adequate supply of water has continued to be a major concern of residents of the El Paso area for cen-turies. During the Spanish colonial period, with the help of a system of *acequias*, the Lower Valley produced grain, beans, fruits, vegetables, and vineyards in abundance. The Rio Grande, however, was a perpetual problem with periodic flooding and droughts bringing untold damage to farms and crops. With the coming of the railroads and the attendant business boom and growth in population, valley farmers began to give serious consideration to a comprehensive system of irrigation to increase production and to

permit farmers to market their commodities for a profit. El Pasoans
pointed to the diversion dams and canals being constructed upriver in New Mexico and Colorado, siphoning away water from El
Paso. This meant that the town's future would be jeopardized
unless prompt and decisive action was taken to ensure a water supply in the years ahead. The river was the problem, as Sonnichsen
puts it, but it was also the answer if something could be done to
stabilize the water supply.[51]

In 1888 Anson Mills proposed the construction of a dam three
miles above El Paso about 60 feet high and 450 feet wide, to create
a lake in the Upper Valley fifteen miles long by seven miles wide,
at a cost of $300,000. Mills insisted it would provide irrigation
water for about 200,000 acres of valley land. His proposal brought
a howl from the residents of the Mesilla Valley, Las Cruces, and
Doña Ana. These communities favored building a dam at Fort
Selden, above Las Cruces. The battle between El Paso and Las
Cruces was on. Although the federal government vetoed the Fort
Selden project, Las Cruces vowed to keep up the fight. "If there is
no new ditch at Las Cruces," said one resident, "there will be no
dam at El Paso." By this time the Mexican government had
entered the picture with protests that the diverting of water from
the river, which was international in character, was causing great
damage to crops and farms on the Mexican side. Significantly, the
Mills project came to be known as the International Dam, but bill
after bill in Congress supporting the project passed the Senate only
to be voted down in the House of Representatives.[52]

In the 1890s a British syndicate obtained a charter from the
Territory of New Mexico to construct a dam at Elephant Butte,
about 125 miles north of El Paso. Although the British promised
to make the entire area "the garden spot of the West," the project
was doomed when the United States Justice Department obtained
an injunction, subsequently upheld by the United States Supreme
Court, to prevent the British syndicate from building. At that
point the United States Bureau of Reclamation stepped into the
picture and recommended that the Twelfth Irrigation Congress,
scheduled to meet in El Paso in 1904, make the final decision on
the matter of the dam site.[53]

Prior to the meeting of the Irrigation Congress, a joint commission composed of representatives from Texas, New Mexico, and

Mexico was named to study the irrigation problem and make its recommendation. The Texas representatives, all El Pasoans, were Félix Martínez, Alfred Courchesne, J. A. Smith, A. P. Coles, and Zach White. The leadership of Martínez was decisive. He had made and lost a fortune in New Mexico, and had become a successful El Paso businessman and real estate owner. The joint commission recommended that the dam be erected at Elephant Butte on a site selected by B. M. Hall, supervising engineer of the Reclamation Service.[54]

The Irrigation Congress held its opening session on 15 November 1904 in a new convention hall El Paso had built for the event. Delegates were treated to a concert by the Mexico City Regimental Band, a bullfight in Juárez, and a football game between Mesilla Park A&M and El Paso Athletics, which ended in a scoreless tie. Although engineer Hall spoke convincingly in favor of the Elephant Butte site which the joint commission had recommended, the sessions during the next three days became increasingly acrimonious over the question of how the water was to be distributed. Finally on 18 November Maj. Richard Burges, an El Paso lawyer, offered a motion that the United States recommend "an equitable division of waters," a motion adopted unanimously. Owen White reveals that Burges was not even a delegate to the convention but that Julius Krakauer, who was sitting beside him, suggested that he make the motion. "They won't know whether you are a delegate or not!" Krakauer was right.[55]

A compact, signed by the Mexican delegation on 18 November, endorsed the Elephant Butte project with a stipulation that Mexico was to be given without cost water needed for all previously irrigated areas. This agreement then was approved by delegations from Texas and New Mexico. Subsequently, in 1906 in a treaty with Mexico, the United States guaranteed to deliver to Mexico 60,000 acre feet of water annually from the proposed new reservoir.[56]

Although Congress in 1907 finally authorized construction of the dam and appropriated $1 million to get the project started, another three years passed before construction began. In the meantime, Martínez and Burges took turns lobbying in Washington, D.C., trying to get the project under way. "Have a talk with President Theodore Roosevelt," wrote Martínez to Burges, "and be sure to thank Teddy for his interest in reclamation and what it means to this whole country." Nothing had been done, however, by the time Roosevelt left office in March 1909. Several months later William Howard Taft, his successor, fired Gifford Pinchot, Roosevelt's conservation specialist. Pinchot had been in close touch with El Paso's civic leaders, and it appeared that the project had received a fatal blow. One last chance remained to get it off dead center – the approaching meeting in El Paso in the fall of the two presidents, William Howard Taft and Porfirio Díaz.[57]

By 1906 Porfirio Díaz was rounding out thirty years in power, and there was mounting discontent with his regime. Significant revolutionary activity had begun along the United States-Mexican border, particularly in El Paso, a superb location as a base for antigovernment operations. Since 1905 Ricardo Flores Magón, the premier intellectual precursor of the Mexican Revolution, had been publishing his inflammatory anti-Díaz newspaper, *Regeneración*, and from his revolutionary party headquarters in El Paso was making preparations for an attack on Ciudad Juárez. These plans, however, were detected, and on the night of 19 October 1906 Mexican and American officials arrested the leaders. Although Flores Magón escaped to Los Angeles, he was later caught and jailed in the summer of 1908. No doubt other antigovernment leaders had taken note of the possibilities offered by the border area; no doubt the same idea had occurred to Porfirio Díaz's advisers. Perhaps a spectacular move – a personal appearance in the border area – might restore some of the dictator's lost popularity, and remind his opposition that in spite of his years, he was still in control. The invitation of Pres. William Howard Taft to the Mexican president to meet in El Paso in October 1909 was readily accepted.[58]

The meeting of Presidents Taft and Díaz on 16 October 1909 was described by the *El Paso Herald* as the "Most Eventful Diplomatic Event in the History of the Two Nations." For this first meeting in history between a president of the United States and a president of Mexico, nothing was left to the imagination. According to newspaper accounts, it was "a veritable pageant of military splendor, social brilliance, courtly formality, official protocol, and patriotic fervor." Following Taft's arrival on the morning of 16 October a presidential breakfast was held at the St. Regis Hotel at a price of twenty-five dollars a plate. Guests included Mayor Joseph U. Sweeney of El Paso, and the governors of Texas and Chihuahua. Taft was then driven to the Chamber of Commerce Building.[59]

198

Prior to President Díaz's arrival, members of the El Paso Committee took the fullest advantage of the opportunity of the moment to present their case regarding the Elephant Butte dam project. President Taft then asked the committee to provide him with details of the proposal and promised that he would give the matter his personal attention – a hopeful sign that the project was still alive. President Díaz arrived at 11:00 A.M., and after formal introductions spent about twenty minutes with the American president. Whether the Chamizal dispute between the United States and Mexico was mentioned is not known, since official reports indicated that nothing of political or diplomatic significance was discussed. Díaz then returned to Juárez, followed by Taft an hour later, and all preparations were completed for the meeting of the two presidents at the Mexican customhouse. There, after a brief interview, they stepped outside to the front of the building under a scarlet canopy and posed for the cameramen. Their photograph was used to good advantage by Díaz in Mexico because of the striking contrast between Taft's plain appearance and Díaz's military bearing and chest full of medals.[60]

The banquet at the Juárez customhouse dwarfed all other events surrounding the visit. The entire building had been transformed into a reproduction of one of the famous salons of Versailles. There were rich red draperies, paintings of George Washington and Miguel Hidalgo, three train carloads of flowers brought from Guadalajara, a gold and silver service that had belonged to Maximilian and was valued at a million dollars, cut glass from Chapultepec Castle valued at $200,000, and fine linens from the presidential palace. The Mexican government reportedly had spent $50,000 remodeling and decorating the customhouse for the occasion. Then came soft music, conversation, with Taft remembering some of the Spanish he had learned in the Philippines, and toasts by each president to the other one. With the presentation of gold goblets to the presidents from Félix Martínez as gifts from the City of El Paso, the evening came to an end. Taft then returned to El Paso to board a train for San Antonio. The regime of Porfirio Díaz, at all times mindful of its image at home and abroad, had put on quite a show – Porfirian pageantry in the grand manner. That night no one would have dreamed that nineteen months later his administration would be overthrown with the capture of Ciudad Juárez by victorious revolutionary forces.[61]

With regard to the Elephant Butte dam project, President Taft was true to his word, and in April 1910 Burges wrote Martínez that Secretary of the Interior R. A. Ballinger was giving the project his support. In the ensuing months the first contracts for construction were let, and the secretary indicated that the completion of the dam was a high priority. A thousand workers were employed, and the project was finally completed in 1916. Dedication ceremonies were held on 20 October, with more than 300 El Pasoans in attendance.[62]

The capacity of Elephant Butte lake was 2.6 million acre feet, and for a time it was the largest man-made lake in the United States. The dam is 308 feet high and 1,700 feet long; planned irrigation in Texas, New Mexico, and Mexico was 160,000 acres; the cost of the dam itself was $5 million, and the cost of irrigation ditches and diversion dams was another $10 million. Valley landowners were to pay for the project in ten years. Each landowner was a stockholder in the project and bought a water right for every acre of land held. Thus at long last, the capricious old river had been brought under control and its waters channeled to make El Paso's valleys green. No longer would it overflow its banks destroying property, crops, and homes; no longer would it shift channels and create boundary disputes. As to the significance of Elephant Butte dam in the development of El Paso, Owen White has written: "Just as it had been a foregone conclusion from the beginning that the building of the railroads would bring prosperity to El Paso, so now it became a certainty that the construction of the dam would bring an equal or even greater prosperity to the Rio Grande Valley."[63]

Specifically, the construction of the dam, with its promise to revolutionize agriculture throughout the region, convinced investors, financiers, and businessmen that El Paso had a great future. The area's economic base was significantly broadened from one largely limited to railroads, mining, ranching, and trade, to one offering a much greater diversification. Transportation and mining remained important, of course; but added to these were oil refining, natural gas, lumber and construction materials, metal working, textiles, manufacturing, real estate, banking, and tourism.

Significant changes also occurred in valley agriculture as small farms, manual labor, and vineyard culture gave way to much larger holdings using powerful and expensive farm machinery in the cultivation of cotton and alfalfa. Here then was the economic base that brought two decades of industrial growth, the building of an impressive downtown and beautiful residential areas, the expansion of municipal facilities, services, and conveniences, and an increase in population that reached 100,000 by 1925. Pierre N. Beringer, in an article written in 1910, summarized the significance of Elephant Butte dam:

> The Southwest is a big country, where they do big things, and the Elephant Butte dam, located in the Rio Grande Valley, is no exception to this rule, being the most enormous undertaking of this nature in the memory of mankind. A complete explanation of what this will mean to the city of El Paso and the surrounding country would require a special volume. No part of North America produces such an abundance nor so great a variety of crops as are made possible when the arid lands of the Southwest are properly irrigated.[64]

For more than a hundred years a major irritant in United States-Mexican relations was a tract amounting to about four hundred acres in South El Paso called El Chamizal, whose ownership was a matter of dispute caused by the capricious Rio Grande. The name is derived from the Mexican word *chamiza*, the desert weed or brush that covered the uninhabited portions of the area. A survey made by a joint commission in 1852 and 1856 fixed the dividing line at what is now Eighth Avenue in South El Paso through the present campus of Bowie High School and just south of East Paisano. The river, however, continued to wear away at the southern bank, and in 1864 there occurred a most violent flood. The river left its original channel and formed a new one, leaving a tract of about four hundred acres on the north bank of the river in South El Paso.[65]

The controversy began to attract attention in both Mexico City and Washington, D.C. Land values in the valley greatly increased and hundreds of claims against Mexico amounting to some $470 million were made by American citizens. At length in 1884, a treaty was signed between the two nations providing that the center of the normal channel of the river would continue to be the boundary if the changes were brought about by gradual erosion, or accretion. If, on the other hand, a change resulted from a sudden and abrupt force of the current thus cutting a new bed, or avulsion, the boundary would remain fixed at the middle of the original bed. Subsequent negotiations between the two countries failed to solve the Chamizal controversy. Meanwhile property values in the tract increased, squatters moved in, and land titles remained uncertain. When railroads, which always had regarded the tract as a potential site for terminal facilities, refused to take the gamble, local corporate and national interests by the turn of the century demanded a solution.[66]

In 1910, possibly as a result of a commitment made by President Taft in his meeting in El Paso with President Díaz, the United States and Mexico signed a treaty for the arbitration of the Chamizal problem. A three-member commission was appointed, composed of Anson Mills of the United States, Fernando Beltrán of Mexico, and Eugene Lafleur of Canada, who was to serve as presiding commissioner. The body was instructed to decide solely and exclusively whether the international title to the Chamizal tract was in the United States or in Mexico – the entire tract, in other words, was to be awarded to one or the other of the disputing nations.[67]

In reality the award of the arbitration commission was made by Lafleur since the American and Mexican commissioners vigorously upheld the claims of their respective nations. Lafleur divided the Chamizal between the two, arguing that the river had moved by slow erosion, or accretion, before 1864, and by rapid erosion, or avulsion, after that date, and that Mexico should have title to the tract south of the riverbed as it had existed in 1864. The Mexican commissioner, deciding that half a loaf was better than nothing, supported Lafleur's ruling, but the United States rejected the decision on the grounds that the commissioners had violated instructions. Anson Mills later wrote, "I recorded my conviction that it would be 'as impossible to locate the channel of the Rio Grande in the Chamizal tract in 1864 as to relocate the Garden of Eden or the lost continent of Atlantis.'" The Chamizal problem remained unsolved, and for half a century cries of "Yankee imperialism" came from south of the border.[68]

El Paso High School, built in 1917, was designed by noted architect Henry C. Trost. (Courtesy El Paso Public Library)

Playing a dominant role in El Paso's growth during the first third of the twentieth century was Henry C. Trost, who arrived in El Paso in 1903 to become the city's foremost pioneer architect. Influenced by the work of Louis Sullivan and Frank Lloyd Wright, as well as the Spanish mission and pueblo styles, Trost designed more than two hundred buildings in El Paso and became an innovator in the use of reinforced concrete. His structures ranged from office buildings, hotels, churches, and schools, to apartments and residences. Most familiar of the Trost structures in the downtown area are the Mills Building, which he claimed to be "the tallest all-concrete structure in the world"; the Caples Building; the Roberts-Banner Building; Hotel Paso del Norte, Zach White's dream hotel with its Tiffany dome, ornamental marbled columns, and stained glass windows; the Toltec Building; Hotel Cortez; Hilton Hotel; and Bassett Tower. Outstanding among Trost's designs outside the downtown area are El Paso High School, the residence of Joseph F. Williams at 323 West Rio Grande, where the

1915 historic meeting took place between Gen. Hugh Scott and
Francisco "Pancho" Villa, and the W. W. Turney house at 1205
Montana (later the El Paso Museum of Art), Temple Mount Sinai,
and his own residence at 1013 West Yandell.[69]

As the downtown district grew upward, the residential areas
grew outward. Most of the city's growth, which increased fivefold
during those years, was northeasterly toward Fort Bliss. Grandview
and Government Hill were laid out in 1906, followed by Logan
Heights, Altura Park, Manhattan Heights, El Paso Heights, Morn-
ingside Heights, Hollywood Heights, Military Heights, and above
all, Austin Terrace with its fabulous James G. McNary home. On
the west side to the east of Mesa Street, Pete Kern, a jeweler who
had made and lost a fortune in Alaska gold fields, and reportedly
something of an eccentric, drew the attention of El Pasoans to his
subdivision by erecting a high symbolic gate at Kansas and Robinson streets. It contained swastikas, signs of the zodiac, mythologi-
cal figures, and more than three hundred lights. Since residential
development on both sides of the mountain made a connecting
road necessary, both candidates in the mayor's race in 1915, C. E.
Kelly and Tom Lea, advocated the construction of a scenic drive
around the mountain.[70]

El Paso's mining industry in the period from 1900 to 1910
sustained substantial growth and its custom smelter became the
world's largest. Harry M. Scott, editor of the prestigious *Mining
World*, called El Paso "the most important mining center in the
country." On the other hand, the Federal Copper Company, built
in 1901 on a site now occupied by Memorial Park, got caught in
the price wars and was forced to shut down after two years of
operation. A local company, organized in 1909 to operate a tin
mine twelve miles north of El Paso, experienced a peak year in
1911, but ran into financial difficulties a short time later. However,
one of Charles Longuemare's fondest dreams came true when the
State School of Mines was founded in 1913 "for the purpose of
teaching the scientific knowledge of mining and metallurgy." With
land donated by citizens of El Paso, including the reservation and
buildings of the El Paso Military Institute, the Board of Regents of
the University of Texas in April 1914 formally established the
Texas School of Mines and Metallurgy just east of Fort Bliss.
Courses were offered in mining law, copper and lead smelting, the

cyanide process, ore dressing, internal combustion engines, air compression, and first aid. One faculty member served as "tutor in Spanish." The first catalogue listed twenty-seven male students; two coeds enrolled in 1916.[71]

In October 1916 the destruction of the Main Building by fire coupled with a water supply problem on the mesa resulting from the huge buildup of troops at Fort Bliss necessitated relocating the school. It was moved to a new site a mile and a half north of the downtown area on twenty-three acres donated by five El Pasoans. The unique Bhutanese style of architecture adopted in 1917 and used since that time (with several modifications) was the idea of Mrs. S. H. Worrell, wife of the dean. She was impressed by an article on Bhutan in the April 1914 issue of the *National Geographic Magazine* and had noted the similarity between that country's terrain and that of the school's new site. The idea was accepted and by the end of 1918, five buildings had been completed. Designed as a branch of The University of Texas in 1919, the school two years later was named the College of Mines and Metallurgy (later Texas Western College), the forerunner of The University of Texas at El Paso.[72]

The victory of the reformers in the early years of the century turned out to be only partial at best, as they continued to encounter stiff resistance from the old frontier code of rugged individualism that permitted a man to carry a gun, gamble his earnings, visit the girls, or drink himself into a stupor so long as others suffered no injury in the process. Many still pointed to the practical revenue aspects of allowing vice for a price, while others objected to what they considered overly zealous moralizing on the part of the reformers. To be sure, El Paso's geographical isolation might work for a while in behalf of "the sporting element," but the impact of the Progressive movement throughout the nation with its emphasis on moral reform at the local level would in time demand an end to officially-sanctioned vice and a cleanup of the city's lingering "Sin City" reputation. Little progress could normally be expected with "the Ring" in firm control under Joseph U. Sweeney and C. E. Kelly, but in the mayor's race in 1915, which featured the heaviest voting in the city's history, the reform movement under the leadership of Tom Lea broke the power of "the Ring," and the crusade against vice was carried forward. Naturally, it could not be eliminated entirely, but by 1917 clearly the old wide-open days were a thing of the past.[73]

Speaking for all those who mourned the passing of the old order was Owen P. White, who poured forth his sentiments on the matter in his most fervent style. Gone were the blonde heads of the ladies from Utah Street no longer to be seen at the Myar Opera House; gone were the whir of the roulette wheel, the rattle of the poker chips, and the banging of the piano that had enticed the transient cowpuncher and the itinerant prospector into the arms of the frescoed beauties of Louis Vidal's dance hall. As a result, El Paso's males had to change their habits. Instead of being able to enjoy themselves in a free and unrestrained manner, they now had to live according to the rules their wives, who had been taking annual trips back East, brought home and inserted into the family curriculum. White continued:

> Men, who a short fifteen years before, had been content to sit on their heels and roll their own while they conversed freely and openly with the world, now found themselves confined in a close pasture where etiquette demanded that they smoke perfectos at four bits a throw and associate only with other unfortunates whose genealogies, like their own, were beginning to appear in the new issues of the herd books of Dun and Bradstreet. These poor men now shaved daily, boasted on the cold plunge every morning, changed their clothes by the clock, and began to play golf. This was the end.[74]

III. The Bicultural
International Community

Benito Juárez Monument
in Ciudad Juárez.
(José Cisneros, 1989)

CHAPTER EIGHT

El Paso and Ciudad Juárez, 1910-1945

THE complicated, confusing, cataclysmic convulsion known as the Mexican Revolution (spelled always with a capital "R") is one of the most important historic movements of the twentieth century. Much of it can be told only in astronomical terms – a million lives were lost; property losses ran to more than a billion dollars; few of the major revolutionary leaders escaped violent death; treachery and betrayal were commonplace. Basically, it was a revolt to overthrow the dictatorship of Porfirio Díaz, who for more than thirty years had maintained himself in power largely through the establishment of a political system based on alliances with state governors, *hacendados*, industrialists, financiers, the Catholic hierarchy, and foreign capitalists.[1]

A swinging bridge over the Rio Grande linked a revolutionary camp on the Mexican side with the smelter area of El Paso. (Courtesy El Paso Public Library)

Although the Mexican Revolution traditionally dates from the movement initiated by Francisco Madero in 1910, significant revolutionary activity had begun along the United States-Mexican border in 1906, particularly in El Paso, because of its supreme strategic location. Here was a railroad center with links to the prosperous ranches of Chihuahua and the mines of Sonora and Coahuila; here was a large Mexican population whose loyalties had remained with the land of their birth and who still harbored resentments against the policies of the Díaz regime; here in spite of existing American neutrality legislation was a potential source of arms, munitions, and provisions; here across the river was Ciudad Juárez, with a federal garrison, customhouse, and several banks. As a center and a base for revolutionary operations, therefore, the El Paso-Ciudad Juárez area offered almost unlimited possibilities.[2]

The Mexican Revolution began in 1910 under the leadership of Francisco Madero, a mild-mannered little man from a wealthy Chihuahua family who desired only a democratic and constitutional government for Mexico. After a slow start, the movement gathered strength in Chihuahua, and was followed by spontaneous rebellions throughout the country. In Chihuahua, under the effective leadership of Abraham González, Pascual Orozco, and Francisco "Pancho" Villa, the nucleus of a revolutionary army, made up of workers from the farms, ranches, mines, lumber camps, and railroad yards, was assembled. Guerrilla raids were launched against government forces in the towns, and trains were seized to transport rebel troops, horses, and equipment.[3]

In January 1911 González arrived in El Paso and on the fifth floor of the Caples Building established a revolutionary junta. Here he enlisted recruits for the rebel cause, commissioned Dr. Ira J. Bush, medical officer for Madero's army, and arranged for the purchase of arms and munitions to be smuggled across the border. Timothy Turner, assigned to cover the Madero movement for the El Paso *Herald*, enthusiastically told about his invitation to attend the meetings of González's junta. He wrote:

> The plotters sat around on the edges of beds or sometimes on the floors. There was always a litter of saddles and ammunition bandoliers and a bustle of filibusters and Mexican plotters coming and going, whispering in knots in the halls, with that unmistakable but intangible suppressed excitement, promising, amid these sordid surroundings, of great things to come.[4]

Under existing United States neutrality statutes, Madero's agents could legally purchase American munitions for exportation to Mexico. This interpretation of the neutrality legislation was clearly stated on 24 January 1911 by Philander C. Knox, secretary of state in the Taft administration. Knox ruled that any individual could purchase as many guns and as much ammunition as desired and export them to any country, whether or not that country was involved in revolution or war. He added that such materials could not be used to equip a military expedition organized on United States territory to fight against a government at peace with the United States. This meant that Francisco Madero or his agents could legally purchase American munitions to outfit an army organized and maintained in Mexico. They could not, however, use the same equipment to outfit an army organized in the United States to invade Mexico or to attack the Mexican government.[5]

With considerable support for the Madero movement in El Paso, the city became a principal headquarters for the sale of arms and munitions to the Mexican rebels. Guns and ammunition were purchased from the Francis Bannerman and Sons surplus arms company of New York, shipped through Galveston to the Shelton Payne Arms Company, a sporting goods dealer in El Paso, and stored in private residences until they could be smuggled across the river. Included with these was the famous old muzzle-loading McGinty cannon known as "the Blue Whistler," which was hidden in a hole in the backyard of an El Paso residence until it was loaded with other material into farm wagons. These were then driven thirty-five miles downriver and carried across to Mexico without incident. The Shelton Payne Arms Company did not charge the Mexican rebels a commission for handling their weapons and, on some occasions, even loaned them money to pay the freight bills.[6]

Francisco Madero, who had remained in hiding in San Antonio, New Orleans, and Dallas, decided in February 1911 that his presence on Mexican soil was needed. He arrived in El Paso, crossed the river near Ysleta, and assumed personal command of the revolutionary forces. By this time some thirty American soldiers of fortune had joined the movement, together with Giuseppi Garibaldi, grandson of the Italian liberator, and Benjamin Viljoen, a veteran of the Boer War. After suffering a demoralizing defeat at Casas Grandes, Madero brought his army to Ciudad Juárez, where he hoped to establish his provisional capital. He made camp on the banks of the Rio Grande across from the El Paso smelter. Soon a swinging foot bridge across the river carried a two-way pedestrian traffic – El Pasoans visiting Madero's camp to take pictures, and his troops coming to El Paso to buy uniforms, clothing, and shoes. Madero checked in at the Sheldon Hotel, which overnight became a revolutionary hotbed of rebels, agents, detectives, spies, informers, and newsmen.[7]

On 23 April an armistice was announced so that a peace conference between the rebel leaders and government agents could be held. The setting impressed a *Times* reporter, who wrote:

A prettier or more picturesque spot for holding the Mexican peace conference than the one selected opposite Hart's Mill could not have been found elsewhere on the border. It is a miniature valley carpeted with green grass and shaded by a luxuriant growth of cottonwood trees. The

*The Blue Whistler cannon won a degree of fame during
the Mexican Revolution. (Courtesy El Paso Public Library)*

restless murmuring waters of the Rio Grande rushing over
Hart's dam, sweep along at the foot of the valley, lying
within the shadow of Orozco Hill. The place will hereafter
be known as Peace Grove.[8]

There was no peace, however, as federal negotiators refused to
accept Madero's demand that Díaz resign. The result was military
action, largely instigated by Orozco and Villa, who were convinced
that the government was stalling and that the city could be taken
without difficulty. The battle of Ciudad Juárez began on 8 May
with rebel forces advancing on the city from all sides, followed by
three days of dynamiting, shelling, burning, and fierce hand-to-
hand fighting. The city's supply of water and electricity was cut
off, gaping holes were made in the walls of the adobe structures,
and buildings in the heart of the city were extensively damaged.
For El Pasoans it was the greatest show they had ever seen. In
spite of repeated city officials' warnings of flying bullets, people
stood on the river banks and roof tops and on box cars to witness
the action. With the taking of the federal garrison on the third
day of the battle, Gen. Juan Navarro surrendered. This was the
drop that overflowed the bucket, as one historian has put it,

leading to Díaz's resignation and departure for Europe. Overnight the triumphant Madero became the toast of El Paso, feted and dined by city officials and businessmen at the Sheldon Hotel, and honored with a victory banquet at the Toltec Club.[9]

El Paso business interests quickly perceived that the city could play an important role in the movement Madero had initiated. Not only could it serve as a sanctuary for Mexican revolutionaries as in the past, but as a sales center for arms, munitions, clothing, and supplies, as well as providing facilities for the safe keeping of Mexican cash holdings. Thanks to the first battle of the Revolution just across the river, El Paso found itself in the national spotlight, and there was every reason to believe that the city would be making headlines for some time to come. In appreciation for the service provided by the newspapermen, the Chamber of Commerce gave them a banquet at the Sheldon Hotel.[10]

Madero became president, but lacked the strong hand and emotional stability to pacify the country. He proved to be a bitter disappointment to the El Paso business community, as anti-Madero revolutionary activities on the border continued without abatement. In October 1911 El Paso supporters of Bernardo Reyes, a former Díaz official, reportedly were planning to initiate a revolt in that city against Madero. Moreover, in Ciudad Juárez, followers of the Emiliano Zapata movement to restore the lands illegally stolen from the villages in the state of Morelos, resorted to looting and burning. But the most significant revolutionary movement on the border in 1912 was led by Pascual Orozco, the former Madero leader. Disenchanted with the slow progress of Madero's revolution, Orozco, with financing from the Chihuahua aristocracy, championed the cause of Francisco Vásquez Gómez, an early Madero leader who had broken with his chieftain when he was denied the vice presidency. Using a colorful flag as their symbol, Orozco's supporters came to be known as Red Flaggers. They captured Ciudad Juarez, and the smuggling of guns and ammunition was now renewed. This time the chief supplier was Krakauer, Zork, and Moye, hardware distributors. But by now El Pasoans had become much more concerned with the safety of American lives and property than with making headlines across the nation.[11]

The *vasquista* threat in Ciudad Juárez soon had local, state, and federal officials at odds with one another. Mayor C. E. Kelly

*El Pasoans could watch the Battle of Juárez from
their own city. (Courtesy El Paso Public Library)*

of El Paso and Gov. Oscar B. Colquitt of Texas adopted the hard
line and demanded strong action by the federal government, including military intervention. In an angry letter to President Taft,
Kelly attributed the "deplorable state of affairs in El Paso to the
continued anarchy in the city of Juárez," and maintained that the
increased United States forces in the area had been used primarily
"to prevent American citizens from defending themselves." According to Kelly, federal officials spent too much time trying to avoid
irritating the Mexicans rather than protecting American lives and
property. "I do not propose to maintain order in the City of
Juárez," Kelly concluded, "but I do intend to protect life and property in the corporate limits of El Paso, Texas."[12]

Mayor Kelly's complaints brought a show of force by the federal
government. Col. Edgar Z. Steever ordered all troops at Fort Bliss
into the city, and El Paso took on the appearance of an armed
camp with additional units from San Antonio, plus a company of
the Texas National Guard, the sheriff's posse, and eleven Texas
Rangers. The Taft administration, however, resorted to economic
pressure rather than military force, and declared an arms embargo
in March 1912. It had the desired effect of bringing about the defeat
of Orozco by government forces under the command of Victoriano
Huerta, a former Porfirian general. Thus, as historians Harris and
Sadler have noted, the *orozquistas* ultimately failed because they lost

A Mexican revolutionary outpost was located on
the Rio Grande bank opposite the El Paso smelter.
(Courtesy El Paso Public Library)

the battle of El Paso—that is, in contrast to Madero, they were
prevented from obtaining munitions as the result of the cooperation of the United States and Mexican governments.[13]

In spite of the failure of the Orozco rebellion, the political
situation in Mexico rapidly reached a crisis with the approach of
the year 1913. Disgruntled army officers openly plotted Madero's
overthrow, and the United States ambassador, Henry Lane
Wilson, spokesman for American business interests in Mexico,
made no effort to conceal his lack of confidence in the Madero
regime and its ability to control the situation. The long-expected
coup came on 9 February 1913 in Mexico City. This marked the
beginning of a bloody affair known as the "Ten Tragic Days." It
brought about Madero's downfall and the installation of the tough
old soldier, Victoriano Huerta. The whole sordid affair was climaxed on the night of 23 February when Madero and his vice-
president, José María Pino Suárez, were shot to death. The assassination, as covered by the Times, was the biggest single news story
in the paper's history.[14]

Taking up arms against the dictatorial Huerta was Venustiano
Carranza and his Constitutionalist movement, which quickly
received effective support from Alvaro Obregón in Sonora and
Pancho Villa in Chihuahua. Huerta's most formidable opponent,

however, was Pres. Woodrow Wilson of the United States. He denounced the Mexican president as immoral, dictatorial, and counter-revolutionary, and therefore refused to extend diplomatic recognition to his government. In the hope that he could bring about Huerta's downfall by measures short of intervention, Wilson lifted the arms embargo of the previous administration to permit the purchases of war materials by Huerta's enemies, Carranza, Obregón, and Villa. The *Times* later reported that Villa spent around $15 million a year in the period from 1913 to 1915 in arming and equipping his Division of the North.[15]

Using Ciudad Juárez as his headquarters, Villa collected revenues from confiscated cattle, hides, and cotton, from the mines of Chihuahua, and from the recreational facilities on the border. Waging fierce guerrilla warfare, his forces captured Parral and Torreón. There he extracted a forced loan of some three million pesos for the primary purpose of preparing an offensive directed at the northern frontier. Villa's spies in Ciudad Juárez provided him with information regarding the size and strength of government forces in the city, enabling him to execute one of the boldest military actions of the Revolution. After capturing a southbound government train near Ciudad Chihuahua, Villa boarded his troops and horses into box cars, forced the engineer to turn the train around, and made him send telegrams to the federal commander in Ciudad Juárez stating that the *villistas* in Chihuahua had forced the train's return. In the predawn hours of 15 November the train entered the city. Villa, with a minimum of bloodshed, quickly brought the entire area under control. The *Times's* nine "extras" had kept El Pasoans informed about one of the greatest coups in Mexican military history. El Paso now had another Mexican hero who had put the city back on the front pages and whose expected purchases of arms and equipment would provide a needed stimulant to the local economy.[16]

Revolutionary activities in Chihuahua during 1912 and 1913 brought a stream of Mexican immigration to El Paso. This time the primary motivating factor was political, as opposed to the economic motives of earlier periods. Rich and poor alike came to avoid persecution, as well as the violence and destruction that the Revolution left in its wake. A number of Americans were forced to flee for their safety, and 1,500 Mormons came to escape Orozco's Red

*Thousands of refugees fled Mexico
to El Paso during the Revolution.
(Courtesy El Paso Public Library)*

Flaggers. Thousands of affluent Chihuahua families fled, including the eighty-four-year-old Luis Terrazas, who managed to salvage a portion of his wealth and bring it to El Paso in twenty horse-drawn wagons. Don Luis rented an entire floor of the recently completed Hotel Paso del Norte prior to his move to Albert B. Fall's mansion on Arizona Street. Fall, soon to be elected to the United States Senate from New Mexico, had for years been closely linked with the Terrazas, Creel, and Guggenheim interests of Chihuahua. Others who were able to salvage something settled in Sunset Heights or Golden Hill Terrace. One of the principal streets in Sunset Heights still bears the name of Porfirio Díaz.[17]

On the other hand, Chihuahua's impoverished and destitute were forced to settle in overcrowded Chihuahuita, where conditions would "shame the holes of Calcutta." For years this *barrio,* where most Mexican-Americans in El Paso lived, had been the worst slum in the country. It was characterized by privation, starvation, disease, and crime, conditions intensified and perpetuated with the influx of thousands of destitute refugees. Although some of the older residents had managed to move out of the *barrio,* they were quickly replaced by the new arrivals. The result was that the Second Street boundary between Anglo El Paso and Chihuahuita became more firmly fixed than ever before. But it was this *barrio* that spawned the foremost novel of the Revolution, *Los de Abajo* (The Underdogs), written by Mariano Azuela, an impoverished refugee. The hero Demetrio, a Mexican peasant, was forced to join the Revolution. He fought bravely but lost everything, a victim of the historical forces around him that he could neither comprehend nor control.[18]

President Wilson's measures short of war failed to bring about Huerta's downfall, and by April 1914 Wilson's patience was wearing thin. Seizing upon an incident in Tampico involving the arrest of American sailors, he ordered the landing of marines at Veracruz, thus pushing the two nations to the brink of war. El Paso officials voiced great concern over the possibility of race riots throughout the city should Villa attack El Paso. Fears subsided, however, and the crisis passed when Villa declared, "It's that little drunkard Huerta's fight; let him fight it." Diplomatic negotiations between the United States and Mexico continued long enough to allow Constitutionalist forces, supported by United States arms, to bring about Huerta's resignation in July 1914. This was followed by the return of a semblance of calm and tranquility on the border, at least for the time being.[19]

Because of strained relations that developed between Carranza and Villa after Huerta's resignation, Gen. John J. Pershing, the ranking American officer in the area, invited Villa and Obregón to El Paso for conversations, an event which once again placed the city on the front pages. There were parades, shouts of "Viva Villa," receptions at the country club, Pershing's home, and Fort Bliss, as well as meetings with local dignitaries. Villa had become the man of the hour in El Paso and the hero of two nations. His relations with Carranza, meanwhile, continued to deteriorate, resulting in a complete break between the two leaders and several months of anarchy in Mexico as the various factions quarreled and fought. Finally, Obregón's forces defeated the *villistas* at Celaya in April 1915 and placed Carranza in an extremely favorable position to assume the executive power.[20]

In the fall of 1915 a series of incidents and developments not only strained relations between the United States and Mexico, but also fanned the flames of racial hatreds and animosities to unprecedented heights along the entire border. One of these was the revelation of the *Plan de San Diego*, a bizarre Mexican scheme calling for the "liberation" of Texas, New Mexico, Arizona, Colorado, and California, followed by the extermination of all Anglo males over the age of sixteen in this area. Angry El Pasoans demanded additional troops at Fort Bliss, rapidly becoming the largest military post in the nation.[21]

Fears of a *huertista* uprising seemed to be confirmed with the appearance in the El Paso area of both Huerta and Orozco. Having been informed of secret meetings between Huerta and German agents, United States officials arrested both Huerta and Orozco for violation of neutrality laws, and they were jailed in El Paso. Orozco escaped, but was killed by a party of ranchers near Sierra Blanca, Texas. To prevent demonstrations, his body was removed from the train before it reached the Union Depot. In view of the tension in El Paso, Huerta was kept under custody at Fort Bliss, but because he was a sick man (dying of cirrhosis of the liver), he was moved to a house at 415 West Boulevard (now West Yandell). There, after surgery, he died on 13 January 1916.[22]

Villa's power and influence declined rapidly after his defeat at the battle of Celaya in April 1915. He still remained hopeful that the cordial relations he had enjoyed with Gen. Hugh L. Scott, now chief of staff of the United States Army, would prejudice the American government in his favor. In a meeting between Villa and Scott in Juárez the previous January, Villa had agreed to cancel an attack on Naco, Sonora, because it might endanger Americans across the border in Arizona. Then in August, the two met again, this time in the home of J. F. Williams on Rio Grande Street. Because Scott was one of the few men that he respected and heeded, Villa agreed to rescind an order to confiscate all foreign-owned mines and smelters in the territory under his control.[23]

By October 1915 President Wilson clearly was leaning toward Carranza. Learning of this development in Ciudad Juárez, a tired and disillusioned Villa gave a *Times* reporter what he termed "the most important interview of my life." "My own forces have recently been diminished," Villa began:

> We haven't the men and money that we once had. All the men who have made money out of our cause have left us, and they have left us because they think no more money is to be made out of it. They have gone to other lands, where they are living upon the profits which they

accumulated by turning the patriots' agony and the widows' and orphans' sorrow into a means of making money. I am here in Juárez, but this is as far as I shall go – north! Mexico is my country. I shall not run away from it. Here I have lived and here I have fought. Here I shall fight and here I shall live. Here maybe I shall die, and that probably soon, but I am content. They may kill me in battle; they may murder me on the highway; they may assassinate me while asleep in my bed, but the cause I have fought for these past twenty-two years will live. It is the cause of liberty; the cause of human freedom; the cause of justice – long delayed and long denied to my suffering countrymen.[24]

Following the recognition of Carranza's government by the United States, the wrath of Pancho Villa found expression in January 1916 in the murder of sixteen American mining engineers by *villistas* near Santa Ysabel, Chihuahua. With the arrival of the caskets, tensions in El Paso rose to the breaking point, resulting in fist fights, violence, and the city's first genuine race riot. Every policeman in the city was sent to Overland Street to control the mob; otherwise, every Mexican in Chihuahuita, Mayor Tom Lea later said, would have been massacred. Local officials and the press pleaded for calm and restraint, and the Chamber of Commerce became extremely apprehensive that the mob activity would give the city a bad reputation. Although the police were able to prevent any further attacks on Mexican-Americans, the atmosphere remained charged, a clear indication that if further trouble occurred, the city might explode again.[25]

More trouble did occur. On 9 March 1916 the *villistas* launched a surprise attack on Columbus, New Mexico, and tensions in El Paso mounted again. This time, however, there were no race riots, since it soon became known that General Pershing had been ordered to pursue Villa into Mexico. This Punitive Expedition, with some 4,000 men, including infantry, cavalry, and field artillery, was the second military intervention in Mexico by the United States within the space of two years. Relations between the two countries again neared the breaking point. Early in May Gen. Hugh Scott and General Obregón, representing the Mexican government, met at the Paso del Norte Hotel and agreed on a plan of gradual withdrawal of American forces. Although President Wilson endorsed the plan, Carranza rejected it, insisting on immediate withdrawal.

The Punitive Expedition therefore remained in Mexico, where skirmishes were fought between American troops and *carrancistas* at Carrizal. Pershing's forces failed to find Villa, and with the growing possibility by late 1916 of American involvement in the war in Europe, American troops were withdrawn in February 1917. Although border conditions gradually returned to normal and tensions eased, traditional racial attitudes had been badly scarred by the events along the border during the Mexican Revolution.[26]

A decade of warfare had left Ciudad Juárez a shambles. "A few years ago," wrote Ernest Peixotto in 1916,

> the city was a thriving enough Mexican town, deriving a rather large if illicit revenue from gambling joints, a cockpit, a bullring, and a jockey club, whose activities would not be tolerated on the American side of the river. But the various revolutions have crippled it sorely. At every turn you come upon ruins – houses riddled with bullet holes or breached with shot and shell; a public library razed to the ground, a mere heap of stones; a post office badly damaged; and opposite the Juárez monument, a brick building, roofless, with gaping walls and windows.[27]

Despite the efforts of the Juárez Chamber of Commerce, business conditions during the next three years failed to improve. On 15 June 1919 Pancho Villa's forces attacked the city for the third time since 1910 and controlled the situation until Gen. James B. Erwin, the commanding officer at Fort Bliss, ordered a force of approximately 3,600, including cavalry, infantry, and artillery, to Ciudad Juárez against the *villistas* on the grounds that American lives and property were in jeopardy. This marked the third United States intervention in Mexico in five years. After twenty-four hours of fighting, the *villistas* were forced to withdraw, and a semblance of order was restored. By that time the first United States Army Border Air Patrol had been established to conduct reconnaissance flights, giving El Pasoans a greater feeling of security than they had known for the past five years.[28]

The stage was thus set for 10,000 El Pasoans to give President-elect Alvaro Obregón an enthusiastic welcome when he visited the city in October 1920. At the banquet given in the Mexican leader's honor, Gov. William P. Hobby of Texas, much to the embarrassment of the Wilson administration, called for the immediate recognition of Obregón's government by the United States, then added:

"I want Mexico and Texas to be pals. In fact, I want them to be the Mutt and Jeff of the Western Hemisphere." In view of the governor's enthusiastic though inappropriate comment, a decade of bitter and bloody border conflict surely had come to a close, at least as far as El Paso and Texas were concerned.[29]

In 1914 hostilities began among the major nations of Europe in a conflict now known as World War I. Involved were the Allied Powers – Great Britain, France, and Russia against the Central Powers, primarily Germany and the Austro-Hungarian Empire. Although officially neutral, the United States remained from the first economically and sentimentally tied to the Allied cause, while stoutly defending the right to trade with belligerent nations. In early 1917 when the military situation favored the Central Powers, the German High Command, convinced that a lightning-like blow would bring the Allies to their knees, on 31 January 1917 proclaimed unrestricted submarine warfare. The result was the breaking of diplomatic relations with Germany by the United States. Shortly after, public opinion throughout the Southwest was brought to a fever pitch when the contents of the so-called Zimmermann telegram revealed that in return for a formal alliance with Germany, Mexico, on the successful conclusion of the war by the Central Powers, would receive back the lands she had lost to the United States in 1848. Anti-German sentiment throughout the Southwest reached an all-time high when on 6 April 1917 the United States declared war against Germany and the Austro-Hungarian Empire.[30]

Fort Bliss contributed significantly to the national effort, serving as a depot post for enlistments, and as a training post for both infantry and cavalry officers. A number of units trained at the post saw action in France. As might be expected of a city with a strong military tradition, El Paso rallied to the colors, registered more than 9,000 for the draft, and supported Liberty Bond drives. On the other hand, the transition from anti-Mexican hysteria during the Mexican Revolution to anti-German hysteria, writes Shawn Lay, a local historian, came with remarkable ease. The local press commented on the un-Americanism of persons of German ancestry, vehemently denounced the Hohenzollerns, and featured cartoons depicting the Kaiser gorging himself on ox-horns full of blood. The German language instructor at the local high school found that his contract had been canceled. A Home Defense League, organized to keep watch on the loyalty and patriotism of the local citizenry, as time went by took on the character of a vigilante organization.[31]

With the entry of the United States into the war El Paso officials eagerly anticipated the expansion of Fort Bliss to include a cantonment, or division training center, and wasted no time in calculating the economic impact. They had not reckoned, however, with Newton D. Baker, the secretary of war, whose abhorrence of the presence of liquor and prostitution near military posts knew no bounds. Baker was convinced that both evils were readily available at the Pass of the North. El Paso reformers supported his position, of course, and thus the exigencies of war, as historian Christian has noted, gave the city the alternative of forsaking its traditional lenient attitude toward pleasures of the palate and the flesh or running the risk of losing its military endowment. But all hopes of a cantonment were dashed when Secretary of War Baker announced on 2 June: "El Paso must clean up. I am in receipt of daily reports showing social conditions to which our soldiers are subjected which can no longer be tolerated." Citing illegal sales of alcohol to soldiers and unrestricted prostitution around army camps, Secretary Baker went on to warn that if conditions in El Paso did not improve, the city might find itself without *any* troops.[32]

In response to the secretary's charges, city officials began a crackdown on vice. Local police were sent into the red light district to evict the prostitutes, and it was soon reported that half of them had departed, with the remainder scattered throughout the city and Ciudad Juarez. Even so, the *Times* complained that the efforts to clean up the city were weak and half-hearted, and that many local officials had ties to the bootleggers and prostitutes. When El Pasoans learned that the city might still receive a divisional cantonment of 30,000 men if the cleanup campaign was intensified, additional steps were taken by the city and county against vice. A city ordinance forbade the sale of liquor to soldiers; the county launched an intensive drive against suspect roadhouses; and the city police force formed two special "purity squads" to search for prostitutes in hotels and rooming houses. In March 1918 a special vigilance group known as the Committee of Twenty-Five was formed to aid in the war on vice. Despite many commendations

received by the city during 1918, the desired and promised cantonment never appeared.[33]

In the meantime, the prohibition issue had come to the forefront when the county commissioners voted three to two to hold a
local option election on the prohibition of alcohol on 30 January
1918. Overnight the city split into two camps – the drys, including
the self-proclaimed forces of morality and patriotism supported by
the newspapers and churches; and the wets, including the brewers,
saloon and restaurant owners, Mexican-Americans, and Anglos
who resided in the older parts of the city, many of whom viewed
prohibition as an unwarranted incursion into their private lives.
As a result of the election, the forces of morality and superpatri-
otism were defeated; the city voted down prohibition 2,421 to
2,207, and El Paso County ballots rendered the same verdict by
2,668 to 2,497. El Paso, says Shawn Lay, had opted to the right of
an individual to run his own life as he saw fit. The local option
election had revealed a clear contrast between El Paso's Southwestern traditions and the Southern progressive moralism of the
Wilsonian era.[34]

Although prohibition had been defeated in the local option
election, the reformers were not denied for very long. On 5 March
the state legislature by joint resolution ratified the Eighteenth
Amendment, which prohibited the manufacture and sale of alcoholic beverages within the state, and 15 April was established as
the closing date for saloons in Texas. Additionally, by governor's
decree a ten-mile prohibition zone would be placed around all
military training camps in Texas, in effect making El Paso a dry
city. As the prohibition deadline neared, saloonmen and retail
dealers began selling out their stocks – Zach White, it was reported,
bought the entire stock from the bar at the Paso del Norte Hotel
for home use.[35]

As the closing hour approached on the evening of 15 April
more than two hundred saloons, against a backdrop of conviviality, were feverishly engaged in exhausting all their remaining
stocks, and by midnight the last bottle of American and Scotch
whiskeys had been sold. The Gem, the most famous of El Paso's
bars, had the largest crowd of all, more than eight bartenders and
scores of waiters could take care of, so that at length bottles, mix-
ers, chasers, and beer were placed on the bar and the customers

were allowed to serve themselves. At 10:30 P.M. the lights were
turned off, drinks were downed, the crowd filed out, and barricades were placed over the doors. Officially, at least, El Paso was
"bone dry." The Tenderloin on South Utah Street, where the prostitutes had held forth for three decades or more, was gone, never
to return to its former days of glory.[36]

In October 1918, as Americans eagerly awaited the end of the
war in Europe, they were also combating the ravages of the devas-
tating Spanish influenza, which in time would kill ten times as
many Americans as were killed by German bombs and bullets during the war. People in the larger cities died by the thousands as
the epidemic moved from East to West. By mid-October there were
2,000 cases at Fort Bliss, which had already been placed under a
strict quarantine. The disease invaded Chihuahuita, bringing an
extremely high death rate among the Mexican population, particularly the children, who had already been exposed to an epidemic
of whooping cough. City agencies responded to the medical crisis
in an impressive way, as did the United States Public Health Service, the Red Cross, and the Associated Charities. An emergency
hospital was established at Aoy School, and by November the
disease had been brought under control, but not until the community had registered 600 deaths. On 9 November the ban on
public gatherings was lifted, making it possible for more than 8,000
to witness the 11 November Armistice Day parade.[37]

On 16 January 1919 the Eighteenth Amendment, prohibiting
the manufacture, transportation, and sale of alcoholic beverages,
became the law of the land. A supplementary law, the Volstead
Act, defined an alcoholic beverage as any one containing more
than 0.5 percent of alcohol; all processors and purveyors of alcoholic beverages were to cease operations on 16 January 1920.[38]

Strong opposition to the prohibition legislation continued to
be voiced by those who regarded it as an unjustifiable infringe-
ment on personal liberty, or as an unwarranted invasion of states'
rights by the federal government. On the other hand, others living
on the borders of the United States, in spite of their own objections to the legislation, could perceive the enormous profits to be
made in smuggling illegal liquor from Mexico into the United
States. Opportunists could envision the El Paso-Juárez area as a
major oasis for thirst-stricken Americans – an oasis that would

226

bring in tourist dollars from all over the bone-dry United States. The profits to be made from illegal liquor, tourism, and all the well known diversions offered by a Mexican border city were hard to resist. Thus El Paso, for the next fourteen years, exploited for its own interests a national law which was unenforceable from the day it was enacted.[39]

El Paso business interests and officials had mixed feelings about conditions in the sister city across the river and the degree to which the two communities ought to cooperate as the result of the prohibition legislation. "Juárez is our greatest asset," remarked R. Burt Orndorff, president of the Sheldon Hotel Company, "and we are just beginning to realize it. High class tourists from the East on their way to California stop just to see Juárez. They have the money to spend and they want to find a good time our neighbor across the river can give them – a dinner with liquor and other amusements." On the other hand, about the same time American Consul John W. Dye remarked, "Juárez is the most immoral, degenerate, and utterly wicked place I have ever seen or heard of in my travels. Murder and robbery are everyday occurrences and gambling, dope selling and using, drinking to excess and sexual vices are continuous. It is a Mecca for criminals and degenerates from both sides of the border."[40]

While there was considerable truth in Dye's statements, Ciudad Juárez had a multitude of attractions that would interest the American tourist and benefit the El Paso hotel business – watering holes, gambling tables, race track, bullring, cockfights, dance halls, brothels, honky-tonks, lewd shops, dope parlors, and the like. The city's main street was said to have more saloons than any other street in the world, a bar nearly every twenty feet for six long blocks. The availability of liquor brought in bootleggers from all over the United States. As a result, a countless number of running gun battles occurred between smugglers and United States customs officials. Traffic between the two cities became so heavy two new international bridges had to be built to replace the old ones. From July 1919 to July 1920 more than 400,000 American tourists came through El Paso on their way to Ciudad Juárez.[41]

The cafes, cabarets, and saloons were located on or in the vicinity of 16th of September Street. Most famous were the Central Cafe, the Palace Cafe, Harry Mitchell's Mint Bar and Oasis Cafe, the Crystal Palace, Fred Lacarra's Office Cafe, Jimmie O'Brien's Bar, and the Lobby. They offered cocktails, dinner, dancing to a name orchestra, and a floorshow. By 8:00 P.M. most night spots were so crowded that in many cases the cover charge would be raised from two dollars to five dollars per person. Profits for the owners, substantial at first, were steadily reduced as the result of *mordidas* and taxes demanded by state and local officials, plus the wage demands of labor unions. These factors forced a number of establishments to close their doors. But two of the best known spots — Harry Mitchell's Mint Bar and Severo G. González's Central Cafe — weathered the storm. Their guest books read like a Who's Who of celebrities of the twenties — Jack Dempsey, Jim Jeffries, Eddie Rickenbacker, Amelia Earhart, H. L. Mencken, Will Durant, Richard Byrd, Tommy Armour, Billy Mitchell, and Jimmy Walker, to name a few.[42]

Other attractions awaited the American tourist — carnivals, cockfights, bullfights, and horse racing. A large, open-air sports arena, the Juárez Coliseum, was opened in April 1926. This facility could accommodate prize fights, wrestling matches, dog races, bicycle races, and track meets. On opening day Jack Dempsey drew a crowd of 8,000. That afternoon the Manassa Mauler lived up to his nickname as he knocked out four opponents in succession. The brothels were located along the Calle del Diablo. While most of them did not last long, two establishments — the Green Lantern and Irma's — weathered vice squad raids, reform campaigns, and barroom brawls. Through payoffs to the authorities, the prostitutes received protection under the law, and sold their charms through alliances with gangsters, confidence men, narcotics peddlers, thieves, and taxi drivers.[43]

With regard to gambling, most saloons in Ciudad Juárez maintained slot machines. The issue of wide open legalized gambling in the casinos had a checkered career during the Prohibition era when it became a bone of contention involving Mexican officials at the local, state, and federal levels and El Paso business interests. Mexican politicians might condemn the operations of gambling casinos such as the Tivoli, the largest in Juárez, but the revenues it produced and paid were extremely difficult to resist. Consequently the Tivoli was allowed to remain open during most of the twenties. In April 1929 all gambling houses were closed by presidential decree, but within a year the Great Depression had completely eroded funds in state and municipal treasuries. As a result, the governor of Chihuahua, under tremendous pressure from Juárez gambling interests, coupled with the prospect of an 80,000-peso monthly allocation for the state government and 25,000 pesos monthly for the Juárez municipality, issued the license for the Tivoli to reopen. The proceeds would be used to complete the Juárez-Chihuahua highway. Gambling was thus given another two years of life in Ciudad Juárez, although little progress was made on the highway.[44]

During Prohibition most of the beer and liquor sold to Juárez saloons was manufactured by American firms that had relocated across the border. Fortunes were made by Americans and Mexicans alike, and the beverage interests became increasingly powerful and influential in local, state, and federal politics. Equipment owned by the El Paso Brewing Association was moved across the river, and on 15 January 1922 the Juárez Brewery opened its doors with free beer to five thousand people attending the ceremony. D&M Distilleries was established by Louis J. Morris, a naturalized Mexican citizen, who in time sold the company to an enterprising Spanish immigrant, Julián Gómez. In addition, the Mexican Distilling Company was formed by Wayne Russell of Denver, who moved the equipment of a defunct distillery from Lewisburg, Kentucky, to Ciudad Juárez. Russell's product soon gained a reputation as "poor stuff" because of improper aging, and many surmised that most of it was being shipped illegally to his native Colorado. A third distillery, known as the D&W, was formed from the dormant Waterfill and Frazier Distilling Company of Louisville, Kentucky. In the new location the D&W was managed by the self-educated dynamic businessman, civic leader, and political figure, Antonio J. Bermúdez, who made a fortune selling his Waterfill and Frazier whiskey in Mexico and, according to some, in the United States.[45]

The prohibition amendment proved to be almost completely unworkable and unenforceable from the moment it was enacted. Ciudad Juárez overnight became a convenient haven for the smuggling of illegal liquor into the United States, and gunfire between smugglers and United States customs officials became the pattern. While the bootleggers and smugglers encountered some risks, there were tremendous profits to be made. One hundred cases of bourbon purchased in Juárez at the wholesale price of $25, upon delivery in

St. Louis, Kansas City, Denver, or Dallas would sell for $6,000 and up. In El Paso a major trouble spot was Cordova Island. This 1,200-acre tract was no longer an island but, because of the shifting Rio Grande to the south, became a part of Mexico extending into El Paso but outside the city limits of Juárez. Here in 1927 a saloon, dance hall, and gambling casino known as the Hole in the Wall was built. This made it possible for El Pasoans to step over the sandy boundary line for a few libations. Federal officials were powerless to take any action. Finally, El Pasoans decided they would yield on the 9:00 P.M. bridge closing in favor of a twenty-four-hour open bridge if officials in Mexico City would close the place down. The international bridge was at least subject to some measure of traffic control. The Hole in the Wall was closed in January 1931, and a wire mesh fence was constructed to mark the boundary; even then an El Pasoan could pass a quarter through the fence and receive in return a few swallows of Waterfill and Frazier.[46]

Closely related to the problem of liquor smuggling was the traffic in narcotics. Then, as now, lucrative profits were to be made in morphine, opium, cocaine, heroin, and marijuana in the American market. Attempts to curb the traffic were futile on both sides of the river. From time to time huge bonfires destroyed confiscated narcotics and paraphernalia, but little progress was made since many Juárez officials were being paid to ignore the law. Most of the big dealers continued to elude detection and arrest. Furthermore, there was the perennial problem of the undocumented worker. Hoping to find employment, he crossed alone or with friends. Others came with the help of an agent who offered transportation in exchange for smuggling in liquor and drugs. If the alien was caught with contraband cargo, he was subject to criminal charges; if not, he would be deported. Sooner or later he would be back trying to cross the border again.[47]

While American tourist dollars during Prohibition temporarily stimulated the entertainment industry in Ciudad Juárez, created jobs, produced public improvements, built private fortunes, and enriched public officials, Juárez's traditional dependence on El Paso was intensified. An opportunity was lost when the city failed to take advantage of the infusion of American dollars to broaden its economic base and to develop fundamental private sectors that would liberate its people from the uncertain service economy. The cities on the border, commented a Mexican economist, "it is sad to say and a bitter truth, are not only demexicanized and absolute tributaries of our northern neighbors, they amount to nothing but 'sectors of tolerance' or 'red light districts' for American cities."[48]

A growing and prosperous El Paso entered the 1920s with confidence in the future. The population by 1921 had reached 80,000; industrial production had increased 450 percent since 1909; bank clearings had risen; housing construction was booming; and exports to Mexico had reached a higher level than ever before. A local newspaper editor captured the spirit:

El Paso is ever a delight to the confirmed booster. There are so many things hereabouts that stir enthusiasm — climate, business, past performances, and future prospects. One cannot breathe the air and absorb the sunshine these January days without a desire to indulge in superlatives. Almost any time one picks up a newspaper he will find some new reason for boosting the town.[49]

On the other hand, there was deep concern and growing apprehension that many traditional American values — patriotism, morality, and law and order — had been placed on the defensive and were in serious jeopardy. From the pulpits of El Paso's Protestant churches came admonitions that "the world was going to the devil," that "the automobile was replacing the red light district," that dance halls and movie theaters were "cesspools of El Paso," and that those who used tobacco "by their example and influence were sending others to hell." Everywhere, said the preachers, irresistible temptations and invitations to damnation were eating at the roots of the American fabric, its values, and its traditions. Such was the mood, the temperament, and the concern on the part of many El Pasoans at the time of the arrival of the Ku Klux Klan.[50]

By the late summer of 1921 a local chapter of the Klan had been organized and was actively attempting to recruit prominent men in the community. Although opposition came from the newspapers, particularly the *Times*, and from city officials, El Pasoans failed to present a solid front. The Klan, as a result, could boast of three hundred members by September. In public statements it insisted that it was neither racist nor intolerant, but was composed of "decent, respectable American citizens from practically every walk of life," whose sole purpose was "to make El Paso a better and

cleaner city, a better place in which to live and rear our children."
The statements, signed "Frontier Klan No. 100, Knights of the Ku
Klux Klan," were affixed with a Klan seal. Next, the Klan launched
a vocal offensive against prostitution, automobile thefts, burglaries
of private residences, and violations of the law. Efforts to enlist the
support of Protestant ministers resulted in at least some degree of
success, and greatly intensified religious tensions throughout the
community.[51]

The Klan's first entry into the local political scene was a clever
move that involved an extremely controversial issue – the public
schools. For years a major complaint of Anglos was that the Mexican population contributed thousands of children but little tax
money to support the system. There was also deep-seated concern,
particularly among the Protestant clergy, that the Roman Catholic
Church was trying to gain control of the public schools. In January
1922 S. J. Isaacks, a well-known attorney, announced for a position
on the school board; he was soon joined on a three-man ticket by
Charles S. Ward and Dr. J. Hal Gambrell, both incumbents. The
ticket favored more money for the schools, which it said the city
machine had neglected. Not so well publicized was the fact that all
three men on the ticket were members of Frontier Klan No. 100.
Supporting them was the Good Government League, a group of
concerned citizens, many of whom were Klan members.[52]

A second ticket was announced in March, composed of William
H. Burges, Ulysses S. Stewart, and Dr. James B. Brady, all prominent longtime El Pasoans. The campaign became increasingly nasty
and noisy, with charges and countercharges between the league
and city officials, who backed the Burges ticket. The two major
newspapers attacked each other, with the *Herald* supporting Ward,
Isaacks, and Gambrell. The Klan became increasingly active and
eagerly exploited every opportunity to impress the public with its
growing membership.[53]

On the evening of 10 March three *Herald* reporters were invited to witness an initiation, held west of the city near Kern
Place. More than one thousand Klansmen gathered in white hoods
and robes and some three hundred men were to be initiated. The
ceremony featured one large bonfire and numerous smaller fires
about which smaller groups clustered. The new members were admitted into a large circle of costumed Klansmen, as five new fires

flared up with the igniting of cactus plants with kerosene. The greatest secrecy was maintained. The newsmen were kept under heavy guard, license plates were covered, incoming roads were guarded, and whistles and flashlights were used as secret signals. After the ceremony a wooden cross on Mount Franklin was ignited. Then, with the school board campaign heating up, Klan fires blazed again on Mount Franklin on two successive nights.[54]

In an unprecedented turnout, in what one city official termed "the bitterest school election he had ever seen," the Ward, Isaacks, Gambrell ticket prevailed, all three receiving a thousand more votes than any of their opponents. An imposing coalition of recent Anglo arrivals, organized labor, and old-time reformers, writes Shawn Lay, had emerged victorious. For the first time "progressivism," albeit of a definitely intolerant cast, had triumphed at the Pass.[55]

By May 1922, as the result of a resignation of one of the seven members of the school board and his replacement with a Klansman recommended by S. J. Isaacks, the Invisible Empire's domination of the board was complete. True to their campaign promises, the new members voted numerous improvements for the schools, secured a record appropriation for the school system, and renamed some proposed and existing schools after Texas heroes — Bowie, Austin, Crockett, Burleson, Fannin, and Rusk. But changing the name of El Paso High School to Sam Houston High School generated so much opposition that the matter was dropped. The removal of three women principals, all of them Catholics, naturally caused a storm of protest, but when a motion to reconsider received five negative votes, the *Times* perceived that the Klan had "seized the schools."[56]

The results of the elections in the state Democratic primary in July indicated that the Klan in El Paso still had plenty of political clout. Its candidates won seven of fifteen races for county offices, including county school superintendent. Here Lillian Huggett, a high school teacher and daughter of the Reverend William D. Huggett of the Highland Park Methodist Church, won an impressive victory over Frances Culligan, one of the fired Catholic principals. Fully convinced that the Klan was making a serious effort to take over the city, the *Times* denounced the organization and its activities in a blistering editorial. "The eleven months since the Klan announced its existence," the *Times* began, "cover the worst period in all El Paso's history." It continued:

The old El Paso spirit of enterprise, cooperation and neigh-
borly good will, the spirit that built on the sun-baked desert
a mighty city, has been well nigh strangled. Religious intol-
erance, hate, suspicion and anger have entered into every
civic activity, from the deliberations of the Chamber of
Commerce to the political primary.[57]

In October a major assault on the Klan and its secrecy was
made by William H. Fryer, former county attorney, prominent
Catholic layman, and a bitter personal enemy of S. J. Isaacks. In
a deposition Fryer submitted to the Sixty-fifth District Court, the
question was asked whether any of twenty-three names listed had
ever attended a meeting of Frontier Klan No. 100. This strategy
exposed many of the organization's most influential members, and
Klan membership became a liability. Mass resignations resulted
and the recruitment of new members became increasingly difficult.
The former enthusiasm of the Protestant ministers for the organization was dwindling. Such was the situation as the city prepared
for its Democratic primary of February 1923.[58]

The race for mayor matched Preston E. Gardner and four
aldermanic candidates, all members of Frontier Klan No. 100,
against State Sen. Richard M. Dudley and an aldermanic ticket,
none of whom were Klansmen, although one was a former member. The issue in the primary was clean cut – pro-Klan versus anti-
Klan. Everyone expected the balloting to be close; however,
Dudley polled 7,572 votes, while Gardner received 5,752. Two
KKK aldermanic candidates who had qualified for runoffs withdrew
their names. As the *Times* commented, Dudley's triumph had been
"a victory for the old El Paso spirit." Other defeats came in rapid
succession as the Klan lost in a school board election, a city
general election, and a bond issue for street improvements. By the
summer of 1924 Frontier Klan No. 100 had ceased to be a significant influence within either the political or the social life of El
Paso. Its tactics – threats, intimidation, and secrecy – had been
soundly beaten at the ballot box.[59]

In sum, the Klan became a force in El Paso because of the appeal of its program of Americanism, Protestant solidarity, social
morality, and law enforcement – solid values offered in response to
the social tensions produced by the Mexican Revolution, the patriotic fervor of World War I, the morality of Wilsonian Southern

Progressivism, and the problems of enforcing the Prohibition Amendment. Even so, with the exception of the Klan's control of the school board for a while, its influence in El Paso was slight because this was an atypical Texas community. El Paso was isolated, semifrontier, middle class, bicultural, quite unlike the cities of the eastern part of the state with their powerful elites where the Klan made great gains. In El Paso it remained a fringe group, maintained a low profile, and never resorted to the violence that characterized the East Texas Klans. As Shawn Lay notes in his excellent study of the Klan, "it was precisely *because* the Pass was heavily Hispanic and Roman Catholic that residents, including a majority of Protestants, rejected the KKK. In a city that was socially and economically dependent on peaceful coexistence, moderation and common sense prevailed."[60]

By 1925 the city of El Paso had reached a population of 100,000, and most of the community leaders were convinced that the city had a great future. In 1923 a city planning commission was established by ordinance to make growth projections and guidelines so that future development could be charted in an orderly and systematic manner. Employed as consulting plan engineer and landscape architect was German-born George E. Kessler, who brought an outstanding international reputation and forty years of experience as consultant in a number of American cities, particularly Kansas City, Missouri, where had he worked for twenty-five years.[61]

Kessler, engaged as consultant to the newly created Plan Commission, died before he completed his report, but by that time all the maps had been drawn and the commission was well acquainted with his basic ideas. The highest priorities were placed on thoroughfares, the area west of the mountain, Rim Road, parks and recreational facilities, an international highway and bridge, the riverfront, and a civic center. Chihuahuita, which had been described in a 1915 housing report as having conditions as "crude, beastly, and primitive" as could be found anywhere in the United States, was to be transformed into a "section of exotic charm and special interest to visitors and residents." Recommendations for the more distant future included a museum and art gallery, a mountain playground with trails, picnic grounds, summer cottages, a hotel, and a sanatorium. Finally, in the development of the border, close cooperation with Ciudad Juárez was recommended.[62]

By 1925 the commission could point to several accomplishments and improvements: Memorial Park, with its swimming pool,
tennis courts, and flower gardens; Rim Road and the connection
between Kern Place and Scenic Drive; Washington Park with its
zoo, tennis courts, swimming pool, and Dudley Field for baseball;
and the widening of Alameda Street. The new street names near
Memorial Park – Federal, Gold, Silver, and Copper – served as
reminders that the area was built on the site of the old Federal
Copper Smelter. Much of what the Kessler Plan had recommended
remained to be done, but at least city officials, vitally concerned
about development, had a blueprint for the future.[63]

Economic growth continued during the 1920s, although El
Paso's population figure leveled off after 1925. Its importance as a
transportation center was well established with its major rail lines,
including three transcontinental east-west lines and the sixteen
passenger trains that stopped in El Paso daily. In addition, eighteen motor truck lines and four motor coach lines operated out of
El Paso, as well as six airlines utilizing the facilities at Municipal
Airport, completed in 1928. The city could continue to boast that
it had the world's largest custom smelter, and by 1929 a copper
refinery and two oil refineries had been built. Natural gas, as the
result of the organization of El Paso Natural Gas Company, was
flowing from Jal, New Mexico, to El Paso through a sixteen-inch
pipeline. More than two hundred manufacturing enterprises were
in operation, involving lumber mills, cement plants, metal working, textiles, meat packing, leather goods, and food and beverages.
Downtown construction continued in the late 1920s with the completion of the Orndorff Hotel in 1926 (later named the Hussman
and now the Cortez), as well as the Hilton Hotel in 1930 (now the
Plaza), built on the site of the old Sheldon Hotel, the victim of a
fire in 1929. Also completed in 1930 were Bassett Tower and the
Plaza Theatre. The El Paso Chamber of Commerce was quick to
point out to potential investors the opportunities the community
had to offer.[64]

During the 1920s the growing, prosperous city experienced,
like the rest of the nation, the dramatic social changes produced
by the automobile, the liberation of the American woman, the
motion picture industry, and the problems of enforcement of the
prohibition amendment. In a significant retreat from the idealism

and moral reform of the World War I period, the 1920s ushered in the age of the "flivver, the flapper, booze, and the blues." By 1921 nearly 10,000 motor vehicles were driven on the streets of El Paso, and already hundreds of young people had discovered that the open touring car was a convenient contraption for a drive to the movies to see one of Hollywood's latest featured vampires in action, or for engaging in a little sparking on Scenic Drive on a moonlight night, or for taking a "joy-ride" across the river.[65]

The enactment of the Nineteenth Amendment, which gave women the right to vote, sparked a movement that emancipated them from traditional domestic chores and produced an assertive, determined, independent type known as the "flapper." She introduced a new fashion style featuring bobbed hair, dangling earrings and beads, rolled hose, and a hemline above the knee. Taking advantage of her newly found freedom, she joined the Charleston craze, smoked in public, and frequented the night spots in Ciudad Juárez all against a backdrop of clinking glasses, clanking slot machines, and a honky-tonk piano. Not all young women in El Paso copied the flapper style, and not all young men in the city got drunk in Juárez and contracted social disease; nevertheless, the flapper behavior was shocking to the middle and older generations. To those preoccupied with moral values, life had never been so fraught with peril.[66]

As for prevailing social trends, the Hollywood influence offered little hope. Best known of El Paso's movie houses, several of which also featured vaudeville shows, were the Texas Grand, the Crawford, the Grecian, the Alhambra, the Unique, the American, the Bijou, and the Wigwam, all located downtown. Here El Paso audiences could view Rudolph Valentino, Clara Bow, Mary Pickford, Charlie Chaplin, Fatty Arbuckle, and a host of others. On one occasion the Wigwam offered a double feature of *A Vampire's Wiles* and *The Tiger Girl*, which carried the caption – "The Story of a Man Who Listened to a Siren's Song." Gradually, the "talkies" replaced the "silents," and in 1930 the Plaza Theatre, the grandest of them all, was opened to the public.[67]

By that time El Pasoans had been exposed to a new form of entertainment – radio. The pioneer was Station KTSM, which came on the air 22 August 1929. Its first broadcasts originated from the basement of Tri-State Music Company on El Paso Street, explaining the call letters. Soon afterward, the community began to feel the effects of the Great Depression, so that a second radio station was not begun until a decade later.[68]

The stock market crash on Wall Street in October 1929 plunged the nation into the worst economic depression in its history. By 1930 a pattern was well established of business and banking failures, foreclosures on farms and homes, production cutbacks, and personnel layoffs. Although the Hilton Hotel and Bassett Tower were completed in 1930, no new structures of this size would be built for more than two decades. The *El Paso Herald* in 1931 was sold to the *Post* and became the *El Paso Herald-Post*. The First National Bank closed its doors in 1931, and the State National Bank experienced a run but managed to weather the storm. Wages dropped 60 percent, unemployment soared to 25 percent of the labor force, and cotton sold for five cents a pound. Mexican-Americans competed with Anglos for jobs and were often blamed for draining public welfare funds and services. Thousands who were laid off and turned down by the welfare agencies were forced to return to their homeland. These *repatriados* served to intensify the unemployment problem in Ciudad Juárez, already soaring due to the reduction of American tourist dollars. Mexican commuters in many instances were harassed and intimidated at the bridge, and great pressure was placed on Juárez officials to close the bridge at an earlier hour to reduce American spending across the river.[69]

On the other hand, a whole generation of young El Pasoans grew up during the depression without even knowing that times were all that bad. They could not get jobs, did not have much money to spend, and had to wear their clothes and shoes a little longer than usual. Yet they never seemed to have been bothered greatly by the hard times. A gallon of gas could be bought for a dime, which was also the price of a malt, soda, or hamburger. Three bottles of 3.2 beer, which became legal in 1933, cost a quarter. Miniature golf, dance marathons, pinball machines, movies, or swims in a public pool did not cost much, and records and a radio playing the swing and sweet music of the big bands were more than ample for any house party. The first Sun Bowl game was played in 1935, the nucleus for one of El Paso's great annual events—the Sun Carnival; and the second radio station, KROD, came on the air in 1940.[70]

In the presidential election of 1932 the Democrats nominated Franklin D. Roosevelt, governor of New York, who promised a New Deal and effective measures to combat the depression. A vote for Herbert Hoover and the Republicans, the Democrats insisted, was a vote for the continuation of hard times. The Democrats won by a landslide, and with their substantial majority in both houses of Congress, relief and recovery legislation was soon forthcoming. The legalization of 3.2 beer was a stopgap measure until the Eighteenth Amendment could be repealed. The alphabet worked overtime, as the New Deal erected a bewildering number of federal agencies and programs—AAA, PWA, WPA, NRA—to stimulate the economy and put people back to work. Ciudad Juárez, on the other hand, already enduring hardships, was dealt another blow with the repeal of Prohibition.[71]

During the 1920s Fort Bliss underwent a program of expansion, a decision reached by national leaders who were convinced of its great strategic importance. In 1925 a congressional appropriation provided for the establishment of Biggs Field, the Castner Range, and William Beaumont Hospital. The post's cavalry presence was continued in the belief that it was the most practical and effective arm for the patrol of the border. Already the First Cavalry Division had been organized in 1921 with its familiar black and gold shoulder insignia, designed by Gladys Dorcy, the wife of the commander of the Seventh Cavalry Regiment. Since those days the post's economic impact on El Paso has continued to be considerable, and the close relationship between post and city has become a tradition. Many El Pasoans hold fond memories of the dances, the polo matches, and the social relationships between the post's young officers and the daughters of the city's prominent families that have maintained El Paso's "mother-in-law of the army" tradition.[72]

El Pasoans were given another opportunity to witness a Mexican revolution in 1929 when Gen. José Gonzalo Escobar led rebel forces in protest against an attempt by Provisional Pres. Emilio Portes Gil and former Pres. Plutarco Elías Calles to impose their man, Pascual Ortiz Rubio, as successor. While rebel troops came up from the south in preparation for an attack on Ciudad Juárez, the First Cavalry Division, under the command of Gen. George Moseley, put up sandbag barricades near the bridges to defend

American soil if necessary. Once again, as in the old Madero-Villa days, El Pasoans climbed on their rooftops to view the action. The battle for Juárez lasted a day, with General Moseley going to Juárez to negotiate a settlement that left the rebel forces of General Escobar in control of the city. During the next few weeks the movement began to deteriorate. With the capture of Nogales by Federal forces, peace was restored, leaving a legacy of distrust of the United States in Mexico for having interfered with its internal affairs.[73]

In 1938, after five years of extraordinary effort, the monument Cristo Rey (Christ the King), generally regarded as El Paso's most imposing work of art, was completed. It stands on the summit of Sierra de Cristo Rey, formerly Sierra de Muleros (Mountain of the Muleteers) three miles from downtown El Paso in New Mexico where the three states of Texas, New Mexico, and Chihuahua come together. The peak is 4,675 feet above sea level, and the statue of Christ is twenty-seven feet high, one foot higher than the Christ of the Andes between Argentina and Chile. Resting on a 33.5-foot-high cross on a 9-foot base, the entire monument is made of Cordova cream limestone quarried near Austin. The trail winding up the mountain is 5,650 feet long, and along the way are fourteen stations representing the Way of the Cross. The annual pilgrimage is held on the last Sunday of October, the Feast of Christ the King, and the ascent takes two hours.[74]

The monument was the inspiration in 1933 of the Reverend Lourdes F. Costa, for twenty years pastor of the parish in Smeltertown. At length the project received the enthusiastic approval of the bishop of the El Paso Diocese. By 1937 funds had been raised, and Urbici Soler, internationally known sculptor, was engaged to carve the monument. The massive limestone blocks had to be moved up the mountain, and the carving was done on a scaffold with an air chisel. An assistant was stationed far below to help Soler achieve the proper proportions of head, face, and figure. After twelve months of his intermittent toil during storms, lightning, wind, and blazing sun, the monument was completed. Soler did his work well, for his statue of Christ, as one appreciative author has noted, looks as eternal as the peak. Soler remained in El Paso, and for several years taught art courses at the College of Mines.[75]

By the late 1930s war clouds once again dominated the European horizon. Using threats, bluff, and pressure, Adolph Hitler, dictator of Germany, absorbed Austria and Czechoslovakia, and invaded Poland in September 1939, the beginning of World War II. In the Far East, Japan had invaded China in an undeclared war. The Roosevelt administration policy of aiding Britain and China met with considerable opposition in the United States, but the Japanese attack on Pearl Harbor on 7 December 1941 united a nation that had been badly divided for more than a year.[76]

Fort Bliss was an immense facility when the United States entered World War II in late 1941. Its original 1,200 acres had increased to 436,000 acres, making it the third largest post in the country. The First Cavalry Division had an active strength of 4,400, and in addition there were five National Guard units, inducted into federal service in 1940. One of these was the 200th Coast Artillery Regiment (AA) from New Mexico, which was sent to the Philippines in September 1941. It made a heroic but futile defense of Clark Field when the Japanese attacked. After this action the unit was divided and the 515th Coast Artillery Regiment (AA) was created. After fighting in the final defense of Bataan, its survivors endured the famous Death March to Camp O'Donnell.[77]

When the First Cavalry Division received orders in February 1943 assigning it to the Pacific Theater, it turned in its horses and horse equipment, bringing a glorious chapter of American military history to an end. One El Paso veteran some years later described it vividly: "For it was we, the 1st Cavalry Division, who hardly more than ten years ago, here at nearby Fort Bliss saddled up for the last time; and as we unsaddled and unlimbered the limbers, an era came to an end—the horse was gone."[78]

The First Cavalry Division fought in the Admiralties, at Leyte Gulf, and at Manila, suffering heavy casualties in each of these actions, and participated in the occupation of Japan after the war. "No greater record," said Gen. Douglas MacArthur, "has emerged from the war than that of the 1st Cavalry Division." In the meantime, Fort Bliss had become an antiaircraft artillery installation. In 1944 the Anti-Aircraft Artillery School and Anti-Artillery Board were moved from North Carolina to the post, making it the nation's primary center for this type of weaponry.[79]

During World War II Ciudad Juárez, which had suffered considerable economic hardships as a result of the depression and the repeal of Prohibition, experienced some degree of recovery.

Wartime conditions in the United States generated a considerable demand, particularly along the border, for Mexican raw materials, goods, and workers. Juárez tourism received an enormous boost as the city became a mecca for 25,000 or more soldiers at Fort Bliss lured by the availability of mixed drinks and the diversions offered by the night life. As the result of a massive migration from the interior, Juárez's population during the war doubled from about 49,000 in 1940 to 122,000 in 1950, approaching that of El Paso. The Bracero Program, a contract labor agreement initiated by the United States and Mexico in 1942, brought in Mexicans at the rate of 2,000 a month to work the cotton fields in the El Paso area. An estimated two-thirds of the *repatriados* of the depression period then returned to the United States. The Bracero Program stimulated Mexican immigration during the 1940s, both legal and illegal, so that the Mexican population in El Paso represented 45 percent of the total figure. By 1950 almost three-fourths of the Mexican population of El Paso was native-born.[80]

In the gray dawn of 16 July 1945, early risers in El Paso watched the northern sky explode in brilliant white light as the world's first atomic bomb was detonated in a remote section of what came to be White Sands Missile Range, some fifty miles northwest of Alamogordo, New Mexico. The story is told that a rancher went to visit his sheep camp in the San Andrés Mountains in New Mexico. Despite a mountain rainstorm, his sheepherders had started out before dawn that morning. They had not gone far when they saw a terrific flash at the other side of the eighty-mile sweep of prairies. They ran back to the sheep camp, shaken and terrified, and cried to their *patrón*, "The sun has exploded, señor. We saw it. It was so bright that we fell on our knees and our sheep stampeded. Take us back to our families and let us go into the church. It is the end of the world."[81]

Three weeks later atomic bombs obliterated Hiroshima and Nagasaki, Japan, and ushered in the Atomic Age with its awesome scientific developments that have placed a sword of Damocles over the entire human race. The end of World War II came shortly afterward with the surrender of the Japanese Empire in September 1945. For the first time in six years the world was at peace.[82]

The Southwest Metropolis Since 1945

T H E years following World War II marked an era of spectacular growth for the city at the Pass of the North. From a population figure that had fallen below 100,000 in the 1930s, El Paso grew to 130,485 in 1950, 276,000 in 1960, 332,000 in 1970, and 425,000 in 1980. During that time its physical size increased from 29 to 240 square miles, largely as a result of the annexation of the Upper and Lower valleys in the 1950s. By 1980 it was the major metropolitan center of West Texas, and the largest American city on the United States-Mexican border.[1]

After development and construction had been stunted for the past fifteen years, by 1945 the city was in an expansive mood. Yet because of growing pains after World War II, it encountered special problems

*Fort Bliss, originally a tiny cavalry post, is now a
major antiaircraft training center for military personnel
of the Free World. (Courtesy Alfred Gutierrez)*

as the result of geographical location, limited water resources, the
international boundary, and the ethnic composition of the population. What followed, as Patricia Reschenthaler has pointed out in
her study of postwar conditions in El Paso, was a critical era of readjustment in moving from the status of a sprawling, growing town
to a position among the fifty largest cities in the United States.[2]

Playing a dominant role in El Paso's development in the postwar period was Fort Bliss. Historically, it had been a significant
stimulant to the El Paso economy, but its contribution following
the close of World War II would be even greater. During the war
years it had undergone a major transition from cavalry post to anti-
aircraft artillery center. This mission was furthered when in 1946,
a team of German rocket specialists including the renowned
Werner von Braun was brought to Fort Bliss to work on rocket
and missile development. The following year it was designated the
Anti-Aircraft Artillery and Guided Missile Center. By that time
the post covered more than one million acres, had 25,000 military
personnel in training, more than a thousand civilian employees,

and a payroll of $13.5 million per year. An estimated 60 to 70 percent of the money expended by the post and its personnel ended up, either directly or indirectly, in the cash registers of El Paso merchants. Unquestionably, Fort Bliss had become El Paso's largest industry, the updating and expansion of its activities having done more than anything else to assure the future growth of the city.[3]

Most of the older established industries experienced significant growth in the postwar period. The one exception was the cattle business, which was hit by a serious drought and by a quarantine on Mexican beef as a result of hoof and mouth disease. Once this problem was brought under control, regional cattle sales recovered and were bringing in $150 million a year by the early fifties. The cotton industry prospered as 2,000 bales of long-staple cotton were produced annually, selling for about $300 a bale, while the shorter-staple cotton sold for more than $160 a bale. By 1950 cotton production was valued at more than $16 million a year.[4]

The two large copper smelters, Phelps Dodge Company and American Smelting and Refining Company, produced 29 percent of the nation's refined copper besides processing some lead and zinc ores. In response to the vociferous complaints that American Smelting and Refining Company (then known as AS&R and later as ASARCO) was polluting the air, it built a smokestack 612 feet high, and later a second one 828 feet high, at that time the world's tallest, and gave assurances that the sulphur fumes it produced had been brought under control. The three oil refineries processed 23,000 barrels of petroleum daily, and El Paso Natural Gas Company by 1950 had become the largest natural gas transporter in the United States. By that time El Paso had two hundred factories, significant increases in bank deposits and foreign exports, and a tourist trade amounting to $25 million per year. The Bureau of Business Research at The University of Texas in Austin in 1949 confidently forecast a prosperous decade for El Paso.[5]

During the war, in order to ease the manpower shortage, the United States signed an agreement with Mexico establishing the Bracero Program which permitted Mexican laborers, on securing identification cards from American immigration officials, to work on the cotton farms in the Lower Valley. Although thousands complied with the procedure, the program became a catalyst for the entry into the United States of thousands of illegal aliens, or *mojados* (wetbacks), Mexicans who waded across the shallow Rio Grande at night. The Mexican government complained bitterly about the low pay the braceros received – $1.50 for a hundred pounds of cotton picked – and the program came to a halt in 1947.[6]

In the following year, because of the desperate need for cotton pickers, the United States Immigration Service permitted Mexican workers to enter so that they could then be arrested and paroled to the Texas Employment Commission, which assigned them to the cotton fields. The "wetback invasion" began, and within a month 20,000 had entered. The Mexican government responded by stationing troops on the international bridges in an effort to stop the crossings. Finally in 1949 a new agreement was signed prohibiting the recruitment of Mexican workers in border cities, limiting to six months the length of labor contracts, and providing for additional protection of the workers.[7]

The spirit of the agreement was not respected, however, and violations of the law continued. Local politicians and officials ignored the law, trained Border Patrol personnel were lacking, and the area to be policed was too large. Alien laborers infiltrated a number of El Paso industries, particularly the building trades, the cement plant, textile manufacturing, the smelters, refineries, and the hotels and restaurants. Wages were depressed to deprivation levels, much to the annoyance of the local labor unions and the Mexican government. At length, the Eisenhower administration launched "Operation Wetback." This massive deportation drive rounded up 35,000 illegal aliens in El Paso in one week in July 1954. Although the Bracero Program remained in effect until 1964, there were repeated violations. The problem of the illegal, or undocumented immigrant, had become a major issue in United States-Mexican relations, and so it has remained to the present day.[8]

Postwar El Paso was characterized by an acute housing shortage because of the limited construction that had taken place over a period of fifteen years. Half of the existing houses were substandard and/or in need of repairs. The deplorable problem of slum conditions still remained, aggravated by the tremendous influx of Mexican immigrant workers. In June 1945 the *El Paso Herald-Post* called attention to conditions in Smeltertown to the northwest of the downtown area adjacent to the smelter – a cluster of small adobe shacks huddled together; they had dirt floors, garbage piles, and windows without screens or glass. A short time later the slums in South El Paso, known as Chihuahuita, were described in two articles, one by Carey McWilliams in the *Nation* in July 1948, and the second by George S. Perry in the 4 February 1950 issue of the *Saturday Evening Post*. In harsh terms both pointed to the adobe huts with eight people to a room, an appalling lack of bathtubs, showers, toilets, and faucets, and the incidence of disease and death among the children. While most of the blame was placed on the landlords, the public came in for its share of criticism for permitting such conditions to prevail. City officials could no longer ignore South El Paso, and in 1949 built two large federally financed housing projects to replace some of the slums. They routed Paisano Drive, the new express highway connecting the Upper and Lower valleys, so as to eliminate some of the slums of South El Paso. Even so, much remained to be done.[9]

The first major construction project of the postwar period was the depression of the Southern Pacific tracks. For more than sixty years these tracks had split the city up the middle and snarled automobile traffic in the downtown and Five Points areas. Leadership for the project was provided by Mayor Dan Duke, a railroad engineer, who loved to talk of the city's democratic spirit which lifted him "from the deck of a locomotive to the highest office in the voters' power to give." The project, officially called Bataan Memorial Trainway, was completed in 1950 at a cost of $5.5 million, split three ways among the city, the railroads, and the state highway department.[10]

Residential sections had remained as they were in the 1930s. On the west side, the Mesita Addition marked the outer limits of the city, with nothing but cactus, greasewood, and rattlesnakes along North Mesa to the Crossroads; in the northeast, construction had reached Fort Bliss; to the east, the area just beyond the present North-South Freeway marked the city limits. In spite of the conviction of many old timers that the city was already overbuilt, the need for new housing was critical. The first new suburban development, begun in 1946, was Loretto Addition and Shopping Center, built on forty acres of sandhills south of Montana, twenty acres more than the developers thought they could use. A pioneer project, it eliminated alleys and set an example for dozens of others to follow in the 1950s. The results far exceeded the most optimistic predictions, and two additional Loretto projects were shortly completed. The city was on the threshold of a period of spectacular development.[11]

The decade of the 1950s marked the period of El Paso's greatest growth and expansion thus far. Thousands of Americans every year decided to escape from the dreary winters of the Snow-belt sections of the country in favor of the sunshine, mild climate, and economic opportunities to be found in the American South-west. While a number of El Paso's traditional economic activities such as transportation, trade, oil refining, natural gas, construction materials, metal working, real estate, finance, and tourism con-tinued to contribute to its growth, several significant changes took place in the period after 1950. For one thing, the military popula-tion increased by 33 percent, and the armed services became a much larger single employer in the area, a reflection of Cold War tensions and strained relations between the United States and the Soviet Union. Substantial increases were made in the employment sector in public utilities, government, retail sales, services, and manufacturing, particularly in the apparel and leather industries, as Farah and Tony Lama products became famous all over the country. On the other hand, a noticeable decline occurred in El Paso's age-old mining, smelter, and railroad activities, which had contributed so dramatically to the city's economy in former days.[12]

The first major change in the downtown skyline in twenty-five years came with the completion of the El Paso Natural Gas Com-pany's eighteen-story building in 1955. It was followed by El Paso National Bank (now Texas Commerce Bank) with its new building in 1962, the Southwest National Bank (now First City Bank) in 1964, and the State National Bank (now MBank) in 1971. Major arterial projects completed by that time included the Cordova Bridge (now Bridge of the Americas), Interstate 10 east-west from county line to county line, and Transmountain Road, a marvel of engineering one mile above sea level and the deepest cut ever made by the Texas Highway Department.[13]

Other signs of growth in the fifties were a new public library, new hospital facilities for Providence Memorial, Hotel Dieu, and Thomason General, new quarters for the El Paso Museum of Art

Woodrow Bean Transmountain Road, completed in 1970, cuts through the Franklin Mountains and is 5,250 feet above sea level at its highest point. (Courtesy Darst-Ireland Photography)

in the historic Turney home on Montana Street, three television studios, and a 30,000-seat Sun Bowl, later expanded to 52,000. By 1949 the College of Mines had an enrollment of about 2,000 students. That same year, reflecting the fact that the school had grown in enrollment, course offerings, and degree programs oriented toward the liberal arts, its name was changed to Texas Western College, though not without considerable opposition from the engineers, both faculty and students. Taking appropriate note of the city's growth, the local newspapers in special editions in 1956 marked their seventy-fifth anniversaries. The *Times'* fifteen sections and 240 pages was the largest edition in the newspaper's history.[14]

The administration of Mayor Hervey was interested in the possibility of a combined city-county government, and therefore saw the need for annexing land adjacent to the city. The drilling of nine water wells in the Upper Valley in 1952 quickly produced plans from the administration to annex a huge tract of land as far north as the Texas-New Mexico line. In April 1954 the city council annexed twenty-eight square miles and thus laid the foundations for the building of Coronado Shopping Center, the Coronado Country Club, and eight residential subdivisions on the west side during the 1950s. An equal number of subdivisions was built to the northeast, including Mountain Park, the innovative area that featured a blending of the streets and homes with the desert and mountain. In addition, half a dozen subdivisions were built to the east.[15]

By the time the Hervey administration had annexed the Upper Valley, it had already begun to look in the direction of the Lower Valley with its 40,000 residents. In 1952 Ascarate was annexed, but plans for annexing Ysleta encountered strong opposition. Fearing city taxes and zoning which would restrict their rural activities, the residents of Ysleta made known their determination to remain independent. In November 1954 the city council passed a resolution annexing Ysleta. This included an offer to cut city services in half, permit farm zoning, and maintain local bus line franchises. Even so, the Ysleta residents publicly denounced the city officials, labeled Hervey another Hitler, and voted overwhelmingly on 13 March 1955 in favor of incorporation. Two days later, however, the city council ignored Ysleta's action and gave the annexation ordinance final approval. In June the Sixty-fifth District Court judge struck down Ysleta's incorporation action, and El Paso gained forty-four square miles and 40,000 disappointed new citizens. With the building of half a dozen new subdivisions in the Lower Valley, the size and shape of the El Paso community had begun to approach its present form.[16]

In South El Paso, or the Segundo Barrio, the appalling conditions continued to stifle progress. In the 1950s there were still more than 12,000 substandard dwelling units in the area, an average of seven families per toilet, with an average of ten persons per family. Focused here were 70 percent of the city's welfare cases, 50 percent of adult crime, 88 percent of juvenile crime, and 67 percent of infant mortality. From time to time some of South El Paso's families would move to other parts of the city, but invariably they would be replaced by new immigrants from Mexico. "And since these people are often the destitute peons from Mexico's backward areas," wrote George S. Perry, "not the least of the problems they create when they are packed into El Paso's slums is a serious menace to the community's health and sanitation."[17]

By the 1960s, in spite of the defeat of a municipal housing code, there was evidence of a greater concern by city officials and private organizations regarding conditions in South El Paso. As a result, improvements were eventually made. Among them were the paving and lighting of streets, the reduction of infant mortality, the building of schools, public housing, health centers, parks and playgrounds, and a community center. Above all, a strong feeling of community pride developed among the families of South El Paso, and with it grew a determination to preserve the Segundo Barrio as a residential area. They organized La Campaña por la Conservación del Barrio to resist all attempts to replace the tenements with industries and offices, waged war against the "slumlords," and made strident demands for rent controls and better housing. But even by the late 1970s there was so little to show for their efforts that a *Times* reporter in 1977 was led to comment that even Dickens would be appalled by the squalor in the Segundo Barrio.[18]

In the struggle minorities have waged against prejudice and discrimination, a major victory had been won in 1944 when Dr. Lawrence A. Nixon, a black physician, was given the right to cast his ballot in the Democratic primary in El Paso, an election traditionally reserved for whites and tantamount to the general election. His case had extended over twenty years and was carried to the Supreme Court of the United States on three separate occasions. Dr. Nixon's courageous fight for justice and equality and the final vindication of his cause, a story which has been sympathetically told by Conrey Bryson, was followed by other breakthroughs. The "colored" sections on streetcars and buses were eliminated, segregation in the public schools came to an end, the El Paso school district being the first in Texas to desegregate unconditionally, and in 1955 in a case decided by Judge Ewing Thomason a black woman, Thelma White, was admitted to Texas Western College. Dr. Joseph Ray, who has edited Thomason's autobiography, writes that the judge's decision "specifically invalidated Texas constitutional provisions and statutes which required separate schools for Negroes. Texas Western thus became the first white Texas public college or university to open its doors to black students." In addition, in the 1960s the city council passed one ordinance providing for open accommodations and a second providing for open access in the purchase and renting of housing. In

251

the black's struggle for equality and justice in Texas, El Paso had led the way.[19]

The Mexican-American population in the United States traditionally has been categorized as a minority group, but such is not the case in El Paso, where it has comprised at least 50 percent of the total for more than half a century. Yet progress for this group, historically the victim of prejudice and discrimination, has been painfully slow in coming, leaving enormous inequities with the Anglos in every aspect of community life. They have traveled only a short distance, writes Oscar Martínez, in their quest to achieve parity with the Anglo population. Economically and socially, a gulf still separates the two groups.[20]

Dominating the political, social, and economic structure in the postwar decades was the powerful and influential business community – the bankers, merchants, and lawyers, many of whom came from the older established local families. They held the political offices, contributed to the campaigns of candidates who had won their confidence, controlled the decision-making process, and scrupulously followed a party line that what was good for El Paso business was good for El Paso. Their principal mouthpiece was the El Paso Times, owned by wealthy Dorrance D. Roderick, and edited by W. J. Hooten, a man known for his kindly, cautious, conservative approach, and his fear of causing discord or stirring up controversy. In the eyes of the Times the influentials were El Paso's "leading citizens," those who could be counted on for decisions made in the best interests of the community. On the other hand, the principal thorn in the side of the business group was the Herald-Post, a Scripps-Howard paper, whose editor, E. M. Pooley, rarely missed an opportunity to rake "the kingmakers," as he dubbed them, over the coals. In the 1950s readers could almost always expect two differing points of view from the local press on just about any subject.[21]

As to the potential political strength of the Mexican-American community, Carey McWilliams in his 1948 article noted that "the Spanish-speaking group is ripe for organized action and has an endless list of social grievances, many of which date back fifty years. It has only begun to achieve real political maturity, but leaders are emerging and the day of political reckoning cannot be long deferred." As to the possibility of the election of a Mexican-American as mayor, a study of El Paso's influentials reported that they conceded that "the election of a Spanish-name person as mayor was acceptable in principle, and that it should and would happen, but they were not prepared to have it happen in their lifetime."[22]

The day of political reckoning came in 1957 when Raymond Telles was elected mayor, the first Mexican-American to be named to that office in the city's history. Telles was young and attractive, had a distinguished career in the Air Force, and had demonstrated administrative ability as the county clerk. Against the opposition of the *Times* and most of the business community, Telles won with the Mexican-American vote in the Lower Valley and the South Side, which turned out in record numbers, and with the support of the *Herald-Post*, champion of the interests of the "Juan Smiths." In the words of attorney George Rodríguez, what had happened was "a revolution, not an election." It was a blow that the powerful business community found difficult to accept. "How can we hold our heads up in the State of Texas," said one, "when we have a Mexican mayor?"[23]

When Raymond Telles was interviewed at a later date, he revealed details about what happened when he ran for county clerk in 1948. His opponent, ten-year incumbent P. D. Lowery, declared on radio, "I want the people of El Paso to know two things – one of them is that my name is P. D. Lowery and the name of my opponent is Raymond Telles. Secondly, I want the people of El Paso to know that he is a Mexican and I am an Irishman." "It was the first time in the history of El Paso, and I guess Texas," Telles recalled, "that anyone with a Spanish name would even dare consider the idea of launching a campaign for any major county office. I honestly thought I had no chance to win." Telles also recalled when he ran for mayor that Ed Pooley, editor of the *Herald-Post*, supported him, but that the other newspapers and the banks were totally against him. "Ed Pooley would probably have lost his job," said Telles, "if I had not been elected mayor."[24]

The decade of the 1960s in the United States was the most turbulent and divisive since the Civil War. Two major problems agonized the nation, one domestic – racial inequality – and the other international – communist expansion in Southeast Asia. Although the administrations of John F. Kennedy and Lyndon B. Johnson attacked them in the 1960s with courage, dedication, and

determination, by the end of the decade the turmoil these problems produced left a powerful nation badly divided. A significant
beginning in the civil rights movement was made under the leadership of President Kennedy and Martin Luther King, Jr. This was
given great impetus by the president's assassination, and by historic civil rights legislation in the Lyndon B. Johnson administration
in 1964-1965. At that point, however, the principal focus of the
racial struggle shifted to black poverty in the urban areas. Race
riots, burnings, lootings, and killings occurred in the Watts section
of Los Angeles, and in Chicago, Cleveland, Detroit, and elsewhere.
"Black Power" had emerged. Its advocates preached violence and
denounced the more moderate position of cooperation with whites
that had been advocated by black leaders such as King.The commitment of the Kennedy administration to halt communist expansion in South Vietnam was significantly expanded under Lyndon
B. Johnson. The principal enemy was the Viet Cong, a popular
communist movement which received substantial aid from North
Vietnam, China, and the Soviet Union. By 1965 the war had become a quagmire, with some officials expressing doubt that it could
ever be won. It soon became a highly controversial issue debated
across the nation on television, in the press, and on the university
and college campuses led by student activists in a movement
known as the New Left.

Student activists first became involved in the civil rights movement in the South. Then came the Free Speech Movement on the
Berkeley campus, and at length as the American involvement in
Vietnam expanded, the antiwar movement. There were demonstrations, teach-ins, sit-ins, invasions of administrative offices, draft
card burnings, and flights to Canada to escape conscription. The
student movement bred a counterculture, characterized by its contempt of middle-class values and conventions, and what it considered to be artificial and hollow in American society. Then came
long hair, shabby dress, iconoclastic language, permissive sex,
drugs, rock music, and a new vocabulary — hippie, dropout, com-
mune, Black Power, Chicano, and Aztlán, to mention a few. Thus,
during the second half of that turbulent decade, hardly any major
institution of higher learning was immune to some level of disruption from radicals and activists among its own faculty and student
body.[25]

In 1960 Dr. Joseph M. Ray was appointed to the presidency of Texas Western College. With a distinguished academic background in political science and administration, Dr. Ray possessed a deep understanding of the role and function of a university, together with the ingredients that constitute a quality educational program. With a recommendation from a citizens' advisory committee known as Mission '73 that the name of the college be changed to The University of Texas at El Paso, positive steps were taken to upgrade the faculty, to bring eminent scholars to the campus, to encourage research and publication, to expand library holdings, and to establish a reputable regional press. Favorable publicity at the national level came with the institution's sponsorship of the first Peace Corps project and an NCAA basketball championship. In 1967 the name of the institution was changed to The University of Texas at El Paso.[26]

The growing protest on university campuses against the Vietnam war reached El Paso in November 1965 when a young history professor led a small group in an antiwar demonstration in San Jacinto Plaza. A large crowd had gathered; the atmosphere was explosive, with considerable name-calling. President Ray was bombarded with angry phone calls and letters demanding that "the commie professor be fired." Although the professor had been at Texas Western for only one year and therefore did not possess tenure, he had impressive credentials and an effective teaching record. To have discharged him would have been a clear violation of academic freedom. The community failed to understand that in The University of Texas system, only the Board of Regents can discharge a professor, and even here strict procedures must be followed and the principle of academic freedom scrupulously upheld. "Academic freedom," President Ray explained, "is an essential ingredient in the formula for a university. Without it there is no university."[27]

Other crises troubled the institution. The head of the sociology department was linked with the Reies Tijerina movement that called for the takeover, by violence if necessary, of former Spanish land grants in New Mexico. Following an investigation, President Ray reported to the chancellor of The University of Texas System that while the professor leaned toward activism in the area of his research interests, he had done nothing to warrant any change in his status. In addition, there were complaints to President Ray for permitting Texas Western Press to publish an article by a political science professor emphasizing the potential of the Mexican-American vote in El Paso, which the professor labeled "Brown Power." Another article by a political science professor and published by the press took a strong pro-labor stance, condemned right-to-work laws, the low wages, and the poor working conditions that prevailed in El Paso.[28]

By that time the small group of blacks on campus had taken the lead in demanding black adminstrators, black teachers, and black studies. The student newspaper, *The Prospector*, in a series of articles, demanded a "free university" run by students and the legalization of marijuana. The same series condemned the interference of the business community in campus affairs and the exploitation of black athletes.[29]

By the spring of 1968, President Ray had been caught in the middle of a tug-of-war between downtown and the campus. Critics complained to the Board of Regents that the president had cold feet and a weak spine in refusing to fire the left-wing activist professors, and a number of the regents had become critical of the manner in which he had handled the various crises. He submitted his resignation in May 1968. In defending the position and the action he had taken in the controversies of the past three years, he later wrote:

> Protests against faculty members focus upon the president. As the personification of the institution in the public mind, he either must disassociate himself from the beleaguered professor and move against him, or he will have to bear the brunt of the criticism in the professor's behalf; there is rarely any middle ground.[30]

With regard to the community-university relationships, Dr. Ray referred to "the proprietary feeling within the community about *our* university." He continued:

> "*Our children* should not be taught by a revolutionary or a radical like *him*." "Students afar may demonstrate, but surely they can be prevented from doing so at *our* university." "The President and other officials should impose strong discipline to maintain decorum," as defined by the persons making complaints....

The community would do well to accept the fact that
a university of necessity will contain faculty members and
students whose views and activities meet with less than
universal acceptance. Even when there is strong disagreement, we may take a perverse pride in the way *our* university is coming to resemble in this as in other ways the
great universities of the nation.[31]

As the result of the momentum for corrective action provided
by the civil rights movement, there emerged in the Southwest the
Chicano crusade to dramatize the Mexican-Americans' grievances
against the Anglo-American establishment, and to ignite the spark
for the better life for all members of the Mexican-American community. In accordance with the concept of Aztlán, Chicano in-
tellectuals envisaged the reconquest of the American Southwest, a
land taken from them by North Americans. Claiming descendancy
from the ancient Aztecs, the original inhabitants of the American
Southwest, Chicanos called for the reconquest of the area and the
establishment of an independent "mestizo nation."[32]

By the late sixties the impact made by the Chicano Movement
on the university campuses of the Southwest was considerable. It
dwarfed every other protest movement by comparison, whether
antiwar activism or Black Power militancy. Remaining basically a
student activist movement, its demands were unceasing and unre-
lenting—Chicano administrators, Chicano faculty, a Chicano on
the Board of Regents, Chicano involvement in the administrative
decision-making process, Chicano studies, Chicano library materials, and so on.[33]

Chicano tactics involved organizational meetings, emotional
rhetoric, protest demonstrations, control of the student newspaper,
invasion of administrative offices, the erection of barricades, and
confrontrations with university officials and faculty. Activist Chicano scholars in the 1960s wasted no time in gathering an elaborate
arsenal of statistical information in support of their basic contention
that a historical division existed between the Anglo and Chicano
communities along economic, political, and social lines. As Oscar
Martínez notes in his assessment of Chicano progress in El Paso:

This separation is partially explained by the perpetual presence of poor immigrants and continuing job competition

257

from cheap labor in neighboring Ciudad Juárez. Such factors have affected local wages, working and living conditions, and have caused some migration to the interior of the United States. Yet, structural discriminatory barriers such as job exclusion and wage differentials, segregation, lack of educational opportunities, and political domination constitute the major causes of Mexican American underdevelopment. Institutional obstacles have reinforced existing disadvantages and have created many others, thus contributing until recently to a marked absence of progress among local Chicanos.[34]

With regard to economic status of the Chicano from 1910 to 1970, the data indicated a protracted concentration of Chicano workers in low-skill and low-paying jobs. Mobility had been limited and slow, and the number of Chicanos who had moved into white-collar positions was extremely low. Moreover, they were largely absent from influential and policy-making positions in El Paso; few lived in the more exclusive neighborhoods. Their political participation prior to the 1960s had been limited, only one Spanish-surnamed person, Martínez notes, serving as mayor in the one-hundred-year period following the incorporation of El Paso as a city in 1873. This same long-standing underrepresentation was also present in the field of education. Thus, the computerized study of El Paso's influentials by Paul Sweeney and Carey Gelernter in 1978 for the *El Paso Times* revealed that not a single Mexican-American was listed in the top thirty economic "elites" that constituted the city's power structure. "We try to pick big operators, substantial people," said a board chairman of a major bank. "The businessman is a white man. This is the United States."[35]

Although by no means were all Mexican-Americans willing to be labeled "Chicano," or to endorse the movement, some readily agreed that there was an urgent need to publicize existing grievances. As one Mexican-American administrator explained:

To me the word "Chicano" is not concerned with a place where the person was born, or whether he is necessarily a Mexican-American. I think a Chicano is a state of mind. The true sense of the word, I think, is that a person is aware that there are injustices, that people are deprived of equal opportunities, that there needs to be a better distribution of opportunity and a chance to make a living, to advance, and to have the necessities of life and even the niceties of life. If a person is involved in that struggle and has an attitude that defines the need to provide all these things which I mentioned, then I think he could classify himself as a Chicano.[36]

Another local Mexican-American official put it this way: "I use the term 'Chicano' as a tool – the Chamber of Commerce crowd understands the word, and so I think we need the movement. I think everyone ought to take a turn being a Chicano, and then go back and get into the mainstream." Still another Mexican-American had this to say:

> I agree with the Aztlán concept if it means the preservation of Mexican culture – but saying that we are going to conquer and bring back the area to our people – I don't know that we would be capable of governing it! If we as a people, whether we call ourselves Spanish-speaking, Mexican-American, or what – if we could sift through the whole background and take out all of the good and put it together and use it as a tool to make things better, this would be giving victory to our heritage by remaining with that heritage, but assimilating into the mainstream of Main Street U.S.A.[37]

On the other hand, some Mexican-Americans were quick to denounce in no uncertain terms the Chicano Movement as divisive, unprofessional, unsophisticated, arrogant, overly aggressive, and lacking direction. "I don't like the name – it is divisive," said one Mexican-American legislator. "Our opponents laugh and say we are fighting among ourselves. The Chicano Movement limits our stroke, our power, because there is no difference between being Chicano, Mexican-American, Mexican surnamed, Latin American, or what." Another Mexican-American, a federal official, insisted that the only way the Hispanic community will ever really progress is to get into the political process. "If you are not out there in that political business," he continued, "you really are not entitled to yell and scream that you are being had by the system. We are going to have to achieve a far greater degree of sophistication than we have now."[38]

Unquestionably, the Chicano Movement produced some beneficial results, though progress was much slower than Chicano leaders desired. Thus, as Martínez notes, "it has allowed the

Chicano community to achieve unprecedented – albeit still limited –
social, economic, and political heterogeneity, leading to varying degrees and shades of integration, acculturation, and assimilation in the
mainstream by middle and upper elements within the group." Even
so, he concludes, El Paso Chicanos have traveled only a short distance in their quest to achieve parity with the Anglo population.[39]

By the 1980s the pace of the movement had slowed considerably, and the term "Hispanic," as used by the federal government
in the 1970s to categorize Cubans, Puerto Ricans, and Mexican-
Americans, has gained acceptance throughout the Southwest, with
the term "Chicano" largely limited to university campuses. But the
term "Hispanic" does an injustice to Mexican-Americans, whose interests differ widely from those of the Cubans and Puerto Ricans,
leaving the term "Mexican-American" as the most accurate one to
identify an American citizen of Mexican descent. Hopefully, the
1990s will offer challenges and opportunities that the Mexican-
American community has never before experienced. There is every
reason to expect that it will play a far greater role in community
affairs in the future than in the past. Perhaps in time all the labels
will be set aside and fall into disuse.[40]

The Tigua settlement of Ysleta del Sur, it will be recalled,
made a firm commitment around the turn of the century to halt
the trend toward Mexicanization and to preserve its tribal identity
as a distinct Indian community. Although the last native speakers
died in the 1930s, the Tigua language has survived in words,
phrases, rituals, and songs, and the native crafts, particularly the
making of pottery, have continued to the present time. Traditional
elements in Tigua civil government and religion have persisted.
On the other hand, the Indians continued to suffer from extreme
poverty, living in adobe structures in the advanced stages of deterioration without water or utilities. Unemployment was widespread
and the children in many cases were so ill clothed that they had
to drop out of school. Homes were facing foreclosure for the failure
of the Tiguas to pay their city taxes.[41]

Coming to the assistance of the proud but destitute Tiguas in
the middle 1960s was El Paso attorney Tom Diamond. Through
his efforts, Texas recognized the tribal status of the Tiguas in 1967
and established the Tigua Indian Reservation, one of two reservations in the state. The following year the federal government

*Beyond El Paso's downtown skyline are Ciudad
Juárez and the Juárez Mountains in Mexico.
(Courtesy Darst-Ireland Photography)*

granted recognition of the tribe and turned the care of the Indians
over to the Texas Indian Commission. With the receipt of approximately $11 million from the state, the Tiguas built a modern 114-
unit complex on land granted to the reservation, a museum, and
an arts and crafts center with a restaurant. As a result, says a recent study, this sorely treated group of American indigenes whose
ancestors trekked down the Rio Grande three hundred years ago,
carrying only their most prized possessions on their backs, has at
last been released from bondage. Yet the Tiguas continue to be
victimized by the poverty of the area in which they live.[42]

During the 1970s El Paso experienced the same spectacular rate
of growth that had characterized the fifties and sixties. A population increase of more than 100,000 brought the figure to 425,000
in 1980, and the half million mark was confidently predicted
before the end of the present decade. Life style and climate continued to attract the newcomers. The *El Paso Herald-Post* proudly
boasted in its edition of 3 December 1977, that "the sun shone today for the 382nd consecutive day; it failed to shine only twenty-
five of the past 5,583 days." Most of the population ignored the

261

historic neighborhoods, bought homes in the suburbs, and patronized the shopping centers and malls such as Cielo Vista, Sunrise,
Northgate, and Bassett. Downtown El Paso remained as the center
for governmental, legal, and financial establishments, while Mexican shoppers from Ciudad Juárez kept the core area merchants in
business until they were hit by successive peso devaluations.[43]

The community's leaders, promoters, and influentials continued to emphasize industrial development and an approach that
"what was good for El Paso business was good for El Paso." The
city, they said, should focus its energies and resources so that it
could become another Phoenix. The newly formed El Paso Development Corporation early in the 1970s pointed out that "the western tip of Texas has always depended on copper, cotton, cattle,
and climate, and more recently on the clothing industry as the
basis of livelihood for the people living here." The five C's and the
expansion of Fort Bliss, said the Development Corporation, have
contributed greatly to the city's growth, but if it is to reach its
potential, it must seek and acquire new industry.[44]

Although a number of firms located in El Paso during the
1970s, the hope that El Paso could become another Phoenix failed
to materialize. A former mayor in 1978 declared, "We want to be
like Phoenix, but we don't have the kind of business leadership we
need." A bank president added, "I hate to express it publicly, but
it's true that our leadership has been sort of mediocre. We didn't
have the influx of well educated people in the industrial and commercial world. Phoenix did." And still another businessman remarked, "We haven't done a selling job of what we've got. Phoenix
has done a better job."[45]

On the other hand, many felt that in view of El Paso's limited
water resources it was just as well that the city failed in its attempt
to rival Phoenix. Emphasizing the cult of bigness, they argued, was
basically the wrong approach. Even so, growth continued during
the seventies as the population figure leaped toward a half million
and a number of significant projects lifted El Paso from small city
to metropolitan status. One of these was a facility many city planners had envisaged for a decade or more as a natural for El Paso
in view of its border location and the proximity of Ciudad Juárez
— a civic center complex to capitalize on the tourist and convention business.[46]

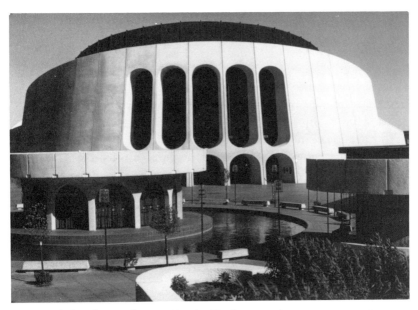

*Built with bonds voted in 1968, the Performing Arts
and Convention Center in downtown El Paso attracts
major entertainment events and large meetings.
(Courtesy Darst-Ireland Photography)*

After two successive failures, a $15 million bond issue for a
civic center in the downtown area (with no increase in property
taxes) was passed in June 1968, behind Mayor Judson Williams's
strong leadership. The complex consisted of a theatre/auditorium
seating more than 2,500, plus an assembly hall and exhibition
facility accommodating 6,000 which could be divided for smaller
groups. Offices for the Chamber of Commerce and various other
city departments were provided, as well as parking underneath.
Local flavor was suggested in the roof of the theatre/auditorium
which was to be designed in the shape of a Mexican sombrero. At
long last, guest artists would be able to perform in a facility other
than the Coliseum or Liberty Hall, often the objects of uncompli-
mentary remarks from guest performers in the past.[47]

The Exhibition Hall was completed and dedicated in November 1972. Shortly thereafter structural problems began and continued for the remainder of the decade—flaws in the ring girder
that supported the roof system of the theatre, cracks in the floor of

the Exhibition Hall, roof leaks, fumes in the underground parking garage, unsatisfactory lighting, and so on. There were lawsuits, countersuits, hard feelings, and frustrations involving lawyers, city officials, architects, contractors, and suppliers. Not until the end of the decade were all the construction problems finally hurdled. In spite of its difficult birth, comments Sonnichsen, the Civic Center did as much as anything to make a big city out of El Paso. "Who could have foreseen," he adds, "when the first train pulled in a hundred years before in 1881 and brought a frontier village into the mainstream of American life, that this ugly duckling would develop into a civic swan?"[48]

An extremely important and imaginative project in the seventies was the incorporation of the entire Franklin Range by the city for the purpose of conserving its rich mountain-desert vegetation, wildlife, Indian relics, and unspoiled beauty. This range, about three miles wide and fifteen miles long, runs in a north-south direction, and features three main peaks – South Franklin Mountain, whose altitude is 6,700 feet; North Franklin Mountain, at 7,900 feet the highest in the range; and Anthony's Nose at the north end, with an altitude of 6,900 feet. On the western slope is Tom Mays Park, whose main features are Aztec Caves, Mundy Gap, and Cottonwood Springs. Also on the western slope of South Franklin Mountain is the celebrated Thunderbird, an enormous formation of red rhyolite in the shape of a spread eagle. Transmountain Road, completed in 1970, cuts between North and South Franklin mountains, and reaches its peak of 5,250 feet above sea level at Smugglers' Pass in Fusselman Canyon.[49]

The plan envisaged by local and state officials called for the systematic development of the entire area north of Transmountain Road. There would be trails, picnic areas, amphitheatre, and resort facilities, all of which might not be completed until late in the century. In 1977 the City of El Paso annexed the entire range and instituted condemnation proceedings against private developers. Two years later an act of the Texas Legislature established the area as a state park. By that time the Wilderness Park Museum had been completed at the eastern terminus of Transmountain Road. It offers a Diorama Hall and impressive displays of projectile points, hammerstones, metates, jewelry of sea shells and turquoise, baskets, and pottery. On the Nature Trail are replicas of a pueblo ruin, a

The city of El Paso is wrapped around the Franklin Mountains. (Courtesy Darst-Ireland Photography)

kiva, and a pithouse, all part of a city museum for which the El Paso Archaeological Society acts in a sponsoring role.[50]

In December 1971 the Chicano Movement on the campus of The University of Texas at El Paso came to a climax when activists staged a demonstration in front of the Administration Building protesting what they felt was the refusal of the administration to meet Chicano demands. Thirty students were arrested when they attempted to take possession of the building. President Joseph Smiley, having weathered the Chicano storm for three years, resigned. In Austin the Board of Regents, appraising the situation on the UTEP campus as "extremely volatile," appointed Dr. Arleigh B. Templeton president, thus bypassing the customary mechanism of a search committee in the selection process. The Chicano fervor subsided as Dr. Templeton took firm control, raising faculty salaries, increasing enrollment, appointing qualified Mexican-Americans to high-level administrative positions, establishing the institution's first doctorate, and initiating a building program.[51]

265

In June 1969 a bond issue created El Paso Community College, designed to accommodate 16,000 students and to offer programs in general education, arts and sciences, vocation-technical training, community services, and continuing education. By 1979 three modern campuses had been built — Valle Verde in the Lower Valley, Transmountain in northeast El Paso, and Rio Grande in downtown. The county-wide college is governed by a locally elected board of trustees and is fully accredited by state and regional educational agencies. By the end of the seventies El Paso, with its Civic Center, educational institutions, museums, libraries, zoological park, symphony, ballet, and theatres, had become a leading cultural center of the Southwest.[52]

Although progress for the Mexican-American community traditionally has been slow and gradual, a number of substantial gains came about in the seventies. For one thing, in 1971 a Mexican-American girl was named Sun Queen. The following year the El Paso schools adopted a bilingual education program, and Affirmative Action, a federal program designed to end discrimination practices, went into effect in 1973. In a historic decision U.S. District Judge William S. Sessions ruled on 23 December 1976 that the El Paso Independent School District was guilty of maintaining and fostering a dual school system. He ordered that discrimination against Mexican-American children must end. In 1977 Ray Salazar became the second Mexican-American to be elected mayor since the city was incorporated, but he was overwhelmingly defeated by a well-organized Anglo vote when he ran for re-election. By 1978 the number of aldermanic districts was increased to six, and single-member-district representation in city council elections was approved. Much to the displeasure of the Mexican-American community, however, the new system failed to guarantee the election of at least three Mexican-American representatives. No doubt progress would continue to come slowly, but the seventies had offered greater challenge and opportunities to the Mexican-American community than it had ever experienced in the past.[53]

The decade of the seventies was featured by a growing interest in the history of the El Paso area, much of it no doubt generated by C. L. Sonnichsen's *Pass of the North*, published in 1968. In observance of the centennial of the city's incorporation, the El Paso County Historical Society in 1973 organized a celebration known as "Aniversario" and published a useful volume of articles under the title, *El Paso: A Centennial Portrait.* In that same year Conrey Bryson published his delightful *The Land Where We Live.* The centennial of the Magoffin Homestead was observed in 1975, and in the following year during the American Bicentennial arrangements were made for the purchase of the property by the state and the city, and for its restoration and preservation by the Texas Historical Commission.[54]

In 1977 a major step forward was taken with the establishment of the El Paso Community Foundation for the funding of local charitable and educational projects. In that same year Jonathan R. Cunningham, director of the city's Department of Planning, Research, and Development, initiated a movement for the preservation of local historic sites. Interest in such programs had been generated by the loss in a fire of the historic St. Regis Hotel early in 1977, after it had been recommended for the National Register of Historic Places. An impressive brochure entitled *El Paso's Forgotten Past* was published by the Department of Planning, Research, and Development. It included a brief history of the area, a historic sites inventory, photographs of the city's most significant historic and archeological sites, and recommendations for a landmark commission and historic preservation master plan, all to be implemented by local ordinance. In 1978 the Landmark Ordinance was approved by the city council, and a Historic Landmark Commission was appointed. The El Paso County Historical Commission, the local extension of the Texas Historical Commission, became active about that time in the expansion of its historic marker and monument program.[55]

El Paso's Four Centuries celebration in 1981, one of the most important events in the city's history, commemorated four centuries of history from the time the first Spanish expedition came up from southern Chihuahua through the Pass of the North on its way to New Mexico. Most of the activities were on a lighter side, climaxed with a gigantic four-day birthday party at the Civic Center which was launched in spectacular fashion when a restored steam locomotive puffed into the Union Depot with black smoke, whistle, and bell. Public interest and attendance at the Civic Center far exceeded expectations. The opportunity to educate the local population on El Paso's history and cultural heritage was not overlooked. A textbook was written for the public schools, and presentations were given in the schools utilizing a basic map of the Rio Grande and four plastic overlays showing the major developments for each of the four centuries. A display at Coronado Bank showed copies of original documents in the Archivo de Indias in Sevilla, Spain, concerning the activities of sixteenth-century Spaniards in the El Paso area. Two series of articles on El Paso history appeared, one in *Password*, the quarterly journal of the El Paso County Historical Society, and the other in the *El Paso Times* in the spring of 1981. Finally, the *New York Times* covered the celebration in its edition of 18 July 1981. Thus the secret of El Paso's rich and fascinating history of four hundred years was revealed to the nation and to the world.[56]

By 1980 El Paso had a population of 425,000, and reached a half million by 1987. It had become a major metropolitan center of West Texas and the largest city on the United States-Mexican border. A strong and stable economy had been built, based primarily on retail sales, manufacturing, government, and service industries such as finance, transportation, communication, and the legal and medical professions. Retail sales (automobiles, appliances, and clothing) exceeded $2.5 billion a year during the mid-1980s, 40 percent spent by Mexican shoppers. Manufacturing exceeded $2 billion, the major industries being apparel, food processing, and building materials. Traditional industries such as smelting, refining of metals, and petroleum refining remained important. Government, particularly Fort Bliss, contributed $750 million, as did the various service industries.[57]

The leading industry to emerge in recent years is electronics assembly, the result of the economic revolution on the border produced by the maquila industry, or twin plant (in bond) program. U.S. raw materials are converted in an El Paso plant into component parts which are then delivered to a plant in Juárez for assembly. The product is then shipped back to the U.S., is assessed a duty only on the value added in Mexico, and is returned to the El Paso plant for inspection, finishing, packaging, and distribution. The program has brought to the border General Electric, General Motors, Sylvania, and RCA, to name a few. The 250 plants which have been established in Juárez to date have brought about the building of more than a hundred in El Paso, employing 8,000 workers.[58]

El Paso's principal industry, as it has been for years, is Fort Bliss, officially the United States Army Air Defense Center. At the present time it covers more than 1,700 square miles, or more than a million acres, and owns a billion dollars' worth of land, structures, and equipment. The total number of military personnel, dependents, retirees, and civilian employees is about 100,000, or one-fifth of El Paso's population. One out of every five dollars flowing through the city's economy therefore begins at the military base, the total impact at the present time amounting to more than $690 million. In the 1980s, as in the past, as an El Paso newspaper put it, Fort Bliss was El Paso's best economic friend.[59]

In March 1980 Dr. Haskell Monroe became president of The University of Texas at El Paso, and shortly afterwards announced that his first priority would be a new library. Completed in 1984, the massive six-story structure was built at the south end of the campus facing Interstate 10 and is the one that most resembles a Bhutanese lamasery. Dr. Monroe encouraged donors to establish professorships and chairs, and initiated a program of academic scholarships to attract gifted and talented students. For years the university has enrolled more students from Mexico than any other comparable institution. By 1983 Hispanics comprised the largest ethnic group on campus, a reflection of the community's Hispanic majority, and it became the largest single producer of Hispanic engineers in the country. It was indeed fitting that historian Haskell Monroe during his tenure should write:

> The institution that we now know as UTEP opened its doors seventy years ago, offering twenty courses in a single field of study. Now it ranks as eighth largest among Texas' public universities, offering hundreds of courses in eighty fields of study. More than 40,000 degrees have been awarded since the first commencement in 1916....
> The school came into being because the people of El Paso pressed the Legislature to create it in 1913 and provided the money to buy the land and buildings for it. The close association between community and this institution has continued over the years.[60]

In 1987 Dr. Monroe accepted the position of chancellor of the University of Missouri, but his enthusiasm for a Diamond Jubilee celebration was actively nurtured by his successor, Dr. Diana Natalicio, former department chairman, dean, and vice president.[61]

In 1969 the Texas Tech Regional Academic Health Center, a function of the Texas Tech School of Medicine in Lubbock, was established in El Paso on Alberta Street. Instrumental in bringing the center to El Paso was Judson Williams, at the time chairman of the Texas Tech Board of Regents. The facility consisted of forty-five full-time professors, as well as twenty-seven local physicians who were part-time visiting instructors. The center offered eight fully accredited residency programs in internal medicine, making it possible for a medical student, after completing the first two years, to attend the Health Center and receive practical experience to supplement classroom work. The center worked closely with Thomason General Hospital, and in 1985 when the county facility ran short of funds for its clinics, Texas Tech assumed control with Thomason as a major component of its School of Medicine. A $6.9 million building across the street from the Health Center was completed to house Thomason's outpatient clinics, now drawing more than 100,000 clinic visits a year. Although the Health Center has been called one of the best-kept secrets in El Paso, its partnership with Thomason General has made it one of the city's most important medical facilities. Its trauma center holds an accreditation from a national agency that no other El Paso hospital has.[62]

Like most of the Southwest, El Paso has always lived on the edge of water scarcity, and has long been concerned about an adequate water supply for future needs. For centuries surface water — namely, the Rio Grande — was the single source of supply that made survival possible through irrigation. Then in 1916 Elephant Butte dam was completed in New Mexico to provide a measure of control over the river's capricious behavior. Although the average rainfall rarely amounts to more than eight inches per year, paradoxically the area is floating on an underground lake of water, now its main source of supply. Within recent years the City of El Paso has used groundwater almost exclusively, with 94 percent pumped from the ground, and 6 percent coming from the Rio Grande. Projections are for continuing depletion of groundwater since pumpage exceeds the rate of replenishment by rainfall and percolation into underground aquifers.[63]

The two main groundwater sources in the area are the Mesilla Bolson and the Hueco Bolson. The Mesilla Bolson straddles the New Mexico-Mexico boundary, while the Hueco Bolson is located

The campus of The University of Texas at El Paso is
distinguished by its Bhutanese architectural style.
The six-story Library, lower left, was completed in
1984. (Courtesy University of Texas at El Paso)

271

between the Franklin and Hueco mountains. It supplies the El
Paso-Juárez area with three times the amount provided by the
Mesilla Bolson. The largest water user in El Paso County is the
city, with other municipal and industrial users including Fort Bliss,
an electric utility, a natural gas company, two oil refineries, a copper refinery, several golf courses, and a dairy. By far the greatest
user in El Paso is the home owner, who consumes more than 80
percent of the total amount pumped from the Hueco Bolson. In
the summer half the total goes for lawn or garden irrigation, swimming pools, and household appliances. Such usage, plus the prospects of a growing population and expanding economic development, have in recent years become matters of the greatest concern
to those whose responsibility is an adequate supply of water for
the future.[64]

In 1978 El Paso's Public Service Board, which governs the city's
water system, became interested in drilling for water in the Mesilla
Bolson, the aquifer in southern New Mexico. This action meant
that the board has decided to challenge the constitutionality of a
New Mexico law embargoing the exportation of water under the
jurisdiction of the state. On 5 September 1980 the PSB authorized
its attorneys to file suit against New Mexico, immediately raising
the fundamental question of who does and who should control
water – state or federal government. New Mexico then declared the
Mesilla Bolson a closed basin, meaning that anyone desiring to
drill for water there must file an application with the state engineer.
The PSB then submitted 326 applications to drill, most of them in
the Mesilla Bolson on public land administered by the federal
Bureau of Land Management. United States Judge Howard Brat-
ton of Albuquerque in 1983 ruled in favor of El Paso and declared
the embargo unconstitutional, but the New Mexico state legislature passed a new law circumventing the ruling by requiring the
approval of the state engineer to drill. The law also authorized him
to reject any application that "impairs existing water rights, is con-
trary to the conservation of water in New Mexico, or is otherwise
detrimental to the public welfare of the citizens of the state." In
December 1987 all 326 El Paso applications were rejected, and
there the matter rests at the present time.[65]

Since this water war between El Paso and New Mexico touches
on the sensitive matter of control over a vital resource, it has pro-

duced bitter words causing a growing gulf between the two sides. El Paso newspapers have stressed the scarcity of water and the interdependence of the El Paso-southern New Mexico region, while the New Mexico newspapers have emphasized the state's need for water, the importance of state control over water resources, and the greed of El Paso. Prof. Ira G. Clark, an eminent authority on water in New Mexico, defends New Mexico's position, stating that the El Paso case is but "the tip of the iceberg," meaning that if El Paso should win its case, New Mexico would be overwhelmed from all sides with requests for water. El Paso's remaining hope, it appears, is to get the case into the federal courts. Attorneys for the PSB are convinced that it is impossible to get a fair hearing before any elected judge in New Mexico. The dispute, which has become an all-out war, is far from over.[66]

A major concern of the El Paso community during the 1980s has been the revitalization of the city's deteriorating downtown area. In December 1980 the City Council designated an eighty-eight-block zone extending from Interstate 10 to Paisano Drive and from St. Vrain Street to the Union Depot as a tax increment financing district, or TIF. Property taxes in the zone would be frozen at 1981 levels for the five entities involved—city, county, school district, community college, and Thomason Hospital. The taxes collected on the increased appraised value of the properties would then be used as security on the issuance of $40 million in bonds to finance downtown improvements. A TIF board of directors would approve and implement a master plan of public works projects extending over a twenty-five-year period.[67]

After a master plan was approved, a lawsuit was instituted by two of the taxing entities—the school district and the community college—challenging the legality of the TIF and delaying City Hall's plans for four years. With the TIF involved in litigation, the private sector joined City Hall's effort to revitalize the downtown area. In 1982 Franklin Land and Resources, Inc., a subsidiary of El Paso Electric Co., announced plans for renovating both the Cortez Hotel as an office building and the old historic landmark, the Paso del Norte Hotel. An expenditure of $50 million was made to restore the del Norte's 1912 lobby and to double the number of rooms by adding a seventeen-story tower to the original structure. It opened its doors in June 1986 as a member of the Westin chain, the *Herald-Post*

joyfully exclaiming that "new life had come for a grand old gal."
Hopefully, it would serve as a catalyst for a revitalized downtown.[68]

In 1987 the constitutionality of the TIF was upheld, and a
compromise was arranged to appease the school district—five representatives instead of one were to serve on the TIF board that
oversees all development plans. City council members would also
serve on the board, along with one representative from each of the
other entities. Private money would be required to supplement
public funds to obtain the approval of any project. Two have been
approved to date—the renovation of the Plaza Theatre, now the
property of the El Paso Community Foundation, and the moving
of the Museum of Art to the downtown site of the Greyhound
Bus Station. Other projects considered include expansion of the El
Paso Convention and Performing Arts Center (formerly the Civic
Center), downtown shopping center and parking garage, expansion
of the public library, decorative lighting from San Jacinto Plaza to
Juárez, and twelve bronze sculptures to depict the history of El
Paso, based on Tom Lea's *Twelve Travelers*.[69]

El Paso's most historic area is its Lower Valley, dating back to
the sixteenth century. Here Juan de Oñate in 1598 took possession
of the land for his king; here Spanish and Tigua refugees founded
the Ysleta and Socorro missions in the 1680s; here was the route
of the Camino Real; and here Spanish officials established the
presidio of San Elizario in 1789. After the area became part of
Mexico in 1821, the shifting Rio Grande formed what was called
"La Isla," and when the river became a boundary in 1848 the three
Mexican towns of Ysleta, Socorro, and San Elizario were a part of
the United States. Americans organized El Paso County in 1850
with San Elizario as the first county seat. Living conditions have
always been primitive and poverty widespread in this agricultural
region, and the capricious Rio Grande on many occasions has
destroyed the adobe houses and crops. Twice it has destroyed both
the Ysleta and Socorro missions; the present structures built in the
mid-nineteenth century serve not only as places of worship but
also as symbols and reminders that the religious heritage of the
area dates back to the seventeenth century.[70]

Although preservationists and developers for years have been
interested in the tourist possibilities of a Mission Trail project
featuring the historic structures of the Lower Valley, basic needs

El Paso's face was changed in the 1960s with construction of Interstate 10, crossing the city from east to west with links from south to north. (Courtesy Darst-Ireland Photography)

such as supplying water to the 28,000 residents of the illegal subdivisions known as *colonias* understandably has been the top priority. Meanwhile, urban sprawl has plagued the Mission Trail, a lack of systematic planning having produced a hodgepodge of junkyards, mobile homes, and stores and residences in various degrees of deterioration. The Mission Trail Association, organized several years ago, seeks to obtain a master plan to repair and preserve the historic treasures and to enlist the support of the private sector in investing in a variety of tourist attractions. Hopefully, such a project would not only preserve and dramatize the area's history, but it would also help to alleviate some of the traditional poverty that has characterized the Lower Valley.[71]

In the past forty years the City at the Pass has become a metropolis. Its physical size increased from 29 to 240 square miles, and its population from 130,000 to more than a half million. The Hispanic population was 57 percent of the total in 1970 and 62 percent in 1980. While the Anglos continued to control the political, social, economic, and educational structure, the Hispanics made significant strides and will undoubtedly play a much greater role in

275

the life of the community in the future. Many of El Paso's traditional industries such as mining and smelting, petroleum refining, transportation, natural gas, agriculture, and tourism remained important, but a number of new industries such as apparel, leather, food processing, construction materials, and electronics moved to the forefront. Three skyscrapers appeared on the downtown landscape, and countless numbers of subdivisions were built on the west side, the northeast, east, and down the Lower Valley. Shopping centers and malls followed the residential subdivisions, and an arterial highway system involving Interstate 10, North-South Freeway, and Transmountain Road carried vehicular traffic from one end of the city to the other. Somehow the schools, hospitals, and churches managed to keep pace with the city's rapid growth, and there was a greater emphasis in the 1970s on quality-of-life projects and the improvement of the city's educational, cultural, recreational, and entertainment facilities.[72]

Finally, the awakening interest during the 1980s in the area's rich history was most gratifying. There were restoration projects — the Magoffin Homestead, the Paso del Norte Hotel, the Cortez Hotel, the Palace Theatre, the Union Station, and the Socorro Mission. The Plaza Theatre was saved from demolition. Five historic districts were established, and more than a dozen historic markers were placed around the city. The historical society erected dioramas in its museum and published articles in *Password*. Dozens of historical books were published by Texas Western Press and Mangan Books. There were exhibits at the public library, and financial assistance was found for the Tiguas. The city was taking pride in its past as it looked confidently to the future.

CHAPTER TEN

The International
Metroplex Since 1961

T H E spectacular growth which El Paso experienced in the post-
World War II years was shared by its twin sister across the river.
Ciudad Juárez underwent a population explosion with the arrival of
tens of thousands of Mexican families at the border in search of the
better life. By 1960 the city had become the fourth largest in Mexico,
with a population of 276,000, a figure which for the first time equaled
that of El Paso. Ciudad Juárez's economy had benefited greatly from
the impetus which the war had provided, and peso devaluations attracted increasing numbers of American shoppers. Once again its
tourist industry experienced the boom times of the past years as U.S.
servicemen and Americans patronized the city's entertainment centers and night life. While the economic relations between the two

cities continued to be featured by a high degree of interdependence, El Paso's more diversified economy placed Ciudad Juárez in a dependent status, and it continued to be a victim of the fierce competition offered by its American twin.[1]

Lying in the very heart of the El Paso-Juárez metropolitan area was the Chamizal problem, for more than fifty years a disturbing and nagging irritant in United States-Mexican relations. Following the refusal of the United States to accept the decision of the arbitration commission of 1911 to divide the tract between the two countries, numerous attempts to arrive at a settlement proved fruitless. Mexico continued to insist that the award of the arbitration commission should be implemented, whereas the United States remained firm in contending that the Canadian and Mexican commissioners in 1911 had exceeded their authority. In the meantime, property values in the disputed area increased enormously although land titles remained in a questionable status. The Mexican press became increasingly emotional over the issue as every effort to find a solution ended in failure. For half a century the cries of "Yankee imperialism" grew louder south of the border.[2]

The election of John F. Kennedy in 1960 inaugurated a new era in United States-Mexican relations. Desirous of improving ties with Mexico in order to strengthen the position of the United States throughout the hemisphere, particularly in view of Fidel Castro's communist regime in Cuba, President Kennedy focused his attention on the Chamizal problem. He was critical of the rigid legal position the United States had maintained since it rejected the findings of the arbitration commission in 1911, pointing out that after agreeing to arbitration, the United States backed down and refused to accept the report. He added that it should therefore erase "the black mark" that resulted from its refusal to comply. Fully aware that the problem had become much more complicated during the half century since the award, he nevertheless concluded that with the passing of time the problem would become worse rather than better, and the best way out would be to settle the issue once and for all.[3]

In June 1962 President Kennedy visited Mexico on a trip he regarded not as just a ceremonial affair and an exchange of pleasantries, but as an opportunity to discuss problems of mutual concern. In the course of the discussion with Mexican Pres. Adolfo López

Mateos, a Mexican diplomat raised the question of the Chamizal, an issue which the U.S. Department of State had deliberately kept off the agenda because of its complexity. Even so, both presidents agreed that any problem causing discord between the two countries should be subject to full discussion. The settlement of the nagging dispute in South El Paso could strengthen the position of the United States throughout the hemisphere. As a result, the two presidents agreed that further conversations should be held in the interest of effecting a settlement of the Chamizal problem.[4]

In July 1962 Thomas G. Mann, United States ambassador to Mexico, arrived in El Paso to confer with Joseph F. Friedkin, United States commisssioner on the International Boundary and Water Commission, and with local officials. Ambassador Mann later returned to El Paso to explain to them the proposals the United States intended to submit to Mexico. On 14 January 1963 the United States and Mexico formally exchanged ratifications of a new Chamizal Treaty. During the ensuing months Ambassador Mann and Commissioner Friedkin consulted with local officials and with the property owners in the disputed tract. The results of these talks, wrote Gladys Gregory, seemed to indicate that fully 90 percent of the people contacted in El Paso were favorable to the project as it had been developed to this point. On 29 August 1963 the Chamizal Convention was signed in Mexico City by Ambassador Mann and the secretary of foreign relations for Mexico, Lic. Manuel Tello.[5]

The Chamizal settlement accepted the principle involved in the 1911 award and divided the disputed territory. Mexico received 630 acres—366 from the Chamizal and 264 from the United States territory east of Cordova Island. This neck of land was then divided equally, with each nation receiving 193 acres. In addition, a new river channel was to be built, together with new bridges. The United States would also have to purchase properties and assume responsibility for relocating 4,500 United States citizens residing in the disputed area. It should be noted, therefore, that had the United States accepted the 1911 award, more than $40 million would have been saved. Finally, the two commissioners on the International Boundary and Water Commission—Joseph F. Friedkin of the United States Section and Joaquín Bustamante Redondo of the Mexican Section—were charged with the enormous task of implementing the treaty provisions.[6]

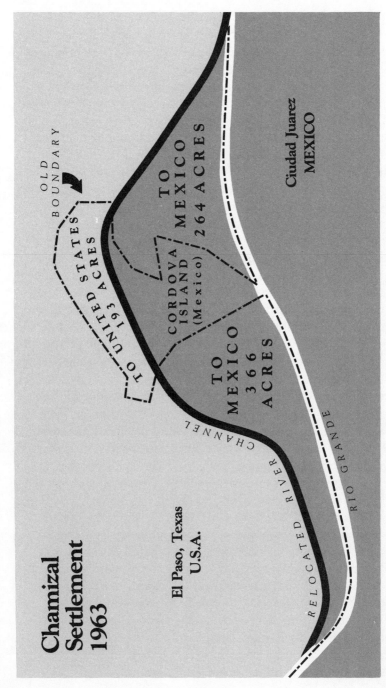

Chamizal
Settlement
1963

El Paso, Texas
U.S.A.

OLD
BOUNDARY

TO UNITED STATES
193 ACRES

CORDOVA
ISLAND
(Mexico)

TO
MEXICO
264 ACRES

TO
MEXICO
366
ACRES

RELOCATED RIVER CHANNEL

RIO GRANDE

Ciudad Juarez
MEXICO

The Chamizal Treaty settled the disputed boundary by awarding 823 acres to Mexico and 193 acres to the United States.

The rechanneled Rio Grande marked the new boundary
between the United States and Mexico after the Chamizal
settlement. (Courtesy Darst-Ireland Photography)

In Mexico the Chamizal Convention was approved by the
proper congressional channels in record time, but such was not
the case in the United States, where a two-thirds majority vote of
the Senate was required. Strong opposition was voiced by Sen.
John Tower of Texas, who questioned the constitutionality of
dismembering a state without its permission, and who therefore
suggested that the passage of the treaty be subject to approval by
the Texas Legislature. On the other hand, Senator Tower stated
that he felt the settlement to be mutually beneficial. What concerned him, he said, was that this might establish a precedent for
any future national government moves to transfer territory to a
foreign nation. El Paso Congressman Ed Foreman said that he
"seriously questioned giving up this land which has been in our
peaceful possession for over one hundred years, to Mexico." Arguing in support of the treaty was Thomas C. Mann, former ambassador to Mexico and now special presidential adviser on Latin
American affairs. Strong endorsements also came from Texas Sen.
Ralph Yarborough, and above all, Lyndon B. Johnson, who

declared a short time after President Kennedy's assassination, that
it would forever stand as a fitting tribute and appropriate
memorial to the president whose leadership had made the settlement of this agonizing dispute a reality.[7]

At the local level the reaction was, for the most part, favorable, although there was some criticism of the so-called "Kennedy
give-away." Mayor Judson Williams was quoted in Mexico City as
saying that the signing of the agreement could lead to better relations between the United States and Latin America. Most local
officials felt that the settlement would make possible the improvement and beautification of an undeveloped area along the border,
and that it would stimulate the economy of the two cities. Federal
Judge Ewing Thomason, a former mayor and member of Congress
who knew the problem well, expressed the prevailing attitude in
these words:

> We wrestled with the Chamizal for fifty years and it would
> be an eyesore for another hundred years if we don't make
> a settlement now. I visualize the time when El Paso and
> Juárez will be a tremendous development. I would like to
> see the agreement followed by a real drive to get rid of the
> slums, a fine beautification program, and a great monu-
> mental free bridge.[8]

Pres. Lyndon Johnson met López Mateos at Bowie High
School on 24 September 1964 in a ceremony commemorating the
settlement; in October 1967, Johnson and the new president of
Mexico, Gustavo Díaz Ordaz, met in Ciudad Juárez in a ceremony
marking the official transfer of the Chamizal to Mexico. Then on
13 December 1968 in a colorful ceremony, Presidents Johnson and
Díaz Ordaz, standing in the center of the new Bridge of the Americas, brought to an end a thorny problem that had been disturbing United States-Mexican relations for more than a century.
Since that time both nations have built public parks and memorials on the lands each received in the settlement. The Chamizal
National Memorial, administered by the National Park Service,
has impressive grounds, a museum, and a theatre, where a variety
of cultural activities is presented throughout the year. On the
Mexican side are a spacious customhouse, large park, monument,
waterfalls, landscaping, and miniature replicas of Indian pyramids.[9]

The administration of Adolfo López Mateos decided that the Mexican federal government could no longer ignore the growing border market and the potentialities of the purchasing power of the neighboring American region. The Border Development Program was thus inaugurated with Antonio J. Bermúdez, well-known ex-mayor of Ciudad Juárez and prominent businessman, selected to administer it. Long associated with border problems, Bermúdez was well qualifed for his new assignment. His views on border development and on the relations between El Paso and Ciudad Juárez, as well as the United States and Mexico, are provocative and merit attention:

> The basic relationship between the United States and Mexico must be one of true friendship, understanding, and mutual respect. Since the United States is a stronger, richer, and more powerful country, it has a moral obligation to be good friends with Mexico. Historically speaking, the most progressive periods in Mexican history have been those in which relationships have been cordial and featuring complete respect and understanding.
>
> Such an approach is even more important and necessary on the border where two civilizations, two distinct cultures, meet. The border is not just one between the United States and Mexico, but between the United States and Latin America. By contributing to the progress of the border the United States can extend its influence automatically from the Río Bravo to the Tierra del Fuego.
>
> Each city needs to promote its own business and economy, but neither can exist without the other, because the two are interdependent. Each city must develop and progress, but not at the expense of the other. Each should contribute to the progress of the other, and Juárez should benefit more from its tourist trade than El Paso.
>
> In the past border cities have been too isolated from the central government, but this is no longer true. Traditionally, the United States sells more to Mexico than Mexico sells to the United States, but with the development of the border, we can take care of ourselves and be economically self-sufficient.[10]

In 1961 the Mexican federal government launched the Programa Nacional Fronterizo, or PRONAF, to "create a gigantic continental shop window." This involved the investment of millions of

With the boundary realignment and the opening of the Cordova boundary crossing point, the Mexican government built a shopping complex and antiquities museum in the ProNaf Center. (Courtesy Darst-Ireland Photography)

pesos in commercial and cultural facilities designed to improve the appearance of Ciudad Juárez and to promote the sale of Mexican products. An investment of 494 million pesos from the public and private sectors went into sixteen border communities, with Ciudad Juárez receiving 30 percent of the total. It resulted in an attractive and impressive new entrance to the city from El Paso, which in time included a statue of Abraham Lincoln, a large shopping center complex, hotels, motels, restaurants, an arts and crafts center, a beautiful Museum of Art and History, a convention building, country club, racetrack, and *charro* ring. While PRONAF unquestionably improved the appearance of Ciudad Juárez and perhaps enticed some American tourists into staying over for a couple of nights instead of the customary one day, the overriding objective of the program, that of increasing the sale of Mexican products and reducing the flow of pesos to the American side, fell short of its planners' predictions. By 1970 Juárez residents were spending more in El Paso and Americans were spending less in Ciudad Juárez than they had five years earlier.[11]

Ciudad Juárez suffered additional economic losses in the early 1970s. While liquor, drugs, and prostitution continued to attract American dollars, they no longer provided the magnet they had in former days with the emergence on the American side of topless bars, X-rated movies, sexual permissiveness, and the availability of drugs. In addition, the legalization of mixed drinks in Texas, the revocation of the Chihuahua law which had permitted the so-called "quickie" divorces, the United States crackdown on the drug traffic, and the suspension of the international streetcar service reduced spending on both sides of the border. Bridge crossings declined from 41 million in 1973 to 28 million in 1975.[12]

In the meantime, in 1971 the Mexican government returned to at least a partial trade basis for many border communities with its *artículos gancho* ("lure" or "enticement") program. This permitted the importation of numerous foreign commodities duty-free for resale in Mexican shops at equal or lower prices than in the United States. Shopping centers in Ciudad Juárez such as the Rio Grande Mall could offer these "lure" items along with merchandise produced in Mexico to keep Mexican pesos from being spent in El Paso. The result was that Ciudad Juárez, until 1976, experienced a far greater volume of business in the importation and sale of *artículos gancho* than any other border city. The peso devaluation that year changed the exchange ratio from 12.5 pesos to 23, thus drastically reducing the purchasing power of large numbers of people and making the cost of American merchandise prohibitive. Merchants in downtown and South El Paso dependent on the Juárez trade suffered a sales drop of 50 percent or more. On the other hand, there was a substantial increase in the traffic flow from El Paso to Ciudad Juárez to take advantage of the new low prices in the curio shops, bars, and restaurants. Once again, the border community could rely on its traditional tourist-related economic base, though in view of Juárez's burgeoning population, the opportunities it offered were becoming more circumscribed all the time.[13]

The most important economic development in the El Paso-Juárez area within recent years was the establishment in 1965 of the *maquiladora*, or twin plant program, officially known as the Border Industrialization Program (BIP). At a time in the 1960s when a wave of investment by United States firms in "offshore" production facilities was taking place to reduce operating costs, the Mexican government decided to establish its own program to attract such firms to Mexican cities on the northern border. Legislation permitted the importation into Mexico free of duty all machinery,

Vehicular traffic enters the United States from Mexico
at this crossing point leading into the downtown business
district. (Courtesy Darst-Ireland Photography)

equipment, raw materials, and components to be used in an "offshore" plant. The only limiting requirement was that the total production from the plant must be exported from Mexico, that at
least 90 percent of the labor had to be Mexican nationals, and
that there be compliance with Mexican minimum wages and conditions of work. Since a bond had to be deposited by the United
States firm covering the items permitted free entry, the *maquiladoras* are frequently called in-bond plants. A twin plant, established
on the American side of the border, would handle the assembly or
processing of the components produced by the in-bond plant.[14]

The development of the *maquiladora* program, rather modest at
first, became impressive during the 1970s. By 1974 sixty-two plants
in Ciudad Juárez were employing more than 10,000 workers, and
by the middle 1980s some 180 plants located in seven industrial
parks were employing more than 85,000 workers. This number far
exceeds any other location in Mexico. More than half the plants
are engaged in the electrical and electronics industries, with clothing and footwear in second place. By the 1980s seventy-nine related
industrial locations or major expansions had been established in

El Paso, employing 5,000 persons, thus benefiting both sides of the border. By 1988 the *maquiladora* program, with its more than 100,000 workers in Juárez and more than 8,000 in El Paso, had wrought an economic revolution on the border.[15]

To be sure, a number of criticisms of the *maquiladora* program have been voiced from various quarters. For one thing, about 85 percent of the workers are women. BIP firms prefer females because of their alleged dexterity, adaptability, patience, cheerfulness, and obedience to assembly-line work that is extremely monotonous and tedious. Most of the male job seekers have failed to find work, leaving the primary goal of the program largely a fiction. In addition, with women working and men unemployed, social tensions have forced the unemployed male into heavy drinking, narcotics, and "another woman" to relieve his resentment, frustration, and wounded *machismo*. As one informant put it, "The BIP is destroying Mexican family life along the border."[16]

American labor unions complain about the loss of jobs for Americans every time a *maquiladora* locates on Mexican soil. Such views have been effectively challenged by national, state, and local proponents of the program, who argue that twin plants actually increase employment in communities such as El Paso because they create hundreds of secondary positions to supplement those in the local American assembly plant. Another argument is that the program, which permits the exploitation of Mexican labor by American companies, substantially increases Mexico's dependence on the United States. In reply to this charge, however, it should be pointed out that the Mexican government has concluded that the benefits derived from BIP outweigh its disadvantages. It therefore hopes that in the future the twin plants will consume more Mexican raw materials, that these plants in time will move into the manufacture of heavy industrial products and equipment, and that new plants can be built in the interior of the country away from the border.[17]

In addition to the more than 85,000 employees in the twin plant program, perhaps 30,000 or more Juárez residents cross the bridge daily to work in El Paso. Possibly half of these are United States citizens who reside in Ciudad Juárez because of the cheaper living expenses. The others are the so-called "green-carders," who have acquired permanent resident alien status. Because they prefer living in Ciudad Juárez, the green card is little more than a work permit. Naturally, the system has its supporters, namely El Paso business interests, as well as its opponents, the labor unions, who have labeled the system "an international racket for employers." Pressures mount for placing restrictions on the system during periods of high unemployment in the United States, when numerous greencarders are erroneously apprehended as undocumented aliens.[18]

Also crossing from Ciudad Juárez are Mexican nationals with *micas*, permits to shop in El Paso within a seventy-two-hour limit, but not to work in El Paso. To attempt to estimate the number who hold this shopping permit is virtually impossible, but they unquestionably provide El Paso households with the vast majority of their full- and part-time maids. As the saying goes, the Mexican maids are El Paso's worst kept secret. They come by the thousands to El Paso because they can earn forty dollars a week, much more, of course, than they can earn in Ciudad Juárez. Just how many Mexican maids work in El Paso is unknown, but there are probably more maids per home in the city than anywhere else in the nation. So far as the Border Patrol is concerned, they are a low level priority, and the city's bus system would be in deep trouble if the immigration officials made an effort to stop the flow. The household maid industry in El Paso is a unique blend of people from a rich and powerful nation with those from a developing country who, in most cases, do not speak the same language. It is an industry, says City Planner Nestor Valencia, that is part of the fiber of the community, a special relationship involving people of different races and classes who need each other. Although the maids are legally entitled to the minimum wage and Social Security, they are reluctant to apply for fear of being caught as undocumented workers, so everyone stays quiet and accepts the system as part of the good life in El Paso.[19]

The poorest of all living conditions on the border, writes Oxford professor and border specialist John W. House, are found in the slum *barrios* straggling up the ravines west of Ciudad Juárez. This area is the city's *periferia*, the outlying neighborhoods where thousands of destitute Mexicans from the interior have settled since the 1960s. Squatters took over public and private lands, and since that time the unsightly *barrios*, have come to be accepted as a permanent feature of border life. Located on the edge of the city are

*This industrial park in Ciudad Juárez is indicative
of the city's major role as a maquiladora or twin
plant center. (Courtesy Darst-Ireland Photography)*

more than fifty *colonias*, where more than 50,000 residents live in
cardboard, cinder block, and adobe shacks. Efforts to provide utilities have been largely ineffective. If there is a health clinic, it is dirty
and unkempt. If there are toilets with plumbing installed in the out-
house behind the shacks, they will not flush. There are blowing
dust, unpaved streets, uncontrolled burning at surrounding land-
fills, and pollution from the cement plant. A steady job for a head
of a family which pays as much as fifty dollars a month is an exception to the rule. Most of the earnings go for food, which consists
of beans, tortillas, and pasta. Milk, fruits, and vegetables are luxury
items. Whether the total number of infant deaths from dehydra-
tion caused by diarrhea has been recorded is highly questionable.
For the *barrio* people life is bleak, and the future is grim. But as
one *colonia* mother expressed it, "This is the best that we can do,
and it will not help us to get depressed." As she looked out toward
El Paso, she added, "I can reach out and hold prosperity in my
palms, but this is the closest we will come to it." Another writer
commenting on the *colonias* found it difficult to hide his cynicism:

> Perched on the hills above Juárez, gathered like armies of
> refugees in exodus, gypsies in the un-Promised land, without
> roads, electricity, gas, sewers, or water, these *paracaidistas*
> [parachutists or squatters] are privileged spectators to scen-
> ic wonders…of good roads, neon lights, glittering automo-
> biles, palatial homes, and kidney-shaped swimming pools.[20]

Tourists visiting Mexico for the first time are invariably impressed with the extremes and contrasts to be seen, and Ciudad
Juárez is no exception. Along with the widespread grinding poverty
to be found in the *colonias*, there are more than a thousand million-
aires. They live in sumptuous homes in the fashionable Campestre
(Country Club) area, or in mansions along 16th of September
Street. They entertain European nobility, travel to Spain and Italy,
send their children to the private schools of El Paso, and to the
Ivy League or California universities, and do their shopping in
Dallas, New York, and El Paso's largest shopping malls. The enormous gap between the few rich and the many poor has been partially closed with the development of a middle class — shopowners,
clerks, foremen, nurses, teachers, government employees, many of
whom have a high school education, regular employment, and
earnings of about $300 a month. This class has been hit hard in
recent years by the peso devaluations, so that while these people
are much better off than those in the *colonias*, the gap between
middle class and rich Juárenses remains so great that it will not be
bridged for many years to come.[21]

A political development of major significance on the northern
frontier of Mexico has been the emergence of the Partido Acción
Nacional, or PAN. In July 1983 this political party brought an end
to the fifty-year supremacy of the Partido Revolucionario Institu-
cional (PRI) in Ciudad Juárez when the PAN's candidate for mayor,
Francisco Barrio Terrazas, was swept into office by a two-to-one
margin. Labeling his party as probusiness and progressive, Barrio
promised more honesty and efficiency in government. He criticized
the federal government for its lack of understanding of border
problems, and promised to improve conditions by integrating the
border more closely with the national economy. The PAN had
emerged as a significant political force on the northern frontier,
placing the PRI on the defensive for the first time in fifty years.
The popular Barrio became the PAN's candidate for governor of

Chihuahua in 1986, but in elections held that summer a PRI-controlled state electoral commission declared that the PRI candidates had swept all state and local offices. The Panistas cried fraud and corruption, dramatizing their grievances with protest demonstrations and a week-long blockade of the Bridge of the Americas. The election results stood, but the PRI had lost considerable credibility both at home and abroad with national elections only two years in the future.[22]

For every United States citizen living in Ciudad Juárez and employed in El Paso, and for every green card and *mica* holder who crosses the bridges and works in El Paso, literally thousands upon thousands of Mexican nationals cross into the United States illegally seeking a better life. This alien tide, victims of the severest economic crisis Mexico has experienced in the past fifty years, has resulted in a "silent invasion" of the United States. One authority has labeled it "perhaps the greatest illegal flow in world history."[23]

Although the causes of this phenomenal migration are complex, most experts point to push-pull factors, while disagreeing somewhat among themselves as to the relative importance of each. The primary long-run "pull" force, writes economist Vernon Briggs, Jr., is the obvious difference between the economies of the United States and Mexico. Nowhere, he says, does a political border separate two nations with a greater economic disparity. Thus, life in the United States for Mexican migrants obviously represents a considerable improvement over the life left behind. Moreover, the immigration policy of the United States historically has been largely determined by the demand for cheap labor. Mexicans have been welcomed as workers but not as settlers, and thus until recently it has not been against the law in the United States to hire an illegal alien. Added to these "pull" factors are the long-run "push" factors — the widespread poverty which is a way of life in Mexico, along with unemployment and underemployment throughout Mexico's struggling economy. All of these factors have served to bring a flood-tide to the border, so that Juárez's population by 1985 had soared to 800,000, almost twice that of El Paso.[24]

The typical illegal alien from Mexico is male, usually unmarried, under thirty years of age, unskilled, rural, poorly educated, speaks little if any English, and is most likely to find work in an unskilled occupation as either a farm or non-farm worker. In the

past, his original intention probably was to work for several
months, save a few dollars, and then return to Mexico. However,
once he found employment in the United States, the temptation
became much greater for him to remain on the job and send part
of his earnings back home. Within recent years several hundred
illegal aliens each day have crossed the Rio Grande into El Paso.
Arrests in the El Paso sector amount to about 16,000 each month
and have been increasing each year. The problem has become extremely complex and controversial. Some argue that the illegals are
good for the El Paso economy, while others insist that they cost
millions of tax dollars, they contribute to crime, they take jobs
away from Mexican-Americans who are United States citizens, and
they give Hispanics a bad image. But the most serious charge is
that the United States has lost all control over its borders.[25]

The United States Border Patrol, established in 1924, is assigned the task of protecting the border, preventing illegal entry,
and apprehending undocumented aliens. As Los Angeles newsman
Rubén Salazar put it shortly before his death in 1970, "there is no
law against hiring wetbacks, only against being a wetback." To
carry out its functions in the El Paso area, the Border Patrol makes
use of river guards, patrol wagons, and train inspectors. Nowhere
on the Rio Grande are the wire fences major obstacles, and the
barrios are only a short distance away. To be sure, the Border Patrol
employs sensing devices, mobile ground and air patrols, and checkpoints; but to control the border effectively, it has been said, would
require "the entire National Guard of five or six states on full-time
duty." Illegal aliens frequently receive assistance, naturally at a
price which they can ill afford, from coyotes – document forgers,
contact men, planners, and arrangers – who handle all the details
in getting the illegal across the river. A guide leads a group which
wades the river at dusk through the fence to a cheap hotel or
motel, then loads them into a van or camper where they are frequently crammed into hidden compartments and kept in conditions
bordering on suffocation for hours on end. The smuggling rings
are highly organized, inhuman, and extortionate. "If not a slave
trade," comments one authority, "the smuggling of undocumented
aliens comes very close to it." Yet the risk of apprehension de-
creases substantially with each successive illegal entry. Of those
who are caught and accept "voluntary departure" to Mexico, about

one-third will return in a few days. The chances are that sooner or later they will succeed in getting across the border.[26]

In November 1986, in response to the growing concern over the problem of the illegal alien, Congress passed, after years of wrangling, the Immigration Reform and Control Act. It contains two principal provisions: (1) employer sanctions, making it unlawful for any person to hire any alien not authorized to work in the U.S.; and (2) an amnesty provision enabling any alien who had been living illegally in the U.S. since 1982 to obtain temporary legal residency, to be converted to a permanent residency status after eighteen months, providing the alien had a minimal understanding of English and a knowledge of U.S. history and government.[27]

A vast administrative machinery became necessary to implement the law. The numbers applying for amnesty were small at first, but 23,000 had been approved for temporary legal residency in El Paso by November 1988. On the other hand, the provision dealing with employer sanctions proved to be much more controversial. Mexican-American organizations stated that the provision would result in nationwide discrimination against all "foreign-appearing" workers and would have a disastrous effect on the labor force throughout the Southwest. Local housewives denounced the law, claiming that "hiring illegal aliens was a way of life in El Paso." Although Border Patrol officials were claiming in 1988 that the number of illegal alien crossings had been significantly reduced, a bilateral commission in November 1988, after a two-year study of the problem, stated that such was not the case. "Short of intolerable methods, the United States cannot stem the flow alone," said former assistant secretary of state William Rogers, chairman of the commission. "Economic development in Mexico," he said, "is the only longterm realistic solution."[28]

A fundamental factor on the border is the degree of economic interdependence between the Mexican cities on the Rio Grande and their United States counterparts, an interdependence described as being "on a scale rarely found along any other world frontier." Thus, El Paso is not only a border city – it is half of the largest international metropolitan complex on the United States-Mexican border. "The two national parts of this metropolitan unit are closely articulated and interdependent," says geographer D. W. Meinig. "The two linguistic cultures live in intimate association or

*The proximity of El Paso to Ciudad Juárez is indicated by this
border crossing point over a bridge over the rechanneled Rio Grande
into downtown El Paso. (Courtesy El Paso Public Library)*

at least daily awareness of one another. Bilingualism is widespread."
As one prominent El Pasoan put it, "El Paso and Juárez are Siamese
twins joined together at the cash register. They are welded together,
and you cannot do anything in El Paso that does not affect Juárez."
Ellwyn Stoddard adds, "We depend on one another for survival. To
try to separate us will kill both of the Siamese twins." Or to put it
another way, "If one sneezes, the other gets the flu."[29]

Southwest authority Carey McWilliams has referred to the
border separating Mexico and the United States as one of the
most unrealistic in the Western Hemisphere. "The Rio Grande," he
says, "does not separate people – it draws them together." As an El
Paso witness before a 1968 Immigration Commission hearing explained, "The drawing of an arbitrary line through 750,000 people
does not separate them culturally, socially, and most of all, economically. Because it is estimated that eighty-five percent of all the

wages earned by commuters in the El Paso area are spent in El Paso we have a selfish interest." Simple but significant statistics that dramatize the interdependence of the two cities are the northbound bridge crossings in 1985 from Juárez to El Paso — 12 million vehicles and 32 million pedestrians.[30]

In testimony before the Texas Senate Subcommittee on Mass Transit and the Texas House Committee on Transportation in October 1974, Mayor Fred Hervey of El Paso described the El Paso-Juárez relationship in graphic terms:

> The cities of El Paso and Ciudad Juárez jointly constitute a contiguous urbanized metropolitan area of nearly one million people. This urbanization is bisected by a thin Rio Grande River which marks the international boundary between Mexico and the United States. Culturally, socially, and economically, there is a complete fusion between both cities today.
>
> We have 82 million crossings both ways between El Paso and Ciudad Juárez each year. Although the physical division is relatively insignificant, there is a vast difference in the governmental systems of both cities and both countries. This difference creates one of the most significant problems faced by border cities along the United States-Mexico international border.
>
> Simply stated, we have two national states with two governmental systems in which the local, state, and federal jurisdictions have different roles, authority, and responsibility.
>
> On the Mexican side, cities lack certain local autonomy and must rely on their state and national governments to bring about changes in major decision making.
>
> Local government in the United States has much more authority to administer and regulate certain aspects of its own affairs.[31]

Mayor Hervey then continued with an analysis of the transportation problem between the two cities:

> To a large extent our federal government contends that the international transportation problem now facing El Paso is a local matter. On the Mexican side, their federal government has jurisdiction and control over the planning and administration of international transportation. Consequently in El Paso and Ciudad Juárez, it is difficult to undertake any transportation planning and program implementation.

Due to the lack of a federal international transportation agency to develop and implement international
treaties, our efforts to establish and improve binational
mass transit operations have become a hit and miss crisis-
oriented procedure.[32]

Of the multitude of problems shared by the two border cities,
whether poverty, unemployment, illegal aliens, health, narcotics,
peso devaluations, or pollution, none is more important in the
semi-arid El Paso-Juárez environment than water – the lifeblood of
man, animals, and the land. The water supplies of the El Paso-
Juárez area consist of groundwater from the lower Mesilla Valley
and the Hueco Bolson with surface water from the Rio Grande
playing a minor role. The area has 1.3 million inhabitants, and
population is projected to double in the next twenty years. Both
cities depend largely on shared groundwater reservoirs for their
municipal water supplies. In view of the heavy water usage in the
El Paso-Juárez area, a recent study concludes:

The area faces significant groundwater problems. The
amount of fresh groundwater is limited and natural re-
charge is not sufficient to meet even present water requirements. The fresh groundwater reserves are being mined
and in their place is encroaching saline water. This condition will continue through the year 2000. While there is sufficient fresh groundwater in the El Paso area to meet the
needs through the year 2000, joint management of this
groundwater resource by Texas, Mexico, and New Mexico is
necessary to ensure an adequate water supply for the future.
Questions which must be addressed concern interstate and
international import and export of groundwater.[33]

An additional complication is that in the border region, the
heaviest groundwater user in the United States, the laws and institutions are woefully inadequate to control the exploitation of
the groundwater resources. The absence of a framework for either
resolving disputes or managing the resources raises the specter of
strained relations between the two countries. Ecologists therefore
insist that steps must be taken immediately to improve the allocation and management of transboundary groundwaters in general
and the United States-Mexican border region in particular.[34]

A simple and logical first step, they argue, is to place a greater
amount of authority in the hands of the International Boundary

and Water Commission, a binational agency, first created in 1894 as the International Boundary Commission, later changed in 1945 to its present name. With an outstanding record for resolving groundwater problems in the past, the ecologists point out, it should therefore be given wider authority to manage and regulate both the surface and groundwater resources along the border as to their quality, quantity, and allocation. Just how this recommendation will be received by the two governments concerned, or by the private sector, particularly in the United States, is highly uncertain at the moment, but what is involved here is the future of the border region as it approaches the twenty-first century.[35]

In recent years, particularly during the cooler months, El Pasoans driving to work in the downtown area have been horrified at the evil yellow pall clinging to the ground along the historic Pass of the North and hiding from view the mountains of Mexico. This villain hanging over the western section of the city is border pollution caused by the emissions of a metropolitan complex and held in place by an atmospheric phenomenon known as "inversion." This is caused by a ground temperature warmer than that in the air — a "lid on a pot," as one expert puts it. A poll of El Pasoans in the 1970s revealed their extreme displeasure — 86 percent were concerned with the city's air problems, 78 percent thought "the government" should "do something," and 63 percent were willing to pay higher taxes to abate pollution. But as one authority has noted, in all likelihood a poll focusing on those areas downwind of the offending smelter stacks would show different values.[36]

In September 1973 the first binational symposium on air pollution, organized under the auspices of the local office of the Pan American Health Organization, was held on the campus of The University of Texas at El Paso. It concluded that El Paso had eight major point emissions of pollutants — the copper, lead, and zinc smelter, the municipal solid waste site, two cement plants, two petroleum refineries and two large brick plants. Other sources were unpaved streets and emissions from some 227,000 registered vehicles, with particularly high levels of pollution from vehicles to be found at the border checkpoints. Ciudad Juárez is overall the more polluted city, with domestic and industrial smoke, a cement plant, hot mix asphalt, and the municipal refuse dump contributing the most.[37]

In 1972 a joint air quality monitoring activity along the
United States-Mexican border was established. Health authorities
of Ciudad Juárez, El Paso, and Las Cruces, with the collaboration
of the local office of the Pan American Health Organization, set
up a program covering a fifty-mile radius centered in the El Paso-
Juárez area. This airshed, writes environmental engineer Arthur
W. Busch, covers more than 2 million persons in an interdependent economic activity reflected by an average of 1 million vehicles
crossing and 3.3 million people crossings each month. It generated
considerable public interest in the pollution problem, as did the
ASARCO smelter case, when it was disclosed that the lead content in the blood of some eight thousand children living near the
smelter had been raised to higher risk levels. The American company paid damages when contamination was established. Even so,
in spite of these efforts, the problem remains, and environmen-
talists candidly confess that not much can be done. Vehicles are
the primary source, and no doubt there will be more of them,
rather than fewer, in the future.[38]

For many years a widely held notion on the border contends
that "it is difficult for people who do not live in a border city to
understand the problems of the border." Legislators, tourist and
convention people, and city promoters complain bitterly about the
ignorance and indifference that exists about El Paso and local border problems. At best, they say, Washington, D.C., and Mexico
City tend to place local and regional border problems within a national and international context. "The ignorance of most congress-
men about border problems is terrible," former congressman Richard
White has said. "As far as they are concerned we on the border
might as well be living on the moon." Few listen when Congressman Ron Coleman harangues the House about border problems,
but he says he refuses to give up. Congressman Kiki de la Garza
adds, "You keep trying even though you know they are not really
interested. Some day they will realize the importance of our area."[39]

Many of the same attitudes prevail at the state level. "They
still think we are Rosa's Cantina – a little border village," says Rep.
Paul Moreno. "They can't understand," adds Rep. Jack Vowell, "why
we make a big hullabaloo over what they see as a pile of rock."
Thus, local lawmakers in the Texas legislature have concluded that
El Paso is the victim of geography that has caused it to be labeled

"a stepchild," and that El Pasoans are basically different from most other Texans. El Paso's twin across the river feels much the same way. Legislators complain that they are maligned and misunderstood by the rest of the country, including the state and federal governments. "Juárez is an island," says Barrio, the Panista leader. "There always has been a problem between the border and the federal government."[40]

The failure of the two border communities to obtain the attention and recognition of their respective governments at the federal and state levels these past two decades has brought local officials on both sides together in another attempt to coordinate their efforts and keep the lines of communication open in the solution of mutual border problems. Traditionally, the process of interaction between the two cities has been carried on by the local influentials, or elites, but in this undertaking, as border expert Ellwyn Stoddard notes, some interesting differences in attitudes, values, ideals, and objectives have come to the surface on many an occasion. He explains:

> The Cd. Juárez elite have, for the most part, been educated in American schools, can speak English well, and understand how the American system works. They have endeavored to make strong friends on the United States side of the border and they look to the United States as a source of ideals, values, and ideas, in addition to any economic benefits which accrue from border tourism or related activity. The El Paso influentials did not look to Mexico for new values, social contacts, intellectual challenges or new ideas. They recognized the importance of being good neighbors and were willing to help Cd. Juárez develop into a more vital community. In general, they did not speak Spanish well; they had few close friends in Cd. Juárez and they visited there rather infrequently. In short, they had worked out a *modus vivendi* with the city but had not internalized much of Mexican culture.

Stoddard concludes that "when successful bicultural relations occur between the border elites it is because the Mexican influentials have deferred to the values and informal demands of the American influentials on a near unilateral basis." It is evident that cultural differences between the twin border communities are as great as their economic disparity.[41]

The various attempts in the past twenty years to create region-
ally responsive bodies to consider common social and economic
problems have in general promised considerably more than they
subsequently delivered. In October 1965, coming in the wake of
the Chamizal settlement, officials and businessmen from El Paso
and Juárez created the Border Cities Association as a forum for
discussing border problems. Then in January 1967 a new official
body, the United States Commission for Border Development and
Friendship, was established in Washington, D.C. Raymond Telles,
former mayor of El Paso and former ambassador to Costa Rica, was
named chairman. Feuding between the two groups ensued, with the
result that the commission, which apparently never understood
what its mission was, had its funds cut and ceased operations in
1969. Two years later the Border Cities Association died of inertia.[42]

In August 1973 the international streetcar service, which had
been operating for more than three quarters of a century, came to
a halt as a result of a labor dispute. The Mexican government, in
an effort to curtail the spending of Mexican pesos in El Paso, then
intervened and refused to allow the service to be restored. This
created a local binational "transportation war." Feverish negotiations between officials in the two cities ensued, but a tentative
agreement concluded by local officials that gave Ciudad Juárez
more benefits than in the past was rejected by Mexico City largely
because of the influence of Juárez business interests working
through their local Chamber of Commerce. A new organization
known as the Inter-City Group was formed, but in spite of firm
pledges and high hopes, it could not get the service restored. René
Mascareñas Miranda, a former mayor of Ciudad Juárez and a
member of the group, voiced his disgust with the powerlessness of
border cities to solve local problems. "It is all a matter of the brutal
centralization of our federal government," he exclaimed. "You in
the United States have considerably more autonomy. I am frustrated. I am trying to solve things on a local level, but we are
unable to settle anything." Another association made up of border
city mayors and known as the Organization of United States
Border Cities was then formed, but when it too failed to solve the
problem, the tracks on both sides were torn up, and what had
been billed as the only international streetcar service in the world
was sent to the car barn. There it remains to this day.[43]

The concept of the binational commission for dealing with border problems, in spite of numerous failures in the past, still remained strong. In 1977 the Southwest Border Regional Commission was created to study and promote economic development. Shortly afterward followed a Mexican counterpart called the Coordinating Commission of the National Program for the Borders and Free Zones. As to their effectiveness in dealing with border problems, John House notes: "It would be unwise to assume that either will be granted more than information or consultative power in relation to the international neighbor. It will be entirely within the verdict of history if all decision making continues to be centralized in Washington, D.C., and Mexico City, whether or not this may be to the detriment of the dwellers on both sides of the Rio Grande."[44]

Thus, while border economic development is the primary concern of these commissions, they have never possessed effective decision-making authority nor funds. They serve only as forums or formal mechanisms for supervising the work of four state border commissions established by California, Arizona, New Mexico, and Texas. In recent years the governors of the states bordering on the United States-Mexico boundary have been meeting periodically to discuss problems of mutual concern. At the local level since 1973 two groups – the El Paso Intercity Group and the Juárez Grupo-Intercitadino, each with about thirty members – have been working to keep the lines of communication open, to ease the aches and pains of border life, to provide a vehicle for the discussion of border problems, to offer common sense and practical solutions, and to plan for the future. Envisaged is the establishment of a Border Region, administered by a director and a binational United States-Mexico commission. In all probability the demand for an effective international planning commission will increase in the coming years. As one scholar has said, "United States-Mexico relations should not be left to protocol visits between presidents in Washington, D.C., Mexico City, or Cancún. In short, border region relations are too important to be left to presidents."[45]

In addition to the roles of state governors, mayors, and businessmen in the affairs of the border region, mention should be made of the research efforts in recent years by Borderlands specialists who have called attention to existing problems and the need for cooperative action. Although there was a time when the Borderlands area was the special province of the historians, for the past decade it has drawn the attention of a diversified group of social scientists, specialists in mental and physical well-being, experts in pollution control, land and water utilization, and the generation and utilization of energy. More than once the Borderlands has been described as a remarkable research laboratory, an area for research aimed at the understanding of fundamental border problems. As Jorge Bustamante, president of El Colegio de la Frontera Norte, in Tijuana, Baja California, has suggested:

> The border provides to social scientists, to people interested in analyzing the problems of the border, a natural laboratory to understand those international implications of the relations between the two countries being manifested in the day-to-day interactions between peoples and institutions of the border area.[46]

In 1976 under the leadership of Ellwyn Stoddard, professor of sociology and anthropology at The University of Texas at El Paso, there was organized the Association of Borderlands Scholars, a springboard for border specialists — historians, political scientists, geographers, sociologists, economists, scientists, and engineers. Under the sponsorship of the association, there was published in 1983 *Borderlands Sourcebook*, a veritable encyclopedia on the area written by specialists in the field. The University of Texas at El Paso has established the Center for Inter-American and Border Studies. As a former director has noted, "Latin America begins just one thousand yards from UTEP, making the study of Mexico and its neighbors to the south a natural part of the University's mission."[47]

In cooperation with Texas Western Press, the center has published a number of important monographs on border topics — *Air Pollution Along the United States-Mexico Border*, edited by Howard Applegate and C. Richard Bath; *Environmental Problems of the Borderlands*, by Applegate; *Air Quality Issues in the El Paso/Cd. Juárez Border Region*, edited by Willard P. Gingerich; and a reissue of *The U.S.-Mexico Border Region: Anticipating Resource Needs and Issues to the Year 2000*, edited by César Sepúlveda and Albert E. Utton. In addition, the center has issued in recent years copies of papers on border topics under the headings of Border Perspectives, and Border Issues and Public Policy. Thus, through conferences, research, and publication, the university is attempting to direct attention to the United States-Mexico border region and the enormous problems which it will be facing as it approaches the twenty-first century. Hopefully, the effort will provide a greater degree of understanding, cooperation, and coordination of activities between the two countries at the national, state, and local levels. At stake is the future of what promises to be one of the world's most dynamic areas.[48]

As has been noted, the El Paso area historically is the product of two diverse cultural traditions – that of the Spanish-Mexican North and the Anglo-American Southwest. That there should be occasional friction between the two is understandable if it is recalled that for centuries the rivalry, antagonism, and conflict between their respective parents, Spain and England, was a major theme in the history of modern Europe. By the nineteenth century this cultural clash entered a new phase on the continent of North America which involved the United States and Mexico, children respectively of their English and Spanish parents. In the El Paso area American and Mexican forces fought in 1846 at the battle of Brazito, and the Treaty of Guadalupe Hidalgo of 1848 fixed the boundary between the United States and Mexico at the Rio Grande. That there would be conflict in the future was inevitable – the Salt War, Santa Ysabel, and the Columbus Raid. Yet to date neither of these highly diverse cultures has absorbed the other. Rather there exists a distinctive border culture neither Latin American nor North American, but something of both. As James Lawrence McConville points out in his provocative article, "El Paso-Ciudad Juárez: A Focus of Inter-American Culture,"

> Here in this area is a zone of cultural contact, and cultural diffusion between the two countries can consequently be expected. If the confrontation of opposing civilizations results in the partial disintegration of the values and norms of these border inhabitants, what does this suggest about future inter-American relations? If Juareses are not Mexicans, and El Pasoans are not Americans, what are they? It is tempting to predict that the time may come when the two cities may share more characteristics with each other than they do with their parent countries. If so, how will compromises of the subtle but important difference between Anglo-American and Hispanic-American civilizations be made?[49]

Most people in the El Paso-Juárez area agree that it is different, unique, or special, and that it is the border that makes it so. "You assume El Paso is a part of Texas and a part of the United States," says sociologist Ellwyn Stoddard,

> but that is a mistake. We are more a part of the border culture than we are American or Mexican. We are a hybrid of Mexican and American cultures and we belong to neither one. We have been taught that there is a legal and political boundary and that two countries line up and touch it. Only after twenty-five years as a border specialist could I get rid of that idea.

Many others agree, pointing out that El Paso is intertwined economically, culturally, and socially with the northern frontier of Mexico, which has created a blend. "The cultures are different," says Bishop Raymundo Peña, "but they intertwine. They create a nice tapestry with threads of different colors giving the whole border a culture that is unique in itself."[50]

Because the two border cultures in the El Paso-Juárez area are strong and have their roots deep in Texas and Mexico, each has influenced the other. The Hispanic cultural influence is particularly noticeable in El Paso in its architecture (hacienda, patio, vigas, tile, and ornamental iron), in the food (caldillo, burritos, chiles rellenos, and guacamole), in the dress (guayaberas and embroidered sundresses), in the music (mariachi, ranchero, and salsa), the dance (folklórico and flamenco), and luminarias. On the other hand, the Anglo influence in Ciudad Juárez, much more commercial than artistic, is seen in the discos, McDonald's, Kentucky Fried Chicken, Pepsi, Coca-Cola, and Hollywood-produced movies. Then at times the two cultural influences come together in a combination known as Tex-Mex. "There is a little bit of Tex-Mex in everyone," a director of El Paso's Arts Resources Department has said. Moreover, the language of the border has produced what is called Spanglish, or Chicano English (Me voy a shopping, watch-i-carro, quieres ir a tomar un drink, ay-te-watcho). A favorite dish on the border is a concoction known as the Mexican plate. Cowboy boots and a guayabera are worn in combination. Hispanics attend football games and Anglos attend bullfights. The El Paso-Juárez border complex is a fascinating place *con mucho ambiente*. Perhaps the lifestyle is "laid-back" as some maintain; certainly it is relaxed, casual, leisurely, informal, friendly, and pleasant.[51]

Finally, it may be asked, does El Paso have a personality? Is it unique, as has often been said? Does it have distinctive characteristics? Has it an individual style? To begin with, El Paso is a leading urban center of the American Southwest, like Phoenix, Tucson, and Albuquerque, with which it has a great deal in common. In his study, *The Urban Southwest*, Bradford Luckingham presents a profile history of these four cities as they evolved from frontier settlements to metropolitan centers. They began as railroad towns; in the 1890s they were "sin cities"; they became health meccas, tourist resorts, and gateways to Mexico; they had a common concern about water, and frequently went to the federal government for help; they developed into cultural centers, each with a university; they had military installations, particularly air bases; after World War II they experienced spectacular increases in population and economic growth, with Phoenix moving far out in front of the others. While each city has a sizeable Hispanic population, Anglos have remained the dominant group. Although the Hispanics helped to build the cities, says Luckingham, the power and the prestige belonged to the Anglos.[52]

On the other hand, while these four Southwestern cities have much in common, each has maintained a degree of individuality that makes it in certain respects different from the other three. This is particularly true of El Paso, the most different of the four. The following points, then, are offered in support of El Paso's distinctive characteristics that give it a uniqueness not shared by the other three:

1. *El Paso is historic.* Four centuries of history at the Pass of the North have produced an international metropolitan complex, the product of the interaction of two cultural traditions – the Spanish-Mexican North and the American Southwest. Spanish civilization arrived at the Pass of the North in the sixteenth century and laid the foundations for more than two centuries of Spanish rule in the Southwest. Six settlements were subsequently established along the south bank of the Rio Grande, one of which, El Paso del Norte, became the future Ciudad Juárez. The three settlements of Ysleta, Socorro, and San Elizario at a later date were placed on the Texas side as a result of the shifting river, giving Ysleta its claim to being

the oldest town in Texas, and El Paso its claim that its Lower
Valley is where Texas history begins. With the establishment of
the Rio Grande as the international boundary between the United
States and Mexico in 1848, Anglo-Americans founded five settlements north of the river, one of which, Franklin, became the
future El Paso, Texas. With the three settlements of Ysleta, Socorro,
and San Elizario, El Paso became a bicultural community, and has
remained so ever since. The city's history, therefore, is one of its
greatest resources, and it is important that projects such as the
Mission Trail receive strong local support.[53]

   2. *El Paso is multi-cultural but primarily bicultural.* The community is a conglomerate of many cultures – sixty-five ethnic groups,
according to a recent study – but Mexican-Americans and Anglos
comprise the two largest groups. Although Mexican-Americans
traditionally have been regarded as a national minority, they have
been a majority group in El Paso most of the twentieth century,
and today they constitute more than 60 percent of the city's population. While most city officials and business interests insist that
relations between Anglos and Mexican-Americans are good, and
that the stereotypes, prejudice, and discrimination no longer exist,
many Mexican-Americans disagree. They point out that while
many of the old barriers have been removed, a gulf exists between
the two, and there are two El Pasos. While Mexican-Americans
have moved up into the middle class, established businesses, entered politics or the professions, the Anglos still maintain their
control over the political, social, and economic system, and continue to hold the top executive positions in finance, business, and
government. Even so, the Mexican-Americans in the future will be
playing a much greater role in community affairs than they have
in the past.[54]

   3. *El Paso has a long military tradition.* Fort Bliss has a proud
record of service of more than a century and a quarter since it was
first established in 1854. It served as a frontier outpost during most
of the nineteenth century, then as an infantry garrison in the
1890s. Cavalry regiments were added during the Mexican Revolution, and following World War I the famous First Cavalry Division
was organized. By World War II Fort Bliss was one of the nation's
largest military posts, and in 1957 it was designated United States
Army Air Defense Center in recognition of its antiaircraft and

missile programs. Relations between the city and the post have always been close, and El Paso's reputation as the mother-in-law of the army has been well established for many years. The impact which Fort Bliss has had on the local economy in recent years is enormous, and it will no doubt remain, as it has been in the past, El Paso's largest and most important industry. Some of the most distinguished names in the annals of American miltary history have served at Fort Bliss, none more famous than General of the Army Omar N. Bradley, who spent his last years there.[55]

4. *El Paso is in Texas, but it should be in New Mexico.* Although the El Paso area was a part of the province of New Mexico in the Spanish colonial period, history and topography were ignored in 1850 when the Texas Legislature organized El Paso County, and the Senate of the United States fixed the thirty-second parallel as the boundary between Texas and New Mexico, the result of political compromise. "That right-angled Texas-New Mexico boundary, like many others of its era," comments geographer D. W. Meinig, "was the product of a Congressional committee which had little knowledge of the country involved. Although El Paso was fully Southwestern in character, it was placed on Texas soil and thus was politically divorced from the region it served, a geographical discordance which was of major importance to the political balance of power within New Mexico.... It is less 'Texas' in a general sense than other regions of the state." On occasion, the irrationality of the Texas-New Mexico boundary rises to the surface, as it has in recent years as a result of the current water dispute between El Paso and New Mexico.[56]

5. *El Paso is an international community.* Not only is El Paso a city – it is half of the largest international metropolitan complex along the United States-Mexican border. One cannot help but recall one El Pasoan's comment, "El Paso and Juárez are Siamese twins joined together at the cash register. They are welded together, and you cannot do anything in El Paso that does not affect Juárez." The growing interdependence of the two cities will undoubtedly increase with the development of the twin plant program, thus stimulating the demand for the establishment of a regional binational commission with the authority to offer practical, common sense solutions to border problems at the local level in a spirit of partnership. Finally, the El Paso-Juárez international

307

metropolitan complex, the geographic center of the Borderlands and the heart and soul of its distinctive culture, possesses the expertise, the facilities, and the potential to become the historical, cultural, and intellectual center of the Borderlands area. Such is the challenge that faces this unique international complex and its distinctive culture as it approaches the twenty-first century. A principal measurement of the future will be how much this area does to recapture its past and to preserve its individuality.[57]

Notes

INTRODUCTION

1. For an important essay on the major developments among historians regarding the interpretation of the term "Borderlands," see David J. Weber, "John Francis Bannon and the Historiography of the Spanish Borderlands: Retrospect and Prospect," *Journal of the Southwest* 29 (Winter 1987): 332-63. See also Ralph H. Vigil, "Historical Overview," in Ellwyn R. Stoddard, Richard L. Nostrand, and Jonathan P. West, eds., *Borderlands Sourcebook: A Guide to the Literature on Northern Mexico and the American Southwest* (Norman, 1983), 28.
2. Vigil, "Overview," 5.
3. T. Zane Reeves, "The U.S.-Mexico Border Commissions: An Overview and Agenda For Further Research," UTEP Center for Inter-American and Border Studies (El Paso, 1984), 2.
4. Stanley R. Ross, "Introduction, Appendix I," Ross, ed. *Views Across the Border* (Albuquerque, 1978), 361.
5. Quoted in Ross, "Introduction," 10.
6. Ibid., 381.

CHAPTER I
THE PASS OF THE NORTH:
FIRST SETTLEMENTS

1. Herbert C. Morrow, "The Mission Trail" (El Paso, 1981), 6; J. Lawrence McConville, "A History of Population in the El Paso-Ciudad Juárez Area" (Master's thesis, University of New Mexico, 1966), 1-4.
2. Morrow, "The Mission Trail," 7; Owen P. White, *Out of the Desert* (El Paso, 1923), 227.
3. Earl M. P. Lovejoy, *El Paso's Geologic Past* (El Paso, 1980), 7.
4. Morrow, "The Mission Trail," 7.
5. Lovejoy, *El Paso's Geologic Past*, 9.
6. Thomas C. O'Laughlin, *The Keystone Dam Site* (El Paso, 1980), 23-26; Michael Whalen, *Settlement Patterns of the Eastern Hueco Bolson* (El Paso, 1977), 6-8.
7. O'Laughlin, *The Keystone Dam Site*, 25-26.

8. Ibid., 26; Whalen, *Settlement Patterns*, 7.

9. John Francis Bannon, *The Spanish Borderlands Frontier, 1513-1821* (New York, 1970), chap. 2.

10. Frederick W. Hodge and Theodore H. Lewis, eds., *Spanish Explorers in the Southern United States, 1528-1543* (New York, 1965), 99, 102; Cleve Hallenbeck, *Alvar Núñez Cabeza de Vaca – The Journey and Route of the First European to Cross the Continent of North America, 1534-1536* (Port Washington, N.Y., 1971), 203. According to Donald E. Chipman's definitive article on Cabeza de Vaca's route, he crossed northern Chihuahua about seventy-five miles south of El Paso as he headed westward toward the Pacific coast. See his "In Search of Cabeza de Vaca's Route Across Texas: An Historiographical Survey," *Southwestern Historical Quarterly* 91, no. 2 (October 1987): 146.

11. Bannon, *The Spanish Borderlands Frontier*, 16.

12. Ibid., 18-20. A residential development, shopping center, and high school have been named for the explorer.

13. Ibid., 29.

14. Herbert E. Bolton, ed., *Spanish Exploration in the Southwest, 1542-1706* (New York, 1963), 145; George P. Hammond and Agapito Rey, eds., *The Rediscovery of New Mexico, 1580-1594* (Albuquerque, 1966), 77.

15. Hammond and Rey, eds., *The Rediscovery of New Mexico*, 14.

16. Ibid.

17. Ibid., 19.

18. Bolton, ed., *Spanish Exploration in the Southwest*, 170-76.

19. Hammond and Rey, eds., *The Rediscovery of New Mexico*, 168; Bolton, ed., *Spanish Exploration in the Southwest*, 176.

20. Bannon, *The Spanish Borderlands Frontier*, 33.

21. Ibid.

22. Bolton, ed., *Spanish Exploration in the Southwest*, 201.

23. Morrow, "The Mission Trail," 37; Gaspar Pérez de Villagrá, *History of New Mexico* (Los Angeles, 1933), 126.

24. Villagrá, *History of New Mexico*, 127.

25. Charles Wilson Hackett, ed., *Historical Documents Relating to New Mexico, Nueva Vizcaya, and Approaches Thereto, to 1773* (Washington, 1923-1937), 1:210; Carlos E. Castañeda, *Our Catholic Heritage in Texas* (Austin, 1936-1958), 1:244-45; Villagrá, *History of New Mexico*, 129-36. The Spanish league varied greatly, from 2.6 miles to 3.1 miles.

26. Hackett, *Historical Documents*, 1:210.

27. Bannon, *The Spanish Borderlands Frontier*, 41.

28. Mrs. Edward E. Ayer, trans., *The Memorial of Fray Alonso de Benavides 1630* (Albuquerque, 1965), 14; Frederick W. Hodge, George P. Hammond, Agapito Rey, eds., *The Revised Memorial of Fray Alonso de Benavides 1634* (Albuquerque, 1945), 174.

29. Rex Gerald, "An Introduction to Missions of the Paso del Norte Area," *Password* 20 (Summer 1975): 49.

30. Vina Walz, in her "History of the El Paso Area, 1680-1692," (Ph.D. diss., University of New Mexico, 1951), 16, argues convincingly that the 8 December 1659 date is an error, citing contemporary sources indicating that the friar could not have been in El Paso del Norte on that day, and that the original date of 1657 or 1658 had been altered in copying; see also Archives of the Archdiocese of Santa Fe (microfilm, UTEP Library, MF525R45F951). For a correction of the errors which historians have made in the past regarding the

founding of the Guadalupe mission, see Bud Newman, "Fray García de San Francisco, Founder of El Paso," *Password* 29 (Winter 1984): 179-86.

31. France V. Scholes, ed., "Documents for the History of the New Mexico Missions in the 17th Century," *New Mexico Historical Review* 4 (1929): 195-201; Fernando Ocaranza, *Establecimientos Franciscanos en el Misterioso Reino de Nuevo México* (México, 1934), 65-68; Michael C. Meyer, *Water in the Hispanic Southwest* (Tucson, 1984), 38.

32. Walz, "History of the El Paso Area," 18-21.

33. Ibid., 27-30.

34. Ibid., 28; H. H. Bancroft, *History of the North Mexican States* (San Francisco, 1884), 1:374.

35. Walz, "History of the El Paso Area," 30; H. H. Bancroft, *History of Arizona and New Mexico* (San Francisco, 1889), 182, n. 10.

36. Walz, "History of the El Paso Area," 32-34. For the Tiguas, see Nicholas P. Houser, "The Tigua Settlement of Ysleta del Sur," *The Kiva* 35 (Winter 1970): 23-39; and Rex E. Gerald, "A History of the Tigua Indians of Ysleta del Sur, Texas" (Manuscript, Special Collections Department, University of Texas at El Paso, 1970).

37. Walz, "History of the El Paso Area," 36. A recent excavation southeast of the present Socorro mission may have found the site of the 1683 structure. See Thomas Rowland, "The Search for the Old Socorro Mission" (Master's thesis, University of Texas at El Paso, 1984), 57.

38. Walz, "History of the El Paso Area," 67, 76; Rex Gerald, "Human Occupation ot the El Paso del Norte Area," David A. Horr, ed., *American Indian Ethnohistory — Indians of the Southwest — Apache Indians* (New York, 1974), 3:18-19.

39. Gerald, "An Introduction to the Missions of the Paso del Norte Area," 53-54.

40. Bolton, ed., *Spanish Exploration in the Southwest*, 315-17; Castañeda, *Our Catholic Heritage in Texas*, 1:269-72.

41. Bolton, ed., *Spanish Exploration in the Southwest*, 317. Castañeda maintains that French traders had reached the Pecos by 1684, preceding by a year La Salle's settlement on Matagorda Bay; see his *Our Catholic Heritage in Texas*, 2:321.

42. Jack D. Forbes, *Apache, Navaho, and Spaniard* (Norman, 1971), 200-225; Walz, "History of the El Paso Area," 166-68.

43. Walz, "History of the El Paso Area," 168.

44. Ibid., 121-23; Anne E. Hughes, *The Beginnings of Spanish Settlement in the El Paso District* (Berkeley, 1914), 368.

45. Walz, "History of the El Paso Area," 161, 192.

46. Elizabeth A. H. John, *Storms Brewed in Other Men's Worlds* (College Station, 1975), 112.

47. Ibid., 113.

48. J. J. Bowden, *Spanish and Mexican Land Grants in the Chihuahuan Acquisition* (El Paso, 1971), 164-65.

49. Oakah L. Jones, Jr., *Pueblo Warriors and Spanish Conquest* (Norman, 1966), 38-45; Forbes, *Apache, Navaho, and Spaniard*, 236-37.

50. J. Manuel Espinosa, "Population of the El Paso District in 1692," *Mid-America* 23 (January 1941): 61-62; Forbes, *Apache, Navaho, and Spaniard*, 243.

51. Jones, *Pueblo Warriors and Spanish Conquest*, 46-62.

52. Espinosa, "Population of the El Paso District in 1692," 62, 84.

53. Declaration of Fray Juan Alvarez, 12 January 1706, in Hackett, ed., *Historical Documents* 3:377-87.

54. Hughes, *The Beginnings of Settlement in the El Paso District*, 391.

CHAPTER II
THE EL PASO AREA
IN THE 18TH CENTURY

1. Morrow, "The Mission Trail," 39-40, 48.

2. Rex Gerald, "Portrait of a Community," *American West* 3 (Summer 1966): 40; Carey McWilliams, *North from Mexico* (New York, 1968), 294.

3. Alexander von Humboldt, *Political Essay on the Kingdom of New Spain* (London, 1822), 2:312.

4. Morrow, "The Mission Trail," 48; see documents signed by Lt. Gov. Don Javier de Uranga, Archives of the Ayuntamiento of Ciudad Juárez (microfilm, UTEP Library, MF495R47F151-73; hereafter cited as Juárez Archives); von Humboldt, *Political Essay* 2:317.

5. William M. Pierson to assistant secretary of state, El Paso del Norte, 30 November 1872, Despatches from United States Consuls in Ciudad Juárez (El Paso del Norte), 1850-1906, General Records of the Department of State, Record Group 59, National Archives (microfilm, UTEP Library M184R2). Consul Pierson's fascinating sketches of Lower Valley agricultural methods were first published by Helen Orndorff in her article, "The Development of Agriculture in the El Paso Valley – The Spanish Period," *Password* 5 (October 1960): 138-47. See also Alice White, "The Beginning and Development of Irrigation in the El Paso Valley," *Password* 2 (November 1957): 106-14.

6. Pierson to assistant secretary of state, El Paso del Norte, 30 November 1872, Despatches from United States Consuls in Ciudad Juáez.

7. Idem to idem, ibid. See also Herbert C. Morrow, "Valley Vineyards A Rich Historical Heritage," *Cactus Points* (Fall 1984): 12.

8. Max Moorhead, *New Mexico's Royal Road* (Norman, 1958), 55; Morrow, "The Mission Trail," 69.

9. Moorhead, *New Mexico's Royal Road*, 39.

10. Robert Ryal Miller, ed., "New Mexico in Mid-Eighteenth Century: A Report Based on Governor Vélez Capuchín's Inspection," *Southwestern Historical Quarterly* 79 (October 1975): 170-71.

11. Ibid.

12. Max Moorhead, *The Apache Frontier* (Norman, 1968), 3-6; Donald E. Worcester, *The Apaches* (Norman, 1979); Florence and Robert Lister, *Chihuahua, Storehouse of Storms* (Albuquerque, 1966), 53-55. Jack D. Forbes argues that the primary villain in New Mexico in the eighteenth century was the Spaniard and not the Apache, pointing out that the peaceful and stable relationship which had been established in the seventeenth century between Apaches and Pueblo Indian groups was greatly disturbed when the Spaniards arrived on the scene and attempted to win over the Pueblo tribes and place them under Spanish protection. See his *Apache, Navaho, and Spaniard*, 281-84.

13. That is, "Oh, Chihuahua...how many Apaches!" This is a chapter title in Fernando Jordán, *Crónica de un país bárbaro* (Chihuahua, 1975), 179; see also Sean Galvin, ed., *The Kingdom of New Spain by Pedro Alonso O'Crouley – 1774* (San Francisco, 1972), 52; for a presidio commander's frustration with the Apache problem, see James M. Daniel, ed., "Diary of Pedro José de la Fuente," *Southwestern Historical Quarterly* 60 (October 1956): 260-81, and 83 (January 1980): 259-78.

14. Max Moorhead, *The Presidio* (Norman, 1975), 27, 36, 38.

15. Guillermo Porras Muñoz, ed., *Diario de Don Pedro de Rivera* (México, 1945), 67-68. The reference to the "east bank" for the towns of Socorro, Ysleta, Senecú,

and San Lorenzo is puzzling, and raises the question whether "east" is a misprint or the river shifted to the south in the 1720s as it would a century later.

16. Moorhead, *The Presidio*, 40, 45-46.
17. Muñoz, ed., *Diario de Don Pedro de Rivera*, 67-68; Carlos E. Castañeda, *Our Catholic Heritage in Texas* (Austin 1936), 2:329-30.
18. John, *Storms Brewed in Other Men's Worlds*, 273; Moorhead, *The Presidio*, 49.
19. Declaration of Fray Miguel de Menchero, Santa Bárbara, 10 May 1744, in Hackett, ed., *Historical Documents*, 3:406-7; Oakah Jones, Jr., *Los Paisanos: Spanish Settlers on the Northern Frontier of New Spain* (Norman, 1979), 120. Utilizing Tjarks's factor of 4.30 for Spanish and caste families and 3.85 for Indian families, the total population of the El Paso area in Menchero's report comes to 2,469 compared with Tjarks's figure of 2,260 for the years 1746-1748. See Alicia V. Tjarks, "Demographic, Ethnic and Occupational Structure of New Mexico, 1790," *The Americas* 35 (July 1978): 51, 53.
20. Declaration of Fray Menchero, Hackett, ed., *Historical Documents*, 3, 406-7; Morrow, "The Mission Trail," 49.
21. Henry W. Kelly, "Franciscan Missions of New Mexico, 1740-1760," *New Mexico Historical Review* 15 (October 1940): 363; Tjarks's figure for 1750 is 3,090. See her "Demographic, Ethnic and Occupational Structure of New Mexico," 60.
22. Report of the Reverend Father Provincial of the Province of El Santo Evangelio, Convent of San Francisco, March 1750, in Hackett, ed., *Historical Documents*, 3:446-47.
23. See document quoted in Armando B. Chávez, *Historia de Ciudad Juárez Chihuahua* (México, 1970), 153-54. Confirmation of the *ejido* lands belonging to the towns of San Lorenzo, Senecú, Socorro, Ysleta, and San Elizario was granted by the Ayuntamiento of Chihuahua on 13 February 1824. See Juárez Archives (microfilm, UTEP Library, MF495R3F005-006).
24. See document signed by Diego Tiburcio de Ortega, alcalde mayor, Limpia Concepción del Socorro, 13 May 1751, Juárez Archives (microfilm, UTEP Library MF513R1F436). The name Diego Tiburcio de Ortega appears in the census of 1692.
25. Report of Father Manuel de San Juan Nepomuceno y Trigo, 1754, in Hackett, ed., *Historical Documents*, 3:460-61.
26. Ibid.; Paul Horgan, *Great River* (New York, 1954), 1:348; John L. Kessell, *Kiva, Cross, and Crown* (Washington, D. C., 1979), 507-12.
27. Eleanor Adams, ed., *Bishop Tamarón's Visitation to New Mexico* (Albuquerque, 1954), 34-35.
28. McConville, "A History of Population in the El Paso-Ciudad Juárez Area," 37; Bancroft's figure for 1760 is 4,982. See his *History of Arizona and New Mexico*, 279. A literal translation of *gente de razón* is "people of reason, or education, or culture." Thus, the term means those of some European or mixed blood—in other words, non-Indians.
29. Adams, ed., *Bishop Tamarón's Visitation to New Mexico*, 35-36.
30. Bancroft, *History of Arizona and New Mexico*, 281-82; Letter of Tomás Vélez Capuchín, Santa Fe, 8 September 1762, Juárez Archives (microfilm, UTEP Library MF495R40F164-66).
31. Letter of Tomás Vélez Capuchín, El Paso del Río del Norte, 16 October 1764, Juárez Archives (microfilm, UTEP Library, MF513R9F275-76).
32. Rex Gerald, "Portrait of a Community," *American West* 4 (Summer 1966): 38-41; Description of El Paso del Río del Norte, 1 September 1773, in Hackett, ed., *Historical Documents*, 3:507; Meyer, *Water in the Hispanic Southwest*, 58-59.

33. Donald Cutter, ed., "An Anonymous Statistical Report on New Mexico in 1765," *New Mexico Historical Review* 50 (October 1975): 351-52.
34. Ibid.
35. Bannon, *The Spanish Borderlands Frontier*, 190-91; Moorhead, *The Presidio*, 47.
36. Lawrence Kinnaird, ed., *The Frontiers of New Spain* (New York, 1967), 1-3.
37. Moorhead, *The Presidio*, 56-59.
38. Kinnaird, ed., *The Frontiers of New Spain*, 82-83.
39. *Dictamen* of Rubí, 10 April 1768, Archivo General de Indias, Audiencia de Guadalajara, 104-6-13. Typed copy in author's possession. See also Sidney Brinkerhoff and Odie B. Faulk, eds., *Lancers for the King* (Phoenix, 1965), for an English translation of the *Royal Regulations*.
40. Mary Lu Moore and Delmar L. Beene, eds., "The Interior Provinces of New Spain—The Report of Hugo O'Conor, January 30, 1776," *Arizona and the West* 13 (Autumn 1971): 265-82; Paige Christiansen, "Hugh Oconor's Inspection of Nueva Vizcaya and Coahuila, 1773," *Louisiana Studies* 2 (Fall 1963): 157-75; David M. Vigness, "Don Hugo Oconor and New Spain's Northeastern Frontier, 1764-1776," *Journal of the West* 6 (January 1967): 27-40.
41. W. H. Timmons, ed., "Defending Spain's Northern Frontier—The El Paso Area," *Password* 26 (Summer 1981): 78-80.
42. Alfred B. Thomas, "Antonio de Bonilla and Spanish Plans for the Defense of New Mexico, 1772-1778," *New Spain and the Anglo-American West* (New York, 1969), 1:186.
43. *Informe* de Antonio María Daroca, December [?], 1773, Archivo General y Público de la Nación, Provincias Internas, vol. 102 (microfilm, UTEP Library, MF478R53a F148); *Informe* de Daroca, July [?] 1774, Juárez Archives (microfilm, UTEP Library, MF495R45F154); Thomas, "Antonio de Bonilla and Spanish Plans for the Defense of New Mexico," 199; Moore and Beene, eds., "The Report of Hugo O'Conor," 277.
44. Moorhead, *The Presidio*, 74.
45. Fray Francisco Atanasio Domínguez to Provincial Fray Isidro Murillo, El Paso del Norte, 4 November 1775, in Eleanor B. Adams and Fray Angélico Chávez, eds., *The Missions of New Mexico, 1776* (Albuquerque, 1975), 270.
46. Moorhead, *The Presidio*, 75-76.
47. Ibid., 79-84.
48. Ibid., 84.
49. Ibid., 91-94; William A. DePalo, Jr., "The Establishment of the Nueva Vizcaya Militia during the Administration of Teodoro de Croix, 1776-1783," *New Mexico Historical Review* 48 (July 1973): 223-49.
50. Thomas, "Antonio de Bonilla and Spanish Plans for the Defense of New Mexico," 187; Pedro Galindo Navarro to Croix, 28 July 1780, Alfred B. Thomas, ed., *Forgotten Frontiers: A Study of the Spanish Indian Policy of Don Juan Bautista de Anza Governor of New Mexico 1777-1787* (Norman, 1969), 185.
51. Thomas, "Antonio de Bonilla and Spanish Plans for the Defense of New Mexico," 188.
52. John, *Storms Brewed in Other Men's Worlds*, 584.
53. Protest of the Citizens of El Paso del Norte, 13 April 1780, Spanish Archives of New Mexico, 1621-1821 (microfilm, UTEP Library, MF454R11F21-33).
54. Sr. Teniente Gobernador to the Comandante General, El Paso del Norte, 20 June 1780, ibid. (microfilm, UTEP Library, MF454R11F34-37).
55. Geographical Description of New Mexico by Fray Juan Agustín de Morfi, 1782, in Alfred B. Thomas, ed., *Forgotten Frontiers* (Norman, 1969), 109-10; von Humboldt, *Political Essay*, 2:313.

CHAPTER III
SPAIN'S LAST YEARS, 1783-1821

1. John Walton Caughey, *Bernardo de Gálvez in Louisiana, 1776-1783* (Gretna, Louisiana, 1972), chap. 12.
2. Bannon, *The Spanish Borderlands Frontier*, 186-87.
3. Edward H. Spicer, *Cycles of Conquest* (Tucson, 1974), 239-40; Moorhead, *The Presidio*, 101, 108.
4. Marc Simmons, "New Mexico's Smallpox Epidemic of 1780-1781," *New Mexico Historical Review* 41 (October 1966): 319-26; Gordon Bronitsky, "Indian Assimilation in the El Paso Area," *New Mexico Historical Review* 62, no. 2 (April 1987): 157; W. H. Timmons, ed., "The Population of the El Paso Area – A Census of 1784," *New Mexico Historical Review* 52 (October 1977): 312-13. The Tjarks study on the population of New Mexico in the eighteenth century, which did not make use of the Juárez Archives, assumes incorrectly that the El Paso settlements maintained a population figure of 5,000 from 1760 to 1790. See her "Demographic, Ethnic and Occupational Structure of New Mexico," table 2, 60-61.
5. Timmons, ed., "The Population of the El Paso Area," 313-14. See also the chart on El Paso's ethnic structure in Tjarks's article, 84.
6. Timmons, ed., "The Population of the El Paso Area," 313-14. The predominantly agrarian character of the El Paso economy is given graphic emphasis in Tjarks's article, table 15, page 86.
7. Census of the El Paso Area, 9 May 1787, Juárez Archives (microfilm, UTEP Library, MF513R12F142); Census of the El Paso Area, 1788, ibid. (microfilm, UTEP Library, MF495R47F120ff); Census of the El Paso Area, 31 December 1789, Spanish Archives of New Mexico (microfilm, UTEP Library, MF454R12F242); Census of the El Paso Area, 1795, Juárez Archives (microfilm, UTEP Library, MF495R39F307). See also Oakah L. Jones, Jr., *Los Paisanos, Spanish Settlers on the Northern Frontier of New Spain* (Norman, 1979), 122. Bancroft notes that a terrible epidemic in 1784-1785 took 1,200 lives in the El Paso area, most of which were probably Indians. See his *North Mexican States and Texas* (San Francisco, 1884), 1:658, n. 42.
8. Peter Gerhard, *The North Frontier of New Spain* (Princeton, 1982), 243; Luis Navarro García, *Don José de Gálvez y la Comandancia General de las Provincias Internas del Norte de Nueva España* (Sevilla, 1964), 492; Juárez Archives (microfilm, UTEP Library, MF495R47F37, 59, 116, 117, and MF495R48F9). Eugene O. Porter found the removal order in the Juárez Archives, published it in his *San Elizario – A History* (Austin, 1973), but misread the date, which should be 14 February 1789 instead of 14 February 1780; Rex Gerald, *Spanish Presidios of the Late Eighteenth Century in Northern New Spain* (Santa Fe, 1968), 25. For a detailed description of the presidio of San Elizario, see Roscoe P. and Margaret B. Conkling, *The Butterfield Overland Mail, 1857-1869* (Glendale, 1947), 2:51; and 3: plate 50.
9. Census of the El Paso Area, December 1804, Juárez Archives (microfilm, UTEP Library, MF495R48F83); Census of the El Paso Area, December 1805, ibid. (microfilm, UTEP Library, MF495R48F156); Census of the El Paso Area, December 1806, ibid. (microfilm, UTEP Library, MF495R49F114ff); Jones, *Los Paisanos*, 140.
10. School Census of 1806, Spanish Archives of New Mexico (microfilm, UTEP Library, MF454R16F194); School Census of 1807, ibid. (microfilm, UTEP Library, MF454R16F363); Jones, *Los Paisanos*, 138.

11. Marc Simmons, *Spanish Government in New Mexico* (Albuquerque, 1968), 104-6; Jones, *Los Paisanos*, 145.

12. Bannon, *The Spanish Borderlands Frontier*, 217. For further details on Anglo-Americans in Santa Fe prior to Pike, see Ernest R. Liljegren, "Zalmon Coley: The Second Anglo-American in Santa Fe," *New Mexico Historical Review* 62 (July 1987): 263-86.

13. Donald Jackson, ed., *The Journal of Zebulon Pike* (Norman, 1966), 1:409-10.

14. Ysidro Rey to Joachín del Real Alencaster, El Paso del Norte, 31 August 1806, Spanish Archives of New Mexico (microfilm, UTEP Library, MF454R16F217); Joseph Manrrique to Ysidro Rey, San Elizario, 23 August 1807, Juárez Archives (microfilm, UTEP Library, MF495R49F232).

15. Bannon, *The Spanish Borderlands Frontier*, 217-18.

16. W. H. Timmons, *Morelos of Mexico: Priest, Soldier, Statesman* (El Paso, 1970), 31-35.

17. Charles R. Berry, "The Election of the Mexican Deputies to the Spanish Cortes, 1810-1822," in Nettie Lee Benson, ed., *Mexico and the Spanish Cortes* (Austin, 1966), 11.

18. H. Bailey Carroll and J. Villasaña Haggard, ed., *Three New Mexico Chronicles* (New York, 1967), 56-58; Berry, "The Election of the Mexican Deputies," 16; Richard V. Baquera, "Paso del Norte and Chihuahua, 1810-1821: Revolution and Constitutionalism," (Master's thesis, University of Texas at El Paso, 1978), 34-40.

19. Timmons, *Morelos of Mexico*, 35.

20. Ibid., 36-39.

21. Ibid., 58-60.

22. Simmons, *Spanish Government in New Mexico*, 43; Francisco R. Almada, *Resumen de Historia del Estado de Chihuahua* (México, 1955), 149-50; Baquera, "Paso del Norte and Chihuahua, 1810-1821," 45-50.

23. Almada, *Resumen*, 150; Luis Navarro García, *Las Provincias Internas en el siglo XIX* (Sevilla, 1965), 63; Baquera, "Paso del Norte and Chihuahua, 1810-1821," 59.

24. Junta de Seguridad to the Commander of the Presidio of El Paso del Norte, 16 April 1811, Archivos del Ayuntamiento de Ciudad Chihuahua (microfilm, UTEP Library, MF491R133); Commander of the Presidio of El Paso del Norte to the Junta de Seguridad, 2 May 1811, ibid.

25. Infidencia de Felipe Montoya, 1811 (copy in W. H. Timmons Collection, box 2, Special Collections Department, UTEP); Salcedo to Manrrique, 2-6 February 1811, Spanish Archives of New Mexico (microfilm, UTEP Library, MF454R17F364-74).

26. Berry, "The Election of the Mexican Deputies," 18-20; José Manrrique to the lieutenant governor of El Paso del Norte, 14 January 1814, Juárez Archives (microfilm, UTEP Library, MF495R34).

27. Simmons, *Spanish Government in New Mexico*, 44-45; José Manrrique to the Ayuntamiento of Chihuahua, 8 January 1814, Archivos del Ayuntamiento de Ciudad Chihuahua (microfilm, UTEP Library, MF491R136).

28. Rafael Montes to José Manrrique, 4 June 1814, Spanish Archives of New Mexico (microfilm, UTEP Library, MF454R17F846-930); Manrrique to Rafael Montes, 27 March 1814, Juárez Archives (microfilm, UTEP Library, MF495R34); Manrrique to Pedro Quiñones, 20 July 1814, ibid.; Simmons, *Spanish Government in New Mexico*, 208-9.

29. *Bando* of Rafael Montes, 15 October 1815, Spanish Archives of New Mexico (microfilm, UTEP Library, MF454R18F250).

30. For pertinent documents regarding the Trespalacios conspiracy, see José María Ponce de León, ed., *Reseñas históricas del estado de Chihuahua* (Chihuahua, 1910), 94-145.

31. Census of the El Paso Area, December 1806, Juárez Archives (microfilm, UTEP Library, MF495R49F114); Census of 1815, Cleofas Calleros Collection (microfilm, El Paso Public Library), reel 1; Census of 1816, ibid., reel 2; Ralph E. Twitchell, *The Leading Facts of New Mexico History* (Cedar Rapids, 1917), 3:193.

32. Lawrence and Lucia Kinnaird, eds., "Secularization of Four New Mexican Missions," *New Mexico Historical Review* 54 (January 1979): 35-37; David Weber, *The Mexican Frontier, 1821-1846* (Albuquerque, 1982), 57.

33. José Miguel de Yrigoyen to Cura Interino Vicario del Paso del Norte, Durango, 15 September 1812, Cleofas Calleros Collection (microfilm, El Paso Public Library, reel 1); Letters Signed by Juan Tomás Terrazas and Juan Rafael Rascón, El Paso del Norte, 1 April 1814, ibid.; Antonio García de Texada to Juan Rafael Rascón, Chihuahua, 12 October 1814, ibid.; Juan Tomás Terrazas to Juan Rafael Rascón, San Elizario, 5 November 1814, ibid.

34. Report of Visitador Juan Bautista Ladrón del Niño de Guevara, 1817, Archives of the Archdiocese of Santa Fe (microfilm, UTEP Library, MF525R45F920-1063); Angélico Chávez, ed., *Archives of the Archdiocese of Santa Fe, 1678-1900* (Washington, D. C., 1957), 193.

35. Report of Visitador Juan Bautista Ladrón del Niño de Guevara, October 1820, Archives of the Archdiocese of Santa Fe (microfilm, UTEP Library, MF525R45F285-302); Chávez, ed., *Archives of the Archdiocese of Santa Fe*, 190.

36. Report of Guevara, October 1820, Archives of the Archdiocese of Santa Fe (microfilm, UTEP Library, MF525R45F285-302); Chávez, ed., *Archives of the Archdiocese of Santa Fe*, 190.

37. Michael C. Meyer and William L. Sherman, *The Course of Mexican History* (New York, 1979), 293-94.

38. Almada, *Resumen*, 158-59.

39. Instructions of the Junta Preparatoria, 5 July 1820, Spanish Archives of New Mexico (microfilm, UTEP Library, MF454R20F394-400).

40. Tomás Bernal to Alejo García Conde, 25 September 1820, Archivos del Ayuntamiento de Chihuahua (microfilm, UTEP Library, MF491R140); Carroll and Haggard, eds., *Three New Mexico Chronicles*, xix.

41. Bernal to García Conde, 25 September 1820, Archivos del Ayuntamiento de Chihuahua (microfilm, UTEP Library, MF491R140).

42. Alejo García Conde to the Interim Governor of New Mexico, 16 March 1821, Spanish Archives of New Mexico (microfilm, UTEP Library, MF454R20); Mariano Orcasitas to Alejo García Conde, 29 August 1821, Archivos del Ayuntamiento de Chihuahua (microfilm, UTEP Library, MF491R140); Carroll and Haggard, eds., *Three New Mexico Chronicles*, 179, n. 161.

43. Meyer and Sherman, *The Course of Mexican History*, 294-96.

44. David Weber, "An Unforgettable Day: Facundo Melgares on Independence," *New Mexico Historical Review* 48 (January 1973): 29; Weber, *The Mexican Frontier*, 8; Almada, *Resumen*, 161-62.

45. In light of the considerable amount of political activity on the northern frontier during the era of Mexican independence, the following quote from H. H. Bancroft's *History of Arizona and New Mexico* (pp. 307-8) is of interest: "It is to be regretted that nothing is known of political events and sentiments in New Mexico during the war of independence in 1811-1821. There is no indication

that the great national struggle sent even a ripple of excitement to the northern interior; and we may reasonably conclude that officials and people here, as in California, were content to await the issue, in which they took but slight interest, and of which in its details they were to a great extent kept in ignorance."

CHAPTER IV
THE MEXICAN PERIOD, 1821-1848

1. V. H. Timmons, "The El Paso Area in the Mexican Period, 1821-1848," *Southwestern Historical Quarterly* 84 (July 1980): 2-3. Permission has been granted to the author by Dr. L. Tuffly Ellis, former director of the Texas State Historical Association and editor of the *Southwestern Historical Quarterly*, to reprint portions of this article.
2. Ibid., 3.
3. Ibid., 1-2; for a brief summary of economic activities in El Paso del Norte in 1831 see Robert Potash, ed., "Notes and Documents," *New Mexico Historical Review* 24 (October 1949): 332-40; see also Timmons, "The El Paso Area in the Mexican Period," 1-2, and W. H. Timmons, "The Church of Ysleta—Recent Documentary Discoveries," *Password* 28 (Fall 1983): 113-16.
4. Census for Socorro, Ysleta, and San Elizario, February-April 1841, Juárez Archives (microfilm, UTEP Library, MF513R32F262-320).
5. Bowden, *Spanish and Mexican Land Grants*, 11.
6. Ibid., 85, 87.
7. Ibid., 77-78. Heath's name appears in the Mexican documents as Juan Gid.
8. Ibid., 79-80, 82, 87, 89.
9. Ibid., 94-95.
10. J. J. Bowden, "The Ponce de León Land Grant," *Southwestern Studies* no. 24 (El Paso, 1969); Juan María Ponce de León to governor of Chihuahua, El Paso del Norte, 16 April 1850, Juárez Archives (microfilm, UTEP Library, MF 495R61F078.
11. Timmons, "The El Paso Area in the Mexican Period," 4-5; Donald Worcester, *The Apaches: Eagles of the Southwest* (Norman, 1979), 38-40. For an entertaining biography of Kirker see William C. McGaw, *Savage Scene: The Life and Times of James Kirker, Frontier King* (New York, 1972).
12. Moorhead, *New Mexico's Royal Road*, 64-65, 75; Max L. Moorhead, ed., Josiah Gregg's *Commerce of the Prairies* (Norman, 1954), 332-33; Richard Onofre Ulibarri, "American Interest in the Spanish-Mexican Southwest, 1803-1848" (Ph.D. diss., University of Utah, 1963), 85. For the volume of trade in 1844 (most of it handled by Mexican merchants), see Ward Alan Minge, "Frontier Problems in New Mexico Preceding the Mexican War, 1840-1846" (Ph.D. diss., University of New Mexico, 1965), 246-53.
13. Edward J. Glasgow to William E. Connelley, 2 November 1906, "Letters of J. F. Crosby & Others to James W. Magoffin, 1852-1880," Josiah F. Crosby Papers (Barker Texas History Center, University of Texas at Austin).
14. Gregg's *Commerce of the Prairies*, 332; Decree of 26 August 1842, Manuel Dublán and José María Lozano, eds., *Legislación Mexicana: o, colección completa de las disposiciones legislativas expedidas desde la independencia de la república* (México, 1876-1890), 4:256.
15. *El noticioso de Chihuahua*, 7 November 1835. In 1836, A. (Archibald?) Stephenson of El Paso del Norte was charged with merchandising *sin guía*, and was

fined the amount of the cargo he had in his possession when he was apprehended. Juárez Archives (microfilm, UTEP Library, MF495R56F49). For details on corruption among customs officers, particularly in New Mexico, see Gregg's *Commerce of the Prairies*, 79-80, n. 20.

16. Ralph P. Bieber, ed., James Josiah Webb, *Adventures in the Santa Fe Trade, 1844-1847* (Glendale, California, 1931), 192.

17. In particular, see Juárez Archives (microfilm, UTEP Library, MF495R7, 11, 12, 13, 58, and 59); Archivos del Ayuntamiento de Chihuahua (microfilm, UTEP Library, MF491R182, 183); Archivos de Janos (microfilm, UTEP Library, MF498R27, 28).

18. List of United States Consular Officers, 1789-1939 (microfilm, UTEP Library, MF587R17); circular dated San Lorenzo, 20 May 1831, Juárez Archives (microfilm, UTEP Library, MF495R54F86); William Elsey Connelley, *Doniphan's Expedition and the Conquest of New Mexico and California* (Kansas City, Mo., 1907), 196; Frederick C. Chabot, *With the Makers of San Antonio* (San Antonio, 1937), 55-56; Strickland, "Six Who Came to El Paso," 27; J. W. Magoffin to Samuel Magoffin, 3 December 1832, "Letters of J. F. Crosby & Others to James W. Magoffin"; José María Ronquillo to the *jefe político* and *comandante militar* of the Territorio del Nuevo México, 19 July 1835, Juárez Archives (microfilm, UTEP Library, MF495R5); J. A. Escudero, *Noticias estadísticas del estado de Chihuahua* (México, 1834), 143, 169; Stella M. Drumm, ed., Susan Shelby Magoffin, *Down the Santa Fe Trail and into Mexico, 1846-1847* (Santa Fe, 1975), xix.

19. Circular of Governor José J. Calvo, Chihuahua, 25 February 1835, Juárez Archives (microfilm, UTEP Library, MF495R35F143); David J. Weber, *The Taos Trappers: The Fur Trade in the Far Southwest, 1540-1846* (Norman, 1971), 222; José María Ronquillo to the *jefe político* and *comandante militar* of the Territorio del Nuevo Mexico, 19 July 1835, Juárez Archives (microfilm, UTEP Library, MF495R5); José María Ronquillo to Cayetano Justiniani, 20 July 1835, Archivos de Janos (microfilm, UTEP Library, MF498R26).

20. J. W. Magoffin to William B. Jones, 30 January 1839, consulate general, Mexican Correspondence (National Archives); Archivos del Ayuntamiento de Chihuahua (microfilm, UTEP Library, MF491R183); "Lista de las cantidades con que voluntariamente han contribuido los señores," 22 August 1842, ibid.; George Wilkins Kendall, *Narrative of the Texan Santa Fe Expedition* (London, 1844), 1:329-30, 398; 2:79, 85; Connelley, *Doniphan's Expedition*, 197; Moorhead, *New Mexico's Royal Road*, 174. Magoffin's wife died in January 1845; in 1850 he married her sister, María Dolores Valdez. See Strickland, "Six Who Came to El Paso," 28-29.

21. Strickland, "Six Who Came to El Paso," 35; James Magoffin Dwyer, Jr., "Hugh Stephenson," *New Mexico Historical Review* 29 (January 1954): 3; Connelley, *Doniphan's Expedition*, 280; William E. Connelley, *The Founding of Harman's Station* (New York, 1910), 97-98.

22. Memorandum of Julián Bernal, Villa del Paso, 18 March 1835, Juárez Archives (microfilm, UTEP Library, MF495R5F183); *Dictamen* of Manuel Simón de (?) Chihuahua, 6 May 1836, ibid. (microfilm, UTEP Library, MF495R56F154-66); "Minuta de los efectos extranjeros y el pais que manifiesta *sin guía* D. A. Stevinson [sic]," El Paso del Norte, 10 December 1836, ibid. (microfilm, UTEP Library, MF495R56F46-52); *Juez de paz* of (?) to the prefect of El Paso del Norte, 13 June 1843, ibid. (microfilm, UTEP Library, MF495R12F45); *Carta de seguridad* no. 638 (1 January 1841) and no. 870 (20

January 1846) for Hugh Stephenson, consulate general, Miscellaneous Record Books (National Archives); Moorhead, *New Mexico's Royal Road,* 173.

23. "Padrón de los extranjeros que hay en esta Real del Barranco," Villa del Paso, 2 April 1844, Juárez Archives (microfilm, UTEP Library, MF495R13F4); Alfonso Anderson to John Black, 10 January 1847, consulate general, Mexico Correspondence.

24. The official government newspaper of Chihuahua carries the title *El noticioso de Chihuahua* in the 1830s; *La luna* from 1840 to 1842; *Revista oficial,* 1842 to July 1845; *La restauración,* July 1845 to January 1846; *El provisional,* 1846; and *El faro,* 1847 until the American occupation.

25. Printed circular of Governor José Joaquín Calvo, 1 December 1835, Juárez Archives (microfilm, UTEP Library, MF495R35F165); *El noticioso de Chihuahua,* 29 July 1836. The El Paso Public Library has one of the two known signed copies of the Treaty of Velasco of 14 May 1836.

26. Joaquín Velarde (?) to (?), El Paso del Norte, 4 July 1836, Juárez Archives (microfilm, UTEP, MF495R10).

27. William C. Binkley, *The Expansionist Movement in Texas* (Berkeley, 1925), 70-77.

28. Ibid., 78-88.

29. Carlos María Bustamante, *El gabinete mexicano* (México, 1842), 2:3, 9, 216; Daniel Tyler, "Anglo-American Penetration of the Southwest: The View from New Mexico," *Southwestern Historical Quarterly* 75 (January 1972): 335.

30. Kendall, *Narrative of the Texan Santa Fe Expedition,* 2:40.

31. Ibid., 41.

32. Ibid.

33. Moorhead, *New Mexico's Royal Road,* 144-45.

34. Ibid., 133-34, 143-44.

35. Charles W. Davis to John Black, 11 May 1844, consulate general, Mexico Correspondence. The names of eight Americans with details about each are given in "Padrón de los extranjeros que hay en esta Real del Barranco," Villa del Paso, 2 April 1844, Juárez Archives (microfilm, UTEP Library, MF495R13F4).

36. Almada, *Resumen,* 220; "Estado que manifiesta el número de hombres...," El Paso del Norte, September 1845, Juárez Archives (microfilm, UTEP Library, MF495R60F223).

37. Meyer and Sherman, *The Course of Mexican History,* 342-47.

38. Amado de la Vega to the prefect of El Paso del Norte, 14 April 1846, Juárez Archives (microfilm, UTEP Library, MF495R38F246-47).

39. José María de Irigoyen to the prefect of El Paso del Norte, 22 May 1846, ibid. (microfilm, UTEP Library, MF495R38F46); "Lista de los individuos de esta municipalidad desde la edad de 16 a 40...," San Lorenzo, 20 July 1846, ibid. (microfilm, UTEP Library, MF495R14F34); Mauricio Ugarte to the governor of New Mexico, 26 August 1846; Gabino Cuilty to the governor of Chihuahua, 29 August 1846; Sebastián Bermúdez to the governor of Chihuahua, 25 August 1846, in Ponce de León, *Reseñas históricas,* 332-36.

40. Thomas Hart Benton, *Thirty Years' View* (New York, 1875), 2:683-84.

41. The story of Magoffin's "bloodless conquest" has been told in great detail by Connelley, Horgan, Keleher, and Twitchell, to name a few. Twitchell's *The Conquest of Santa Fe* (Española, N. Mex., 1967) has a copy of the Magoffin Papers, which include Magoffin's claim of $37,780.96 for services rendered. He eventually received $30,000. While most authorities give Magoffin credit for

about everything he said he did, it is noteworthy that Max Moorhead, in his *New Mexico's Royal Road*, 161, presents documentary evidence that suggests that Magoffin's role was not all that he claimed it to be.

42. Circular of José de Arellano, Chihuahua, 25 August 1846, Juárez Archives (microfilm, UTEP Library, MF495R14F86); George Rutledge Gibson, *Journal of a Soldier under Kearny and Doniphan, 1846-1847*, ed. by Ralph P. Bieber (Glendale, Calif., 1935), 98.

43. Sebastiàn Bermúdez to the governor of Chihuahua, 25 August 1846, in Ponce de León, *Reseñas históricas*, 332-33; José Muñoz to the prefect of El Paso del Norte, 26 September 1846, Juárez Archives (microfilm, UTEP Library, MF495R38F125).

44. Moorhead, *New Mexico's Royal Road*, 162.

45. Connelley, *Doniphan's Expedition*, 198-99; Susan Magoffin, *Down the Santa Fe Trail*, xxvii; Sebastián Bermúdez to the governor of Chihuahua, 27 September 1846, in Ponce de León, *Reseñas históricas*, 336.

46. Documents concerning Magoffin's capture and an inventory of his personal effects are in the Juárez Archives (microfilm, UTEP Library, MF495R60F49-55, 139, 150, 172).

47. Armando Chávez, *Historia de Ciudad Juárez, Chihuahua* (n.p., 1970), 225; Connelley, *Doniphan's Expedition*, 385.

48. Abraham Robinson Johnston, Marcellus Ball Edwards, and Philip Gooch Ferguson, *Marching with the Army of the West, 1846-1848*, ed. by Ralph P. Bieber (Glendale, Calif., 1936), 228-38; Almada, *Resumen*, 224; Moorhead, *New Mexico's Royal Road*, 19; Connelley, *Doniphan's Expedition*, 101-2; Ramón Alcaraz, *The Other Side; or Notes for the History of the War between Mexico and the United States*, trans. by Albert C. Ramsey (New York, 1850), 171. For the most probable location of the Brazito battlefield, see George Ruhlen, "The Battle of Brazito – Where Was It Fought?" *Password* 2 (May 1957): 60.

49. Ralph A. Smith, "The 'King of New Mexico' and the Doniphan Expedition," *New Mexico Historical Review* 38 (January 1963): 29-32; Worcester, *The Apaches*, 43.

50. "Junta militar del distrito…con el caracter de consejo de guerra," El Paso del Norte, 27 December 1846, Juárez Archives (microfilm, UTEP Library, MF495R14F233-35); Johnston, Edwards, and Ferguson, *Marching with the Army of the West*, 243; Gibson, *Journal of a Soldier*, 313; Magoffin, *Down the Santa Fe Trail*, 211. One must make allowances for Susan Magoffin's Spanish – "Bermúdez" is spelled "Belmudis."

51. Johnston, Edwards, and Ferguson, *Marching with the Army of the West*, 245; Gibson, *Journal of a Soldier*, 323; Sonnichsen, *Pass of the North*, 1:117-22; John P. Bloom, "Johnny Gringo at the Pass of the North," *Password* 4 (October 1959): 134-40.

52. John T. Hughes to W. L. Marcy, El Paso, 25 January 1847, in Connelley, *Doniphan's Expedition*, 393.

53. Ibid., 395-96; Gibson, *Journal of a Soldier*, 321-23; Johnston, Edwards, and Ferguson, *Marching with the Army of the West*, 241; U.S. Congress, House Reports, 36th Cong., 1st sess. (Serial 1068), doc. no. 321, p. 45; Bowden, *Spanish and Mexican Land Grants*, 89.

54. Johnston, Edwards, and Ferguson, *Marching with the Army of the West*, 50; Moorhead, *New Mexico's Royal Road*, 165-68; Connelley, *Doniphan's Expedition*, 395-98.

55. Gibson, *Journal of a Soldier*, 99; Alcaraz, *The Other Side*, 173-74.

56. Gibson, *Journal of a Soldier*, 101; Almada, *Resumen*, 224; Carlos María de Busta-mante, *El nuevo Bernal Díaz del Castillo; o sea, historia de la invasión de los Anglo-Americanos en México* (México, 1949); Ponce de León, *Reseñas históricas*, 325.

57. Almada, *Resumen*, 225; Connelley, *Doniphan's Expedition*, 107; Moorhead, *New Mexico's Royal Road*, 141, 173, 177, 180-81; Luis Rivas to Baltasar Padilla, 14 January 1848, Archivos de Janos (microfilm, UTEP Library, MF498R32); Florence and Robert Lister, *Chihuahua, Storehouse of Storms*, 114-15.

58. Meyer and Sherman, *The Course of Mexican History*, 348-51.

59. Treaty of Guadalupe Hidalgo, 2 February 1848, William M. Malloy, ed., *Treaties, Conventions, International Acts, Protocols and Agreements between the United States and Other Powers, 1776-1909* (Washington, D.C., 1910), 1:1110, 1113.

60. Official position of the Chihuahua delegation, Querétaro, 5 February 1848, "Algunos documentos sobre el Tratado de Guadalupe y la situación de México durante la invasión Americana," *Archivo Histórico Diplomático Mexicano*, no. 31, ed. by Antonio de la Peña y Reyes (México, 1930). One of the members of the Chihuahua delegation was Ramón Ortiz. *Ejidos* are communal land holdings.

61. Johnston, Edwards, and Ferguson, *Marching with the Army of the West*, 62-68; M. H. Thomlinson, "The Dragoons and El Paso, 1848," *New Mexico Historical Review* 23 (July 1948): 223.

62. Timmons, "The El Paso Area in the Mexican Period," 27-28.

CHAPTER V
AMERICAN EL PASO, 1848-1854

1. Ferol Egan, *The El Dorado Trail* (New York, 1971), 114-24; W. H. Timmons, "American El Paso: The Formative Years," *Southwestern Historical Quarterly* 87 (July 1983): 1-2. Permission has been granted to the author by Dr. L. Tuffly Ellis, former director of the Texas State Historical Association and editor of the *Southwestern Historical Quarterly*, to reprint portions of this article. "The Great Western," who answered to the name Sarah, although her surname is somewhat uncertain, was six feet tall, handy with a gun, and generous with her affections. She served as nurse, laundress, and cook during the Mexican War and became El Paso's first hotelkeeper. See Nancy Hamilton, "The Great Western," *Women Who Made the West* (Garden City, N.Y., 1980), 186-97.

2. Mabelle E. Martin, ed., "From Texas to California in 1849 – Diary of C. C. Cox," *Southwestern Historical Quarterly* 29 (October 1925): 130-31.

3. Mabelle E. Martin, "California Emigrant Roads through Texas," ibid., 28 (April 1925): 301; Timmons, "The El Paso Area in the Mexican Period," 24-27; Strickland, "Six Who Came to El Paso," 10-13, 26-29, 34-37.

4. Timmons, "The El Paso Area in the Mexican Period," 24, 26-27.

5. Ibid., 26-28; Strickland, "Six Who Came to El Paso," 11.

6. William L. Marcy to James K. Polk, 31 July 1848, U.S. Congress, H. Exec. Doc. 76, p. 4, 30th Cong., 1st sess. (1848), serial set 521; Jefferson Van Horne to Assistant Adjutant General, 9th Military Department, 10 September 1849, U.S. Congress, S. Exec. Doc. 24, pp. 33-34, 31st Cong., 1st sess. (1850), serial set 554; Van Horne to Assistant Adjutant General, 9th Military Department, 1 October 1849, Office of the Commissary General and Office of the Quarter-master General, National Archives (microfilm copy in the State Records

Center and Archives, Santa Fe; this material is hereafter cited as NA, Santa Fe); W. H. Timmons, "American El Paso," 3.

7. Van Horne to Assistant Adjutant General, 9th Military Department, 23 September 1849, U.S. Congress, S. Exec. Doc. 56, p. 3, 31st Cong., 1st sess. (1850), serial set 561; John Munroe to Van Horne, 28 December 1849, ibid., 4-5.

8. Van Horne to Assistant Adjutant General, 9th Military Department, 1 October 1849, Office of the Commissary General and Office of the Quartermaster General (NA, Santa Fe); Moorhead, *The Presidio*, 90.

9. Thomas L. Brent to Assistant Adjutant General, 9th Military Department, (?) November 1849, Office of the Commissary General and Office of the Quartermaster General (NA, Santa Fe).

10. Petition of James W. Magoffin, et al., 20 November 1849, ibid.; Emilio Langberg to Van Horne, 20 November 1849, ibid.

11. William S. Henry to Assistant Adjutant General, 9th Military Department, 20 February 1850, ibid.

12. John Russell Bartlett, *Personal Narrative of Explorations and Incidents in Texas, New Mexico, California, Sonora, and Chihuahua* (New York, 1854), 1:194; Strickland, "Six Who Came to El Paso," 11-12; T. Frank White to John R. Bartlett, 23 December 1850, Mexican Boundary Commission Papers of John Russell Bartlett, 1850-1853, John Carter Brown Library, Brown University (microfilm, UTEP Library, MF497).

13. Bartlett, *Personal Narrative*, 1:191; W. W. H. Davis, *El Gringo; or New Mexico and Her People* (New York, 1973), 376; Strickland, "Six Who Came to El Paso," 37.

14. Edwin V. Sumner to Charles M. Conrad, 27 March 1852, as quoted in Robert W. Frazer, "Purveyors of Flour to the Army: Department of New Mexico, 1849-1861," *New Mexico Historical Review* 47 (July 1972): 220-22.

15. Bowden, "The Ponce de León Grant," 5-6, 46.

16. Strickland, "Six Who Came to El Paso," 14-15.

17. Van Horne to Roger Jones, 1 September 1850, Records of the War Department, Office of the Adjutant General, Record Group 94, Selected Letters Received from Major Jefferson Van Horne, National Archives (microfilm, UTEP Library, MF463); Van Horne to Jones, 1 October 1850, ibid.

18. Van Horne to Jones, 21 November and 27 December 1850, ibid.; Strickland, "Six Who Came to El Paso," 21-23.

19. Strickland, "Six Who Came to El Paso," 8, 17; Deed Records, Book A, 202 (Records of the El Paso County Clerk's Office, El Paso, Texas).

20. Electus Backus to Lafayette McLaws, 12 July 1851 (NA, Santa Fe).

21. Ibid.

22. Charles W. Ogden et al. to Edwin V. Sumner, 4 August 1851, ibid.; Benjamin F. Coons to Sumner, 26 August 1851, ibid.; Gouverneur Morris to Don Carlos Buell, 27 August 1851, ibid.; "Statement of Indian Depredations," October 1853 (?), in Robert W. Frazer, ed., *Mansfield on the Condition of the Western Forts, 1853-1854* (Norman, 1963), 70.

23. Bowden, "The Ponce de León Grant," 6-8.

24. Quoted in Paul Horgan, *Great River: The Rio Grande in North American History* (New York, 1954), 2:802-3; Bartlett, *Personal Narrative*, 1:193; Strickland, "Six Who Came to El Paso," 29.

25. Strickland, "Six Who Came to El Paso," 30-32; Bowden, *Spanish and Mexican Land Grants*, 94-95; James Magoffin to John Russell Bartlett, 24 April 1853, Bartlett Papers (microfilm, UTEP Library, MF497); Bartlett, *Personal Narrative*,

2:384; Magoffin to the Committee of El Paso County, 5 August 1852, Governors' Papers: Peter H. Bell (Archives Division, Texas State Library, Austin); Hugh Stephenson et al. to Millard Fillmore, 20 December 1851, ibid.

26. Bartlett, *Personal Narrative*, 1:192-93; Roscoe P. Conkling and Margaret B. Conkling, *The Butterfield Overland Mail, 1857-1869* (Glendale, California, 1947), 2:82; Stephenson to the Local Committee, 5 August 1852, Governors' Papers: Bell.

27. James D. Lucas to John M. Clayton, 18 May 1849, Despatches from United States Consuls in Ciudad Juárez (El Paso del Norte), 1850-1906 (microfilm, UTEP Library, M184); Joaquín de Arellano to the *jefe político* of Cánton Bravos, Chihuahua, 18 April 1849, Juárez Archives (microfilm, UTEP Library, MF495R15 F155); Manuel Armendáriz to the *jefe político* of Cantón Bravos, (?) June 1850, ibid. (microfilm, UTEP Library, MF495R5F171-73); James A. Lucas to the *jefe político* of Cánton Bravos, 18 June 1850, ibid. (microfilm, UTEP Library, MF495R5F169); John S. Lucas to Americans and Foreigners Now Residing in El Paso del Norte, 3 June 1850, ibid. (microfilm, UTEP Library, MF495R5F170).

28. J. A. Lucas to the *jefe político* of Cantón Bravos, 18 June 1850, Juárez Archives (microfilm, UTEP Library, MF495R5F169); David R. Diffenderffer to the *prefecto* of Cantón Bravos, 25 May 1852, ibid. (microfilm, UTEP Library, MF495R62F070); Diffenderffer to Marcy, 1 March 1854, Despatches from United States Consuls in Ciudad Juárez.

29. Diffenderffer to Daniel Webster, 1 August 1851, Despatches from United States Consuls in Ciudad Juárez (microfilm, UTEP Library, M184); Diffenderffer to Volney E. Howard, 8 December 1852, ibid.; Diffenderffer to Marcy, 23 July 1853, ibid.; Juan N. Zubirán to the *jefe político* of Cantón Bravos, 20 August 1851, Juárez Archives (microfilm, UTEP Library, MF495R16F144-45).

30. Zubirán to the *jefe político* of Cantón Bravos, (?) November 1851, Juárez Archives (microfilm, UTEP Library, MF495R61F159); Diffenderffer to Marcy, 1 February and 1 March 1854, Despatches from United States Consuls in Ciudad Juárez (microfilm, UTEP Library, M184); Diffenderffer to Edward Everett, 18 January 1853, ibid.

31. Diffenderffer to Marcy, 23 July 1853, Despatches from United States Consuls in Ciudad Juárez (microfilm, UTEP Library, M184); James Tucker to Jefferson Davis, 4 August 1853, ibid.; Diffenderffer to Marcy, 7 January 1855, ibid.; J. Morgan Broaddus, Jr., *The Legal Heritage of El Paso* (El Paso, 1963), 50-51.

32. Moorhead, *New Mexico's Royal Road,* 75, 113, 140; Moorhead, ed., Josiah Gregg, *Commerce of the Prairies*, 265-67; Timmons, "The El Paso Area in the Mexican Period," 6.

33. Owen White, *Out of the Desert: The Historical Romance of El Paso* (El Paso, 1923), 42; Michael Dennis Carman, "United States Customs and the Madero Revolution," *Southwestern Studies* no. 48 (El Paso, 1976): 6-7; Diffenderffer to Marcy, 1 March 1854, 8 January 1855, Despatches from United States Consuls in Ciudad Juárez (microfilm, UTEP Library, M184).

34. William Campbell Binkley, *The Expansionist Movement in Texas, 1836-1850* (Berkeley, 1925), 27; Van Horne to Assistant Adjutant General, 9th Military Department, 23 September 1849, U. S. Congress. S. Exec. Doc. 56, p. 3, 31st Cong., 1st sess. (1850), serial set 561; Munroe to Van Horne, 28 December 1849, ibid., 4-5.

35. Charles A. Hoppin to Peter H. Bell, 3 January 1850, Governors' Papers: Bell.

36. "Governor Bell's Message," of 26 December 1849, published in *State Gazette* (Austin), 29 December 1849; Binkley, *Expansionist Movement in Texas*, 177.

37. Bell to the Senate, 3 January 1850, Governors' Papers: Bell; Kenneth Franklin Neighbours, *Robert Simpson Neighbors and the Texas Frontier, 1836-1859* (Waco, Texas, 1975), 87-89.
38. "From El Paso," *State Gazette*, 27 April 1850; Grace Long, "The Anglo-American Occupation of the El Paso District" (Master's thesis, University of Texas, 1931), 129; William H. Emory, *Report on the United States and Mexican Boundary Survey*, 91, H. Exec. Doc. 135, 34th Cong., 1st sess. (1856), serial set 861; Binkley, *Expansionist Movement in Texas*, 181.
39. Broaddus, *Legal Heritage of El Paso*, 34, 47-48, 52; Neighbours, *Robert Simpson Neighbors*, 90. Henry L. Dexter's correspondence, 1854-1869, most of it with his sister, was published by Art Leibson in the *El Paso Times*, 16-28 September 1957.
40. Neighbours, *Robert Simpson Neighbors*, 90-91, 96-98; Binkley, *Expansionist Movement in Texas*, 185, 188-89.
41. Binkley, *Expansionist Movement in Texas*, 190, 208-15.
42. Ibid., 208-15.
43. *Congressional Globe*, 31st Cong. 1st sess. (1850), 165.
44. Ibid., 165-66.
45. Ibid., 170-71; Binkley, *Expansionist Movement in Texas*, 209-10.
46. *Congressional Globe*, 31st Cong., 1st sess. (1850), 244-45.
47. Ibid., 247, 1381.
48. Ibid., 436-38.
49. Binkley, *Expansionist Movement in Texas*, 212-13.
50. Ibid., 214.
51. *Congressional Globe*, 31st Cong., 1st sess. (1850), 1520, 1555-56; Binkley, *Expansionist Movement in Texas*, 214.
52. Binkley, *Expansionist Movement in Texas*, 215; *State Gazette*, 16 November and 14 December 1850. See also Holman Hamilton, *Prologue to Conflict: The Crisis and Compromise of 1850* (Lexington, Ky., 1964), 133-50, a scholarly study emphasizing the leadership role of Stephen A. Douglas.
53. P. M. Baldwin, "A Historical Note on the Boundaries of New Mexico," *New Mexico Historical Review* 5 (April 1930): 124.
54. Ernest Wallace, *The Howling of the Coyotes: Reconstruction Efforts to Divide Texas* (College Station, Tex., 1979), 50-53, 66; John Middagh, *Frontier Newspaper: The El Paso Times* (El Paso, 1958), 88, 89-94. J. J. Bowden has called attention to an unusual situation that developed in the 3600 block of Doniphan Drive when the Rio Grande shifted its bed, leaving a small tract of New Mexico land lying east of the highway. In 1927 the Supreme Court of the United States ruled that the boundary was a fixed line, that the river had moved physically but not legally. The tract then became the site of several cocktail lounges, mixed drinks being at the time legal in New Mexico but not in Texas. Many El Pasoans will no doubt remember Tom Burchell's and Billy Crews's establishments. See J. J. Bowden, "The Texas-New Mexico Boundary Dispute Along the Rio Grande," *Southwestern Historical Quarterly* 63 (October 1959): 221-37.
55. Odie B. Faulk, "The Controversial Boundary Survey and the Gadsden Treaty," *Arizona and the West* 4 (Autumn 1962): 201-2; Luis G. Zorrilla, *Historia de las relaciones entre México y los Estados Unidos de América, 1800-1958* (México, 1977), 1:219-20; Personal Journal, 13 and 22 November and 2 December 1850, 21 February 1851, Bartlett Papers.
56. Robert M. Utley, *The International Boundary: United States and Mexico: A History of Frontier Dispute and Cooperation, 1848-1963* (Santa Fe, 1964), 9-10;

Faulk, "The Controversial Boundary Survey," 204-5; William E. Goetzmann, *Army Exploration in the American West, 1803-1863* (New Haven, 1959), 175-77; Paul Neff Garber, *The Gadsden Treaty* (Gloucester, Mass., 1959), 16-17; J. Fred Rippy, *The United States and Mexico* (New York, 1926), 113-15.

57. Bowden, *Spanish and Mexican Land Grants*, 49-50; Faulk, "The Controversial Boundary Survey," 214; Bartlett, *Personal Narrative*, 1:214-15.

58. Utley, *The International Boundary*, 10-11; Faulk, "The Controversial Boundary Survey," 206.

59. Goetzmann, *Army Exploration*, 177-78; Utley, *The International Boundary*, 12, 14.

60. Utley, *The International Boundary*, 13-15; Goetzmann, *Army Exploration*, 127-38.

61. Bartlett, *Personal Narrative*, 1:160-61; Broaddus, *Legal Heritage of El Paso*, 34, 43-44, 47-48.

62. Petition of the Citizens of El Paso County to His Excellency Gov. P. H. Bell, 29 April 1852, in Dorman H. Winfrey and James M. Day, eds., *The Indian Papers of Texas and the Southwest* (Austin, 1966), 3:159-60.

63. Utley, *The International Boundary*, 16; Rippy, *The United States and Mexico*, 115.

64. Magoffin to Bartlett, 24 April 1853, Bartlett Papers.

65. Rippy, *The United States and Mexico*, 119.

66. James Morton Callahan, *American Foreign Policy in Mexican Relations* (New York, 1932), 227, 229; Garber, *The Gadsden Treaty*, 103-104, 131, 145; Faulk, "The Controversial Boundary Survey," 224-25; White, *Out of the Desert*, 74.

67. "Posts Recommended," in Frazer, ed., *Mansfield on the Condition of Western Forts*, 28; "Statement of Indian Depredations," October 1853 (?), ibid., 70-75; Conkling and Conkling, *The Butterfield Overland Mail*, 2:79; Long, "The Anglo-American Occupation of the El Paso District," 86-88.

68. Robert A. Griffen, ed., *My Life in the Mountains and on the Plains: The Newly Discovered Autobiography by David Meriwether* (Norman, 1966), 237-38; Almada, *Resumen de historia*, 241.

69. Almada, *Resumen de historia*, 242; Bowden, *Spanish and Mexican Land Grants*, 50; Long, "The Anglo-American Occupation of the El Paso District," 117; Diffenderffer to Marcy, 8 June 1854, Despatches from United States Consuls in Ciudad Juárez (microfilm, UTEP Library, M184).

70. Timmons, "American El Paso: The Formative Years, 1848-1854," 36.

CHAPTER VI
THE CONTINENTAL CROSSROADS, 1849-1881

1. W. H. Emory, *Report on the United States and Mexican Boundary Survey*, 41.

2. W. F. Smith, *Report of Routes from San Antonio to El Paso*, Sen. Exec. Doc. 64, 31st Cong., 1st sess. (1850), serial set 562, p. 50; Goetzmann, *Army Exploration*, 232; W. Turrentine Jackson, *Wagon Roads West* (Berkeley, 1952), 37-41.

3. Smith, *Report*, 23; Stephen B. Oates, *John Salmon "Rip" Ford's Texas* (Austin, 1963), xxvi, 126-29.

4. Goetzmann, *Army Exploration*, 233.

5. Randolph B. Marcy, *Report of a Route from Fort Smith to Santa Fe*, Sen. Exec. Doc. 129, 33rd Cong., 1st sess. (1855), serial set 737, pp. 43-44.

6. John Pope, *Report of Explorations of a Route for the Pacific Railroad*, H. Exec. Doc. 129, 33rd Cong., 1st sess. (1855), serial set 737, pp. 43-44.

7. Wayne R. Austerman, *Sharps Rifles and Spanish Mules: The San Antonio-El Paso Mail, 1851-1881* (College Station, Tex., 1985), 19-32; Robert H. Thonhoff,

"San Antonio Stage Lines, 1847-1881," *Southwestern Studies* no. 29 (El Paso, 1971): 9-11; for interesting details on Big Foot Wallace, see C. G. Raht, *The Romance of Davis Mountains and Big Bend Country* (Odessa, Tex., 1963), 128-29.

8. Strickland, "Six Who Came to El Paso," 8; Thonhoff, "San Antonio Stage Lines," 15-16; Nancy Hammons, *A History of El Paso County, Texas to 1900* (El Paso, 1983), 40-41.

9. Lewis Burt Lesley, ed., *Uncle Sam's Camels* (Cambridge, 1929), 170-71.

10. John C. Reid, *Reid's Tramp* (Austin, 1935), 139-61.

11. Joseph Leach, "Stage Coach Through the Pass – The Butterfield Overland Mail Comes to El Paso," *Password* 3 (October 1958): 130-34.

12. Waterman L. Ormsby, *The Butterfield Overland Mail* (San Marino, Calif., 1972), 77-78.

13. Leach, "Stage Coach Through the Pass," 131.

14. Anson Mills, *My Story* (Washington, D.C., 1918), 49-52.

15. Owen White, *Out of the Desert*, 50-52; Nancy Hamilton, "Ben Dowell: El Paso's First Mayor," *Southwestern Studies* no. 49 (El Paso, 1976): 19.

16. White, *Out of the Desert*, 51. For three colorful descriptions of the El Paso area in the 1850s see Lansing Bloom, ed., "The Rev. Hiram Walter Read, Baptist Missionary," *New Mexico Historical Review* 17 (April 1942): 101-47; Julius Froebel, *Travel in Central America, Northern Mexico and the Far West of the United States* (London, 1859), 322-33; and Albert Richardson, *Beyond the Mississippi: From the Great River to the Great Ocean* (Hartford, 1867), 237-44.

17. Rex Strickland, ed., W. W. Mills's *Forty Years at El Paso, 1858-1898* (El Paso, 1962), 22-23.

18. Hammons, *A History of El Paso County*, 43-44; Strickland, ed., Mills's *Forty Years at El Paso*, 28.

19. Sonnichsen, *Pass of the North*, 1:154.

20. For details on the two votes cast against secession by the Mills brothers, see Anson Mills, *My Story*, 62; Strickland, ed., Mills's *Forty Years at El Paso*, 37; Hamilton, "Ben Dowell," 29-30.

21. James W. Magoffin to Gov. Edward Clark, Fort Bliss, 28 April 1861, Governors' Papers: Edward Clark, Texas State Archives, Box 301-35 (9); Hammons, *A History of El Paso County*, 45; Strickland, ed., Mills's *Forty Years at El Paso*, 38-39.

22. Strickland, ed., Mills's *Forty Years at El Paso*, 50; Mills's personal account should be supplemented with Eugene O. Porter, ed., "Letters Home: W. W. Mills Writes to his Family," published in the four issues of *Password* 17 (1972); David R. Diffenderffer to W. H. Seward, 29 May 1863, Despatches from United States Consuls in Ciudad Juárez (microfilm, UTEP Library, M184R1).

23. Hammons, *A History of El Paso County*, 46-48.

24. Ibid.; for an analysis of Sibley's weaknesses as a general and as a strategist, see Martin Hardwick Hall, *Sibley's New Mexico Campaign* (Austin, 1960), 54.

25. Sonnichsen, *Pass of the North*, 1:156; quoted in Hammons, *A History of El Paso County*, 48. The only thing the Confederates could salvage in the retreat to El Paso were the six Union cannons, one of which eventually became the property of the McGinty Club and the Pioneers Association of El Paso. It was placed at the disposal of Francisco Madero's revolutionary forces in 1911, and is now on permanent loan to Eastwood High School. See Conrey Bryson, *Down Went McGinty* (El Paso, 1977), 62-63.

26. Ibid.; J. L. Waller, "The Civil War in the El Paso Area," *The West Texas Association Year Book* 22 (October 1946): 9.

27. Quoted in F. S. Donnell, "The Confederate Territory of Arizona, as Compiled from Official Sources," *New Mexico Historical Review* 17 (April 1942): 162-63.
28. Hammons, *A History of El Paso County*, 49-50.
29. Broaddus, *The Legal Heritage of El Paso*, 80-81; Larry D. Ball, *The United States Marshals of New Mexico and Arizona Territories, 1846-1912* (Albuquerque, 1978), 38.
30. Ibid.; Strickland, "Six Who Came to El Paso," 41-42.
31. John L. Waller, *Colossal Hamilton of Texas* (El Paso, 1968), 66; Broaddus, *The Legal Heritage of El Paso*, 85; Evelyn R. Rosen, "Henry Cuniffe: the Man and his Times," (Master's thesis, University of Texas at El Paso, 1961), 65; John S. Watts to Don Mariano Samaniego, El Paso, Tex., 18 June 1872, Juárez Archives (microfilm, UTEP Library, MF495R69F157-61); Strickland, "Six Who Came to El Paso," 34.
32. Lydia Spencer Lane, *I Married a Soldier or Old Days in the Old Army* (Philadelphia, 1893), 170; Strickland, "Six Who Came to El Paso," 34.
33. Austerman, *Sharps Rifles and Spanish Mules*, 201-6.
34. Ibid., 208-10, 215-16, 244, 255; Thonhoff, "San Antonio Stage Lines," 26-32.
35. Austerman, *Sharps Rifles and Spanish Mules*, 282.
36. Meyer and Sherman, *The Course of Mexican History*, 377-81.
37. David R. Diffenderffer to Lewis Cass, El Paso del Norte, 10 April 1858, Despatches from United States Consuls in Ciudad Juárez (microfilm, UTEP Library, M184R1); Diffenderffer to Cass, El Paso del Norte, 17 March 1860, ibid.; James Magoffin to Gov. Sam Houston, Magoffinsville, 24 May 1860, Governors' Papers: Sam Houston, Texas State Archives, Box 301-32 (53).
38. Meyer and Sherman, *The Course of Mexican History*, 384-85.
39. Ibid., 389, 396.
40. Ibid., 395-96.
41. Diffenderffer to Seward, Washington, D.C., 29 May 1863, Despatches from United States Consuls in Ciudad Juárez (microfilm, UTEP Library, M184R1); H. L. Cuniffe to W. H. Seward, El Paso del Norte, 10 October 1864, ibid.; Cuniffe to Seward, El Paso del Norte, 22 December 1865, ibid.; Benito Juárez to Pedro Santacilia, El Paso del Norte, 18 August 1865, Alfredo Escalante, trans., "Letters from Benito Juárez Written While at El Paso del Norte, 1865-1866" (seminar paper, UTEP, 1962); Juárez to Gen. James Carleton, 6 September 1865, ibid. It should be noted that the photograph of Juárez and friends in Sonnichsen's *Pass of the North* vol. 1 between pages 226 and 227, and in Strickland's *Forty Years at El Paso* by W. W. Mills on page 198 is not Juárez, but rather is Don José María Uranga, Jefe Político and Comandante del Cantón Bravos. See Armando B. Chávez, *Historia de Ciudad Juárez, Chih.*, 262.
42. Juárez decree of 8 November 1865, Escalante, "Letters from Benito Juárez"; Cuniffe to Seward, El Paso del Norte, 31 March 1866, Despatches from United States Consuls in Ciudad Juárez (microfilm, UTEP Library, M184R1); I. S. Bartlett, "President Juárez at Old El Paso," *Pan American Bulletin* 41, no. 5 (November 1915): 646-58; Olga P. Wilson, "Benito Juárez in Old El Paso del Norte," seminar paper, Sul Ross College, 1941).
43. Meyer and Sherman, *The Course of Mexican History*, 398-99.
44. McConville, "A History of Population in the El Paso-Ciudad Juárez Area," 67; some Tiguas were involved in this move to the Mexican side, according to Nancy Hamilton, in her "Ben Dowell," 74 n. 8.
45. William M. Pierson to secretary of state, El Paso del Norte, 4 December 1872, Despatches from United States Consuls in Ciudad Juárez (microfilm, UTEP

Library, M184R2); Broaddus, *The Legal Heritage of El Paso*, 95-96. Owen White, in his *Out of the Desert*, 76, writes: "The less we say about Mills, the better this book will be."

46. Complaint of Ysleta Citizens to Gov. J. W. Throckmorton, 18 November 1866, Governors' Papers: Throckmorton, Texas State Archives, Box 301-53 (4).

47. List of Registered Voters, El Paso County, 1867-1869, Texas State Archives.

48. A. M. Gibson, *The Life and Death of Colonel Albert Jennings Fountain* (Norman, 1965), 53. The Thirteenth amendment abolished slavery; the Fourteenth made the Negro a citizen of the U.S.; and the Fifteenth gave the Negro the right to vote.

49. Ibid., 53-54.

50. Carl H. Moneyhon, *Republicanism in Reconstruction Texas* (Austin, 1980), 91-92; Ernest Wallace, *The Howling of the Coyotes*, (College Station, Tex., 1979), 50-53.

51. Gibson, *The Life and Death of Colonel Albert Jennings Fountain*, 54-55.

52. Ibid., 55-56.

53. Ibid., 77-79; Strickland, ed., Mills's *Forty Years at El Paso*, 147-48.

54. Moneyhon, *Republicanism in Reconstruction Texas*, 179-80; Sonnichsen, *Pass of the North*, 1:195.

55. Petition of Luis Cardis and Charles Howard to the Texas Legislature, San Elizario, 19 February 1873, Memorials and Petitions, Texas State Archives.

56. Sonnichsen, *Pass of the North*, 1:196-97.

57. Hamilton, "Ben Dowell," 47-50.

58. Hammons, *A History of El Paso County*, 56; Broaddus, *The Legal Heritage of El Paso*, 123-24.

59. Rex Strickland, *The Turner Thesis and the Dry World* (El Paso, 1963), 10, 13-14; Austerman, *Sharps Rifles and Spanish Mules*, 310-12. For details on the first Masonic lodge established in the El Paso area, see John Denny, *One Hundred Years of Freemasonry in El Paso, 1854-1954* (El Paso, 1956).

60. For the origin of the word "greaser," see Arnoldo de León, *They Called Them Greasers* (Austin, 1983), 16-17; Frank L. Halla, "El Paso, Texas and Juárez, Mexico: A Study of a Bi-Ethnic Community, 1846-1881" (Ph.D. diss., University of Texas at Austin, 1978), 52.

61. Halla, "El Paso, Texas and Juárez, Mexico," 53; for details on Ortiz see Fidelia Miller Puckett, "Ramón Ortiz: Priest and Patriot," *New Mexico Historical Review* 25 (October 1950): 265-95.

62. Halla, "El Paso, Texas and Juárez, Mexico," 56; R. P. Daguerre, "Alexandre Daguerre and Family" (MS in Southwest Collection, El Paso Public Library); Nancy Hamilton, "The Daguerre Family," *El Paso Herald-Post*, 9, 10, and 11 January 1974. For biographical sketches of Ortiz, Samaniego, and Ochoa, see Strickland, ed., Mills's *Forty Years at El Paso*, 186, 188.

63. Mark Wasserman, *Capitalists, Caciques, and Revolution: The Native Elite and Foreign Enterprise, 1854-1911* (Chapel Hill, N.C., 1984), 38; Sonnichsen, *Pass of the North*, 1:381.

64. Halla, "El Paso, Texas and Juárez, Mexico," 57-58.

65. William M. Pierson to assistant secretary of state, Despatches from United States Consuls in Ciudad Juárez, El Paso del Norte, 19 October, 15, 26, and 30 November 1872, and 5, 11, and 17 March 1873 (microfilm, UTEP Library, M184R2). Consul Pierson's pencil sketches of Lower Valley agriculture which he forwarded to the State Department are descriptive and fascinating. He drew the sketches himself, he said, because the consulate could not afford an artist.

66. Walter P. Webb, *The Texas Rangers* (Austin, 1965), 345-46; C. L. Sonnichsen, *The El Paso Salt War* (El Paso, 1961), Foreword.
67. Sonnichsen, *The El Paso Salt War*, chaps. 3-5.
68. Ibid., chaps. 7-9; Solomon Schutz to the Department of State, El Paso del Norte, 6 March 1878, Despatches from United States Consuls in Ciudad Juárez (microfilm, UTEP Library, M184R2).
69. Goetzmann, *Army Exploration in the American West*, 304.
70. There have been numerous discrepancies in the past with regard to the date of the arrival of the railroad in El Paso, as well as the date of the celebration. The *Herald-Post's* Diamond Jubilee Edition of 28 April 1956 is no doubt correct when it gives 19 May 1881 as the date the railroad arrived, and 26 May 1881 as the date of the celebration. For the race between the Southern Pacific and the Texas and Pacific to reach El Paso first, see Edward A. Leonard, "Rails to the Pass of the North," *Password* 23 (Fall 1978): 88-90. The story is told that the Southern Pacific foreman sent fifty kegs of whiskey into the Texas and Pacific camp, with the result that the construction gang celebrated for so long that it allowed the Southern Pacific crew to reach Sierra Blanca first. A highway marker called "El Borracho Draw" commemorates the event. Letter of Willa Hargrove to the author, 22 February 1981.
71. Austerman, *Sharps Rifles and Spanish Mules*, 257; for Hague's impressions of his trip to El Paso in a stage coach, see his letters to his wife in 1871, in Lillian Hague Corcoran, "He Brought the Railroads to El Paso – the Story of Judge James P. Hague," *Password* 1 (May 1956): 47-50.
72. James B. Gillett, *Six Years with the Texas Rangers* (Austin, 1921), 322-23; El Paso *Lone Star*, 30 July 1884. The Pierson Hotel was not completed until after the railroads arrived.
73. Joseph Leach, "Farewell to Horse-Back, Mule-Back, 'Foot-Back' and Prairie Schooner: The Railroad Comes to Town," *Password* 1 (May 1956): 40; Edward A. Leonard, "Rails at the Pass of the North," *Southwestern Studies* no. 63 (El Paso 1981): 7. Sonnichsen gives the date of the "Great Day" as 26 May 1881, in his *Pass of the North*, 1:227.
74. Leach, "Farewell to Horse-Back," 41.
75. Ibid., 42.
76. El Paso *Lone Star*, 30 July 1884.

CHAPTER VII
FROM FRONTIER TOWN
TO WESTERN COMMUNITY, 1881-1917

1. See, for example, El Paso Bureau of Information, *The City and County of El Paso, Texas the Future Great Metropolis of the Southwest* (El Paso, 1886), and El Paso Chamber of Commerce, *Prosperity and Opportunities in El Paso* (El Paso, 1911).
2. *El Paso Times*, 1 January 1882; Jo Ann Hovious, "Social Change in Western Texas: El Paso, 1881-1889" (Master's thesis, University of Texas at El Paso, 1972), 23-25; Appendix, Map I.
3. Hovious, "Social Change," 33-34, 39-42; see also Fire-Map, C. L. Sonnichsen and M. G. McKinney, *The State National Bank Since 1881* (El Paso, 1971), between pages 82-83.
4. For all the details on "Sin City," see Sonnichsen, *Pass of the North*, 1: chap. 12; and H. Gordon Frost, *The Gentlemen's Club* (El Paso, 1983); for the

Chinese, see Nancy Farrar, "The Chinese of El Paso," *Southwestern Studies* no. 33 (El Paso, 1972), 4-22; and Cleofas Calleros, *El Paso Then and Now* (El Paso, 1954), 51-54.

5. Clyde Wise, Jr., "The Effects of the Railroads Upon El Paso," *Password* 5 (July 1960): 92.

6. Otis C. Coles interview in *El Paso Times*, 5 July 1925; Wise, "Effects of the Railroads," 95-96.

7. White, *Out of the Desert*, 160-64; William I. Latham, "Early El Paso Churches," *Password* 27 (Fall 1982): 99-114.

8. Edith L. Morrel, *The Rise and Growth of Public Education in El Paso, Texas* (El Paso, 1936), 38ff.; Hovious, "Social Change," 122-24; Wise, "The Effects of the Railoads," 96-97; Mario T. García, *Desert Immigrants* (New Haven, 1981), 110.

9. Tom Diamond, et al., "Pueblo de la Ysleta del Sur," 42; this story, first published in Owen White's *Out of the Desert*, 185, has become a classic. John Middagh, in his *Frontier Newspaper: The El Paso Times* (El Paso, 1958), 30, writes that "El Paso, with fewer than 1,000 votes, had convinced 2,252 citizens that El Paso was the logical site for the courthouse."

10. García, *Desert Immigrants*, 155; Oscar J. Martínez, "The Chicanos of El Paso: An Assessment of Progress," *Southwestern Studies* no. 59 (El Paso, 1980): table 8; for a revealing comparison of Mexican-American and Anglo-American populations in El Paso County, 1860-1900, see Arnoldo De León, *The Tejano Community, 1836-1900* (Albuquerque, 1982), 43.

11. *Lone Star*, 30 July 1884.

12. James M. Day, "El Paso: Mining Hub for Northern Mexico, 1880-1920," *Password* 24 (Spring 1979): 21-24.

13. Donald V. Brady, "The Theatre in Early El Paso," *Southwestern Studies* no. 13 (El Paso, 1966), 5-24. Myar learned about El Paso from his sister-in-law, who had married El Pasoan Herman Kayser.

14. *Times*, 17 December 1887; Brady, "The Theatre in El Paso," 27-32.

15. Ward Bros., *Souvenir of El Paso, Texas and Paso del Norte, Mexico* (Columbus, Ohio, 1887).

16. Bryson, *Down Went McGinty*, chaps. 3-10, passim.

17. As quoted in Leon Metz, *Fort Bliss* (El Paso, 1981), 39.

18. Ibid., 40. Still standing as reminders of the old Fort Bliss site near Hart's Mill are two apartment buildings which served as officers' quarters.

19. George Ruhlen, "The Genesis of New Fort Bliss," *Password* 29 (Winter 1974), 198-214. The author is the grandson of the post's builder. See also Garna L. Christian, "Sword and Plowshare: The Symbiotic Development of Fort Bliss and El Paso, Texas, 1849-1918" (Ph. D. diss., Texas Tech University, 1977), 82.

20. Lansing B. Bloom, ed., "Bourke on the Southwest," *New Mexico Historical Review* 13 (April 1938): 205-7; J. Walter Fewkes, "The Pueblo Settlements near El Paso, Texas," *American Anthropologist* 4 (January 1902): 57-75; Bronitsky, "Indian Assimilation in the El Paso Area," 155. As a result of the political activities of I. G. Gaal, a Hungarian immigrant, which had caused a riot in 1890, Ysleta voted to abolish the town corporation in 1895. The vote was 52 to 1! See Nancy Hamilton, "The Ysleta Riot of 1890," *Password* 24 (Fall 1979): 101-11. See also De León, *The Tejano Community*, 44-45.

21. W. H. Timmons, "The Church in Ysleta—Recent Documentary Discoveries," *Password* 28 (Fall 1983): 113-16.

22. Frederick A. Ober, *Travels in Mexico and Life Among the Mexicans* (Boston, 1884), 598-99.

23. Walter B. Stevens, *Through Texas* (Missouri Pacific Railway, 1892), 62-63.
24. Maude M. Austen, *'Cension: A Sketch from Paso del Norte* (New York, 1896), 32-33; Chávez, *Historia de Ciudad Juárez*, 295.
25. Rudolf Eickemeyer, *Letters from the Southwest* (New York, 1894), 8, 10, 25; Cleofas Calleros, *El Paso Then and Now*, 31-32. According to Calleros, six baby alligators were shipped to A. Munsenburger, a mining man, in 1890 by a Louisiana friend as a joke. The city council put them in the public square, soon to be named San Jacinto Plaza.
26. Eickemeyer, *Letters from the Southwest*, 19, 22, 33.
27. Ibid., 43-46.
28. Ibid., 70.
29. García, *Desert Immigrants*, 2-3, 46.
30. Ibid., 34-35; Elizabeth Broadbent, "Mexican Population in Southwestern United States," *Texas Geographic Magazine* 5, no. 2 (Autumn 1941): 20; Oscar J. Martínez, *Border Boom Town: Ciudad Juárez since 1848* (Austin, 1978), 29-30.
31. García, *Desert Immigrants*, 37, 46; Martínez, "The Chicanos of El Paso," 6.
32. García, *Desert Immigrants*, 6-7.
33. Edward J. M. Rhoads, "The Chinese in Texas," *Southwestern Historical Quarterly* 81, no. 1 (July 1977): 11-13; Farrar, "The Chinese of El Paso," 5-22.
34. Rhoads, "The Chinese in Texas," 13-14.
35. Ibid., 15-18; Farrar, "The Chinese of El Paso," 22. A recent archaeological investigation of the Cortez parking lot site at the corner of Main and Mesa streets concludes: "This site may contain one of the largest collections of Chinese material culture available for study in the United States.... Certainly, information on a range of activities once carried out by El Paso's resident Chinese population is preserved under the Cortez parking lot." See Edward Staski and David Batcho, "A Preliminary Report on Archaeological Testing of the Cortez Parking Lot Site, Mill Block 3, West Half" (New Mexico State University, 1983), 12.
36. *Statistical Abstract of El Paso, Texas* (El Paso, 1973), 12; Marilyn T. Bryan, "The Economic, Political and Social Status of the Negro in El Paso," *Password* 13 (Fall 1968): 74, 76.
37. Bryan, "The Economic, Political and Social Status of the Negro in El Paso," 75-77.
38. Ibid., 77.
39. Theodore D. Harris, ed., *Negro Frontiersman – The Western Memoirs of Henry O. Flipper* (El Paso, 1963), vii-viii; Eugene O. Porter, "Lord Beresford and Lady Flo," *Southwestern Studies* no. 25 (El Paso, 1970), 22.
40. Christian, "Sword and Plowshare," 164, 169, 171-72.
41. Floyd S. Fierman, *Some Early Jewish Settlers on the Southwest Frontier* (El Paso, 1960); and his "The Schwartz Family of El Paso," *Southwestern Studies* no. 61 (El Paso, 1980), 6-7, 10-13.
42. Sarah E. John, "Trade Will Lead Man Far: Syrian Immigration to the El Paso Area, 1900-1935" (Master's thesis, University of Texas at El Paso, 1982), chap. 2. Many of these immigrants were Lebanese, who were under Syrian jurisdiction until 1920.
43. White, *Out of the Desert*, 197-200; for a political analysis of the election, see Jack C. Vowell, Jr., "Ballots, Bombast and Blackguardism: The El Paso City Election of 1889," *Password* 1 (November 1956): 118-26.
44. For biographical sketches of Waters Davis and the Burges brothers, see Broaddus, *The Legal Heritage of El Paso*, 216-18. See also J. F. Hulse, *Texas Lawyer:*

The Life of William H. Burges (El Paso, 1982), 39-49. During this period the era of the gunfighter in El Paso came to an end with the death of the notorious John Wesley Hardin at the hands of John Selman, who was later shot and killed by George Scarborough.

45. John Middagh, *Frontier Newspaper*, 102-4.
46. *El Paso Herald*, 10 and 11 November 1904. No doubt Sheriff J. H. Boone's announced intention to enforce the antigambling legislation was decisive. Playing a key role in organizing the crusade against gambling were the churches and women's organizations.
47. Jack C. Vowell, Jr., "Politics at El Paso, 1859-1920" (Master's thesis, University of Texas at El Paso, 1952), 121-22.
48. White, *Out of the Desert*, 206-7; Middagh, *Frontier Newspaper*, 129-33.
49. See the El Paso Chamber of Commerce publications, *Story of a City*, (1910) and *Prosperity and Opportunities in El Paso* (1911).
50. For further details see G. L. Seligmann, Jr., "The El Paso and Northeastern Railroad's Economic Impact on Central New Mexico," *New Mexico Historical Review* 61 (July 1986): 217-31; Leonard, *Rails at the Pass of the North,* 37-39; Middagh, *Frontier Newspaper*, chap. 7; Dorothy Jensen Neal, *The Cloud-Climbing Railroad* (Alamogordo, N. Mex., 1966); and *The Lodge, 1899-1969* (Alamogordo, N. Mex., 1969).
51. Alice White, "The Development of Irrigation in the City of El Paso," *Password* 4 (January 1959): 37-38; Helen Orndorff, "Agriculture in the El Paso Valley, 1870-1914," *Password* 12 (Fall 1967): 83-85; Sonnichsen, *Pass of the North,* 1:384.
52. *El Paso Times* Jubilee Edition, 29 April 1956.
53. Ibid.
54. Ibid.
55. Ibid.; White, *Out of the Desert*, 224.
56. Ira G. Clark, "The Elephant Butte Controversy: A Chapter of the Emergence of Federal Water Law," *The Journal of American History* 61, no. 4 (March 1975): 1030.
57. Félix Martínez to Richard F. Burges, El Paso, 13 May 1908, Richard Burges Papers, Microfilm Copy, El Paso Public Library.
58. Richard M. Estrada, "Border Revolution: The Mexican Revolution in the Ciudad Juárez-El Paso Area, 1906-1915" (Master's thesis, University of Texas at El Paso, 1975), 32-44.
59. *El Paso Herald*, 16 October 1909; Charlotte Crawford, "The Border Meeting of Presidents Taft and Díaz," *Password* 3 (July 1958): 91.
60. Crawford, "The Border Meeting of Presidents Taft and Díaz," 91-94.
61. Ibid., 95. Other than the two presidents, the most conspicuous individuals at the meeting were Félix Martínez and Enrique Creel, governor of Chihuahua whose wife was a Terrazas. See *Crónica de la entrevista Díaz-Taft* (México, 1910); W. Dirk Raat, *Revoltosos: Mexico's Rebels in the United States, 1903-1923* (College Station, Tex., 1981), 176-79.
62. Burges to Martínez, Washington, D.C., 23 April 1910, Burges Papers; *El Paso Times*, 29 April 1956.
63. *El Paso Times*, 29 April 1956; White, *Out of the Desert*, 225. Conrey Bryson has called my attention to a quote which describes the dam in graphic language: "It stores more water than the world famous Assuan dam on the Nile.... It holds water enough to fill a stand-pipe eleven feet in diameter reaching from El Paso to the moon, or to cover Massachusetts to a depth of

six inches!" See Frederick Simpich, "Along Our Side of the Mexican Border," *The National Geographic Magazine* 38 (July 1920): 65.

64. El Paso Chamber of Commerce, *Prosperity and Opportunities in El Paso* as quoted in Lloyd C. and June-Marie F. Engelbrecht, *Henry Trost—Architect of the Southwest* (El Paso, 1981), 75.

65. Sheldon B. Liss, *A Century of Disagreement: The Chamizal Conflict* (Washington, D.C., 1965), chap. 1; Gladys Gregory, "The Chamizal Settlement—A View from El Paso," *Southwestern Studies* no. 2 (El Paso, 1963), 5-11; see also Luis G. Zorrilla, *Historia de las relaciones entre México y los Estados Unidos* (México, 1977), 2: chap. 14; and César Sepúlveda, *La frontera norte de México* (México, 1976), chap. 11.

66. Liss, *A Century of Disagreement*, chap. 2.

67. Ibid., chap. 4.

68. Ibid., 32-35. Liss points out that one of the reasons for Díaz's downfall was his inability to get the Chamizal for Mexico. He adds that Victoriano Huerta, who became president of Mexico in February 1913, would have conceded the Chamizal to the United States in return for U.S. recognition of his regime. Pres. Woodrow Wilson refused. See pp. 49-50. See also Anson Mills, *My Story*, 298.

69. Engelbrecht, *Henry C. Trost Architect of the Southwest*, 31-85, passim.

70. Conrey Bryson, "In Skagway They Still Remember Pete Kern," *Password* 19 (Fall 1974): 126-32; Vowell, "Politics at El Paso," 139-40.

71. Francis L. Fugate, *Frontier College* (El Paso, 1964), 6-18; Patrick Rand, "The Federal Smelter," *Password* 22 (Fall 1977): 109-15; Conrey Bryson, "The El Paso Tin Mine," *Password* 3 (January 1958): 4-13.

72. Fugate, *Frontier College*, 27-29.

73. Vowell, "Politics at El Paso," 141.

74. Owen P. White, "El Paso: 'The Right Thing' on the Frontier," in Duncan Aikman, ed., *The Taming of the Frontier* (Freeport, N.Y., 1967), 22-23.

CHAPTER VIII
EL PASO AND CIUDAD JUAREZ, 1910-1945

1. The scholarly literature on the Mexican Revolution is considerable. In addition to the general works of Katz, Knight, and Ruiz, mention should be made of the more specialized works of Almada, Beezley, Cumberland, Hall, Meyer, Quirk, Raat, Ross, and Womack. For the general reader, W. W. Johnson's *Heroic Mexico* is a well-written narrative, and Timothy Turner's *Bullets, Bottles, and Gardenias* provides the flavor.

2. Estrada, "Border Revolution," Introduction.

3. William H. Beezley, *Insurgent Governor* (Lincoln, 1973), 37.

4. Mardee Belding de Wetter, "Revolutionary El Paso: 1910-1917," *Password* 3 (April 1958): 50; I. J. Bush, *Gringo Doctor* (Caldwell, Idaho, 1939), 178-80; Timothy Turner, *Bullets, Bottles, and Gardenias* (Dallas, 1935), 24.

5. Michael Dennis Carman, "United States Customs and the Madero Revolution," *Southwestern Studies* no. 48 (El Paso, 1976): 40-41; W. Dirk Raat, *Revoltosos: Mexico's Rebels in the United States, 1903-1923* (College Station, Tex., 1981), 232.

6. Carman, "United States Customs and the Madero Revolution," 51; Bush, *Gringo Doctor*, 180-85. For details on the McGinty cannon, see *El Paso Herald*, 6 June 1911; and Bryson, *Down Went McGinty*, 58-59.

7. William Weber Johnson, *Heroic Mexico* (New York, 1968), 51; Turner, *Bullets, Bottles, and Gardenias,* 50; de Wetter, "Revolutionary El Paso," 55-56.

8. Quoted in de Wetter, "Revolutionary El Paso," 56.

9. *El Paso Times,* 8-10 May 1911; Estrada, "Border Revolution," 80-84; Johnson, *Heroic Mexico,* 69; Stanley R. Ross, *Francisco I. Madero* (New York, 1955), 166.

10. Turner, *Bullets, Bottles, and Gardenias,* 70; de Wetter, "Revolutionary El Paso," 58-59; John Middagh, *Frontier Newspaper: The El Paso Times* (El Paso, 1958), 159.

11. Raat, *Revoltosos,* 243; Charles H. Harris III and Louis R. Sadler, "The 1911 Reyes Conspiracy: The Texas Side," *Southwestern Historical Quarterly* 83 (April 1980): 325-26; Estrada, "Border Revolution," 92-94, 96-103.

12. C. E. Kelly to William Howard Taft, El Paso, Tex., 11 March 1912, El Paso Public Library, Southwest Collection, Vertical File – Pioneers – C. E. Kelly; Huntington Wilson to C. E. Kelly, 20 March 1912, *Records of the Department of State Relating to Internal Affairs of Mexico, 1910-1929* (microfilm, UTEP Library, M274R17F812.00/3357); C. E. Kelly to Secretary of State, El Paso, 26 March 1912, ibid., (microfilm, UTEP Library, M274R17F812.00/3474); Don M. Coerver and Linda B. Hall, *Texas and the Mexican Revolution* (San Antonio, 1984), 44-46.

13. Coerver and Hall, *Texas and the Mexican Revolution,* 47; de Wetter, "Revolutionary El Paso," 108-9; Charles H. Harris III and Louis R. Sadler, "The 'Underside' of the Mexican Revolution: El Paso, 1912," *The Americas* 39, no. 1 (July 1982): 82-83.

14. Johnson, *Heroic Mexico,* 96-107, 108-15; Middagh, *Frontier Newspaper,* 161.

15. Mark Gilderhus, *Diplomacy and Revolution* (Tucson, 1977), 9; *El Paso Times,* 19 July 1915; Estrada, "Border Revolution," 125.

16. Estrada, "Border Revolution," 117-18; Middagh, *Frontier Newspaper,* 164.

17. de Wetter, "Revolutionary El Paso," 112, 117; Richard Estrada, "The Mexican Revolution in the Ciudad Juárez-El Paso Area, 1910-1920," *Password* 24 (Fall 1979): 66.

18. García, *Desert Immigrants,* 131, 137, 141-43; Estrada, "The Mexican Revolution in the Ciudad Juárez-El Paso Area," 65.

19. Gilderhus, *Diplomacy and Revolution,* 10-11; Shawn Lay, *War, Revolution and the Ku Klux Klan* (El Paso, 1985), 22-23.

20. Christian, "Sword and Plowshare," 333; Johnson, *Heroic Mexico,* 289-91.

21. Coerver and Hall, *Texas and the Mexican Revolution,* 85-86; Charles H. Harris III and Louis R. Sadler, "The Plan of San Diego and the Mexican-United States War Crisis of 1916: A Reexamination," *The Hispanic American Historical Review* 58, no. 3 (August 1978): 381-408.

22. Christian, "Sword and Plowshare," 344-49. For details concerning Huerta's and Orozco's last days, see Michael C. Meyer, *Huerta: A Political Portrait* (Lincoln, 1972), 221-29. Huerta was first buried in Concordia Cemetery, but later was moved to Evergreen Cemetery.

23. de Wetter, "Revolutionary El Paso," 149, 151; Middagh, *Frontier Newspaper,* 175-76.

24. *El Paso Times,* 9 October 1915; Estrada, "Border Revolution," 136-37.

25. Lay, *War, Revolution and the Ku Klux Klan,* 16-17, 25; de Wetter, "Revolutionary El Paso," 154.

26. Historians of the Columbus Raid are now essentially in agreement that it was not as irrational or irresponsible as it was once thought, but there are still differences in opinion as to its motivation. The various theses include: Villa's desire not only to retaliate against the Americans but also to provoke their

intervention in Mexico, thus creating a situation on which he could capitalize; his intention to loot Columbus and the nearby Thirteenth Cavalry encampment for munitions, remounts, and provisions; his desire for vengeance against certain Columbus businessmen who had allegedly defrauded him of money and arms; and finally, the provocative theory that German agents manipulated Villa into attacking Columbus in order to embroil the United States in a war with Mexico. See Charles H. Harris III and Louis R. Sadler, "Pancho Villa and the Columbus Raid: the Missing Documents," *New Mexico Historical Review* 50 (October 1975): 343. Friedrich Katz recently has offered evidence to suggest that the primary motivation was Villa's firm belief that Woodrow Wilson had concluded an agreement with Carranza that would virtually convert Mexico into a U.S. protectorate. See his "Pancho Villa and the Attack on Columbus, New Mexico," *The American Historical Review* 83, no. 1 (February 1978): 102. For the Punitive Expedition, see the works of Clendenen, Braddy, and Tompkins.

27. Ernest Peixotto, *Our Hispanic Southwest* (New York, 1916), 95-96.
28. Coerver and Hall, *Texas and the Mexican Revolution*, 127; Stacy C. Hinkle, "Wings Over the Border," *Southwestern Studies* no. 26 (El Paso, 1970), 5-6.
29. Coerver and Hall, *Texas and the Mexican Revolution*, 133.
30. For details on the Zimmermann telegram, see Friedrich Katz, *The Secret War in Mexico* (Chicago, 1981), 350ff; and Gilderhus, *Diplomacy and Revolution*, 58-62.
31. Christian, "Sword and Plowshare," 426-28; Lay, *War, Revolution and the Ku Klux Klan*, 34-37. During the war El Pasoans displayed their patriotism by bringing the Liberty Bell to the city for an hour and a half, erecting a Liberty statue in Pioneer Plaza, and constructing an auditorium, later known as Liberty Hall, for selling Liberty Bonds. It was at this time that because of the fear of the Germans an "English only" law was passed for Texas schools. In later years it was used against the Mexican-Americans.
32. Christian, "Sword and Plowshare," 433; Lay, *War, Revolution and the Ku Klux Klan*, 38.
33. Lay, *War, Revolution and the Ku Klux Klan*, 40.
34. Ibid., 41-45.
35. Ibid., 45; Edward L. Langston, "The Impact of Prohibition on the Mexican-United States Border: The El Paso-Ciudad Juárez Case" (Ph.D. diss., Texas Tech University, 1974), 42-43.
36. Ibid., 46-48.
37. Bradford Luckingham, "Epidemic in the Southwest, 1918-1919," *Southwestern Studies* no. 72 (El Paso, 1984), 1-17.
38. Langston, "The Impact of Prohibition," 2-3.
39. Ibid., 4-5.
40. Martínez, *Border Boom Town*, 57, 59.
41. Ibid., 57-58.
42. Langston, "The Impact of Prohibition," 91-92; Frank Mangan, *El Paso in Pictures* (El Paso, 1971), 108-9.
43. Langston, "The Impact of Prohibition," 126-27.
44. Ibid., 159-63.
45. Ibid., 227-34.
46. Ibid., 248-51, 259-66.
47. Ibid., 266-70, 278-84.
48. Quoted in Martínez, *Border Boom Town*, 67.

49. *El Paso Times,* 19 January 1921.
50. Lay, *War, Revolution and the Ku Klux Klan,* 106-7.
51. Ibid., 75.
52. Ibid., 92-94.
53. Middagh, *Frontier Newsapaper,* 201-2.
54. Lay, *War, Revolution and the Ku Klux Klan,* 106-7.
55. Ibid., 103.
56. Ibid., 112-14; *El Paso Times,* 20 May 1922.
57. *El Paso Times,* 30 September 1922.
58. Lay, *War, Revolution and the Ku Klux Klan,* 133-36.
59. *El Paso Times,* 25 and 26 February 1923. For insights on the mayor's race in 1923 with all of its emotionalism, see R. M. Dudley, Scrapbook, July 1922-March 1923, Southwest Collection, no. 562, El Paso Public Library. For more on the El Paso spirit, see R. E. Sherman's speech given in 1923, in William J. Hooten, *Fifty-Two Years a Newsman* (El Paso, 1974), 54-55.
60. Lay, *War, Revolution and the Ku Klux Klan,* 155-59.
61. El Paso City Plan Commission, *The City Plan of El Paso, Texas* (El Paso, 1925), 6-7 (hereafter cited as the *Kessler Plan*).
62. *Kessler Plan,* 12-15; Martínez, *Border Boom Town,* 45-46.
63. *Kessler Plan,* 18; Rand, "The Federal Smelter," 109-15.
64. El Paso Chamber of Commerce, *El Paso, Texas — Predestined to Become the Commercial and Industrial Center of the Scenic Southwest* (El Paso, 1930), 11-21.
65. Lay, *War, Revolution and the Ku Klux Klan,* 66.
66. Ibid., 67.
67. Ibid., 66; Mangan, *El Paso in Pictures,* 100.
68. Mangan, *El Paso in Pictures,* 100.
69. *El Paso Times,* 5 and 25 September 1931, 8 October 1932; *El Paso Herald-Post,* 22 June and 26 October 1931; C. L. Sonnichsen and M. G. McKinney, *The State National Since 1881* (El Paso, 1971), 87-89; Martínez, *Border Boom Town,* 89, 93-94; R. Reynolds McKay, "Texas Mexican Repatriation During the Great Depression" (Ph. D. diss., University of Oklahoma, 1982), 117. For an excellent summary of the repatriation problem during the depression that emphasizes the El Paso-Ciudad Juárez area, see Yolanda Leyva, "The Repatriation of Mexicans During the Great Depression: The Case of El Paso and Cd. Juárez" (seminar paper, University of Texas at El Paso, 1987).
70. Mangan, *El Paso in Pictures,* 117-19.
71. Sonnichsen, *Pass of the North* (El Paso, 1980), 2:40-41; Martínez, *Border Boom Town,* 93.
72. Metz, *Fort Bliss,* 117-23.
73. Middagh, *Frontier Newspaper,* 243-44.
74. El Paso Chamber of Commerce, "Cristo Rey The Christ of the Rockies," ms., n.d.
75. Ibid. See also Charles H. Binion, *An Introduction to El Paso's Scenic and Historic Landmarks* (El Paso, 1970), 19-23.
76. Sonnichsen, *Pass of the North,* 2:48-49. For the role of El Paso's Congressman R. E. Thomason during World War II, see Joseph M. Ray, ed., *Thomason, The Autobiography of a Federal Judge* (El Paso, 1971), 57.
77. Perry D. Jamieson, "A Survey History of Fort Bliss," W. H. Timmons, ed., *Four Centuries at the Pass* (El Paso, 1980), 87-88. See also Bertram C. Wright, *The 1st Cavalry Division in World War II* (Tokyo, 1947) for all the campaigns in the Southwest Pacific.

78. Jamieson, "A Survey History of Fort Bliss," 88.
79. Ibid.
80. Martínez, *Border Boom Town*, 96, 110; see also his "The Chicanos of El Paso," 6.
81. Ruth Laughlin, *Caballeros* (Caldwell, Idaho, 1947), 382-83. It is interesting to note that the headline in the *El Paso Herald-Post* read: "Army Ammunition Explosion Rocks Southwest Area," an indicaton of the secrecy that had guarded the development of the atomic bomb during the war years.
82. Sonnichsen, *Pass of the North*, 2:53.

CHAPTER IX
THE SOUTHWEST METROPOLIS SINCE 1945

1. Bureau of Business and Economic Research, *Statistical Abstract of El Paso, Texas* (El Paso, 1986), 1-1; Bradford Luckingham, *The Urban Southwest* (El Paso, 1982), 108.
2. Patricia Reschenthaler, "Postwar Readjustment in El Paso, 1945-1950," *Southwestern Studies* no. 21 (El Paso, 1968): 3.
3. Ibid., 7-8.
4. Ibid., 20-21.
5. Ibid., 11-14, 19.
6. Martínez, *Border Boom Town*, 110-13.
7. Reschenthaler, "Postwar Readjustment in El Paso," 23.
8. Martínez, *Border Boom Town*, 113.
9. *El Paso Herald-Post*, 7, 8, and 9 June 1945; Carey McWilliams, "The El Paso Story," *The Nation*, 10 July 1948; George Sessions Perry, "El Paso," *Saturday Evening Post*, 4 February 1950.
10. Perry, "El Paso."
11. Mangan, *El Paso in Pictures*, 119. Loretto Shopping Center was woefully short on parking. Chelmont Shopping Center, built several years later, became the model.
12. John M. Richards, *Economic Growth in El Paso, 1950-62* (El Paso, 1964), 26, 31-32, 33, 45-46.
13. Mangan, *El Paso in Pictures*, 140, 147-48; Sonnichsen and McKinney, *The State National Since 1881*, 157-59. Transmountain Road has been officially named Woodrow Bean Transmountain Road in recognition of the leadership provided by County Judge Woodrow Bean in building it and other projects such as the Cordova Bridge, Thomason Hospital's new building, and the Sun Bowl.
14. *El Paso Herald-Post*, 28 April 1956; *El Paso Times*, 29 April 1956; Fugate, *Frontier College*, 103.
15. Christopher M. Wallace, "Water out of the Desert," *Southwestern Studies* no. 22 (El Paso 1969): 28-31; Mangan, *El Paso in Pictures*, 143.
16. Wallace, "Water out of the Desert," 31-32. One of the upshots of the annexations was the phenomenon of having two of the ten most populous school districts in the state—El Paso and Ysleta—within the city.
17. El Paso Department of Planning, "A Short History of South El Paso," (El Paso, 1967), 30; Perry, "El Paso."
18. El Paso Department of Planning, "A Short History of South El Paso," 36-37; Tom Butler, "The Barrio," *El Paso Times*, 24 April 1977, 1, 17.
19. Conrey Bryson, "Dr. Lawrence A. Nixon and the White Primary," *Southwestern Studies* no. 42 (El Paso, 1974), 85-86; Joseph M. Ray, ed., *Thomason, The Autobiography of a Federal Judge* (El Paso, 1971), 116.

20. Oscar J. Martínez, "The Chicanos of El Paso," *Southwestern Studies* no. 59 (El Paso, 1980), 39.
21. William V. D'Antonio and William H. Form, *Influentials in Two Border Cities* (University of Notre Dame Press, 1965), 132-33. Although the two newspapers had separate ownership, under an arrangement that became popular during the depression years, they had the same printing plant and advertising/circulation agency, and were housed in the same building, with the same telephone switchboard. This led many people to believe that the conflicts between editors were staged as a sales gimmick. Such was not the case.
22. McWilliams, "The El Paso Story"; D'Antonio and Form, *Influentials in Two Border Cities*, 138.
23. D'Antonio and Form, *Influentials in Two Border Cities*, 142; Paul Sweeney and Carey Gelerntner, "EP Influentials Elude Mexican-Americans," *El Paso Times*, 24 December 1978; Hooten, *Fifty-Two Years a Newsman*, 149.
24. Taped interview with Raymond Telles, 22 October 1975, Institute of Oral History, University of Texas at El Paso (hereafter cited as IOH, UTEP).
25. For further details, see any up-to-date textbook in American history, such as Richard N. Current, T. Harry Williams, Frank Friedel, Alan Brinkley, *A Survey of American History*, 6th ed. (New York, 1983), chap. 30.
26. Joseph M. Ray, *On Becoming a University* (El Paso, 1968), 89-91.
27. Ibid., 41.
28. Samuel D. Myres, *The Education of a West Texan* (El Paso, 1985), 193-94.
29. *The Prospector*, 16 February, 1 August, 15-25 October 1968.
30. Ray, *On Becoming a University*, 37.
31. Ibid., 40-41.
32. For an informative introduction to the Chicano movement, see the series of articles by Bob Ybarra in the *El Paso Herald-Post*, 27-31 December 1971. See also Oscar J. Martínez, "The Chicanos of El Paso," 38, and Carlos E. Cortés, "The New Chicano Historiography," in Ellwyn R. Stoddard, Richard L. Nostrand, and Jonathan P. West, eds., *Borderlands Sourcebook* (Norman, 1983), 60-63.
33. Taped interview with Mike Romo, 8 and 14 October 1975, IOH, UTEP; Richard L. Nostrand, "A Changing Culture Region," in Stoddard, et al., *Borderlands Sourcebook*, 11-12.
34. Martínez, "The Chicanos of El Paso," 38.
35. Ibid., 9-16; Sweeney and Gelerntner, "EP Influentials Elude Mexican-Americans," *El Paso Times*, 24 December 1978.
36. Taped Interview with David Carrasco, 28 April 1976, IOH, UTEP.
37. Taped Interview with Ralph Murillo and Eligio "Kiki" de la Garza, 7 July 1975 and 22 October 1975, IOH, UTEP.
38. Taped Interview with Tati Santiesteban and Fernando Oaxaca, 30 June 1975 and 23 October 1975, IOH, UTEP.
39. Martínez, "The Chicanos of El Paso," 39.
40. Taped Interview with Fernando Oaxaca, 23 October 1975, IOH, UTEP.
41. Bertha P. Dutton, *American Indians of the Southwest* (Albuquerque, 1983), 20-21.
42. Diamond, et al., "Pueblo de la Ysleta del Sur," 53; Texas Indian Reservation, *The Tiguas, A Short History*, 1976.
43. Luckingham, *The Urban Southwest*, 102-15.
44. Ibid., 97. The *El Paso Herald-Post*, 22 September 1975, carried a story entitled "El Paso Ranks 66th in Quality of Life Among 83 Cities in its size category."

45. Quoted in Luckingham, *The Urban Southwest*, 97.
46. Sonnichsen, *Pass of the North*, 2:63.
47. *El Paso Times*, 30 November 1972. Viewing the Civic Center as an obvious tourist attraction, both newspapers began publishing a Tourist and Convention Guide twice a year, in June and in December.
48. Sonnichsen, *Pass of the North*, 2:101.
49. Charles H. Binion, *An Introduction to El Paso's Scenic and Historic Landmarks* (El Paso, 1970), 25-37; Fred W. Bailey, "The Mountains," *El Paso – A Centennial Portrait* (El Paso, 1973), 22-25. The thunderbird is the mascot of nearby Coronado High School.
50. El Paso Industrial Development Corporation, *El Paso Area Fact Book*, "Community Living," 12; see also the Wilderness Park Museum's brochure, "The Best Kept Secret in El Paso."
51. *El Paso Herald-Post*, 3 December 1971; *El Paso Times*, 4 December 1971; Sonnichsen, *Pass of the North*, 2:62; Haskell Monroe, "UTEP Aims for Top Goals," *El Paso Times*, 2 September 1984.
52. El Paso Industrial Development Corporation, *El Paso Area Fact Book*, "Community Living," 7-9.
53. Olaya H. Andrade, "The Hispanic Community," in *Four Centuries at the Pass*, 123; Martínez, "The Chicanos of El Paso," 30, 35-36; Sonnichsen, *Pass of the North*, 2:102. By 1971 the selection process for choosing the sun queen had been drastically altered to involve a significant number of community groups, including, for example, LULAC.
54. *El Paso – A Centennial Portrait*; Conrey Bryson, *The Land Where We Live*; Brochure, "Magoffin Home State Historic Site."
55. Department of Planning, Research, and Development, *El Paso's Forgotten Past* (El Paso, 1977); Patrick Abel, "Historic Preservation," in *Four Centuries at the Pass*, 125-26; El Paso County Historical Commission, *The Historic Past of El Paso County* (El Paso, 1983).
56. For a summary of activities, see W. H. Timmons, "El Paso's 'Mr. History' Says 'Let's Celebrate,'" *The Texas Humanist* 5, no. 1 (September-October 1982); and John M. Crewdson, "In Sister Cities of El Paso and Juárez, 400 Years of History Erase a Border," *The New York Times*, 18 July 1981.
57. El Paso Foreign Trade Association, *Paso del Norte Trade Area* (El Paso, 1986); *El Paso Herald-Post*, 18 June 1987. According to *The El Paso Economic Review* for September-October 1988, El Paso's eight basic industries are mining, construction, manufacturing, transportation, trade, finance, services, and government.
58. "The 'In-Bond' (Maquila) Industry in Ciudad Juárez and El Paso, Texas," *The El Paso Economic Review* 20, no. 1 (January-February 1984); *El Paso Times*, 6 November 1988.
59. Bureau of Business and Economic Research, *Statistical Abstract of El Paso, Texas*, 13-1; *El Paso Times*, 5 May 1987; *El Paso Herald-Post*, 29 July 1988.
60. *El Paso Times*, 2 September 1984; *El Paso Herald-Post*, 7 July 1987.
61. *El Paso Times*, 12 February 1988; Nancy Hamilton, *UTEP: A Pictorial History of The University of Texas at El Paso* (El Paso and Norfolk-Virginia Beach, 1988), 215-17.
62. *El Paso Herald-Post*, 6 June 1982; *El Paso Times*, 9 November 1988.
63. Wallace, "Water out of the Desert," 4-6.
64. Neal E. Armstrong, "Anticipating Transboundary Water Needs and Issues in the Mexico-United States Border Region in the Rio Grande Basin," in César Sepúlveda and Albert E. Utton, eds., *The U.S.-Mexico Border Region: Anticipating*

Resource Needs and Issues to the Year 2000 (El Paso, 1984), 172; Randall J. Charbeneau, "Groundwater Resources of the Texas Rio Grande Basin," ibid., 234-39.
65. Ryan J. Barilleaux, "The Politics of Southwestern Water," *Southwestern Studies* no. 73 (El Paso, 1984): 9-15; Bryan Woolley, "Texas Says N.M. Law Doesn't Hold Water," *Dallas Times Herald*, 12 September 1988.
66. Barilleaux, "The Politics of Southwestern Water," 39-45; Ira G. Clark, *Water in New Mexico* (Albuquerque, 1987), 675-80; Woolley, "Texas Says N.M. Law Doesn't Hold Water."
67. *El Paso Times*, 9 December 1983.
68. Ibid., 1 May 1985; *El Paso Herald-Post*, 13 May 1986.
69. *El Paso Times*, 20 and 21 January 1987, 22 June 1988.
70. See chaps. 1-4.
71. *El Paso Herald-Post*, 9 April 1988; *The Dallas Morning News*, 20 November 1988.
72. *Statistical Abstract of El Paso, Texas; El Paso Area Fact Book.*

CHAPTER X
THE INTERNATIONAL METROPLEX SINCE 1961

1. Martínez, *Border Boom Town*, 114-15, 158.
2. Sheldon B. Liss, *A Century of Disagreement: The Chamizal Conflict* (Washington, D.C., 1965), 1-36; Gladys Gregory, "The Chamizal Settlement – A View from El Paso," *Southwestern Studies* no. 2 (El Paso, 1963): 5-38.
3. Quoted in Gregory, "The Chamizal Settlement," 4-5.
4. Liss, *A Century of Disagreement*, 84-87.
5. Gregory, "The Chamizal Settlement," 5; Liss, *A Century of Disagreement*, 87-90.
6. Liss, *A Century of Disagreement*, 90-93; Gregory, "The Chamizal Settlement," 41-43. The map on the latter's pp. 26-27 explains the settlement in graphic terms. See Jerry E. Mueller, *Restless River* (El Paso, 1975), 103, for the total costs to the United States. For a discussion of the Chamizal problem by two eminent Mexican scholars, see Zorrilla, *Historia de las relaciones entre México y los Estados Unidos*, 2: chap. 14; and César Sepúlveda, *La frontera norte de México* (México, 1976), chap. 11.
7. Liss, *A Century of Disagreement*, 95-98, 107.
8. Ibid., 105; Gregory, "The Chamizal Settlement," 3-4.
9. E. V. Niemeyer, Jr., "Personal Diplomacy: Lyndon B. Johnson and Mexico, 1963-1968," *Southwestern Historical Quarterly* 90 (October 1986): 163, 181; Martínez, *Border Boom Town*, 116; International Boundary and Water Commission, *Joint Projects of the United States and Mexico* (Washington, D.C., 1981), 9-10.
10. Taped interview with Antonio J. Bermúdez, 21 June 1974, IOH, UTEP.
11. Martínez, *Border Boom Town*, 117, 121; Ellwyn R. Stoddard, *Maquila* (El Paso, 1987), 16-17.
12. Martínez, *Border Boom Town*, 126.
13. Ibid., 128-29; Stoddard, *Maquila*, 17.
14. "The 'In Bond' (Maquila) Industry in Cd. Juárez, Mexico and El Paso, Texas," *The El Paso Economic Review* 20, no. 1 (January-February 1984); Stoddard, *Maquila*, 17-26.
15. "The 'In Bond' (Maquila) Industry in Juárez and El Paso." For complete details on the in-bond plants, see *Statistical Abstract of El Paso, Texas* (El Paso, 1986), 16-10 – 16-51. See also the article on the *maquiladoras* in the *El Paso Times*, 6 November 1988.

16. "The 'In Bond' (Maquila) Industry in Juárez and El Paso"; Stoddard, *Maquila*, chaps. 3-5.
17. By 1986 there were more than a thousand plants in Mexico, 12 percent located in the interior. See Stoddard, *Maquila*, Table 2.
18. John W. House, *Frontier on the Rio Grande* (Oxford, 1982), 154; Martínez, *Border Boom Town*, 141-42.
19. "The Border," *El Paso Herald-Post* (Summer 1983), 83-86.
20. House, *Frontier on the Rio Grande*, 80-81; "The Border," *El Paso Herald-Post*, 51-54; Martínez, *Border Boom Town*, 145.
21. "The Border," *El Paso Herald-Post*, 63-65.
22. Ibid., 10.
23. House, *Frontier on the Rio Grande*, 141-42.
24. Vernon M. Briggs, Jr., "Labor Market Aspects of Mexican Migration to the United States in the 1970s," in Stanley R. Ross, ed., *Views Across the Border* (Albuquerque, 1979), 209-15.
25. Ibid., 208; "The Border," *El Paso Herald-Post*, 79-82.
26. House, *Frontier on the Rio Grande*, 148, 158-62.
27. *El Paso Times*, 6 November 1986.
28. *El Paso Herald-Post*, 1 June 1987, 31 May 1988, 19 August 1988; *El Paso Times*, 7 and 17 November 1988.
29. D. W. Meinig, *Southwest: Three Peoples in Geographical Change, 1600-1970* (New York, 1971), 108-9; taped interview with Ken Flynn, July 1977, IOH, UTEP; "The Border," *El Paso Herald-Post*; Bob Reid, "Inter City Groups," *Cactus Points* (Summer 1983): 16.
30. McWilliams, *North from Mexico*, 59, 61; House, *Frontier on the Rio Grande*, 201; *Statistical Abstract*, 6-11.
31. Quoted in Arthur W. Busch, "Environmental Management: A Basis for Equitable Resource Allocation," in Ross, ed., *Views Across the Border*, 345.
32. Ibid.
33. Charbeneau, "Groundwater Resources of the Texas Rio Grande Basin," in *The U.S.-Mexico Border Region*, 241-42.
34. Utton, "Shared Water Resources in the United States-Mexico Border Region," in *Ecology and Development of the Border Region*, 167-68.
35. Ibid., 171, 177.
36. Busch, "Environmental Management," 356.
37. House, *Frontier on the Rio Grande*, 134-35; Howard G. Applegate and C. Richard Bath, eds., *Air Pollution Along the United States-Mexico Border* (El Paso, 1974), introd.
38. Busch, "Environmental Management," 358; Howard G. Applegate, *Environmental Problems of the Borderlands* (El Paso, 1979), 21.
39. House, *Frontier on the Rio Grande*, 251; "The Border," *El Paso Herald-Post*, 8-9.
40. "The Border," *El Paso Herald-Post*, 6-10.
41. Quoted in House, *Frontier on the Rio Grande*, 251-52.
42. Sonnichsen, *Pass of the North*, 2:114.
43. Martínez, *Border Boom Town*, 124-25; Taped Interview with René Mascareñas Miranda, February-April, 1976, IOH, UTEP. A 1989 *Southwestern Studies* entitled "Standoff at the Pass: A Failure of Microdiplomacy," by Thomas Price gives the details on the international streetcar negotiations.
44. House, *Frontier on the Rio Grande*, 256.
45. T. Zane Reeves, "The U.S.-Mexican Border Commissions: An Overview and Agenda for Further Research," UTEP Center for Inter-American and Border

Studies. Congressman Ron Coleman has introduced a bill to create a U.S.-Mexico Border Commission. See *El Paso Times*, 18 May 1988.

46. Quoted in Ross, ed., *Views Across the Border*, 381.

47. Stoddard, et al., eds., *Borderlands Sourcebook*, xiv; Martínez, brochure, "Latin American and Border Studies."

48. Willard P. Gingerich, ed., *Air Quality Issues in the El Paso/Cd. Juárez Border Region* (El Paso, 1980), preface.

49. James Lawrence McConville, "El Paso-Cd. Juárez – A Focus of Inter-American Culture," *New Mexico Historical Review* 40 (July 1965): 234-35.

50. "The Border," *El Paso Herald-Post*, 12-13.

51. Ibid., 16-17. El Pasoans will recall Tom Lea's fascination with the Tex-Mex theme in *The Wonderful Country*.

52. Luckingham, *The Urban Southwest*, 52, 130-42.

53. W. H. Timmons, "El Paso – Where Texas History Begins," *Password* 31 (Summer 1986): 56-57, 64.

54. "The Border," *El Paso Herald-Post*, 20-21; Luckingham, *The Urban Southwest*, 118.

55. Perry D. Jamieson, "A Survey History of Fort Bliss," in *Four Centuries at the Pass*, 89-90.

56. Meinig, *Southwest*, 21, 50; see also his *Imperial Texas* (Austin, 1969), 113.

57. McConville, "El Paso-Cd. Juárez – A Focus of Inter-American Culture"; Willard P. Gingerich, "The El Paso-Ciudad Juárez Border and Its Future," in *Four Centuries at the Pass*, 129-31; Chávez, *Historia de Ciudad Juárez, Chih.*, 507.

Bibliography

I. BIBLIOGRAPHIC AIDS

Barnes, Thomas C., Thomas H. Naylor, Charles W. Polzer, comps. *Northern New Spain: A Research Guide*. Tucson: University of Arizona Press, 1981.

Beers, Henry Putney. *Spanish and Mexican Records of the American Southwest*. Tucson: University of Arizona Press, 1979.

Caballero, César, comp. "Mexico and the Southwest." El Paso: University of Texas at El Paso Libraries, Special Collections Department, 1984.

Chávez, Angélico, ed. *Archives of the Archdiocese of Santa Fe, 1678-1900*. Washington, D.C.: Academy of American Franciscan History, 1957.

Daguerre, R. P., comp. "List of Archival Accessions," UTEP Special Collections, 1975.

Institute of Oral History. *Guide to the Oral History Collection*. El Paso: University of Texas at El Paso, 1987.

Jenkins, Myra Ellen, ed. "Mexican Archives of New Mexico." Santa Fe: State of New Mexico Records Center, 1969.

_____ "Spanish Archives of New Mexico, 1621-1821." Santa Fe: State of New Mexico Records Center, 1967..

Kielman, Chester V., ed. *The University of Texas Archives: A Guide to the Historical Manuscript Collections in the University of Texas Library*. Austin: University of Texas Press, 1968.

McClure, Charles R., comp. "Guide to the Microfilm Collection of the Periódico Oficial de Chihuahua." UTEP Library, n.d.

McConville, James Lawrence. "General Description of the Spanish Language Archives on Microfilm Held by the UTEP Archives." 1972.

Naylor, Thomas H., and Charles W. Polzer, S.J., ed. *The Presidio and Militia on the Northern Frontier of New Spain*. Tucson: University of Arizona Press, 1986.

Norris, Patrick. *History by Design: A Primer on Interpreting and Exhibiting Community History*. Austin: Texas Association of Museums, 1985.

Polzer, Charles W., comp. "The Documentary Relations of the Southwest." Tucson: Arizona State Museum, The University of Arizona, 1977.

Rittenhouse, Jack. *The Santa Fe Trail – A Historical Bibliography*. Albuquerque: University of New Mexico Press, 1971.

Scurlock, Dan, comp. "Spain in North America." Austin: Texas Historical Commission, 1973.

Stoddard, Ellwyn R., Richard L. Nostrand, and Jonathan P. West, eds. *Borderlands Sourcebook: A Guide to the Literature of Northern Mexico and the American Southwest.* Norman: University of Oklahoma Press, 1983.

Taylor, Virginia H. *The Spanish Archives of the General Land Office of Texas.* Austin: Lone Star Press, 1955.

Twitchell, Ralph Emerson. *The Spanish Archives of New Mexico.* 2 vols. Cedar Rapids: Torch Press, 1914.

Tyler, Daniel. *Sources of New Mexican History, 1821-1848.* Santa Fe: Museum of New Mexico Press, 1984.

II. PRIMARY SOURCES

A. Manuscript Collections

Archives of the Archdiocese of Santa Fe, 1678-1900. 90 rolls. UTEP Library. MF 525.

Archivos del Ayuntamiento de Chihuahua, 1712-1941. 656 rolls. UTEP Library. MF 491.

Archivos del Ayuntamiento de Ciudad Juárez, 1726-1899. 91 rolls. UTEP Library. MF 495. This collection has been refilmed as Ciudad Juárez, Chihuahua Municipal Archives. MF 513.

Archivos de la Catedral de Ciudad Juárez, 1671-1893. 14 rolls. UTEP Library. MF 489.

Archivos Históricos, Manuscritos y Documentos de Janos, 1772-1858. 37 rolls. UTEP Library. MF 498.

Bartlett, John Russell. Papers. The Mexican Boundary Commission Correspondence, 1850-1853. 12 rolls. UTEP Library. MF 497.

Burges, Richard. Papers, 1897-1940. 12 rolls. El Paso Public Library.

Calleros, Cleofas. Collection, 1623-1892. 6 rolls. El Paso Public Library.

Carrizal Collection, 1827-1912. 23 rolls. UTEP Library. MF 505.

Correspondence of J. F. Crosby and Others to James W. Magoffin, 1832-1880. Barker Texas History Center. University of Texas at Austin.

Despatches from United States Consuls in Ciudad Juárez (El Paso del Norte), 1850-1906. 6 rolls. UTEP Library. M 184.

Dexter, Henry L. Papers, 1855-1869. Copy in author's possession.

Dudley, Richard M. Scrapbooks, July 1922-April 1925. El Paso Public Library.

El Paso City Council Minutes, 1881-1908. El Paso Public Library.

Federal Censuses, 1860-1880. National Archives. UTEP Library. 1623/M653, 1623/M593, 1622/T9.

Gardner-Emory Boundary Survey Papers, 1849-1854. DeGolyer Western Collection, Southern Methodist University.

Governors' Papers: Bell, Runnels, Houston, Clark, Throckmorton, Pease, 1850-1868. Texas State Archives.

Hill, Caryl Clyde. Papers, 1832-1916. Barker Texas History Center. University of Texas at Austin.

Institute of Oral History. Taped Interviews. UTEP.

Kemp, Maury. Memoirs. UTEP Library. MF 324.

List of Registered Voters in El Paso County, 1867-1869. Texas State Archives.

Materials in the Archivo de Indias dealing with the History of the Pacific and the American Southwest, 1773-1780. 2 rolls. UTEP Library. MF 490.

Memorials and Petitions, 1866-1873. Texas State Archives.

Mexican Archives of New Mexico, 1821-1846. 42 rolls. State of New Mexico Records Center. UTEP Library. MF 455.

Mills, W. W. Papers, 1856-1922. Barker Texas History Center. University of Texas at Austin.

Phillips, John. Narrative History of Ysleta, 1931. Barker Texas History Center. University of Texas at Austin.

Pioneers Association Biographical Sketchbook, 1932. 1 roll. UTEP Library. MF 503.

Provincias Internas, 1604-1822. Archivo General de la Nación. 85 rolls. UTEP Library. MF 478.

Records of the Department of State Relating to the Internal Affairs of Mexico, 1910-1929. 812.00/3357; 812.00/3474. UTEP Library. M 274.

Records of the El Paso County Clerk's Office, Deed Records. Book A. UTEP Library. Special Collections Department.

Records of the Office of the Commissary General, 1850-1860. 1 roll. State of New Mexico Records Center.

Records of the Office of the Quartermaster General, 1849-1861. 1 roll. State of New Mexico Records Center.

Rubí, Marqués de. "Dictamen," 1768. Archivo de Indias, Audiencia de Guadalajara, 104-6-13. Typed copy in author's possession.

Spanish Archives of New Mexico, 1631-1821. 22 rolls. State of New Mexico Records Center. UTEP Library. MF 454.

United States Department of State. List of United States Consular Officers, 1789-1939. 21 rolls. UTEP Library. MF 587.

Van Horne, Jefferson. Selected Letters, 1849-1851. 1 roll. UTEP Library. MF 463.

B. Published Documents

Adams, Eleanor B., ed. Bishop Tamarón's Visitation of New Mexico, 1760. Albuquerque: University of New Mexico Press, 1954.

Adams, Eleanor B., and Fray Angélico Chávez, eds. The Missions of New Mexico. Albuquerque: University of New Mexico Press, 1956.

Alessio Robles, Vito, ed. Nicolás de Lafora—Relación del viaje que hizo a los Presidios Internos. México, 1939.

Ayer, Mrs. Edward E., ed. The Memorial of Fray Alonso de Benavides—1630. Chicago, 1916.

Bieber, Ralph P., ed., Adventures in the Santa Fe Trade, 1844-1847. Southwest Historical Series, vol. 1. Glendale, Calif.: Arthur H. Clark Co., 1931.

_____. Exploring Southwestern Trails, 1846-1854. Southwest Historical Series, vol. 7. Glendale, Calif.: Arthur H. Clark Co., 1938.

_____. Journal of a Soldier Under Kearny and Doniphan. Southwest Historical Series, vol. 3. Glendale, Calif.: Arthur H. Clark Co., 1935.

_____. Marching with the Army of the West, 1846-1848. Southwest Historical Series, vol. 4. Glendale, Calif.: Arthur H. Clark Co., 1936.

_____. Southern Trails to California in 1849. Southwest Historical Series, vol. 5. Glendale, Calif.: Arthur H. Clark Co., 1937.

Bloom, Lansing B., ed. "Barreiro's Ojeada sobre Nuevo México." New Mexico Historical Review 3 (1928): 73-96, 145-78.

_____. "Bourke on the Southwest." New Mexico Historical Review 13, no. 2 (April 1938): 192-238.

_____. "The Rev. Hiram Walter Reed, Baptist Missionary." New Mexico Historical Review 17, no. 2 (April 1942): 101-47.

Bolton, Herbert E., ed. *Spanish Explorers in the Southwest, 1543-1706.* New York: Charles Scribner's Sons, 1916.

Bravo Ugarte, José, ed. "Informe sobre Misiones – 1793." *México Heróico,* no. 50. México: Editorial Jus, 1966.

Brooks, Clinton E., and Frank D. Reeve, eds. "James A. Bennett: A Dragoon in New Mexico," *New Mexico Historical Review* 22, no. 2 (April 1947): 140-76.

Carroll, H. Bailey, and J. Villasaña Haggard, eds. *Three New Mexico Chronicles.* Albuquerque: University of New Mexico Press, 1942.

Carson, William G. B., ed. "William Carr Lane Diary." *New Mexico Historical Review* 39 (July 1964): 181-234.

Castañeda, Carlos E., ed. *The Mexican Side of the Texas Revolution.* Washington, D.C., 1971.

Coues, Elliott, ed. *The Expeditions of Zebulon Montgomery Pike.* 3 vols. New York, 1895.

Cutter, Donald, ed. "An Anonymous Statistical Report on Nuevo México in 1765." *New Mexico Historical Review* 50 (October 1975): 347-52.

Daniel, James M., ed. "Diary of Pedro José de la Fuente, Captain of El Paso del Norte – 1765." *Southwestern Historical Quarterly* 60 (October 1956): 260-81; and 83 (January 1980), 259-78.

De la Peña y Reyes, Antonio, ed. "Algunos Documentos sobre El Tratado de Guadalupe." *Archivo Histórico Diplomático Mexicano,* num. 31. México: Publicaciones de la Secretaría de Relaciones Exteriores, 1930.

Dillon, Richard, ed. *Benjamin Butler Harris' The Gila Trail.* Norman: University of Oklahoma Press, 1966.

Drumm, Stella M., ed. *Down the Santa Fe Trail and into Mexico – Diary of Susan Shelby Magoffin, 1846-1847.* New Haven: Yale University Press, 1926.

Espinosa, Gilberto, trans. *Villagrá's History of New Mexico.* Los Angeles: Quivira Society, 1933.

Espinosa, J. Manuel, ed. *First Expedition of Vargas into New Mexico.* Albuquerque: University of New Mexico Press, 1940.

_____. ed. "Population of the El Paso District in 1692," *Mid-America* 22 (January 1941): 61-84.

Fierman, Floyd S., ed. "El Paso Merchant and Civic Leader." *Southwestern Studies,* no. 11. El Paso: Texas Western Press, 1965.

Flint, Timothy, ed. *The Personal Narrative of James O. Pattie.* New York: Arno Press, 1973.

Florescano, Enrique, and Isabel Gil Sánchez, comps. *Descripciones económicas regionales de Nueva España – Provincias del Norte, 1790-1814.* México, 1976.

Frazer, Robert W., ed. *Mansfield on the Condition of the Western Forts.* Norman: University of Oklahoma Press, 1963.

_____. *New Mexico in 1850: A Military View.* Norman: University of Oklahoma Press, 1968.

Fulton, Maurice Garland, ed. *Diary and Letters of Josiah Gregg.* 2 vols. Norman: University of Oklahoma Press, 1941.

Galvin, Sean, ed. *The Kingdom of New Spain by Don Pedro Alonso O'Crouley – 1774.* San Francisco: John Howell, 1972.

Galvin, John, ed. *Western America in 1846-1847 – the Original Travel Diary of Lieut. J. W. Abert.* San Francisco: John Howell, 1966.

González Flores, Enrique, ed. *Las constituciones de Chihuahua.* Chihuahua, 1960.

González Flores, Enrique, and Francisco Almada, eds. *Informe de Hugo O'Conor sobre el Estado de la Provincias Internas, 1771-1776.* México, 1952.

Greenwood, C. L., ed. "Letters and Documents—Opening Routes to El Paso, 1849," *Southwestern Historical Quarterly* 48 (October 1944): 262-73.

Griffen, Robert A., ed. *My Life in the Mountains and on the Plains: The Newly Discovered Autobiography by David Meriwether.* Norman: University of Oklahoma Press, 1966.

Hackett, Charles Wilson, ed. *Historical Documents relating to New Mexico, Nueva Vizcaya, and Approaches thereto, to 1773.* 3 vols. Washington, D.C.: Carnegie Institute, 1923-1937.

_____. *Revolt of the Pueblo Indians of New Mexico and Otermín's Attempted Reconquest.* 2 vols. Albuquerque: University of New Mexico Press, 1970.

Hafen, Le Roy R., ed. *Ruxton of the Rockies.* Norman: University of Oklahoma Press, 1950.

Hammond, George P., and E. H. Howes, eds. *Robert Eccleston's Overland to California, 1849.* Berkeley: University of California Press, 1950.

Hammond, George P., and Agapito Rey, eds. *Expedition into New Mexico made by Antonio de Espejo, 1582-1583.* Los Angeles: Quivira Society, 1929.

_____. *Obregón's History.* Los Angeles: Wetzel Publishing Co., 1928.

_____. *Don Juan de Oñate Colonizer of New Mexico, 1595-1628.* 2 vols. Albuquerque: University of New Mexico Press, 1953.

_____. *The Rediscovery of New Mexico, 1580-1594.* Albuquerque: University of New Mexico Press, 1966.

Harris, Theodore D., ed. *Negro Frontiersman—The Western Memoirs of Henry O. Flipper.* El Paso: Texas Western Press, 1963.

Hodge, Frederick, and Theodore Lewis, eds. *Spanish Explorers in the Southern United States, 1528-1543.* New York: Barnes and Noble, 1959.

Hodge, Frederick, George P. Hammond, and Agapito Rey, eds. *Revised Memorial of Fray Alonso de Benavides—1634.* Albuquerque: University of New Mexico Press, 1945.

Hodge, Frederick, ed. *Thomas Falconer's Letters and Notes on the Texas-Santa Fe Expedition.* New York: Dauber and Pine Bookshops, 1930.

Huggins, Dorothy, ed. "To California through Texas and New Mexico: Diary and Letters of Thomas B. and Joseph G. Eastland." *California Historical Society Quarterly* 18 (June 1939).

Jackson, Donald, ed. *The Journal of Zebulon Montgomery Pike.* 2 vols. Norman: University of Oklahoma Press, 1966.

Kephart, Horace, ed. *George F. Ruxton's Wild Life in the Rocky Mountains.* New York: MacMillan, 1937.

Kinnaird, Lawrence, ed. *The Frontiers of New Spain—Nicolás de Lafora's Description, 1766-1768.* Berkeley: Quivira Society, 1958.

Lesley, Lewis Burt, ed. *Uncle Sam's Camels—The Journal of May Humphreys Stacey Supplemented by the Report of Edward Fitzgerald Beale.* Cambridge: Harvard University Press, 1929.

McMaster, Richard K., ed. "The Mansfield Report—1853." *Password* 4, no. 3 (July 1959): 96-112.

Martin, Mabelle E., ed. "From Texas to California in 1849—Diary of C. C. Cox." *Southwestern Historical Quarterly* 29 (October 1925): 128-46.

Martínez, Oscar, ed. *Fragments of the Mexican Revolution.* Albuquerque: University of New Mexico Press, 1983.

Mecham, J. Lloyd, ed. "Supplementary Documents Relating to the Chamuscado-Rodríguez Expedition." *Southwestern Historical Quarterly* 29 (January 1926): 224-32.

Miller, Robert R., ed. "New Mexico in Mid-Eighteenth Century: A Report Based on Governor Vélez Capuchín's Inspection." *Southwestern Historical Quarterly* 79, no. 2 (October 1975): 166-81.

Moore, Mary Lu, and Delmer Beene, eds. "The Report of Hugo Oconor." *Arizona and the West* 13 (Autumn 1971): 265-82.

Moorhead, Max, ed. *Josiah Gregg's Commerce of the Prairies*. Norman: University of Oklahoma Press, 1954.

Morris, Richard, Josefina Z. Vásquez, and Elías Trabulse, eds. *Las Revoluciones de Independencia en México y los Estados Unidos*. 3 vols. México, 1976.

Nasatir, A. P., introd. *Thomas James' Three Years Among the Indians and Mexicans*. Philadelphia: J. B. Lippincott, 1962.

Ponce de León, José M., ed. *Reseñas Históricas del Estado de Chihuahua*. Chihuahua, 1910.

Porras Muñoz, Guillermo, ed. *Diario y Derrotero de lo caminado de D. Pedro de Rivera*. México, 1945.

Porrua Turanzas, José, ed. *Fray Agustín Vetancurt's Teatro Mexicano*. 3 vols. Madrid, 1959-1961.

Porter, Eugene O., ed. "Letters by Ernst Kohlberg." *Southwestern Studies* no. 38. El Paso: Texas Western Press, 1973.

_____, ed. "Letters Home: W. W. Mills Writes to His Family," *Password* 17, nos. 1-4 (1972).

Potash, Robert, ed. "Notes and Documents." *New Mexico Historical Review* 24 (October 1949): 332-40.

Quaife, Milo M., ed. *James B. Gillett's Six Years with the Texas Rangers*. New Haven: Yale University Press, 1925.

Robinson, Jacob S., ed. *A Journal of the Santa Fe Expedition under Colonel Doniphan*. Princeton: Princeton University Press, 1932.

Scholes, France, ed. "Documents for the History of the New Mexican Missions in the Seventeenth Century." *New Mexico Historical Review* 4, no. 1 (January 1929): 45-58; and no. 2 (April 1929): 195-201.

Smith, George Winston, and Charles Judah, eds. *Chronicles of the Gringos*. Albuquerque: University of New Mexico Press, 1968.

Thomas, Alfred B., ed. *After Coronado*. Norman: University of Oklahoma Press, 1966.

_____. "Antonio de Bonilla and Spanish Plans for the Defense of New Mexico, 1772-1778." In *New Spain and the Anglo-American West*, edited by George P. Hammond, 1: 183-209. Lancaster, Pa.: Lancaster Press, Inc., 1932.

_____. *Forgotten Frontiers*. Norman: University of Oklahoma Press, 1969.

_____. "Governor Mendinueta's Proposals for the Defense of New Mexico, 1772-1778." *New Mexico Historical Review* 6 (January 1931): 21-39.

_____. *The Plains Indians and New Mexico, 1751-1778*. Albuquerque: University of New Mexico Press, 1940.

_____. *Teodoro de Croix and the Northern Frontier of New Spain, 1776-1783*. Norman: University of Oklahoma Press, 1941.

Timmons, W. H., ed. "El Paso Documentary: Defending Spain's Northern Frontier—the El Paso Area." *Password* 26, no. 2 (Summer 1981): 78-81.

_____. "The Population of the El Paso Area—A Census of 1784." *New Mexico Historical Review* 52 (October 1977): 311-16.

Weber, David J., ed. *The Extranjeros: Selected Documents from the Mexican Side of the Santa Fe Trail, 1825-1828*. Santa Fe, 1967.

_____. *Foreigners in their Native Land*. Albuquerque: University of New Mexico Press, 1973.

_____. *El México perdido — Ensayos escogidos sobre el antiguo norte de México.* México, 1976.

Worcester, Donald, ed. *Instructions for Governing the Interior Provinces of New Spain, 1786.* Berkeley: Quivira Society, 1967.

Wright, Lyle H., and Josephine M. Bynum, eds. *Waterman L. Ormsby's The Butterfield Overland Mail.* San Marino, Calif., 1972.

C. Government Documents

Congressional Globe. 31st Cong. 1st sess. Washington, D.C., 1850.

Dublán, Manuel, and José María Lozano, eds. *Legislación Mexicana.* 19 vols. México, 1876-1890.

Gammel, H. P. N., ed. *Laws of the State of Texas.* 10 vols. Austin, 1898.

U.S. Congress, *House Executive Document,* no. 76, 30th Cong., 1st sess., 1848. Serial Set 521.

_____, no. 56, 31st Cong., 1st sess. 1850. Serial Set 561.

_____, no. 129, 33d Cong., 1st sess. 1855. Serial Set 737.

_____, no. 135, 34th Cong., 1st Sess. 1856. Serial Set 861.

Journals of the House of Representatives of the State of Texas, 3d sess. 1849.

Journals of the Senate of the State of Texas, 3d Legislature, 2d sess. 1850.

Malloy, William, ed. *Treaties and Conventions of the United States.* 2 vols. Washington, D.C.: Government Printing Office, 1910.

U.S. Congress. *Senate Executive Document,* no. 24, 31st Cong., 1st sess., 1850. Serial Set 554.

_____, no. 64, 31st Cong., 1st sess., 1850. Serial Set 562.

Winfrey, Dorman, and James M. Day, eds. *The Indian Papers of Texas and the Southwest.* 5 vols. Austin, 1966.

D. Newspapers and Contemporary Accounts

Abbot, Gorham D. *Mexico and the United States: Their Mutual Relations and Common Interests.* New York: G. P. Putnam and Sons, 1869.

Alberts, Don E., ed. *Rebels on the Rio Grande — The Civil War Journal of A. B. Peticolas.* Albuquerque: University of New Mexico Press, 1984.

Alcaraz, Ramón. *The Other Side or Notes for the History of the War between Mexico and the United States.* Translated by Albert Ramsey. New York: John Wiley, 1850.

Bartlett, I. S. "President Juárez at Old El Paso." *Pan American Bulletin* 41, no. 5 (November 1915): 646-58.

Bartlett, John Russell. *Personal Narrative of Explorations and Incidents in Texas, New Mexico, California, Sonora, and Chihuahua.* 2 vols. New York: Appleton Co., 1854.

Bell, William A. *New Tracks in North America.* London: Chapman and Hall, 1870.

Benton, Thomas Hart. *Thirty Years' View.* 2 vols. New York: Appleton and Co., 1875.

Bush, I. J. *Gringo Doctor.* Caldwell, Idaho: Caxton Printers, 1939.

Bustamante, Carlos Maria de. *El Gabinete Mexicano.* 2 vols. Mexico, 1842.

_____. *El Nuevo Bernal Díaz del Castillo o sea Historia de la Invasión.* México, 1949.

Crónica de le entrevista Díaz-Taft. México, 1910.

Davis, W. W. H. *El Gringo.* New York: Harper Bros., 1857.

Day, James M., ed. *Morris B. Parker's Mules, Mines, and Me in Mexico, 1895-1932.* Tucson: University of Arizona Press, 1979.

_____, comp. *The Texas Almanac, 1857-1873*. Waco: Texian Press, 1967.

Edwards, Frank S. *A Campaign in New Mexico with Colonel Doniphan*. London: James S. Hodson, 1848.

Eickemeyer, Rudolf. *Letters from the Southwest*. New York: J.J. Little, 1894.

El Paso. Brooklyn: Albertype Co., n.d.

El Paso Bureau of Information. *The City and County of El Paso, Texas*. El Paso: Times Publishing Co., 1886.

El Paso Chamber of Commerce. *El Paso Texas Predestined to Become the Commercial and Industrial Center of the Scenic Southwest*. El Paso, 1930.

_____. *Photographic History of El Paso*. 2 vols. El Paso, 1909.

_____. *Prosperity and Opportunities in El Paso*. El Paso, 1911.

_____. *The Story of a City*. El Paso: El Paso Printing Co., 1910.

El Paso City Directory, 1885-1988.

El Paso Herald-Post, 1881-1988.

El Paso Times, 1881-1988.

Emory, William H. *Report – United States and Mexican Boundary Survey*. Washington, D.C., 1857.

Escudero, José Agustín de. *Memorias del diputado por el Estado de Chihuahua*. México, 1848.

_____. *Noticias estadísticas del Estado de Chihuahua*. México, 1834.

Frank, Jeanie. *I Can Tell It All Now*. El Paso, 1948.

Froebel, Julius. *Travel in Central America, Northern Mexico and the Far West of the United States*. London: Richard Bestle, 1859.

García Conde, Pedro. *Ensayo estadístico sobre el Estado de Chihuahua*. Chihuahua, 1842.

Gillett, James B. *Six Years With the Texas Rangers*. Austin: Von Boeckman-Jones, 1921.

Gilliam, Albert M. *Travels in Mexico during the Years 1843 and 1844*. Aberdeen: George Clark and Son, 1847.

Gooch, Fanny Chambers. *Face to Face with the Mexicans*. New York: Fords, Howard, and Hulbert, 1887.

Guide to El Paso, Texas – A Complete History of the City and Review of Its Business. El Paso, Texas: A. B. McKie and W. M. Edwardy, 1887.

Hamilton, Nancy, ed. "The Diary of C. R. Morehead." *Password* 30 (Fall 1985): 107-14, 142; (Winter 1985), 159-67, 186.

Hendee, Alice J. *El Paso What It Is and Why*. El Paso: El Paso Printing Co., 1914.

Historical and Descriptive Review of El Paso. El Paso: Trade and Commerce Publishing Co., 1890.

Hobbs, James. *Wild Life in the Far West*. Waterford, Conn., 1875.

Hooten, William J. *Fifty-Two Years a Newsman*. El Paso: Texas Western Press, 1974.

Hughes, John T. *Doniphan's Expedition*. Cincinnati: U. P. James Co., 1847.

Humboldt, Alexander von. *Political Essay on the Kingdom of New Spain*. 4 vols. London: Longman, 1811.

Kendall, George W. *Narrative of the Texan Santa Fe Expedition*. 2 vols. London: Wiley and Putnam, 1844.

Kessler, George E. *The City Plan of El Paso, Texas*. El Paso: City Plan Commission, 1925.

Lane, Lydia Spencer. *I Married a Soldier or Old Days in the Old Army*. Philadelphia: J. B. Lippincott Co., 1893.

Lewis, Tracy Hammond. *Along the Rio Grande*. New York: Lewis Publishing Co., 1916.

Liggett, William. *My Seventy-five Years Along the Mexican Border.* New York: Exposition Press, 1964.

Lone Star, 1881-1886.

McNary, James Graham. *This Is My Life.* Albuquerque: University of New Mexico Press, 1956.

Mayer, Brantz. *Mexico: Aztec, Spanish, and Republican.* Hartford: S. Drake and Co., 1852.

Mesilla Times, 1860-1862.

Mills, Anson. *My Story.* Washington, D.C.: Byron S. Adams, 1918.

Ober, Frederick A. *Travels in Mexico and Life Among the Mexicans.* Boston: Estes and Lauriat, 1884.

Payne, D. R. *El Paso Illustrated.* El Paso, 1892.

Periódico Oficial de Chihuahua, 1834-1970.

Perkins, Clifford Alan. *Border Patrol.* El Paso: Texas Western Press, 1978.

Ray, Joseph M. *On Becoming a University.* El Paso: Texas Western Press, 1968.

_____, ed., *Thomason, The Autobiography of a Federal Judge.* El Paso: Texas Western Press, 1971.

Reed, John. *Insurgent Mexico.* New York: Appleton, 1914.

Reid, John C. *Reid's Tramp, Or A Journal of the Incidents of Ten Months' Travel Through Texas, New Mexico, Arizona, Sonora, and California.* Austin: The Steck Co., 1935.

Richardson, Albert D. *Beyond the Mississippi: From the Great Plains to the Ocean.* Hartford, Conn.: American Publishing Co., 1867.

Ruxton, George. *Adventures in Mexico and the Rocky Mountains.* New York: Harper Bros., 1848.

Stevens, Walter B. *Through Texas.* Missouri Pacific Railway, 1892.

Strickland, Rex W., ed. *El Paso in 1854.* El Paso: Texas Western Press, 1969.

_____. *Forty Years at El Paso by W. W. Mills.* El Paso: Carl Hertzog, 1962.

Sullivan, Maude Durlin. *The El Paso Public Library Progress Report.* El Paso: Ellis Bros. Printing Co., 1929.

Texas State Gazette, 1849-1869.

Turner, Timothy G. *Bullets, Bottles, and Gardenias.* Dallas: Southwest Press, 1935.

Vertical File. Southwestern Collection, El Paso Public Library.

The Voice of the Mexican Border. Marfa, Tex.: Marfa Publishing Co., 1933-1934.

Ward Brothers. *Souvenir of El Paso, Texas and Paso del Norte, Mexico.* Columbus, Ohio, 1887.

White, Owen P. *The Autobiography of a Durable Sinner.* New York: G. P. Putnam's Sons, 1942.

Wizlizenus, A. *Memoir of a Tour to Northern Mexico.* Washington, D.C.: Tippin and Streeper, 1848.

E. Taped Interviews, Institute of Oral History, UTEP

Woodrow Bean, no. 23, 9 August 1968.

Border Governors Conference, no. 369, 26-27 June 1980.

Antonio J. Bermúdez, no. 161, 21 June 1974.

David Carrasco, no. 250, 29 April 1976.

Chester Chope, no. 27, 27 July 1968.

Gaspar Cordero, no. 195, 3 July 1975.

Eligio "Kiki" de la Garza, no. 208, 22 October 1975.

Ken Flynn, no. 304, 15 July 1977.

Chris Fox, no. 19A, 22 July 1972.

S. L. A. Marshall, no. 181, 5 July 1975.
René Mascareñas Miranda, nos. 65 and 234, 1 March 1973, and February-April 1976.
Sidney M. Metzger, no. 507, 8 August 1978.
Ralph Murillo, no. 167, 16 July 1975.
Fernando Oaxaca, nos. 196 and 416, 23 October 1975, and 18 September 1976.
Charles V. Porras, no. 212, 18 November 1975.
Belen B. Robles, no. 222, 26-27 April 1976.
George Rodríguez, Sr., no. 177, 29 July 1975.
George Rodríguez, Jr., no. 412, 7 August 1975.
Mike Romo, No. 215, 8 October 1975.
Tati Santiesteban, no. 187, 30 June 1975.

III. SECONDARY MATERIALS

A. Books

Adams, Verdon R. *Methodism Comes to the Pass*. El Paso: Guynes Printing Co., 1975.

Aikman, Duncan, ed. *The Taming of the Frontier*. Freeport, New York: Books for Libraries Press, 1967.

Alexander, Robert E., and Associates. *Urban Development Manual for the City of El Paso: A Handbook for Community Planning*. Los Angeles, 1968.

Almada, Francisco R. *Diccionario Historia Geografía y Biografía Chihuahuenses*. Ciudad Juárez, 1968.

_____. *Gobernadores del Estado de Chihuahua*. México, 1950.

_____. *Resumen de Historia del Estado de Chihuahua*. México, 1955.

_____. *La Revolución en el Estado de Chihuahua*. 2 vols. Chihuahua, 1964.

American Institute of Architects. *Portals at the Pass—El Paso Area Architecture to 1930*. El Paso, 1984.

Applegate, Howard. *Environmental Problems of the Borderlands*. El Paso: Texas Western Press, 1979.

Applegate, Howard, and C. Richard Bath, eds. *Air Pollution Along the United States-Mexican Border*. El Paso: Texas Western Press, 1974.

Austen, Maude M. *'Cension: A Sketch from Paso del Norte*. New York, 1896.

Austerman, Wayne R. *Sharps Rifles and Spanish Mules: The San Antonio-El Paso Mail, 1851-1881*. College Station: Texas A&M Press, 1985.

Austin, Mary. *The Land of Journey's Ending*. Tucson: University of Arizona Press, 1983.

Baerrensen, Donald. *The Border Industrialization Program of Mexico*. Lexington, Mass.: D. C. Heath and Co., 1971.

Bailey, Jesse Bromilow. *Diego de Vargas and the Reconquest of New Mexico*. Albuquerque: University of New Mexico Press, 1940.

Ball, Larry D. *The United States Marshals of New Mexico and Arizona Territories, 1846-1912*. Albuquerque: University of New Mexico Press, 1978.

Bancroft, Hubert Howe. *History of Arizona and New Mexico*. San Francisco, 1889.

_____. *History of Mexico*. 6 vols. San Francisco, 1883-1888.

_____. *History of the North Mexican States and Texas*. 2 vols. San Francisco, 1884-1885.

Bannon, John Francis. *The Spanish Borderlands Frontier, 1513-1821*. New York: Holt, Rinehart and Winston, 1970.

E L   P A S O

Beezley, William H. *Insurgent Governor Abraham González and the Mexican Revolution in Chihuahua.* Lincoln: University of Nebraska Press, 1973.

Benjamin, Thomas, and William McNellie, eds. *Other Mexicos: Essays on Regional Mexican History, 1876-1911.* Albuquerque: University of New Mexico Press, 1984.

Benson, Nettie Lee, ed. *Mexico and the Spanish Cortes, 1810-1822.* Austin: University of Texas Press, 1966.

Binion, Charles. *Scenic and Historic Landmarks.* El Paso: Texas Western Press, 1970.

Binkley, William Campbell. *The Expansionist Movement in Texas.* Berkeley: University of California Press, 1925.

Bishop, Morris. *The Odyssey of Cabeza de Vaca.* New York: Century Co., 1933.

Bobb, Bernard E. *The Viceregency of Antonio María Bucareli in New Spain, 1771-1779.* Austin: University of Texas Press, 1962.

Bolton, Herbert E. *Texas in the Middle Eighteenth Century.* Austin: University of Texas Press, 1970.

Bowden, J. J. *Spanish and Mexican Land Grants in the Chihuahuan Acquisition.* El Paso: Texas Western Press, 1971.

Brack, Gene M. *Mexico Views Manifest Destiny, 1821-1846.* Albuquerque: University of New Mexico Press, 1975.

Braddy, Haldeen. *Pershing's Mission in Mexico.* El Paso: Texas Western Press, 1966.

Brinkerhoff, Sidney, and Odie B. Faulk, eds. *Lancers for the King.* Phoenix: Arizona Historical Foundation, 1965.

Broaddus, J. Morgan. *The Legal Heritage of El Paso.* El Paso: Texas Western Press, 1963.

Brooks, Charles M. *Texas Missions: Their Romance and Architecture.* Dallas: Dealey and Lowe, 1936.

Brown, Leonard E. *Survey of the United States Boundary, 1849-1855.* Washington, D.C.: United States Department of Interior, 1969.

Bryson, Conrey. *Down Went McGinty.* El Paso: Texas Western Press, 1975.

Callahan, James Morton. *American Foreign Policy in Mexican Relations.* New York: Macmillan Co., 1932.

Calleros, Cleofas. *El Paso Then and Now.* El Paso, 1954.

Campa, Arthur L. *Hispanic Culture in the Southwest.* Norman: University of Oklahoma Press, 1979.

Cardoso, Lawrence A. *Mexican Emigration to the United States.* Tucson: University of Arizona Press, 1980.

Carreño, Alberto María. *México y los Estados Unidos de América.* México, 1922.

Casey, Robert J. *The Texas Border.* Indianapolis: Bobbs-Merrill Co., 1950.

Castañeda, Carlos E. *Our Catholic Heritage in Texas.* 7 vols. Austin: Von Boeckman-Jones Co., 1936-1958.

Caughey, John Walton. *Bernardo de Gálvez in Louisiana, 1776-1783.* Gretna, La.: Pelican Publishing Co., 1972.

Chabot, Frederick C. *With the Makers of San Antonio.* San Antonio: Artes Gráficas, 1937.

Chávez, Angélico. *Origin of New Mexico Families.* Santa Fe: Historical Society of New Mexico, 1975.

Chávez, Armando. *Historia de Ciudad Juárez, Chihuahua.* México, 1970.

_____. *Sesenta Años de Gobierno Municipal.* México: Gráfica Cervantina, 1959.

Cisneros, José. *Riders Across the Centuries.* El Paso: Texas Western Press, 1984.

Clark, Ira. *Then Came the Railroads: The Century from Steam to Diesel in the Southwest.* Norman: University of Oklahoma Press, 1958.

_____. *Water in New Mexico: A History of Its Management and Use*. Albuquerque: University of New Mexico Press, 1987.

Clendenen, Clarence C. *Blood on the Border: The United States Army and the Mexican Irregulars*. New York: Macmillan, 1969.

_____. *The United States and Pancho Villa: A Study in Unconventional Diplomacy*. Ithaca: Cornell University Press, 1961.

Coan, Charles F. *A History of New Mexico*. 3 vols. Chicago and New York: American Historical Society, 1925.

Coerver, Don M., and Linda B. Hall. *Texas and the Mexican Revolution: A Study in State and National Border Policy, 1910-1920*. San Antonio: Trinity University Press, 1984.

Conkling, Roscoe, and Margaret Conkling. *The Butterfield Overland Mail, 1857-1869*. 2 vols. Glendale: Arthur Clark Co., 1947.

Connelley, William Elsey. *Doniphan's Expedition*. Kansas City: Bryant and Douglas Co., 1907.

_____. *The Founding of Herman's Station*. New York: Torch Press, 1910.

Corwin, Arthur F., ed. *Immigrants and Immigrants: Perspectives on Mexican Labor Migration to the United States*. Westport, Conn.: Greenwood Press, 1980.

Cunningham, Mary S. *The Woman's Club of El Paso*. El Paso: Texas Western Press, 1978.

D'Antonio, William V., and William H. Form. *Influentials in Two Border Cities*. Notre Dame, Ind.: University of Notre Dame Press, 1965.

De León, Arnoldo. *The Tejano Community, 1836-1900*. Albuquerque: University of New Mexico Press, 1982.

_____. *They Called Them Greasers*. Austin: University of Texas Press, 1983.

Denny, John. *One Hundred Years of Freemasonry in El Paso, 1854-1954*. El Paso: Texas Western Press, 1956.

Dickerson, Patricia W., and Jerry M. Hoffer, eds. *The Trans Pecos Region*. Albuquerque: University of New Mexico Press, 1980.

Dutton, Bertha P. *American Indians of the Southwest*. Albuquerque: University of New Mexico Press, 1983.

Edwards, Aaron William. *My Cloudcroft*. N.p., 1982.

Egan, Ferol. *The El Dorado Trail*. New York: McGraw-Hill, 1971.

Englebrecht, Lloyd C., and June Marie F. Englebrecht. *Henry C. Trost – Architect of the Southwest*. El Paso: El Paso Public Library Association, 1981.

Espinosa, J. Manuel. *Crusaders of the Rio Grande*. Chicago: Institute of Jesuit History, 1942.

Farías Negrete, Jorge. *Industrialization Program for the Mexican Northern Border*. México: Editorial Jus, 1969.

Faulk, Odie B. *Destiny Road – The Gila Trail and the Opening of the Southwest*. New York: Oxford University Press, 1973.

_____. *Land of Many Frontiers*. New York: Oxford University Press, 1968.

_____. *Too Far North – Too Far South*. Los Angeles: Westernlore Press, 1967.

Fernández, Raul A. *The United States-Mexico Border, A Politico-Economic Profile*. University of Notre Dame Press, 1977.

Fierman, Floyd S. *Some Early Jewish Settlers on the Southwestern Frontier*. El Paso: Texas Western Press, 1960.

_____. *Guts and Ruts: The Jewish Pioneer on the Trail in the American Southwest*. New York: KTAV Publishing House, 1985.

Flores Caballero, Romeo. *Evolución de la Frontera Norte*. Monterrey, México: Centro de Investigaciones Económicas, 1982.

Forbes, Jack D. *Apache, Navaho, and Spaniard*. Norman: University of Oklahoma Press, 1960.

Fort Bliss One Hundreth Anniversary. El Paso: Guynes Printing Co., 1948.

Fowler, Harlan D. *Camels to California*. Stanford University Press, 1950.

Frazer, Robert W. *Forts and Supplies – The Role of the Army on the Economy of the Southwest, 1846-1861*. Albuquerque: University of New Mexico Press, 1983.

Frost, H. Gordon. *The Gentleman's Club – The Story of Prostitution in El Paso*. El Paso: Mangan Books, 1983.

Fuentes Mares, José. *Juárez y los Estados Unidos*. Mexico: Editorial Jus, 1964.

Fugate, Francis. *Frontier College: Texas Western at El Paso*. El Paso: Texas Western Press, 1964.

Garber, Paul Neff. *The Gadsden Treaty*. Philadelphia: University of Pennsylvania Press, 1923.

García, Juan Ramos. *Operation Wetback: The Mass Deportation of Mexican Undocumented Workers in 1954*. Westport, Conn.: Greenwood Press, 1980.

García, Mario. *Desert Immigrants: The Mexicans of El Paso, 1880-1920*. New Haven: Yale University Press, 1981.

George, Isaac. *Heroes and Incidents of the Mexican War*. Greensburg, Pa., 1903.

Gerhard, Peter. *The North Frontier of New Spain*. Princeton, N.J.: Princeton University Press, 1982.

Gibson, A. M. *The Life and Death of Colonel Albert Jennings Fountain*. Norman: University of Oklahoma Press, 1965.

Gibson, Lay James, and Alfonso Corona Rentería, eds. *The U.S. and Mexico: Border Development and the National Economies*. Boulder: Westview Press, 1985.

Gilderhus, Mark T. *Diplomacy and Revolution*. Tucson: University of Arizona Press, 1977.

Gilpin, Laura. *The Rio Grande: River of Destiny*. New York: Duell, Sloan, and Pearce, 1949.

Goetzmann, William H. *Army Exploration in the American West*. New Haven: Yale University Press, 1959.

Grieb, Kenneth. *The United States and Huerta*. Lincoln: University of Nebraska Press, 1969.

Griggs, George. *History of the Mesilla Valley or the Gadsden Purchase*. Las Cruces, New Mexico: Bronson Printing Co., 1930.

_____. *Mines of Chihuahua, 1911: History, Geology, Statistics, Mining Companies*. Chihuahua: Imp. El Norte, S.A., 1911.

Hafen, Le Roy R. *The Overland Mail*. Cleveland: Arthur H. Clark Co., 1926.

Haley, P. Edward. *Revolution and Intervention: The Diplomacy of Taft and Wilson with Mexico, 1910-1917*. Cambridge, Mass.: MIT Press, 1970.

Hall, Linda B., and Don M. Coerver. *Revolution on the Border: The United States and Mexico, 1910-1920*. Albuquerque: University of New Mexico Press, 1988.

Hall, Martin Hardwick. *Sibley's New Mexico Campaign*. Austin: University of Texas Press, 1960.

Hallenbeck, Cleve. *Alvar Nuñez Cabeza de Vaca – The Journey and Route of the First Europeans to Cross the Continent of North America, 1534-1536*. Glendale, Calif.: Arthur H. Clark Co., 1940.

Hamilton, Holman. *Prologue to Conflict: The Crisis and Compromise of 1850*. Lexington: University of Kentucky Press, 1964.

Hamilton, Nancy. *UTEP: A Pictorial History of The University of Texas at El Paso*. El Paso and Norfolk-Virginia Beach: Texas-Western Press-Donning Co., 1988.

Hammond, George P., ed. *New Spain and the Anglo-American West*. New York: Kraus Reprint, 1969.

Hammons, Nancy Lee. *El Paso to 1900*. El Paso: University of Texas at El Paso, 1983.

Hansen, Niles. *The Border Economy: Regional Development in the Southwest*. Austin: University of Texas Press, 1981.

Harris, Ruth. *Geography of El Paso County*. El Paso: Technical Institute, 1938.

Hinojosa, Gilberto Miguel. *A Borderlands Town in Transition — Laredo, 1755-1870*. College Station: Texas A&M University Press, 1983.

Horgan, Paul. *Great River*. 2 vols. New York: Rinehart and Co., 1954.

Horn, Calvin. *New Mexico's Troubled Years*. Albuquerque: Horn and Wallace, 1963.

Horr, David A., ed. *American Indian Ethnohistory — Indians of the Southwest*. New York: Garland Publishing Co., 1974.

House, John W. *Frontier on the Rio Grande*. New York: Oxford University Press, 1982.

Hughes, Anne E. *The Beginnings of Spanish Settlement in the El Paso District*. Berkeley: University of California Press, 1914.

Hulse, J. F. *Texas Lawyer: The Life of William H. Burges*. El Paso: Mangan Books, 1982.

Irigoyen, Ulises. *El Problema Económico de las Fronteras Mexicanas*. 2 vols. México, 1935.

Jackson, William Turrentine. *Wagon Roads West*. Berkeley: University of California Press, 1952.

John, Elizabeth. *Storms Brewed in Other Men's Worlds*. College Station: Texas A&M University Press, 1975.

Johnson, William Weber. *Heroic Mexico — The Violent Emergence of a Modern Nation*. New York: Doubleday and Co., 1968.

Jones, Fayette Alexander. *New Mexico Mines and Minerals*. Santa Fe: New Mexico Print Co., 1904.

Jones, Harriott Howze, ed. *El Paso — A Centennial Portrait*. El Paso: Superior Printing Co., 1972.

Jones, Oakah, Jr. *Los Paisanos — Spanish Settlers on the Northern Frontier of New Spain*. Norman: University of Oklahoma Press, 1979.

_____. *Pueblo Warriors and Spanish Conquest*. Norman: University of Oklahoma Press, 1966.

Jordán, Fernando. *Crónica de un País Bárbaro*. Chihuahua, México, 1975.

Katz, Friedrich. *The Secret War in Mexico*. Chicago: University of Chicago Press, 1981.

Keleher, William A. *Turmoil in New Mexico, 1846-1868*. Santa Fe: Rydal Press, 1952.

Kenner, Charles L. *A History of New Mexican-Plains Indians Relations*. Norman: University of Oklahoma Press, 1969.

Kessell, John L. *Friars, Soldiers, Reformers*. Tucson: University of Arizona Press, 1976.

_____. *Kiva, Cross, and Crown*. Washington, D.C.: National Park Service, 1979.

Knight, Alan. *The Mexican Revolution*. 2 vols. Cambridge: Cambridge University Press, 1986.

Ladman, Jerry R., ed. *Mexico: A Country in Crisis*. El Paso: Texas Western Press, 1986.

Laughlin, Ruth. *Caballeros*. Caldwell, Idaho: Caxton Press, 1947.

Lay, Bennett. *The Lives of Ellis P. Bean.* Austin: University of Texas Press, 1960.

Liss, Sheldon B. *A Century of Disagreement: The Chamizal Conflict, 1864-1964.* Washington, D.C.: University of Washington, D.C., 1966.

Lister, Florence S., and Robert H. Lister. *Chihuahua, Storehouse of Storms.* Albuquerque: University of New Mexico Press, 1966.

Loomis, Noel M. *The Texan-Santa Fe Pioneers.* Norman: University of Oklahoma Press, 1958.

Loomis, Noel M., and Abraham Nasatir. *Pedro Vial and the Road to Santa Fe.* Norman: University of Oklahoma Press, 1967.

Lovejoy, Earl M. P. *El Paso's Geologic Past.* El Paso: Texas Western Press, 1980.

Loyola, Sister Mary. *The American Occupation of New Mexico, 1821-1852.* New York: Arno Press, 1976.

Luckingham, Bradford. *The Urban Southwest – A Profile History of Albuquerque, El Paso, Phoenix, Tucson.* El Paso: Texas Western Press, 1982.

MacCallum, Esther Darbyshire. *The History of St. Clement's Church El Paso Texas, 1870-1925.* El Paso: McMath Co., 1925.

McConnell, Joseph Carroll. *The West Texas Frontier or a Descriptive History of Early Times in Western Texas.* 2 vols. Jacksboro, Tex., 1933, 1939.

McGaw, William C. *Savage Scene: The Life and Times of James Kirker, Frontier King.* New York: Hastings House, 1972.

McWilliams, Carey. *North from Mexico.* New York: Greenwood Press, 1968.

Machado, Manuel A. *The North Mexican Cattle Industry, 1910-1975: Ideology, Conflict, and Change.* College Station: Texas A&M Press, 1981.

Mangan, Frank. *El Paso in Pictures.* El Paso: Mangan Books, 1971.

Martin, Jack. *Border Boss: Captain John R. Hughes, Texas Ranger.* San Antonio: Naylor Co., 1942.

Martínez, Oscar J., ed. *Across Boundaries.* El Paso: Texas Western Press, 1986.

_____. *Border Boom Town: Ciudad Juárez, Chihuahua.* Austin: University of Texas Press, 1978.

Meinig, D. W. *Imperial Texas – An Interpretative Essay in Cultural Geography.* Austin: University of Texas Press, 1969.

_____. *Southwest – Three Peoples in Geographical Change, 1600-1970.* New York: Oxford University Press, 1971.

Metz, Leon. *Fort Bliss – An Illustrated History.* El Paso: Mangan Books, 1981.

Meyer, Michael C. *Mexican Rebel: Pascual Orozco and the Mexican Revolution.* Lincoln: University of Nebraska Press, 1967.

_____. *Huerta: A Political Portrait.* Lincoln: University of Nebraska Press, 1972.

_____. *Water in the Hispanic Southwest.* Tucson: University of Arizona Press, 1984.

Meyer, Michael, and William L. Sherman. *The Course of Mexican History.* New York: Oxford University Press, 1979.

Middagh, John J. *Frontier Newspaper: The El Paso Times.* El Paso: Texas Western Press, 1958.

Miller, Darlis. *The California Column in New Mexico.* Albuquerque: University of New Mexico Press, 1982.

Moneyhon, Carl H. *Republicanism in Reconstruction Texas.* Austin: University of Texas Press, 1980.

Moorhead, Max. *The Apache Frontier: Jacobo Ugarte y Loyola and Spanish-Indian Relations in Northern New Spain, 1769-1791.* Norman: University of Oklahoma Press, 1968.

_____. *New Mexico's Royal Road*. Norman: University of Oklahoma Press, 1958.

_____. *The Presidio – Bastion of the Spanish Borderlands*. Norman: University of Oklahoma Press, 1975.

Morrel, Elaine Lewis. *The Rise and Growth of Public Education in El Paso, Texas*. El Paso, 1936.

Moyana Pahissa, Angela. *El Comercio de Santa Fe y la Guerra del 47*. México, 1976.

Mueller, Jerry E. *Restless River*. El Paso: Texas Western Press, 1975.

Navarro García, Luis. *Don José de Gálvez y la Comandancia General de las Provincias Internas del Norte de Nueva España*. Sevilla, 1964.

_____. *Las Provincias Internas en el Siglo XIX*. Sevilla, 1965.

Neal, Dorothy Jensen. *The Cloud-Climbing Railroad*. Alamogordo, New Mex., 1966.

_____. *The Lodge, 1899-1969*. Alamogordo, 1969.

Neighbours, Kenneth F. *Robert Simpson Neighbors and the Texas Frontier, 1836-1859*. Waco: Texian Press, 1975.

Oates, Stephen B. *John Salmon "Rip" Ford's Texas*. Austin: University of Texas Press, 1963.

Ocaranza, Fernando. *Crónica de las Provincias Internas*. México, 1939.

_____. *Establecimientos Franciscanos en el Misterioso Reino de Nuevo México*. México, 1934.

O'Laughlin, Thomas C. *Excavations at the Transmountain Campus El Paso Community College*. El Paso: El Paso Community College, 1979.

_____. *The Keystone Dam Site and Other Archaic and Formative Sites in Northwest El Paso, Texas*. El Paso: El Paso Centennial Museum, 1980.

Owens, M. Lilliana. *Carlos M. Pinto, S. J. – Apostle of El Paso*. El Paso: Revista Católica Press, 1951.

Peixotto, Ernest. *Our Hispanic Southwest*. New York: Charles Scribner's Sons, 1916.

Peyton, Green. *America's Heartland – The Southwest*. Norman: University of Oklahoma Press, 1948.

Porter, Eugene O. *San Elizario – A History*. Austin: Jenkins Publishing Co., 1973.

Prince, L. Bradford. *Historical Sketches of New Mexico*. Kansas City, Mo., 1883.

Purcell, Susan Kaufman. *Mexico-United States Relations*. New York: Praeger, 1981.

Raat, W. Dirk. *Revoltosos – Mexico's Rebels in the United States, 1903-1923*. College Station: Texas A&M Press, 1981.

Raht, Carlyle Graham. *The Romance of Davis Mountains and Big Bend Country*. Odessa: Raht Books, 1963.

Raine, William MacLeod. *Guns of the Frontier*. Boston: Houghton Mifflin Co., 1940.

Reed, John. *Insurgent Mexico*. New York: International Publishers, 1969.

Reeve, Frank D. *History of New Mexico*. 3 vols. New York: Lewis Historical Publishing Co., 1961.

Reisler, Mark. *By the Sweat of their Brow: Mexican Immigrant Labor to the United States*. Westport, Conn.: Greenwood Press, 1976.

Rippy, J. Fred. *The United States and Mexico*. New York: Alfred Knopf Co., 1926.

Rister, Carl Coke. *The Southwestern Frontier, 1865-1881*. Cleveland: Arthur Clark Co., 1928.

Ritch, William G. *Aztlán: The History, Resources and Attractions of New Mexico*. Boston: Lothrop and Co., 1885.

Roa Barcena, José María. *Recuerdos de la Invasión Norteamericana (1846-1848)*. 3 vols. México, 1971.

Roeder, Ralph. *Juárez and His Mexico.* 2 vols. New York: Viking Press, 1947.
Ross, Stanley R. *Francisco I. Madero, Apostle of Mexican Democracy.* New York: Columbia University Press, 1955.
Ross, Stanley R., ed., *Ecology and Development of the Border Region.* México: Anuis/Profmex, 1983.
__________. *Views Across the Border.* Albuquerque: University of New Mexico Press, 1978.
Ruiz, Ramón. *The Great Rebellion.* New York, W. W. Norton, 1980.
Ruth, Kent. *Great Day in the West: Forts, Posts and Rendezvous Beyond the Mississippi.* Norman: University of Oklahoma Press, 1963.
Seligson, Mitchell A., and Edward J. Williams. *Maquiladoras and Migration.* Austin: University of Texas Press, 1983.
Sepúlveda, César. *La Frontera Norte de México.* México, 1976.
Sepúlveda, César, and Albert E. Utton, eds. *The United States-Mexico Border Region: Anticipating Resource Needs and Issues to the Year 2000.* El Paso: Texas Western Press, 1984.
Silverberg, Robert. *The Pueblo Revolt.* New York: Weybright and Talley, 1970.
Simmons, Marc. *Albuquerque: A Narrative History.* Albuquerque: University of New Mexico Press, 1982.
__________. *Spanish Government in New Mexico.* Albuquerque: University of New Mexico Press, 1968.
Sonnichsen, C. L. *The El Paso Salt War of 1877.* El Paso: Texas Western Press, 1961.
__________. *The Mescalero Apaches.* Norman: University of Oklahoma Press, 1958.
__________. *Pass of the North.* 2 vols. El Paso: Texas Western Press, 1968, 1980.
__________. *Tucson – The Life and Times of an American City.* Norman: University of Oklahoma Press, 1982.
Sonnichsen, C. L., and M. G. McKinney. *The State National Since 1881.* El Paso: Texas Western Press, 1971.
Spicer, Edward H. *Cycles of Conquest.* Tucson: University of Arizona Press, 1962.
Stanley, F. *Ciudad Santa Fe – Mexican Rule, 1821-1846.* Pampa, Tex.: Pampa Print Shop, 1962.
Steele, James W. *Frontier Army Sketches.* Chicago: Jansen, McClurg, 1883.
Stoddard, Ellwyn R. *Maquila Assembly Plants in Northern Mexico.* El Paso: Texas Western Press, 1987.
Thomlinson, M. H. *The Garrison of Fort Bliss.* El Paso: Hertzog and Resler, 1945.
Timm, Charles A. *The International Boundary Commission – United States and Mexico.* Austin: University of Texas Press, 1941.
Timmons, W. H. *Morelos of Mexico – Priest Soldier Statesman.* El Paso: Texas Western Press, 1971.
__________, ed. *Four Centuries at the Pass.* El Paso: Guynes Printing Co., 1980.
Tompkins, Frank. *Chasing Villa.* Harrisburg, Pa.: Military Service Publishing Co., 1934.
Toulouse, Joseph H., and James R. Toulouse. *Pioneer Posts of Texas.* San Antonio: Naylor Co., 1936.
Tuck, Jim. *Pancho Villa and John Reed.* Tucson: University of Arizona Press, 1984.
Turner, Timothy G. *Bullets, Bottles, and Gardenias.* Dallas: Southwest Press, 1935.
Twitchell, Ralph E. *The Leading Facts of New Mexico History.* 5 vols. Cedar Rapids: Torch Press, 1911-1917.
__________. *The Military Occupation of New Mexico, 1846-1851.* Denver: Smith-Brooks, Co., 1909.

Tyler, Ronnie C. *The Big Bend: A History of the Last Frontier.* Washington, D.C.: National Park Service, 1975.

Utley, Robert M. *The International Boundary: United States and Mexico.* Santa Fe: Department of Interior, Southwest Region, 1964.

Vanderwood, Paul J., and Frank N. Samponaro. *Border Fury: A Picture Postcard Record of Mexico's Revolution and U.S. War Preparedness, 1910-1917.* Albuquerque: University of New Mexico Press, 1988.

Velázquez, María del Carmen. *Establecimiento y Pérdida del Septentrión de Nueva España.* México, 1974.

Wallace, Ernest. *The Howling of the Coyotes – Reconstruction Efforts to Divide Texas.* College Station: Texas A&M Press, 1979.

Waller, John L. *Colossal Hamilton of Texas.* El Paso: Texas Western Press, 1968.

Wasserman, Mark. *Capitalists, Caciques, and Revolution: The Native Elite and Foreign Enterprise, 1854-1911.* Chapel Hill: University of North Carolina Press, 1984.

Webb, Walter P. *The Texas Rangers – A Century of Frontier Defense.* Austin: University of Texas Press, 1965.

Weber, David J. *The Mexican Frontier, 1821-1846.* Albuquerque: University of New Mexico Press, 1982.

_____. *The Taos Trappers.* Norman: University of Oklahoma Press, 1979.

_____. *New Spain's Far Northern Frontier.* Albuquerque: University of New Mexico Press, 1979.

_____. *Northern Mexico on the Eve of the United States Invasion.* New York: Arno Press, 1976.

West, Ray B., ed. *Rocky Mountain Cities.* New York: W. W. Norton Co., 1949.

Whalen, Michael. *Settlement Patterns of the Eastern Hueco Bolson.* El Paso: El Paso Centennial Museum, 1977.

_____. *Special Studies in the Archeology of the Hueco Bolson.* El Paso: El Paso Centennial Museum, 1980.

Wheat, Carl I. *Mapping the Transmississippi West.* 5 vols. San Francisco: Institute of Historical Cartography, 1959.

White, Owen. *Lead and Likker.* New York: Minton, Balch and Co., 1932.

_____. *Out of the Desert – the Historical Romance of El Paso.* El Paso: McMath Co., 1923.

_____. *Texas: An Informal Biography.* New York: G. P. Putnam's Sons, 1945.

Wilson, Rufus R. *Out of the West.* New York: Press of the Pioneer, 1933.

Winter, Nevin O. *Texas the Marvellous.* Boston: Page Co., 1916.

Wolfskill, George, and Douglas Richmond, eds. *Essays on the Mexican Revolution: Revisionist Views of the Leaders.* Austin: University of Texas Press, 1979.

Worcester, Donald E. *The Apaches: Eagles of the Southwest.* Norman: University of Oklahoma Press, 1979.

Wright, Bertram C. *The 1st Cavalry Division in World War II.* Tokyo: Topan Printing Co., 1947.

Zorrilla, Luis G. *Historia de las Relaciones entre México y los Estados Unidos de América, 1800-1958.* 2 vols. México, 1965-1966.

B. Essays, Articles, and Pamphlets

Allison, William H. H. "John Heath." *New Mexico Historical Review* 6, no. 4 (October 1931): 360-75.

Almada, Francisco. "Los Apaches." *Boletín de la Sociedad Chihuahuense de Estudios Históricos* 2, no. 1 (Junio 1939): 5-15.

_____. "Sucesos y Recuerdos de la Independencia en Chihuahua." *Boletín de la Sociedad Chihuahuense de Estudios Históricos* 4, nos. 7, 8, 9; 5, nos. 2, 3, 5, 6 (1941).

Applegate, Howard, and C. Wayne Hanselka, "La Junta de los Ríos del Norte y Conchos." *Southwestern Studies*, no. 41. El Paso: Texas Western Press, 1974.

Arellano Schetelig, Lorenzo. "Los Prisioneros en Chihuahua." *Boletín de la Sociedad Chihuahuense de Estudios Históricos* 1, no. 10 (March 1939): 332-35.

Austin Urban Research Group. "Economic Studies." Austin, 1971.

Baldwin, P. M. "A Historical Note on the Boundaries of New Mexico." *New Mexico Historical Review* 5 (April 1930), 117-37.

_____. "A Short History of the Mesilla Valley." *New Mexico Historical Review* 13 (July 1938): 314-24.

Barilleaux, Ryan J. "The Politics of Southwestern Water." *Southwestern Studies*, no. 73. El Paso: Texas Western Press, 1984.

Barrick, Nona, and Mary Taylor. "The Mesilla Guard." *Southwestern Studies*, no. 51. El Paso: Texas Western Press, 1984.

Bell, Samuel E., and James M. Smallwood. "The Zona Libre, 1858-1905." *Southwestern Studies*, no. 69. El Paso: Texas Western Press, 1982.

Bender, A. B. "Opening Routes Across West Texas, 1848-1850." *Southwestern Historical Quarterly* 37 (July 1933): 116-35.

Benson, Nettie Lee. "Texas' Failure to Send a Deputy to the Spanish Cortes, 1810-1812." *Southwestern Historical Quarterly* 64 (July 1960): 14-35.

Bieber, Ralph. "The Southwestern Trails to California in 1849." *Mississippi Valley Historical Review* 12 (December 1925): 344-75.

Binkley, William C. "The Question of Texas Jurisdiction in New Mexico under the United States, 1848-1850." *Southwestern Historical Quarterly* 24 (July 1920): 1-38.

_____. "Reports from a Texas Agent in New Mexico, 1849." *New Spain and the Anglo-American West* (Los Angeles 1932), 2: 157-83.

Bloom, John P. "Johnny Gringo at the Pass of the North." *Password* 4 (October 1959): 134-40.

Bloom, Lansing B. "The Chihuahua Highway." *New Mexico Historical Review* 12 (July 1937): 209-16.

_____. "New Mexico under Mexican Administration." *Old Santa Fe* 1, nos. 1 and 2 (July and October 1913).

Bobb, Bernard. "Bucareli and the Interior Provinces." *Hispanic American Historical Review* 34 (February 1954): 20-36.

Books, Willard G. "East Meets West: El Pasoans of Chinese Descent." *Password* 28, no. 2 (Summer 1983): 58-66.

Bowden, J. J. "The Ponce de León Grant." *Southwestern Studies*, no. 24. El Paso: Texas Western Press, 1969.

_____. "The Texas-New Mexico Boundary Dispute." *Southwestern Historical Quarterly* 63 (October 1959): 220-37.

Brady, Donald. "The Theatre in Early El Paso, 1881-1905." *Southwestern Studies*, no. 13. El Paso: Texas Western Press, 1966.

Broadbent, Elizabeth. "Mexican Population in Southwestern United States." *Texas Geographic Magazine* 5, no. 2 (Autumn 1941): 16-24.

Bronitsky, Gordon. "Indian Depredations in the El Paso Area." *New Mexico Historical Review* 62, no. 2 (April 1987): 151-68.

Brown, Gerald B. "Protestantism Comes to El Paso — St. Clement's Episcopal Church." *Password* 1, no. 4 (November 1956): 127-33.

Bryan, Marilyn T. "The Economic, Political, and Social Status of the Negro in El Paso." *Password* 13, no. 3 (Fall 1968), 74-86.

Bryson, Conrey. "Contemporary Civil Rights Issues as Affected by Events in El Paso." *Password* 27, no. 1 (Spring 1982): 26-31.

_____. "The El Paso Tin Mine," *Password* 3, no. 1 (January 1958): 4-13.

_____. "In Skagway They Still Remember Pete Kern." *Password* 19, no. 3 (Fall 1974): 126-32.

_____. *The Land Where We Live.* El Paso: Guynes Printing Co., 1973.

_____. "Dr. Lawrence A. Nixon and the White Primary." *Southwestern Studies*, no. 42. El Paso: Texas Western Press, 1974.

Calleros, Cleofas. *La Antorcha de El Paso del Norte.* El Paso: American Printing Co., 1951.

_____. *El Paso's Missions and Indians.* El Paso: McMath Co., 1951.

_____. *Queen of the Missions.* El Paso: American Printing Co., 1952.

_____. *San Elizario Presidio-Mission.* El Paso, 1960.

Cárdenas, Leonard. "The Municipality in Northern Mexico." *Southwestern Studies*, no. 1. El Paso: Texas Western Press, 1963.

Carman, Michael. "The United States Customs and the Madero Revolution." *Southwestern Studies*, no. 48. El Paso: Texas Western Press, 1976.

Chipman, Donald E. "In Search of Cabeza de Vaca's Route Across Texas: An Historiographical Survey." *Southwestern Historical Quarterly* 91, no. 3 (October 1987): 127-48.

Christian, Garna L. "El Paso's Splendid Little War." *Password* 23, no. 1 (Spring 1978): 5-17.

Christiansen, Paige. "Hugh O'Conor's Inspection of Nueva Vizcaya and Coahuila, 1773." *Lousiana Studies* 2 (Fall 1963): 157-75.

_____. "The Presidio and the Borderlands." *Journal of the West* 8 (January 1969): 29-37.

Clark, Ira G. "The Elephant Butte Controversy: A Chapter in the Emergence of Federal Water Law." *Journal of American History* 61, no. 4 (March 1975): 1006-33.

Corcoran, Lillian Hague. "He Brought the Railroads to El Paso – The Story of James P. Hague." *Password* 1, no. 2 (May 1956): 45-54.

Cosio Villegas, Daniel. "Border Troubles in Mexican-United States Relations." *Southwestern Historical Quarterly* 72 (July 1968): 34-39.

Crawford, Charlotte. "The Border Meeting of Presidents Taft and Díaz." *Password* 3 (July 1958): 86-96.

Daniel, James M. "Expedition of Captain Rubín de Celis from El Paso to La Junta, 1750." *Texas Geographic Magazine* 13, no. 1 (Spring 1949): 11-19.

_____. "The Spanish Frontier in West Texas and Northern Mexico." *Southwestern Historical Quarterly* 71 (April 1968): 481-95.

Day, James M. "El Paso: Mining Hub for Northern Mexico, 1880-1920." *Password* 24, no. 1 (Spring 1979): 17-32.

_____. "El Paso's Texas Rangers." *Password* 24, no. 4 (Winter 1979): 153-72.

DePalo, William A. "The Establishment of Nueva Vizcaya Militia during the Administration of Teodoro de Croix, 1776-1783." *New Mexico Historical Review* 48 (July 1973): 223-49.

Department of Planning Research and Development. "El Paso Parks and Recreation Plan, 1978-2000." El Paso, 1978.

De Wetter, Mardee Belding. "Revolutionary El Paso, 1910-1917." *Password* 3, nos. 2, 3, 4 (April, July, October 1958): 46-59, 107-19, 145-58.

Donnell, F. S. "The Confederate Territory of Arizona, as Compiled from Official Sources." *New Mexico Historical Review* 17 (April 1942): 148-63.

Dwyer, James Magoffin. "Hugh Stephenson." *New Mexico Historical Review* 29 (January 1954): 1-7.

El Paso Chamber of Commerce. *El Paso Photographic History*. 2 vols. El Paso, 1909.

Espinosa, J. Manuel. "Population of the El Paso District in 1692." *Mid-America* 23 (January 1941): 61-84.

Estrada, Richard. "The Mexican Revolution in the Ciudad Juárez-El Paso Area, 1910-1920." *Password* 24, no. 2 (Summer 1979): 55-69.

Farrar, Nancy. "The Chinese in El Paso." *Southwestern Studies*, no. 33. El Paso: Texas Western Press, 1972.

Faulk, Odie B. "The Controversial Boundary Survey and the Gadsden Treaty." *Arizona and the West* 4 (Autumn 1962): 201-26.

_____. "The Presidio: Fortress or Force?" *Journal of the West* 8 (January 1969): 22-28.

Fewkes, J. Walter. "The Pueblo Settlement Near El Paso, Texas." *American Anthropologist* 4 (January 1902): 57-75.

Fierman, Floyd S. "The Schwartz Family of El Paso." *Southwestern Studies*, no. 61. El Paso: Texas Western Press, 1980.

Fisher, Lillian Estelle. "Teodoro de Croix." *Hispanic American Historical Review* 9 (November 1929): 488-504.

Forbes, Jack D. "The Janos, Jocomes, Mansos, and Suma Indians." *New Mexico Historical Review* 32 (October 1957): 319-34.

Frazer, Robert. "Purveyors of Flour to the Army – Department of New Mexico, 1849-1861." *New Mexico Historical Review* 47 (July 1972): 231-38.

French, Robert. "An Economic Survey of El Paso County." Bureau of Business Research, University of Texas, 1949.

Galley, Frank B. "James Baird, Early Santa Fe Trader." *Missouri Historical Society Bulletin* 15, no. 3 (April 1959).

García, Mario T. "Mexican Americans and the Politics of Citizenship: The Case of El Paso, 1936." *New Mexico Historical Review* 59, no. 2 (April 1984): 187-204.

Gerald, Rex. "An Introduction to the Missions of the Paso del Norte Area." *Password* 20, no. 2 (Summer 1975): 47-57.

_____. "Portrait of a Community." *American West* no. 3 (Summer 1966): 38-41.

_____. *Spanish Presidios of the Late Eighteenth Century in Northern New Spain*. Santa Fe: Museum of New Mexico Press, 1968.

Gingerich, Willard, ed. *Air Quality Issues in the El Paso/Cd. Juárez Region*. UTEP Center for Inter-American Studies. El Paso, 1980.

Goetzmann, W. H. "The United States-Mexican Boundary Survey, 1848-1853." *Southwestern Historical Quarterly* 62 (July 1958): 164-90.

Greenleaf, Richard E. "The Nueva Vizcaya Frontier, 1787-1789." *Journal of the West* 8 (January 1969): 56-66.

Gregory, Gladys. "The Chamizal Settlement: A View from El Paso." *Southwestern Studies* 1:2 (Summer 1963).

Hackett, Charles W. "The Retreat of the Spaniards from New Mexico in 1680, and the Beginnings of El Paso." *Southwestern Historical Quarterly* 16 (October 1912): 137-68; (January 1913): 259-76.

Haddox, John. "Los Chicanos, An Awakening People." *Southwestern Studies* no. 28. El Paso: Texas Western Press, 1970.

Hail, Marshall. *Historic Buildings at the Pass of the North*. El Paso, 1967.

Hamilton, Nancy. "Ben Dowell, El Paso's First Mayor." *Southwestern Studies*, no. 49. El Paso: Texas Western Press, 1976.

_____. "The Great Western." In *The Women Who Made the West*, edited by Nellie S. Yost. Garden City, N.Y.: Doubleday, 1980.

_____. "The Ysleta Riot of 1890." *Password* 24, no. 3 (Fall 1979): 101-11.

Harris, Charles H. III, and Louis R. Sadler. "The 1911 Reyes Conspiracy: The Texas Side." *Southwestern Historical Quarterly* 83, no. 4 (April 1980): 325-48.

_____. "Pancho Villa and the Columbus Raid: The Missing Documents." *New Mexico Historical Review* 50 (October 1975): 335-46.

_____. "The Plan of San Diego and the Mexican-United States War Crisis of 1916: A Reexamination." *Hispanic American Historical Review* 58, no. 3 (August 1978): 381-408.

_____. "The 'Underside' of the Mexican Revolution: El Paso, 1912." *The Americas* 39, no. 1 (July 1982): 69-83.

Hartmann, Clinton P. "Scenic Drive, A Road With a View." *Password* 32, no. 3 (Fall 1987): 121-32.

Henderson, Peter V. N. "Mexican Exiles in the Borderlands, 1910-1913." *Southwestern Studies*, no. 58. El Paso: Texas Western Press, 1979.

Herschberger, Charles E. "The Presidential Campaign of 1928 in El Paso County." *Password* 5, no. 1 (January 1960): 5-19.

Hinkle, Stacy C. "Wings and Saddles: The Air and Cavalry Punitive Expedition of 1919." *Southwestern Studies*, no. 19. El Paso: Texas Western Press, 1967.

_____. "Wings Over the Border." *Southwestern Studies*, no. 26. El Paso: Texas Western Press, 1970.

Houser, Nicholas P. "The Tigua Settlement of Ysleta del Sur." *The Kiva* 35 (Winter 1970): 23-29.

International Boundary and Water Commission. *Joint Projects of the United States and Mexico*. Washington, D.C., 1981.

Jones, Harriott Howze. "The Magoffin Homestead." *Password* 11, no. 2 (Summer 1966): 61-69.

Juarrieta, Romolo. "Batalla de Sacramento, 28 de febrero de 1847." *Boletín de la Sociedad de Estudios Históricos* 7, no. 4 (1944).

Katz, Friedrich. "Labor Conditions on Haciendas in Porfirian Mexico: Some Trends and Tendencies." *Hispanic American Historical Review* 54, no. 1 (February 1974): 1-47.

_____. "Pancho Villa and the Attack on Columbus, New Mexico." *The American Historical Review* 83, no. 1 (February 1978): 101-30.

Kelly, Henry W. "Franciscan Missions of New Mexico, 1740-1760." *New Mexico Historical Review* 15 (October 1940): 345-68.

Kerig, Dorothy Pierson. "Luther Ellsworth – United States Consul on the Border during the Mexican Revolution." *Southwestern Studies*, no. 47. El Paso: Texas Western Press, 1975.

Kinnaird, Lawrence, and Lucia Kinnaird. "Secularization of Four New Mexican Missions." *New Mexico Historical Review* 54, no. 1 (January 1979): 35-41.

Knowlton, Clark S., ed. *International Water Law Along the Mexican American Border*. El Paso: Texas Western Press, 1968.

Latham, William I. "Early El Paso Churches." *Password* 27, no. 3 (Fall 1982): 99-114.

Leach, Joseph. "Farewell to Horse-Back, Mule-Back, 'Foot-back' and Prairie Schooner: the Railroad Comes to Town." *Password* 1, no. 2 (May 1956): 34-44.

EL PASO

_____. "Of Time and the Tiguas." *Password* 30, no. 4 (Winter 1985): 169-75.
_____. "Stagecoach Through the Pass – the Butterfield Overland Mail Comes to El Paso." *Password* 3 (October 1958): 130-37.
Leonard, Edward. "Rails to the Pass of the North." *Password* 23, no. 3 (Fall 1978): 87-95.
_____. "Rails at the Pass of the North." *Southwestern Studies*, no 63. El Paso: Texas Western Press, 1981.
Levy, Estelle Goodman. "The Myar Opera House and Other Theaters in Old El Paso." *Password* 5, no. 2 (April 1960): 65-73.
Liljegren, Ernest R. "Zalmon Coley: The Second Anglo-American in Santa Fe." *New Mexico Historical Review* 62, no. 3 (July 1987): 263-86.
Lucker, G. William, and Adolpho J. Alvarez. "Controlling Maquiladora Turnover Through Personal Selection." *Southwest Journal of Business and Economics* 2, no. 3 (Spring 1985): 1-20.
Luckingham, Bradford. "The American Southwest: An Urban View." *Western Historical Quarterly* 15, no. 3 (July 1984): 261-89.
_____. "Epidemic in the Southwest, 1918-1919." *Southwestern Studies*, no. 72. El Paso: Texas Western Press, 1984.
McClure, Charles R. "The Texan-Santa Fe Expedition." *New Mexico Historical Review* 48, no. 1 (1973): 45-56.
McConville, James Lawrence. "El Paso-Ciudad Juárez – a Focus of Inter-American Culture." *New Mexico Historical Review* 40 (July 1965): 233-47.
McGaw, William C. "James Kirker." In *The Mountain Men and the Fur Trade of the Far West*, edited by Le Roy Hafen. 5: 125-45. Glendale, Calif.: Arthur H. Clark Co. (1965-1972).
McKinney, M. G. "The Forgotten Site of Fort Bliss." *Password* 23 (Winter 1978): 143-48.
McMaster, Richard K. *Musket, Saber, and Missile – A History of Fort Bliss.* El Paso, 1966.
Mahon, Emmie Giddings W., and Chester V. Kielman. "George H. Giddings and the San Antonio-San Diego Mail Line." *Southwestern Historical Quarterly* 61 (October 1957): 220-39.
Marshall, Thomas M. "Commercial Aspects of the Texan Santa Fe Expedition." *Southwestern Historical Quarterly* 20 (January 1917): 242-59.
_____. "St. Vrain's Expedition to the Gila in 1826." *Southwestern Historical Quarterly* 19 (January 1916): 251-61.
_____. "The Southwestern Boundary of Texas, 1821-1840." *Texas State Historical Association Quarterly* 14 (1911): 277-93.
Martin, Mabelle E. "California Emigrant Roads through Texas." *Southwestern Historical Quarterly* 28 (April 1925): 287-301.
Martínez, Oscar. "The Chicanos of El Paso – An Assessment of Progress." *Southwestern Studies*, no. 59. El Paso: Texas Western Press, 1980.
Mecham, J. Lloyd. "Antonio de Espejo and his Journey to New Mexico." *Southwestern Historical Quarterly* 30 (October 1926): 114-39.
Moorhead, Max. "The Presidio Supply Program of New Mexico in the Eighteenth Century." *New Mexico Historical Review* 36 (July 1961): 210-29.
_____. "The Private Contract System of Presidio Supply in Northern New Spain." *Hispanic American Historical Review* 41 (February 1961): 31-54.
_____. "The Soldado de Cuera: Stalwart of the Spanish Borderlands." *Journal of the West* 8 (January 1969): 38-55.
_____. "Spanish Transportation in the Southwest, 1540-1846." *New Mexico Historical Review* 32 (April 1959): 107-22.

Morrow, Herbert. "The Mission Trail." El Paso: West Texas Council of Governments, 1981.

_____. "Mission Trail Paints Cultural Landscape." *Cactus Points* (Summer 1983): 10-14.

_____. "Valley Vineyards A Rich Historical Heritage." *Cactus Points* (Fall 1984): 8-13.

Mullin, Robert N. "David Meriwether, Territorial Governor of New Mexico." *Password* 8, no. 3 (Fall 1963): 83-98.

_____. "Stagecoach Pioneers of the Southwest." *Southwestern Studies*, no. 71. El Paso: Texas Western Press, 1983.

Murphy, Retta. "The Journey of Pedro de Rivera, 1724-1728." *Southwestern Historical Quarterly* 41 (October 1937): 125-41.

Myres, Sandra L. "The Ranch in Spanish Texas, 1691-1800." El Paso: Texas Western Press, 1969.

Neighbours, Kenneth F. "The Expedition of Major Robert S. Neighbors to El Paso in 1849." *Southwestern Historical Quarterly* 58 (July 1954): 36-59.

Newman, Bud. "Fray García de San Francisco, Founder of El Paso." *Password* 30, no. 4 (Winter 1984): 179-86.

Niemeyer, E. V., Jr. "Personal Diplomacy: Lyndon B. Johnson and Mexico, 1963-1968." *Southwestern Historical Quarterly* 90, no. 2 (October 1986): 159-86.

Orndorff, Helen. "The Development of Agriculture in the El Paso Valley – The Spanish Period." *Password* 5, no. 4 (October 1960): 139-47.

_____. "Agriculture in the El Paso Valley, 1821-1870." *Password* 10, no. 4 (Winter 1965): 136-44.

_____. "Agriculture in the El Paso Valley, 1870-1914." *Password* 10, no. 4 (Fall 1967): 74-89.

_____. "A Brief History of the Origin of Elephant Butte Dam." *Password* 12, no. 1 (Spring 1967): 43-44.

Palmore, Glenn L. "The Ciudad Juárez Plan for Comprehensive Socio-Economic Development: A Model for Northern Mexico Border Cities." El Paso: UTEP Bureau of Business and Economic Research, 1974.

_____ and Timothy P. Roth. *Statistical Abstract of El Paso, Texas.* El Paso: UTEP Bureau of Business and Economic Research, 1973.

Park, Joseph E. "Spanish Indian Policy in Northern Mexico, 1765-1810." *Arizona and the West* 4 (Winter 1962): 325-44.

Past, Alvin W. "El Paso's Water Shortage Problem." *Password* 9, no. 3 (Fall 1964): 104-12.

Porter, Eugene O. "The Great Flood of 1897." *Password* 18, no. 3 (Fall 1973): 95-103.

_____. "Lord Beresford and Lady Flo." *Southwestern Studies*, no 25. El Paso: Texas Western Press, 1970.

Prestwood, Nadine Hale. "Life in the 1880s in El Paso." *Password* 11, no. 4 (Winter 1966): 162-69.

_____. "El Paso in the Early 1900s." *Password* 18, no. 2 (Summer 1973): 51-58.

Puckett, Fidelia Miller. "Ramón Ortiz: Priest and Patriot." *New Mexico Historical Review* 25 (October 1950): 265-95.

Rand, Patrick. "An Early Trip to Elephant Butte." *Password* 20, no. 3 (Fall 1975), 111-16.

_____. "The Federal Smelter." *Password* 22, no. 3 (Fall 1977), 109-15.

Reid, Bob. "Inter-City Groups Bring El Paso Juárez Together." *Cactus Points* (Summer 1983): 5-7.

Reschenthaler, Patricia. "Post-War Readjustment in El Paso, 1945-1950." *Southwestern Studies*, no. 21. El Paso: Texas Western Press, 1968.

Rhoads, Edward J. M. "The Chinese in Texas." *Southwestern Historical Quarterly* 91, no. 1 (July 1977): 1-36.

Richards, John M. "Economic Growth in El Paso, 1950-1962." El Paso: Texas Western Bureau of Business and Economic Research, 1964.

_____. "Statistical Abstract of El Paso, Texas." El Paso: Texas Western Bureau of Business and Economic Research, 1968.

"The Rio Grande Valley's First Interurban Line." *The Pass Magazine* 1, no. 1 (November 1913): 8-10.

Ruhlen, George. "Brazito – The Only Battle in the Southwest Between American and Foreign Troops." *Password* 2 (February 1957): 4-13.

_____. "The Battle of Brazito – Where Was It Fought?" *Password* 2 (May 1957): 53-60.

_____. "The Genesis of New Fort Bliss." *Password* 19 (Winter 1974): 188-217.

Salinas, Carlos R. *Statistical Abstract of El Paso, Texas.* El Paso: UTEP Bureau of Business and Economic Research, 1986.

Sanger, Donald B. *The Story of Fort Bliss,* El Paso, 1933.

Scholes, France V. "The Supply Service of the New Mexican Missions in the Seventeenth Century." *New Mexico Historical Review* 5, no. 2 (April 1930): 86-210.

Seligmann, G. L., Jr. "The El Paso and Northeastern Railroad's Economic Impact on Central New Mexico." *New Mexico Historical Review* 61 (July 1986): 217-31.

Sheppard, Thomas. *Statistical Abstract of El Paso, Texas.* El Paso: UTEP Bureau of Business and Economic Research, 1977.

Simmons, Marc. "New Mexico's Smallpox Epidemic of 1780-1781." *New Mexico Historical Review* 41, no. 4 (October 1966): 319-26.

_____. "Settlement Patterns and Village Plans in Colonial New Mexico." *Journal of the West* 8 (January 1969): 7-19.

_____. "Spanish Irrigation Practices in New Mexico." *New Mexico Historical Review* 47, no. 2 (April 1972): 135-50.

Simpich, Frederick. "Along Our Side of the Mexican Border." *The National Geographic Magazine* 38 (July 1920): 63-68.

Smith, Ralph. "Apache Plunder Trails Southward, 1831-1840." *New Mexico Historical Review* 37 (January 1962): 20-42.

_____. "Indians in American-Mexican Relations Before the War of 1846." *Hispanic American Historical Review* 43 (February 1963): 34-64.

_____. "King of New Mexico and the Doniphan Expedition." *New Mexico Historical Review* 38 (January 1963): 29-55.

_____. "Scalp Hunter in the Borderlands, 1835-1850." *Arizona and the West* 6 (Spring 1964): 5-22.

Spellman, W. J. "Adjustment of the Texas Boundary in 1850." *Texas State Historical Association Quarterly* 7 (January 1904): 177-95.

Strickland, Rex. "James Baird." In *The Mountain Men and the Fur Trade of the Far West,* edited by Le Roy Hafen, 3: 27-37. Glendale, Calif.: Arthur H. Clark Co. (1965-72).

_____. "Lewis Dutton." In *The Mountain Men,* 3: 147-52.

_____. "Robert McKnight." In *The Mountain Men,* 9: 259-68.

_____. "Six Who Came to El Paso – Pioneers of the 1840's." *Southwestern Studies*, no. 3. El Paso: Texas Western Press, 1963.

_____. "The Turner Thesis and the Dry World." El Paso: Texas Western Press, 1963.

Sullivan, Maud Durlin. "Old Roads and New Highways in the Southwest." *New Mexico Historical Review* 10, no. 2 (April 1935): 143-49.

Sully, John M. "The Story of the Santa Rita Mine." *Old Santa Fe* 3 (April 1916): 138-50.

Texas Indian Reservation. *The Tiguas.* El Paso, n.d.

Thomlinson, M. H. "The Dragoons and El Paso, 1848." *New Mexico Historical Review* 23 (July 1948): 217-24.

Thonhoff, Robert. "San Antonio Stage Line, 1847-1881." *Southwestern Studies,* no. 29. El Paso: Texas Western Press, 1971.

Timmons, W. H. "American El Paso: The Formative Years, 1848-1858." *Southwestern Historical Quarterly* 86 (July 1983): 1-36.

_____. "The Church of Ysleta – Recent Documentary Discoveries." *Password* 28, no. 3 (Fall 1983): 113-16.

_____. "The El Paso Area in the Mexican Period, 1821-1848." *Southwestern Historical Quarterly* 84, no. 1 (July 1980): 1-28.

_____. "The Merchants and the Military, 1849-1854." *Password* 27, no. 2 (Summer 1982): 51-61.

Tjarks, Alicia V. "Demographic, Ethnic and Occupational Structure of New Mexico, 1790." *The Americas* 35 (July 1978): 45-88.

Twitchell, Ralph Emerson. *The Conquest of Santa Fe, 1846.* Española, N. Mex.: Rio Grande Sun Press, 1967.

Tyler, Daniel. "Anglo American Penetration of the Southwest." *Southwestern Historical Quarterly* 75, no. 3 (January 1972): 325-38.

Velázquez, María del Carmen. "La Comandancia General de las Provincias Internas." *Historia Mexicana* 27 (October 1977): 163-76.

Vigness, David. "Don Hugo Oconor and New Spain's Northeastern Frontier." *Journal of the West* 6 (January 1967): 27-40.

Vowell, Jack C., Jr. "Ballots, Bombast, and Blackguardism: The El Paso City Election of 1889." *Password* 1, no. 4 (November 1957): 118-26.

Walker, Billy D. "Copper Genesis: The Early Years of Santa Rita del Cobre." *New Mexico Historical Review* 54 (January 1979): 5-20.

Walker, Dale L. "C. L. Sonnichsen: Grassroots Historian." *Southwestern Studies,* no. 34. El Paso: Texas Western Press, 1972.

Wallace, Christopher M. "Water Out of the Desert." *Southwestern Studies,* no. 22. El Paso: Texas Western Press, 1969.

Waller, J. L. "The Civil War in the El Paso Area." *The West Texas Historical Association Yearbook* 22 (October 1946): 3-15.

Watford, W. H. "Confederate Western Ambitions." *Southwestern Historical Quarterly* 44 (October 1940): 161-87.

Weber, David. "An Unforgettable Day: Facundo Melgares on Independence." *New Mexico Historical Review* 48 (July 1973): 27-44.

_____. "John Francis Bannon and the Historiography of the Spanish Borderlands: Retrospect and Prospect." *Journal of the Southwest* 29, no. 4 (Winter 1987): 332-63.

White, Alice. "The Beginnings and Development of Irrigation in the El Paso Valley." *Password* 2, no. 4 (November 1957): 106-14.

_____. "The Development of Irrigation in the City of El Paso." *Password* 4, no. 1 (January 1959): 31-38.

Wingfield, Clyde J., ed. *Urbanization in the Southwest.* El Paso: Texas Western Press, 1968.

Winther, Oscar O. "The Southern Overland Mail and Stagecoach Line, 1857-1861." *New Mexico Historical Review* 32 (April 1957): 81-106.

Wise, Clyde, Jr. "The Effects of the Railroads Upon El Paso." *Password* 5, no. 2 (July 1960): 91-100.

C. Dissertations, Theses, and Other Unpublished Papers

Adams, Mark, and Gertrude Adams. "A Report on Politics in El Paso." Cambridge, Mass.: Joint Center for Urban Studies of the Massachusetts Institute of Technology, 1963.

Baquera, Richard. "Paso del Norte and Chihuahua, 1810-1821: Revolution and Constitutionalism." Master's thesis, University of Texas at El Paso, 1978.

Baylor, George W. "Historical Stories of the Southwest." El Paso Public Library, 1902.

Berge, Dennis E. "Mexican Response to United States Expansionism, 1841-1848." Ph.D. diss., University of California at Berkeley, 1965.

"Biographical and Historical Sketchbook of the Pioneers Association of El Paso County." Typed manuscript, Special Collections, UTEP Library, 1932.

Blake, Robert Neal. "A History of the Catholic Church in El Paso." Master's thesis, Texas Western College, 1948.

Bowden, J. J. "The Ascarate Grant." Master's thesis, Texas Western College, 1953.

Bridgers, W. W. "Just Chatting." 4 vols. Typed scrapbook, 1934-1936. Southwest Collection, El Paso Public Library.

Brown, Robert B. "Guns Over the Border: American Aid to the Juárez Government During the French Intervention." Ph.D. diss., University of Michigan, 1951.

Bryson, Conrey. "El Paso Water Supply—Problems and Solutions, 1921-1959." Master's thesis, Texas Western College, 1959.

Burrus, Ernest. "Outstanding Historical Dates and Events of Towns, Missions, and Churches in the El Paso Valley." El Paso: Catholic Diocese of El Paso, Texas, 1981.

Bush, Mary Elizabeth. "El Paso County in the First World War." Master's thesis, University of Texas, 1950.

Campbell, Elsie. "Spanish Records of the Civil Government of Ysleta—1835." Master's thesis, Texas Western College, 1950.

Christian, Garna L. "Sword and Plowshare: The Symbiotic Development of Fort Bliss and El Paso, Texas." Ph.D. diss., Texas Tech University, 1977.

Crego, Arthur Van Voorhis. "City on the Mesa: The New Fort Bliss, 1890-1895." Master's thesis, Louisiana State University, 1969.

Cummings, Lewis B. "Zach White, Pioneer Capitalist." Master's thesis, University of Texas at El Paso, 1967.

Daguerre, R. P. "Alexandre Daguerre and Family." El Paso Public Library, Southwest Collection.

Decorme, Gerald, S. J. "Las misiones del Valle del Paso." Ysleta, 1960-1964.

Diamond, Tom. "Pueblo de la Isleta del Sur—Chronology and Related Historical Materials." El Paso, n.d.

El Paso Chamber of Commerce. "Cristo Rey, The Christ of the Rockies." N.d.

El Paso Department of Planning. "El Paso Data Book." El Paso, 1959.

_____. "A Short History of South El Paso." El Paso, 1967.

_____. "A Short History of Ysleta." El Paso, 1966.

El Paso Industrial Development Corporation. "El Paso Area Fact Book." El Paso, 1968-1986.

_____. "Proximity for Progress – El Paso-Juárez Twin Plant Handbook." El Paso, 1971-1974.

El Paso Public Library. Southwest Collection. Vertical File – El Paso History, History of Cd. Juárez, El Paso Pioneers, Mexico, Biography.

Escalante, Alfredo, trans. "Letters from Benito Juárez Written While at El Paso del Norte, 1865-1866." Seminar paper, Texas Western College, 1961.

Estrada, Richard. "Border Revolution – The Mexican Revolution in the Ciudad Juárez-El Paso Area, 1910-1915." Master's thesis, University of Texas at El Paso, 1975.

_____. "Chihuahua and New Mexico, 1810-1821." Seminar paper, University of Texas at El Paso, 1973.

Freeman, Leola. "James Wiley Magoffin." El Paso Public Library, 1951.

García, Mario T. "Obreros: The Mexican Workers of El Paso, 1900-1920." Ph.D. diss., University of California San Diego, 1975.

George, Edward Y., and Robert D. Tollen. "The Economic Impact of the Mexican Border Industrialization Program." No. 20 UTEP Center for Inter-American and Border Studies. El Paso, 1983.

Gerald, Rex. "A History of the Tigua Indians of Ysleta del Sur, Texas." Typed manuscript, Special Collections Department, UTEP Library, 1970.

Halla, Frank L. "El Paso, Texas and Juárez, Mexico: A Study of a Bi-Ethnic Community, 1846-1881." Ph.D. diss., University of Texas at Austin, 1978.

Hansen, Niles. "Border Region Development and Cooperation: Western Europe and the U.S.-Mexico Borderlands in Comparative Perspective." No. 10. UTEP Center for Inter-American and Border Studies. El Paso, 1985.

Harden, Thordis D. "An Historical Appraisal of the Kessler Plan for El Paso." Master's thesis, University of Washington, 1959.

Hardin, Mary Christine. "Framework for El Paso: Downtown Revitalization Strategies." Master's thesis, University of Texas at Austin, 1983.

Hovious, Jo Ann Platt. "Social Change in Western Towns: El Paso, Texas, 1881-1889." Master's thesis, University of Texas at El Paso, 1972.

Ivey, Rosalee. "A History of Fort Bliss." Master's thesis, University of Texas at Austin, 1942.

Jackson, William Turrentine. "A Tale of Two Western Stagecoach Depots." Paper read at The University of Texas at El Paso, 1984.

John, Sarah E. "Trade Will Lead a Man Far: Syrian Immigration to the El Paso Area, 1900-1935." Master's thesis, University of Texas at El Paso, 1982.

Langford, Margaret H. "The Public Image of El Paso." Master's thesis, University of Texas at El Paso, 1969.

Langston, Edward Lonnie. "The Impact of Prohibition on the Mexican-United States Border: The El Paso-Juárez Case." Ph.D. diss., Texas Tech University, 1974.

Lee, Mary Antone. "A Historical Survey of the American Smelting and Refining Company in El Paso." Master's thesis, Texas Western College, 1950.

Leonard, Glen M. "Western Boundary Making: Texas and the Mexican Cession, 1844-1850." Ph.D. diss., University of Utah, 1970.

Leyva, Yolanda. "The Repatriation of Mexicans during the Great Depression: The Case of El Paso and Ciudad Juárez." Seminar Paper, University of Texas at El Paso, 1987.

Long, Grace. "The Anglo-American Occupation of the El Paso District." Master's thesis, University of Texas at Austin, 1931.

McConville, J. Lawrence. "A History of Population in the El Paso-Ciudad Juárez Area." Master's thesis, University of New Mexico, 1966.

McKay, R. Reynolds. "Texas Mexican Repatriation during the Great Depression." Ph.D. diss., University of Oklahoma, 1982.

McLaughlin, Walter V. "First Book of Baptisms of Nuestra Señora de Guadalupe del Paso del Norte." Master's thesis, Texas Western College, 1962.

Minge, Ward Alan. "Frontier Problems in New Mexico Preceding the Mexican War, 1840-1846." Ph.D. diss., University of New Mexico, 1965.

Miyasato Tsuyako, B. "The Japanese in the El Paso Region." Master's thesis, University of Texas at El Paso, 1982.

Newman, S. H. "Reminiscences." Typed manuscript, Special Collections Department, UTEP Library, 1906.

Popp, Linda. "The El Paso Area – Crossroads of Argonaut Trails to California." Seminar paper, University of Texas at El Paso, 1976.

Reeves, T. Zane. "The U.S.-Mexican Border Commissions: An Overview and Agenda for Further Research." No. 13. UTEP Center for Inter-American and Border Studies. El Paso, March, 1984.

Rocha, Rodolfo. "The influence of the Mexican Revolution on the Mexico-Texas Border, 1910-1916." Ph.D. diss., Texas Tech University, 1981.

Rosen, Evelyn R. "Henry Cuniffe: The Man and His Times." Master's thesis, Texas Western College, 1961.

Rowland, Thomas "The Search for the Old Socorro Mission." Master's thesis, University of Texas at El Paso, 1984.

Sandstrum, Allan. "Fort Bliss – the Frontier Years." Master's thesis, Texas Western College, 1962.

Sherman, Edward F. "A Decade of Exploration in the Southwest, 1846-1855." Master's thesis, Texas Western College, 1962.

Sick, Deborah. "Archaeological Testing of 41EP2370, the Kohlberg Parking Lot Site, El Paso, Texas." New Mexico State University, July 1983.

Stanley, Duffy B. "Historic Structures Within the City of El Paso." El Paso Department of Planning and Research, 1971.

Stanton, Mary I. "Historical El Paso." El Paso Public Library.

Staski, Edward, and David Batcho. "A Preliminary Report of Archaeological Testing of the Cortez Parking Lot Site, Mills Block 3, West Half." New Mexico State University, December 1983.

Thompson, Howard. "Makers of El Paso." El Paso Public Library.

Timmons, W. H. "Mexican Independence in Texas: The View from El Paso." Paper read at the annual meeting of the Texas State Historical Association, Austin, 1975.

Ulibarri, Richard O. "American Interest in the Spanish Southwest, 1803-1848." Ph.D. diss., University of Utah, 1963.

Valencia, Nestor A. "Twentieth Century Urbanization in Latin America and a Case Study of Ciudad Juárez." Master's thesis, University of Texas at El Paso, 1969.

Vowell, Jack, Jr. "Politics at El Paso, 1850-1920." Master's thesis, Texas Western College, 1952.

Walz, Vina. "History of the El Paso Area, 1680-1692." Ph.D. diss., University of New Mexico, 1951.

Weber, David J. "'From Hell Itself': The Americanization of Mexico's Northern Frontier, 1821-1846." Paper read at Border Studies Symposium, UTEP, 1983.

White, Katherine H. "The Pueblo de Socorro Grant." Master's thesis, Texas Western College, 1961.

_____. "The Recognized Spanish and Mexican Land Grants of the El Paso Area." Seminar paper, Texas Western College, 1960.

White, Robert R. "Félix Martínez, Border Giant." Paper read at the Joint Meeting of the Texas State Historical Association and the New Mexico Historical Society, El Paso, 1981.

White, Russell A. "El Paso del Norte: The Geography of a Pass and Border Area Through 1906." Ph.D. diss., Columbia University, 1968.

Wilson, Olga P. "Benito Juárez in Old Paso del Norte." Seminar paper, Sul Ross State College, 1941.

Wise, Clyde, Jr. "Joseph Magoffin." Seminar paper, Texas Western College, 1960.

Yeilding, Kenneth. "The Chamizal Dispute: An Exercise in Arbitration." Ph.D. diss., Texas Tech University, 1973.

_____. "The Juan de Oñate New Mexico Entrada, 1596-1598." M.A. thesis, Texas Western College, 1962.

Index

Illustrations by José Cisneros,
design by Vicki Trego Hill,
typesetting by Camille,
all of El Paso, Texas

Type is set in Goudy Old Style,
and Goudy Handtooled.

Printed on acid-free paper
by BookCrafters of Chelsea, Michigan.